Whatever Happened to the Third World?

"*Whatever happened to the Third World* is a concise yet masterful analysis of the sources of economic growth and its implications for poverty reduction in developing countries. Peter de Haan does an excellent job in reviewing past growth theories against recent performance of the shrinking 'Third World'. The volume is a must read both for university students and development practitioners."

—Constantine Michalopoulos, *Advisor to international organisations including the IMF, the World Bank, UCTAD and the EU Commission*

"Peter de Haan's new book is a comprehensive and entertaining tool to understand how people and institutions devised development paths through time. His economics academic insights combined with international field experience provide a brilliant grasp of a challenging matter."

—Eduardo Rodriguez-Veltze, *Former President of Bolivia, La Paz, Bolivia*

"Economic development, international trade and globalisation are such vast fields that it takes an excellent guide as Peter de Haan to understand their meaning and relevance for the Third World. Adding his personal experience, he lively describes how the developing world fared, how successive generations in development economics looked at it, and how they explained what happened. Experts, students and practitioners alike will enjoy this sparklingly written book."

—Arie Kuyvenhoven, *Professor Emeritus of Development Economics, Wageningen University*, and Visiting Professor, *Nanjing Agricultural University, China*

"...Peter de Haan, drawing from his rich life-long experience working on the field as a diplomat and development expert, has written a fascinating book on the development and evolution of the economics of development. This very readable intellectual journey should be a required reading for policy makers, politicians, and students of economic development and the century-long fight on poverty, for an illuminating insight into this fascinating field of human endeavor. Delightful reading!"

—Ronald MacLean-Abaroa, *Former Minister of Finance, Sustained Development, and Foreign Affairs, and four-term elected Mayor of La Paz, Bolivia*

Peter de Haan

Whatever Happened to the Third World?

A History of the Economics of Development

palgrave
macmillan

Peter de Haan
The Hague, The Netherlands

ISBN 978-3-030-39612-1 ISBN 978-3-030-39613-8 (eBook)
https://doi.org/10.1007/978-3-030-39613-8

This Palgrave Macmillan imprint is published by the registered company Springer Nature Switzerland AG.
The registered company address is: Gewerbestrasse 11, 6330 Cham, Switzerland

To Simone

Preface

The World Bank's *Commission on Growth and Development* analysed the spectacular economic growth of thirteen countries. Since 1950, these countries had grown at more than 7% per year for at least a quarter century. The Commission wanted to find out what their secrets of success were; what exactly triggered their rapid economic growth? These countries shared six secrets of success: (i) commitment to growth in combination with effective governance; (ii) high saving and investment rates; (iii) fast export growth; (iv) macroeconomic stability; (v) knowledge and technology import; and (vi) market-friendly policies. In addition, the countries made the most of the global economy. Sustained growth at this pace was not possible before 1950, because since then the world economy became more open and more tightly integrated.

The six secrets of success are all very sensible explanatory factors. This prompts two questions: what is it that made these successful former developing countries adopt the right mix of policies; and, second, why haven't other developing countries adopted similar policies? This book attempts to present the answers that can be given from an economic point of view.

There is a difference between growth and development. Economic growth is expressed in the percentage with which a country's Gross Domestic Product (GDP) has changed from one year to the next. This percentage is, however, a crude indication of a country's economic condition. In the typical developing country, lack of statistical capacity, mismeasurement of the economy, changes in the quality and range of goods, and the contribution of the informal economy to GDP, can all subject real GDP per capita measures to substantial revision. A recent IMF Working

Paper uses satellite-recorded nighttime lights as a supplementary measurement of true GDP per capita.

GDP per capita does not reflect what the purchasing power of a citizen would be. In other words, what products can that citizen buy with the local currency compared with what an American dollar can buy for the same products in America. The purchasing power parity (PPP) measurement makes better comparisons between countries possible.

Development involves growth plus change. For example, GDP per head does not reflect the distribution of income and wealth. Nor does it say much about human development, i.e., how healthy and how well-educated the population is. GDP per head also does not say whether the society is democratic or whether it is ruled by an autocratic leader. It is a big mistake, as one GDP analyst once said, to think that one number (i.e., GDP) serves all purposes.

In short, there is not one exclusive answer to the question what exactly would development include? It depends what one means by development. For example, if one would wish to live in the best country on earth, according to the Organisation of Economic Cooperation and Development (OECD), the ideal country would be Australia, Sweden, or Norway. But for a business person, the country with the most conducive business environment is Singapore, and so on.

Change involves the achievement of more objectives than only GDP growth—perhaps one should speak of quality growth. China, for example, is not just striving after economic growth, the country is aiming at comprehensive development, involving balances between urban and rural development, social and economic development, man and nature, and domestic and international markets.

The United Nations uses the *Human Development Index* (HDI), which is a good instrument, as it measures a country's annual economic growth *and* life expectancy at birth and educational attainment. But even this broader measurement does not include all aspects of what development implies. Measurements should not just capture material progress but also—as Amartya Sen argues—the broadening of people's entitlements (to ensure life sustenance) and capabilities (to promote personal freedom and self-esteem). In *Economics of Development*, Anthony Thirlwall and Penélope Pacheco-López describe the purpose of development in broad terms indeed. They say that development occurs when there is an improvement in basic needs, when economic progress contributes to a greater sense of self-esteem for the country and individuals within it, and when material advancement expands people's entitlements, capacities and freedoms.

Besides the above measurements, there are many others. For example, the OECD introduced the *Better Life Index*, and the annual *World Happiness Report*. Regarding corruption, there is Transparency International's *Corruption Perception Index*. For Africa, there is the *Ibrahim Index of African Governance*. The environmental and sustainability dimension of development has gained justified prominence since scholars, political leaders, and society at large became more and more conscious of the fact that economic growth and the—still growing—world population contribute to pollution, climate change, and the depletion of vital natural resources at a worrying pace. Concerns about the environment and climate change have, for example, been taken on board by the New Economics Foundation's *Happy Planet Index*. A decade ago, the World Bank published *Where is the Wealth of Nations?*, introducing the concept of wealth as a complementary indicator of GDP for monitoring a country's sustainable development. In 2018, the Bank published *The Changing Wealth of Nations*, which addresses development through a comprehensive measure of wealth, underpinning income and well-being.

In sum, there is no shortage in the variety of measurements of growth and development in the widest sense of the terms. This is of great help to all, including myself, who want to find out how developing countries have fared over the past 70 years.

Growth and development belong to the issues that are not fully understood by the economic science. So, both are intriguing subjects, not in the least since both determine to a large extent a country's economic prosperity and political stability. This is not only relevant for individual countries but also between them, as the wider the gap between rich and poor countries, the greater the threats of discontent, mass migration, political instability, and war.

In my book various classifications of countries are being used, ranging from least-developed and low-income countries, emerging market economies, newly industrialising countries, to industrialed—and high-income countries. In most instances I have used the World Bank classification: low-income countries, lower middle-income and upper middle-income countries, and high-income countries. However, depending on the particular context, I use other classifications.

Although development assistance is here and there mentioned, aid's contribution to economic growth and development is not dealt with. This subject deserves a balanced, yet critical, analysis which is beyond the scope of this book. The same also applies to environmental issues relevant to developing countries.

Here and there, I share some of my forty years' experience in development assistance. However, scholarly books, papers, and reports constitute the principal basis of my analysis.

I hope that students and scholars of development economics, economic history, and political science will find this book useful. What follows can also be enjoyed by everyone taking an interest in economic growth and development of developing countries.

The book contains seven chapters and a brief epilogue. Chapter 1 presents an overview of the book's contents. Chapter 2 describes, in fairly broad terms, how the Third World evolved and what categories of countries emerged, ranging from successful ones, via middle-income countries, low-income countries, to fragile and failed states. Chapter 3's title: What preceded development economics, reflects what this chapter is about. Set before World War II, the chapter provides a brief description of what different scholarly disciplines (i.e., geography and economics) had to say about growth and development of colonies and other poor tropical countries. Chapter 4 introduces the first generation of development economists, who developed theories and formulated proposals with a view to help newly-independent developing countries achieving their aim of rapid economic growth. Dissenting views on proposals of the first generation are presented as well. The proposals and actions of their successors—members of the second generation of development economists—are described in Chap. 5, again, including dissenting views. The question arose, whether the second generation would be succeeded by a third generation. In response, Chap. 6 presents not just one, but various schools of thought that greatly contributed to the contemporary broadened growth and development literature. Finally, Chap. 7 attempts to answer the question to what extent developing countries have benefitted from international trade and globalisation.

* * *

The author has worked for forty years in development. First as a Junior Professional Officer at the Pacific Regional Office of the United Nations Development Programme, after which he was appointed Asia Bureau Chief at the Dutch Non-Governmental Organisation NOVIB (now merged with Oxfam). After his time at Oxfam/NOVIB, he briefly managed the European Office of Inter Press Service, a Third World news agency. Subsequently, de Haan was appointed Senior Institutional Development Advisor at the Netherlands Ministry for Development Cooperation, followed by his postings at the Netherlands' Embassy in La Paz, Bolivia, and—subsequently—Lusaka, Zambia. He has written various books about development and economics; the latest one being *From Keynes to Piketty; the Century that Shook up Economics.*

The Hague, The Netherlands
November 2019

Peter de Haan

Acknowledgments

To my delight, all the persons I approached with the request to help me in writing this book, did so. This was very inspiring indeed, not in the least since they were all critical, but fair, in their comments on the drafts I sent them.

My old-time friend, former ambassador Kees Beemsterboer was kind enough to share his constructive comments with me. Dr. Bernard Berendsen, also former ambassador, deserves special thanks, as he had to read the lengthy text of successive drafts of one chapter, before it met with his approval. Emeritus Professor of Development Economics at Wageningen University, Arie Kuyvenhoven, gave me, apart from his advice, valuable additional references, which I gladly accepted. The results are included in this book's text. Dr. Auke Leen, Assistant Professor of Economics, Leiden University, after enthusiastically having accepted my request, gave me inspiring comments. Another friend, and former Ambassador Harry Molenaar, did not spare me with his comments. I thank him, because this is what one must expect from true friends. In the past, another colleague, Jan Bade had written a review of my book *From Keynes to Piketty*. I asked him to review one of the chapters, which he did in a very thorough manner indeed. Needless to say that, again, I benefitted greatly from his comments and suggestions. Peter Kardoes, retired attorney at law, was also prepared to help. Although he said that he did not know much about economics, he, nonetheless, pointed to shortcomings in the text. Alfonso Garcia-Salaues, former colleague at the Netherlands Embassy in la Paz, Bolivia, who now lives in the Hague, helped me a great deal with up-to-date literature, comments, and uplifting discussions during our regular coffee meetings at the Hague's Filmhouse. Dr. Nico van Niekerk, another colleague of mine, gave me such a thorough and wide-ranging commentary on my draft piece on environmental issues, that I took the wise decision not to include it in the book.

I am also deeply grateful for the sterling editing work done by novelist Geneanne Walsh. Despite the fact that my text is certainly not a novel, yet, Geneanne doggedly went through the text, not omitting even the slightest oversight on my part. My son-in-law, Marcus Slingsby, also greatly contributed to the improvement of my English. Thank you, Geneanne and Marcus.

I wrote the book in the Hague and in El Perelló, Spain, where my Spanish wife and I spend the summer months. As it is very warm during summer in Spain, I was lucky to be allowed to write in El Perelló's air-conditioned municipal library. I warmly thank librarian Ysabel Meseguer for the hospitality extended to me. When in the Hague, I visited the well-stocked library of the Institute of Social Studies, many times, in order to work there and to borrow books. From time to time, the books I needed were not available. Librarian Cathelijne van der Ree went out of her way to get me the books from other libraries. I thank her for her unfailing help.

Without the enthusiasm and support of my editors Laura Pacey and Ruth Jenner, this book would not have seen the light. The same applies to Lavanya Devgun, editorial assistant, who was very helpful in correcting my English and in preparing the text for printing. So, Laura, Ruth, and Lavanya: thank you very much indeed! Finally, despite the fact that my wife, Marisales Ramón-Chordá, was also writing a book, she nevertheless found the time to help me with comments and to solve the many problems I encountered in designing Figures, formatting texts, and putting footnotes in the proper place. I am deeply grateful to her.

Contents

1	Introduction	1
2	Whatever Happened to the Third World	39
3	What Preceded Development Economics	99
4	The First Generation of Development Economists	113
5	The Second Generation of Development Economists	161
6	Main Components of the Third Generation	193
7	Trade, Globalisation and Development	253
	Epilogue	299
	Index	305

List of Figures

Fig. 2.1 Countries classification in percentages 1978–2018. (Source: World Development Reports 1978–2018. The 1978 World Development Report (WDR) also includes two categories: (i) capital surplus oil exporters (3) and (ii) centrally planned economies (11). I included the 3 surplus oil exporters in the industrialised (high-income) group. As for the 11 centrally planned economies, given their respective income levels, I included 5 of them in the lower middle-income and 5 in the upper middle-income group. Number 11, the DDR, is included in the high-income group) 42

Fig. 2.2 Countries classification thresholds and average GNI per capita 1978–2018. (Source: World Development Reports 1978–2018). The 1988 WDR distinguishes between lower middle-income and upper middle-income countries. However, the report does not provide a threshold figure for the latter category. I chose $1799.- as the threshold for upper middle-income countries. A further operational classification used by the World Bank is the list of countries in Fragile and Conflict Affected Situations 43

List of Tables

Table 2.1	Latin American and Asian middle-income countries compared 1978–2018	85
Table 5.1	Rules of good behavior for the promotion of economic growth	166

CHAPTER 1

Introduction

1.1 Introduction

Gapminder Institute's founder, Hans Rosling (1948–2017) is fondly remembered. He playfully refuted the conventional wisdom about developing countries, i.e., that they were a hopeless lot, characterised by corruption, squalor, endless poverty, inadequate health care, and low literacy rates. In short, the assumption was, said Rosling, that there was no hope that these countries would ever develop, let alone shed their poverty. Supported by statistical evidence, Rosling demonstrated in his TED lectures and in *Factfulness* that a lot of progress has been made over the past 50 years.[1] Even 'hopeless' sub-Saharan Africa (SSA) took-off, economically speaking—the impossible appeared to be possible! Indeed, SSA is making progress.

Not only is the developing world's past economic record pretty impressive, the same can be said about progress made in poverty alleviation, life expectancy, sanitation, and literacy. For example, the number of the world's poor declined from 1.9 billion in 1990 to 836 million in 2015. China alone managed to lift 600 million people out of extreme poverty over the past forty years. The average child born in 1950 lived 48 years; now this child can expect to live 71 years. Over two billion people have gained access to safe drinking water and toilets. More children go to school. This good news is a reflection of the Millennium Development Goals (MDGs) that have been achieved, thanks to the collective efforts of recipient and donor countries.

P. de Haan, *Whatever Happened to the Third World?*,
https://doi.org/10.1007/978-3-030-39613-8_1

What is a typical Third World country? Thirlwall and Pacheco-López offer a number of similarities and obstacles of Third World countries:

- A high proportion of the labour force engaged in agriculture with low productivity.
- A high proportion of domestic expenditure on food and necessities.
- An export trade dominated by primary products and an import trade dominated by manufactured goods.
- A low level of technology and poor human capital.
- A high birth rate coupled with a falling death rate.
- Savings undertaken by a small percentage of the population.[2]

The Third World, as originally conceived in the early 1950s, has fallen apart. Some countries- in particular East Asian countries, which used to form an integral part of the Third World, took off, while others have not done so well. Unfortunately, quite a number of developing countries deteriorated into fragile or failed states.[3]

On 14 August 1952, French historian Alfred Sauvy introduced the term *Third World* in an article in *L'Observateur*, a French newspaper. Sauvy distinguished the First and Second World as, respectively, the advanced Western world and the Soviet-bloc. In Sauvy's distinction, the Third World consisted of Latin-America, Africa, and Asia. After the first oil price hike by oil producing countries in 1973, a 'Fourth World' emerged, consisting of Most Seriously Affected (MSA) Countries. In addition, oil and natural gas rich countries received a separate categorisation.

Despite the similarities presented above, the Third World was more heterogeneous than one would think at first sight. After all, it included giants such as India and tiny countries such as Malawi. It also included relatively well-developed countries like Brazil, but also undeveloped Nepal. In other words, the term Third World was to some extent defined by what it was not: it was not Europe, it was not America, and neither was it the Soviet Union. Yet, as Branko Milanovic argues, the term was by and large not unreasonable as it allowed us to organise the world in a rather tidy fashion. It also corresponded broadly to a division in economic policies. The Third World was dominated by 'developmentalist' policies, where the state played an active role. State-led development and import substitution were guiding principles in countries as diverse as Brazil, Turkey, India, Tanzania, and Ghana.[4]

A principal explanation for a low level of development is low productivity. When dealing with productivity, economists use the term total factor productivity (TFP).[5] Poor countries typically produce raw materials or, at best, semi-processed goods, with low productivity. Their agricultural productivity is also low—less than one-twentieth of the level of developed countries.[6] What these countries lack is the appropriate type of industrialisation—in particular labour-intensive manufacturing—which would boost their TFP.

Now, what explains this low productivity? There are many possible explanations, ranging from erroneous economic policies, corruption, weak protection of property rights, a lack of entrepreneurial spirit and of a strong work ethic, a lack of credit, problematic access to national and international markets and better technology, and lack of a properly educated and healthy population. There are also political explanations: the elites simply block others from economic opportunities. They monopolise their favoured position in order to maintain the *status quo*.

History also plays its part. During the first wave of globalisation (1870–1914), colonies and other poor countries did not industrialise. In fact, these countries deindustrialised due to the undermining influence of European countries, which had benefitted from the Industrial Revolution. Before the Industrial Revolution, colonies and other poor countries had levels of industrial activity more or less similar to Europe's. But Europe achieved a sixfold increase in industrialisation levels between 1750 and 1913, while Asia and Latin America witnessed a decline to less than one-third of their initial level of industrialisation.[7] And this is where the development gap began.

The only non-Western country that managed to industrialise before 1914 is Japan, promoted by well-educated businessmen and a government intent on modernising Japan after the 1868 Meji Restoration. Poor countries, like Japan, were able to develop as long as they combined the efforts of a forward-looking government that designed and implemented sound economic policies, and a group of dynamic entrepreneurs. Roughly a century later, this was understood by other Asian countries, starting with the four Asian Tigers: Hong Kong, Taiwan, Singapore, and South Korea. Their remarkable economic development refuted neo-Marxist development theories, stating that developing countries would be barred from development.

Around 2050, three of the five largest economies in the world will be in Asia: China, India, and Japan. America obviously belongs to the top five. The question is who will be number five—will it be Germany, Indonesia, Russia, or Brazil? And what will this development imply for the world's geopolitical order? This is what Bruno Maçães projects:

> The new world order shares with the last decade of the previous century the belief in the inevitability of interdependency and connectivity, but it combines it with the recognition of division and conflict, where borders become increasingly diffuse but cultural and civilizational differences do not, giving rise to a permanently unstable compound of heterogeneous elements.[8]

1.2 Global Economic Development

Economic growth of developing countries does not happen in isolation; it is influenced by developments in the world economy. From the start of the decolonisation process in 1945 and up to 1973, when OPEC suddenly increased the price of oil fourfold, the world economy enjoyed a *Golden Age* of robust economic growth, triggered by reconstruction of war-damaged infrastructure, the Marshall Plan, and America's accelerated TFP.[9] This period was one of unparalleled prosperity. World per capita GDP grew by 2.9% per year. World GDP rose 4.9% per year, and world exports increased nearly 8%. This dynamism could be observed in all regions. However, the acceleration was greatest in Europe and Asia.[10] The mood was optimistic; commodity prices soared, from which newly independent developing countries benefitted: between 1950 and 1970, developing countries' real per capita income grew at an average rate of 2.1% per year.

The United Nations declared the 1960s the *Development Decade*. In 1961 the G-77 nonalignment movement among developing countries was established. In 1964, the United Nations Conference on Trade and Development (UNCTAD) was established, providing a forum for developing countries to strengthen their hand in international trade negotiations. The Kennedy Round (1964–1967) included attention for trade interests of developing countries. Before this Round, President Kennedy launched in 1961 the *Alliance for Progress*, a $20 billion economic aid programme for 22 Latin American countries. In addition, the United

States Agency for International Development (USAID), to administer America's aid budget, was created, along with the Peace Corps, a volunteer programme. Other advanced countries, such as Canada, Sweden, and the Netherlands, created separate ministries or agencies to administer their bilateral aid. In October 1970, The UN General Assembly accepted that 0.7% of donor countries' GNP was to be devoted to assist poor countries in their development efforts.[11]

After the 1973 dramatic oil price increase (repeated in 1979) the golden days were over. An initial positive result of the oil price increase was that credit became cheap, as the international financial market was flooded with so-called petro-dollars. However, oil-importing developing countries started to encounter balance-of-payments difficulties. In particular low-income countries faced increasing problems in servicing their debt, financing their investments and importing essential—but expensive—fuels and foodstuffs.

Coinciding with OPEC's price hike, the economies of America and Europe were overheating. Inflation was spinning out of control which negatively affected economic growth and employment. *Stagflation* (a combination of high inflation, high unemployment, and sluggish growth) was the result, plunging all affected countries into a recession. Interest rates rose and international demand fell, hitting developing countries' exports hard. The high interest rates increased their already heavy debt burden. This contributed to indebtedness of many developing countries, leading to defaults, bail-outs, and painful financial and economic restructuring.

The developing world underwent *lost decades* of growth. For some (mainly Latin American countries hit by the debt crisis) it took a decade to overcome the slump; others (in particular sub-Saharan African (SSA) countries) needed much more than a decade to restore economic order. Help was led by the Washington-based International Monetary Fund (IMF) and the World Bank (WB). The so-called Washington Consensus-inspired rescue package was not very effective in putting Latin America's and SSA's economies back on track.

The resumption of economic growth in Latin America and SSA coincided with the start of a fairly long period of stable world economic growth, triggered by a dramatic drop in transportation and communication costs, and by more and more freeing up of international trade. This period became known as The Great Moderation. It began somewhere in the middle of the 1980s and ended in 2008. During this period, two

Not only external economic shocks affected developing countries' economies, there were also endogenous shocks caused by unstable and unanticipated monetary and fiscal policies applied by these countries themselves. Developing countries, not having access to foreign capital, financed their fiscal deficits by printing money, which triggered inflation. Unanticipated changes in fiscal policy, such as fiscal expansion, typically translate into a rise in the interest rate. This higher interest rate led to less investment, which in turn resulted in a dampening effect on output and future economic growth.[12]

historical events took place: in 1989 the fall of the Berlin Wall and, in 1991, the implosion of the Soviet Union. It was hoped that, given the end of the Cold War, a *peace dividend* would ensue, from which developing countries would benefit. Indeed, the expectation was that the funds saved as a result of the drop in military expenditures could be used to fund useful projects in developing countries. But did it happen? During the 1990s, foreign direct investment in developing countries grew sevenfold, but Official Development Assistance (ODA) decreased in per capita terms and measured as a share of receiving country GNP.[13]

Not only ODA was decreasing, some 40 developing countries—among them 33 SSA countries—again encountered mounting difficulties to service their international debt. Most of them were granted debt-relief, promoted by the *Jubilee 2000* international coalition of concerned people that called for the cancellation of Third World debt. *Jubilee 2000* was supported by the then Labour government in Britain and the US Congress; the latter approving $769 million for bilateral and multilateral debt relief. In 1996, well before *Jubilee 2000*, the World Bank, the IMF, and other multilateral, bilateral, and commercial creditors began the Heavily Indebted Poor Country (HIPC) Initiative.[14] HIPC provided debt relief and low-interest loans to indebted developing countries to cancel external debt or reduce debt repayments to sustainable levels. One of HIPCs goals was to re-channel government funds freed from debt repayment into poverty-reduction programs. Each country had to formulate a Poverty Reduction Strategy Paper (PRSP) describing the intended macroeconomic, structural, and social programs to promote economic growth and reduce poverty. When I was posted in Zambia, it was nice to see how the government, NGOs, and civil-society groups participated in the formulation of Zambia's PRSP. To date, HIPC and related Multilateral Debt Relief Initiative (MDRI) programs have benefitted 36 countries (30 SSA countries among them) from $99 billion HIPC and MDRI debt relief. A number of countries also received an additional $1.6 billion in 'topping up' assistance.[15]

The period of the Great Moderation was humming along. But then, in 2008 the Great Recession broke out. Investments dried up, and commodity prices, on which many developing counties still depended as principal export earners, plunged. The same applied to international demand for other products and services. Economic growth stalled and unemployment rose; governments had to tighten their belts, social security budgets were slashed and, as so often, the poor suffered most. Edward Luce maintains that the recession was not as great as the name suggests. He argues: 'Although the short-term market turmoil was worldwide, the so-called global recession was primarily an Atlantic one. Most of the rest of the world continued to expand.'[16] This can be partly explained by China's response. The country countered the Great Recession with a huge fiscal injection of $685 billion, from which exports of developing countries benefitted. For example, a remarkable number of SSA countries achieved commendable economic growth figures. Over the period 2000–2007, two-thirds of their economies grew at more than 5.5% per year. One-third of them even managed to achieve 7% growth per year. However, growth has yet to translate in more equitable income and wealth distribution. SSA remains one of the most unequal regions globally.

Apart from the gradually moving geopolitical power from the West to the East, the question is what the economic prospects of the developing world will be? Since 2008, the weight of developing and emerging economies in the global economy tipped over the 50% mark (expressed in PPP terms) for the first time.[17] By 2010, developing countries accounted for around 42% of global merchandise trade; South-South flows made up about half of the total.

During a good part of the second decade of this century, world economic growth and trade slowed down, caused by the negative effects of the Great Recession and China's gradual transformation from a manufacturing and export-led economy to one based on services and domestic consumption. Yet China and, to an increasing extent, India are attractive export markets for developing countries. However, international trade and world economic growth may be affected by various ongoing international trade disputes and Brexit.

Poverty has decreased over the past fifteen years. However, there are still some 836 million extremely poor people in the world. Following the completion of the Millennium Development Goals, in 2015 even broader and more ambitious development goals have been adopted by the United Nations: the Sustainable Development Goals (SDGs). As for poverty eradication the SDGs are quite clear. Goal 1: End poverty in all its forms everywhere. More specifically, by 2030, extreme poverty should have been reduced to 1%.

1.2.1 Growth Patterns of Developing Countries

Economic growth is the most powerful instrument to reduce poverty and promote development. The other side of the coin is that poverty retards growth. In line with Amartya Sen's thinking, development has occurred when there has been an improvement in basic needs, when economic progress has contributed to a greater sense of self-esteem for the country and individuals within it, and when material advancement has expanded people's entitlements, capabilities and freedoms.[18]

When economies of developing countries are growing well below their growth potential, even modest policy measures will result in growth accelerations. Impressive growth percentages were indeed achieved by a large number of newly independent poor countries. In fact, the 1960s was the best growth decade during the past century for almost all developing countries. However, in many cases the pace of growth could not be sustained; the growth performance turned out to be highly unstable. Periods of growth accelerations were followed by plateaus, or by growth slowdowns.

Based on a sample of 110 countries, Ricardo Hausmann, Lant Pritchett and Dani Rodrik found that 60 countries, including 18 African countries, had at least one period of eight years of growth accelerations between 1957 and 1992.[19] This suggests that achieving rapid economic growth was possible for almost any developing country. However, the question was how to sustain growth. Indeed, during Latin America's lost decade of the 1980s, the continent's annual average growth rate was minus 0.5%. For SSA, the period of negative economic growth was even longer: from 1975 to 2004, SSA's average annual growth was minus 0.1%, aggravated by the HIV/AIDS epidemic which hit SSA hardest.

1.2.2 The Gap Between Rich and Poor Countries

This is the fundamental development question: will poor countries evolve to eventually join the ranks of rich countries. Angus Maddison (1924–2010) estimated that the interregional spread in 1870 was 5:1. Around the beginning of the twenty-first century the gap between the United States and Africa was 20:1.[20]

In 1982, Ian Little observed that between 1958 and 1978, world inequality had slightly increased.[21] Twenty years later, William Easterly wrote: 'For the whole period of 1960 to 1999, the poorest countries did significantly worse than the rich countries, with the poorest two-fifths barely mastering positive growth. The poorest four-fifths of countries in 1960….roughly correspond to what later became known as the Third World. Seventy percent of these Third World countries grew more slowly over the whole period than the median growth of 2.4 percent per capita for the richest countries. They were falling behind, not catching up.'[22]

But Easterly appeared to be too pessimistic. Fourteen years later, Branko Milanovic observes in *Global Inequality*[23] that global income inequality between countries may be declining; in other words a converging process may be taking place.

> ….the most accurate statement would be that the evidence suggests that global income inequality is either stable or in decline. A stronger statement would be to say that there is no evidence of rising global income inequality (and the difference in income between the Western and Asian middle classes has clearly been shrinking).[24]

This development is mainly thanks to China's and India's phenomenal economic growth over the past four decades.[25] Other emerging economies also contributed to this converging trend, albeit to a lesser extent. *The Economist* reported that the geographic scope of catch-up growth is narrowing. Real output per person as a share of that in the US has fallen in the Middle East and North Africa, since 2013 in Latin America, and since 2014 in SSA. Estimates suggest declines in European emerging economies as well, leaving Asia as the last hope of convergence.[26] Another factor is that breakneck growth of emerging economies will not go on forever. This observation may be a bit shortsighted, since there may be room for more growth in emerging economies. After all, more productivity can be created by workers moving from low-productivity sectors to higher ones. And, secondly, productivity can also be boosted within sectors. Such sustained productivity growth would obviously help emerging economies to continue catching up with high-income countries.

We should bear in mind that the Western middle classes have lost their role of growth promoters. Luce observes: 'Within my lifetime, the emerging middle class has gone from virtually nowhere to supplant the established Western middle class as the engine of global growth. Since 1970, Asia's per-capita incomes have increased fivefold. Even in Africa, the worst-performing continent, incomes have almost doubled. The West's median income, meanwhile, has barely shifted in the last half-century.'[27]

Neither should one be blind to another trend: the world's richest 1% now own more wealth than the other 99% put together.[28] The rich enhance their influence in the political domain. Both developments are impinging upon the social fabric of societies but also upon societies' political sustainability.

1.2.3 Inequality Within Countries

Various studies reveal that income inequality within a country negatively affects its growth rate. For example, Milanovic found that a 5 point increase in the Gini ratio (a measurement of inequality) would reduce annual economic growth by 0.5%.[29] Economic growth can contribute to domestic redistribution of income and wealth, but cannot address inequality on its own. Two World Bank staffers, David Dollar and Aart Kraay, studied the relationship between economic growth and income distribution in 80 countries over a period of four decades. They conclude that the income of the poorest 20% of the population rose on a one-to-one basis with overall growth. While the Gini ratio remained the same, the absolute inequality between the incomes of the rich and poor widened.[30]

Large obstacles have to be removed before redistribution of income and wealth in developing countries can bear fruit. Thirlwall and Pacheco-López mention three of them:

1. There is the dualistic nature of many economies, perpetuated by feudal land tenure systems and urban bias in the allocation of investment resources.
2. There is inequality in the provision of education facilities, and a particular lack of facilities in rural areas where the poorest are concentrated.
3. There is disguised rural employment, underemployment and open unemployment in urban areas created by rural-urban migration, a shortage of investment resources and inappropriate production techniques.[31]

1.2.4 What Happened to the Third World

While the growing number of fragile and failed states is worrying, and poverty will not disappear from the face of the earth, the Third World, as we knew it in the 1950s, is gradually disappearing. The 1966 *World Bank Atlas* included 58 low-income countries; their number fell to 34 in 2018. Even more inspiring is the fact that the number of high-income countries has increased considerably: from only 21 in 1966 to 81 in 2018. So, what we are witnessing is a process of differentiation between developing countries. A growing number of them are rapidly emerging as strong and dynamic economies, while the number of low-income countries is shrinking. It is indeed worrying that some former middle-income and low-income countries are deteriorating into fragile or failed states.

Following Japan's example, as of the 1960s and 1970s, the four Asian Tigers pulled away from other Third World countries. Quite a few others followed in their footsteps. China is the most telling example. Towards the end of 1978, the Chinese leader Deng Xiaoping was able to introduce economic reforms. Since then, China's economic growth is simply phenomenal. In the early 1990s, India opened its economy, after which the country achieved high and sustained economic growth figures. Together with Brazil, Russia, and South Africa, the BRICS countries are now important global economic and political actors. In their slipstream, new groups of countries are emerging, such as the 'Next-11': Bangladesh, Egypt, Indonesia, Iran, Mexico, Nigeria, Pakistan, the Philippines, Turkey, South Korea, and Vietnam.

Between the increasing number of fast growers and the decreasing number of low-income countries, there is a fairly steady group of middle-income countries which have difficulties in joining the ranks of high-income countries. They seem to be held back by the so-called middle-income trap.

There are still 34 poor low-income countries; most of them (26) are to be found in SSA. And there is a growing number of fragile and failed states, in which central government is so weak or ineffective that it has little control over much of its territory. There is widespread corruption and criminality; refugees and involuntary movement of populations abound, and their economies are going down the drain.

The Middle-Income Trap
Now, what is the middle-income trap? It is the phenomenon of hitherto rapidly growing economies stagnating at middle-income levels and failing to graduate to the ranks of high-income countries.

Since the 1980s (when globalisation picked up), the world's poorest countries did well: during the 1980s and 1990s their real per capita income increased by more than 160%. This miracle was not spurred by agricultural export; no, it was large-scale standardised manufactured goods that contributed to the increase of per capita incomes. In contrast, middle-income countries, almost all Latin American countries, former Soviet republics, and much of the Middle East, did not do so well: over the same period their real per capita incomes grew by less than 20%. So, these middle-income countries were trapped—caught in the middle. Why is this? This is what Geoffrey Garrett observes:

> The answer seems to be that they have not found a niche in world markets. They have been unable to compete in high-value-added markets dominated by wealthy economies because their work forces are not sufficiently skilled and their legal and banking systems are not sophisticated enough. As a result, they have had little choice but to try to compete with China and other low-income economies in markets for standardized products made with widely available and relatively old technologies. But because of their higher wages, the middle-income nations are bound to lose the battle.[32]

Justin Lin provides yet another explanation: 'After World War II many Latin American countries carried out the 'secondary import substitution' strategy to develop some capital-intensive industries.... Not surprisingly, it resulted in inadequate employment, an unfair distribution of wealth, and a mushrooming of slums. Under the pressure of unemployment and social tension, those countries resorted to so-called democratic politics. The politicians offered temporary social welfare policies to the electorate. But it produced the Latin American middle-income trap, featuring stagnation, failure to narrow the income gap with advanced countries, periodic financial turmoil, and economic crises.'[33] A number of suggestions to overcome the middle-income trap are presented in Chap. 2.

Low-Income Countries and Fragile States
In 1988, I visited Sri Lanka on behalf of a Dutch funding agency to discuss fresh development proposals with Sri Lankan Non-Governmental

Organisations (NGOs). At the time, the security situation was tense on the isle as a result of the Tamil Tigers' armed struggle. Yet, Sri Lanka could be visited according to the Netherlands Embassy's advice. So I went. A few days after my arrival, bombs exploded in the vicinity of government buildings. Tourists were ordered to leave the country immediately. Since I was under the protection of a large Sri Lankan NGO, I could stay. I then realised once again how much damage the civil war did to Sri Lanka in human lives but also in financial and development terms. The World Bank calculated that between 1983 and 1996, the total financial damage of Sri Lanka's civil war was around $4 billion—twice the size of Sri Lanka's GDP in 1996. The Tamil Tigers have been defeated, but now and again, bloody attacks by extremist groups crop up.

In 2018, there were 61 fragile or failed states in the world. The majority is to be found in SSA (34); the remainder in Asia (18), the Middle East and West Asia (7), as well as in Latin America (2).[34] According to the Fund for Peace, a fragile state has several attributes. Common indicators include a state whose central government is so weak or ineffective that it has little practical control over much of its territory; it cannot provide public services; there is corruption and criminality; refugees and involuntary movement of populations abound; and the economy is falling apart. Failed states have the tendency to spread to neighbouring states, creating an opening for jihadist groups to step into the void.

While economic stagnation and poverty may not be the only characteristics of fragile and failed states, they are nevertheless important ones. As Paul Collier (who coined the term fragile state, by the way) once said, growth is not a cure all, but the lack of growth is a kill-all. Of all the fragile and failed states in 2018, 30 are low-income countries, while 21 of them belong to the lower middle-income group. Only 8 are upper middle-income countries. All told, 83.6% of them are low-income or lower middle-income countries.[35]

What can be done? It is important to analyse what the underlying causes would have been why a particular state slid backwards into a situation of near anarchy. A one-size-fits-all approach, typically focused on strengthening the state's capacity, may not be the appropriate one. In *Fixing Failed States*, Ashraf Ghani and Clare Lockhart introduce the notion of a sovereignty gap between de jure state sovereignty and de facto capabilities of states to serve their population and act as responsible member of the international community.[36] The authors argue that outdated one-size-fits-all solutions, involving lots of aid monies, have not brought about the intended results. More suggestions for improvement are presented in Chap. 2.

1.2.5 The Evolution of Development Economics

Around the beginning of the twentieth century, colonial powers started to understand that colonies should no longer be treated as providers of valuable raw materials. It was felt that the citizenry of their colonies deserved to be educated and to receive health services, so as to provide the skilled labour needed for their countries' future development. At the time, this politically-inspired intention coincided with an emerging scholarly interest in the economic development of colonies and other poor tropical countries. The insights, often developed by geographers, are now outdated and here and there politically incorrect, as elaborated in Chap. 3.

Development economics, as a sub-discipline of economics, evolved after the end of World War II (WWII), when a whole range of colonies gained independence. Many of these former colonies were typically poor, agrarian, and overpopulated. For their countries' economic development, the new Asian and African leaders sought advice from the first generation of development economists. From roughly 1950 onwards, this generation called the shots.[37] Economists belonging to the first generation agreed that state-led rapid, yet balanced, economic growth through industrialisation was required to boost development, create employment, and to overcome poverty. Subsequent generations of development economists begged to differ.

The First Generation

In this generation's view, economic development of newly independent countries should be achieved as fast as possible to provide jobs for the growing population and to increase income per capita. Given the lack of private entrepreneurship and poor functioning of markets, the way forward was through state-led capital-intensive industrialisation, as the absence of an industrial sector was *the* reason for poor economic performance. Was it not that developed countries had gained their prosperity thanks to industrialisation? Technical and financial aid would help the development process take off. Development economists belonging to this generation shared the view that there was a need for a structural transformation of low productivity activities in agriculture, petty trade, and the like, to high-productivity manufacturing. The urgency of this transformation was prompted by widespread poverty of rapidly increasing populations longing to catch up with developed countries.

The first generation provided the theoretical basis upon which younger generations further developed their insights and models. The first generation also clarified the role of basic economic notions in the development of newly independent countries, such as the interplay between saving and investment, marginal productivity of capital and labour, sectoral transformation, and import and export.

This first generation, as it turned out, was too confident and too optimistic. They overlooked the thorny realities obtaining in newly independent poor countries. Their governments were typically ill-equipped to implement the many development tasks they were supposed to undertake. Around the beginning of the 1970s, it became clear that state-led industrial development had not lived up to expectations. Investments had not yielded much in terms of output, employment, let alone in consumption.

The leaders of young developing countries had been blinded by nation-building objectives through impressive, but loss-making, industrial establishments rather than driven by purely economic objectives. Worse, the leadership had neglected agricultural development. Agricultural exports were discouraged; agricultural savings were diverted to the loss-making industrial sector through heavy taxation of agricultural exports. Deficiencies in government plans, insufficient resources (including foreign aid), limited capacity of governments' civil service, government-inspired market distortions, and all sorts of institutional weaknesses explained the poor development record. In sum, government had failed.

The Second Generation

The question of how economies grow is one of the most fundamental questions in economics. During the time of the second generation, new growth theories appeared (see Chap. 5). This was important for developing countries because understanding what the factors of economic growth would be, helped to invest in them. When successful, this creates jobs, increases income per capita, and boosts productivity. Economic growth also makes it affordable for governments to invest in people's abilities (i.e., education, technical training), and for people to invest in themselves. And economic growth helps to lift the poor out of misery.

As noted, government had failed to deliver the development goods. The allocative efficiency of the market, including price incentives, and the stimulating role of international trade had been overlooked. 'Getting the prices right' became the second generation's motto. This new generation moved away from the first generation's grand theories towards a micro-economic approach. Disaggregated micro-studies were undertaken in which the units of analysis were, for example, agricultural production and household units which constituted the basis of specific sectoral or fiscal policies but also of adequately guiding policy in the macroeconomic domain.

The first action to take was to remove price distortions and trade protection measures. It was also felt that it was not so much initial conditions but differences in policies that explained the often poor performance of developing countries. In other words: a country was not poor because of a vicious circle of poverty; no, it was poor because its policies were poor. Look at the success of the Asian Tiger countries, second generation economists pointed out, their strategy was moving away from inward-looking policies. Instead—after a period of protecting their emerging industrial sector—the Asian Tigers concentrated on export promotion, responding to market and price incentives.

However, in the early 1980s, it became quite clear that getting the prices right did not necessarily bring about economic development. During the 1970s, most Latin American countries had borrowed heavily—their public sector spending had almost doubled. In 1982, Mexico defaulted and—soon after—other large Latin American countries had to call in financial help. During the 1980s and 1990s, most African countries did not grow at all; their economies shrank. There was an urgent need to restore order in governments' finances. Fundamental policy reform was required, including trimming down overextended governments.

By necessity, addressing government failure remained the main objective; a good second was creating conditions for the market to play its allocative role. The IMF and WB—and in their slipstream bilateral donor agencies—stepped in with stabilisation credits (IMF) and structural adjustment loans (WB), both based upon the *Washington Consensus* philosophy. The implementation met with criticism, as explained in Chap. 5.

A Third Generation?

Institutional economist Douglass North (1920–2015) argued that to get the prices right, and to get the policies right, it is particularly important to also get the institutions right. This catchy statement suggests that institutions would be the common denominator for a third generation of development economists. But it was not to be. Apart from new institutional economics, there are now also other influential schools of thought, ranging from, new economic geography, economic anthropology, to economic history.[38] Insights of new institutional economists, economic historians, and economic geographers are presented in detail in Chap. 6.

Institutions Matter

Douglass North successfully put the role of institutions at center stage in the economic development literature. His message did not fall on deaf ears among donor agencies. During my time at the Netherlands Ministry for Development Cooperation, I was given the task to formulate an institutional development policy for the ministry.

Institutions mould *incentives* that promote (or hinder) economic progress. Surely, people interested to engage in business can be found anywhere, poor developing countries not excluded. However, they will only invest when there are incentives to do so; that is, if government's development policy is sound, property rights are secured, contracts are enforced, investment capital is available, and the environment to do business is favourable. Property rights play a vital role in economic markets. Without these rights, and their protection, people are not prepared to invest, nor will they innovate. The capture of the gains from trade requires the development of a state as a coercive power which can secure property rights and, at the same time, has the power to enforce contracts. North argued that the inability of most societies to develop effective low-cost enforcement of contracts is the most important source of historical stagnation and underdevelopment of many developing countries.

Institutional economists make a distinction between limited access order societies and open access societies. There is a critical tipping point from which the former can evolve into an open access society. Such a tipping point comes when open access in the economic or political domain results in sufficient power of the new entrants to press the elites to accept them. Once this stage is reached, rapid changes will take place, extending to ever-larger segments of society. New institutions are created, providing services for newly emerging organisations, including the protection of their property rights. The tipping point comes when open access in one dimension, say in the economic domain, commands sufficient power to press successfully for open access in the other dimension—the political domain.[39]

New institutional economics revealed a crucial missing link in growth theories: institutions do matter when analysing long-term processes of economic growth or stagnation. This discovery is more and more taken on board by development economists who deal with two basic questions: (1) how to get economic growth started and (2) how to sustain it. Research on these two questions has brought to light that to get economic growth going, institutions may not yet matter as much. But institutions are important to sustain economic growth. There is broad agreement that differences in institutions must be the fundamental source of the wide differences in growth rates observed for countries at low levels of income and for low income—and low total factor productivity levels.

History Matters as Well

The historical approach to the question of growth may be the most promising, as it pays due attention to the role of culture and politics which both may promote or constrain economic growth. However, economic historians are held back by a paucity of data, nor have they managed to arrive at a shared understanding of the nature of economic growth.

In Chap. 6 the works of two prominent economic historians, taking different approaches to the subject matter, are presented. The Darwinian approach explains economic growth in a reproductive Darwinian perspective. Oded Galor is a representative of this approach. The basic idea is that the agents who are doing well in the economy, and thus act as the agents of economic growth, will also have differential reproduction rates. Hence their share in the population keeps rising. The cultural traits which these people represent can be characterised as bourgeois values.

However, other economic historians, such as Joel Mokyr, observe that in Darwinian models culture is static; there is little room in them for learning, persuasion, or imitation. Mokyr underscores the important dynamic part that culture plays in the history of economic growth.

Although not presenting a shared understanding of the history of economic growth; nonetheless, Galor and Mokyr agree that analysing the onset of the Industrial Revolution is key to understanding what has happened since in terms of economic development. They both use notions like demographic transition and the Great Divergence. Both of them also integrate political, institutional, and geographical factors into their analyses; factors missing in standard economic growth models to date. These three factors help to better capture—and better explain—the process of economic growth over the past two centuries.

New Economic Geography

Paul Krugman was instrumental in reviving interest in economic geography, underscoring the role of geography in the process of economic development. When transportation costs are high, Krugman argues, spreading of economic activities takes place. Instead, when these costs are low, peripheral regions can efficiently be served from a central location, as economies of scale at the centre trigger a centre-periphery structure. But if transportation costs continue to fall, the periphery may benefit.

The manufacturing sector can create increasing returns to scale. The production of manufactured goods will concentrate in the location where there is a large market. This will be reinforced by the notion that it is more desirable to live and produce near a concentration of manufacturing production, because it is less expensive to buy the goods that this location provides. However, if transportation costs continue to fall, the importance of being close to markets and suppliers will decline. Peripheral countries offer potential producers the advantage of lower wages. At some point the decline in transportation costs will be sufficient that the lower wage rate in the periphery more than offsets the disadvantage of being remote from markets and supplies. At this point manufacturing will have an incentive to move out from the core to the periphery again, eventually resulting in the convergence of wage rates.

There is no shared understanding to date about the decisive force of geography in explaining economic growth, or stagnation for that matter. Yet, development economists now pay more attention to what economic geographers have to say about development.

Looking back at the evolution of development economics, the challenge is to capture economic growth in its widest sense. One way or the other, insights of other sciences need to be incorporated into growth models to more comprehensively capture what exactly causes growth and to accurately predict what its future trajectory will be.

1.2.6 Trade, Globalisation and Developnment

International trade and globalisation are both solid topics of analysis in economics. Adam Smith (1723–1790) was the first economist to write about the benefits of free trade. Since then, international trade theory evolved. Globalisation is, historically speaking, a more recent phenomenon. There are economists who praise globalisation for its stimulating economic effects, but there are others, who draw attention to globalisation's downsides.

International trade benefits from rules to which trading partners adhere. After the end of WWII, institutions were established to regulate and promote trade between countries, inspired by the positive mood of multilateralism. How they came about, their purpose, the role played by developing countries in their establishment, and their respective 'rules of the game' is succinctly described below.

Given the purpose of this book, two pertinent questions will be dealt with: (1) to what extent did developing countries benefit from international trade and globalisation, and (2) what can be done to let developing countries benefit more from international trade and globalisation?

International Trade Theories

International trade is not, as mercantilists would have it, a *zero-sum game*. It is a prominent engine of growth, as Adam Smith and other classical economists argued. For example, David Ricardo (1772–1823) developed *the law of comparative advantage*, which said that through trade between nations everyone can obtain more of everything than they could produce for themselves. However, Ricardo's law is *static*—once the decision to specialise in a particular good has been made, no further gains were foreseen. A more recent contribution to international trade economics is the *Hekscher-Ohlin Theorem.* It says that poor countries, with a combination of an abundant labour force and scarce capital, will find it cheaper to produce and export labour-intensive goods, whereas rich countries—endowed with more capital goods but with a limited labour supply—would produce and export capital-intensive goods. In the end, this leads to narrowing the wage gap and economic convergence between rich and poor countries.

Then, there is the *Stolper-Samuelson Theorem.* The basic message of it is that even when free trade raises national income, some factors, such as labour, may lose out in the absence of compensation by the government. Needless to say, the Stolper-Samuelson Theorem may well enjoy renewed interest now that a wave of protectionism looms.

Raúl Prebisch's (1901–1986) point of departure was peripheral Latin America, where the benefits from increased productivity had not reached. Prebisch argued that industrialisation, by way of import-substitution, would be the only means by which Latin America could achieve higher productivity levels. If productivity in agriculture could also be increased by technical progress, Prebisch observed, and if real wages could be raised by industrialisation, the disequilibrium between incomes at the centre (i.e., rich countries) and the periphery (i.e., Latin America and other developing continents) could be corrected.

Apart from Ricardo's *static* comparative advantage theorem, international trade can also trigger *dynamic* effects. It depends on what a country specialises in: natural resources or manufacturing. Regarding the latter, manufacturing triggers technological progress, which in turn promotes faster growth. Paul Krugman, as mentioned, incorporated this dynamism in the new trade theory, emphasising increasing returns and the geographic concentration of production.

Globalisation

Globalisation is not exclusively an economic phenomenon; it encompasses more things, such as the international flow of ideas and knowledge, sharing of cultures, global civil society, and the global environmental movement. The first globalisation wave started around 1870 and ended abruptly in 1914, when the First World War broke out. The second globalisation wave started after the end of WWII, from which developing countries also benefitted. For example, by the end of the 1990s, (semi) manufactured exports constituted 70% of total exports from the developing world. And in 2013, the Asian and Pacific region's world market share of (semi) manufactures was 24.5%, while their share of high-tech exports had increased to 30.6%.

Emerging economies, like Brazil, China, and India, play an ever more important role in international trade, to the detriment of traditional industrial economies. It is quite possible that China's economy will surpass America's around 2030. A converging process of global incomes is ongoing. Obviously this will change the geopolitical playing field. In fact, it may be doing so already: the Beijing Consensus is gradually overtaking the Washington Consensus. The question is: will political capitalism eclipse liberal capitalism?

With cyclical ups and downs, globalisation was humming along until 2016 when a majority of the British population voted for Brexit, and until early 2018, when President Trump announced that the US would increase import tariffs on steel and aluminum. Since then, a trade war ensued between the US and China, which negatively affected international trade.

Surely, globalisation contributed to international economic growth, lowering of prices of consumer goods, and to poverty reduction. However, not everybody benefitted. There are downsides to globalisation, among them job losses in industrial countries, as the Stolper-Samuelson Theorem predicted. Another downside is the destabilising impact of financial globalisation, which backfired when countries had not put in place the necessary safeguards to prevent capital flight. These negative effects were initially neglected by free trade-minded policymakers and economists alike. But not by politicians who gained popular support from a growing number of globalisation-skeptics. Trade protection and closing borders for labour migrants are now popular political rallying points. If not properly countered, the positive aspects of globalisation will be lost.

International Trade Institutions

GATT

In the spirit of multilateralism, the General Agreement on Tariffs and Trade (GATT) was established way back in 1947. Ever since then, tariff walls have been broken down in pursuit of international free trade. In addition, technological progress, the lowering of transportation and communication costs, and the spread of private capital flows opened the gates for more international trade and investment. However, on the question of improved access to industrialised markets by developing countries and commodity price stabilisation, GATT disappointed. In short, GATT increasingly became a target of criticism from developing countries, as their concerns were not effectively addressed by GATT. It was felt, not unjustified, that the post-WWII international institutional structure functioned primarily to defend the interests of industrialised countries to maintain the *status quo*.

UNCTAD

In 1961, the Non-Aligned Movement (NAM) was established. The Group of 77 NAM nations (better known as G-77) agreed that a united stance would greatly help to conclude favourable international trade deals. Indeed, G-77 has been instrumental in the establishment in 1964 of the United Nations Conference on Trade and Development (UNCTAD). UNCTAD's objectives were to: (1) create better access to the markets of developed countries; (2) establish a system which would help stabilise commodity prices; and (3) compensate developing countries for fluctuations in export earnings and for deterioration of their terms of trade.

UNCTAD offered developing countries *the* platform to pursue their trade priorities.

But it turned out that G-77 did not share the same trade priorities, which limited their bargaining power. On top of this, developed countries were not particularly eager to offer developing countries trade preferences, especially not regarding agricultural products. This lack of eagerness was inspired by the fact that food security and low food prices are formidable strategic objectives of their governments. Furthermore, in many developed countries the agricultural sector, which was politically well represented, had a big finger in the pie and, thirdly, governments wanted to make sure that their countries' agricultural areas would continue to offer an economic and social environment in which people can work, live, shop, and have access to nearby schools or hospitals.

What has UNCTAD been able to achieve? Some analysts maintain that the Generalised System of Preferences (GSP) is UNCTAD's principal achievement. GSP intends to promote developing countries‘ exports of (semi)-manufactured products through non-reciprocal treatment.[40] Some argue that another achievement is a higher proportion of IMF's Special Drawing Rights reserved for developing countries. This is too much praise, as decisions like these are only made by the IMF Board. In 1980, UNCTAD's Common Fund for Commodities (CFC) was established to finance international buffer stocks and internationally coordinated national stocks. However, to date CFC functions primarily in providing technical assistance to developing country commodity producers.

All told, UNCTAD now plays a smaller role as a political forum than in the 1960s and 1970s. It is focusing on analyses of developing country trade and foreign investment perspectives. UNCTAD had some success in persuading developed countries to grant preferential access to the exports of developing countries, but mainly in the field of manufactured goods, benefitting the larger and more advanced developing countries.[41]

WTO

As of January 1995, the World Trade Organisation (WTO) started its operations; GATT was immersed into the WTO. The WTO allows members to increase import tariffs when a sudden surge in imports puts domestic firms in trouble. WTO itself does not punish violators, but it allows countries that suffer injury as a result of a violation, to retaliate by imposing trade restrictions on the offending country. In fact, the WTO is an institutional response to a practical question: how to sustain a mutually beneficial liberal economy in a world of many sovereign states of different economic strength and sophistication, all of which suffer from internal protectionist pressures.

WTO does not do away with the inequality in the power of nations. Yet it established a procedure for dispute settlement. Evading WTO's appellate body's decision is impossible, unless it is reversed collectively by every single WTO member. The WTO offers poor countries a forum of forcing powerful countries to adhere to internationally agreed rules. WTO also offers these countries the possibility of greater integration into the international trade system. Exceptions to WTO rules apply to developing countries, while additional exceptions are extended to the poorest among them.[42] This was welcomed by developing countries since they wanted to promote their exports and to attract foreign investment. Since the early 1990s, many developing countries made progress in liberalising their trade regimes. Out of 50 countries analysed, Constantine Michalopoulos concludes that 45 showed a decline in their average applied rates—frequently more than half.[43]

Since GATT, special international trade rounds were held. The Kennedy Round and Uruguay Round were such rounds. The most recent one was the Doha Round. This 'Development Round', with a special view to address the agricultural demands of developing countries, should have ended in 2005. The Doha Development Agenda had several important implications for Trade Related Intellectual Property Rights (TRIPS). Another issue was that low-income countries would not be asked to liberalise any of their trade restrictions in either manufactures or agriculture. Industrial countries were only prepared to cut their agricultural subsidies and trade barriers in exchange for access of their manufactured goods and financial services to the markets of developing countries, to which the latter objected. As a consequence, the Doha Round was formally abandoned in 2015.

Many developing countries face WTO restrictions regarding their own industrial policies. For example, it is harder for Latin American and African countries to copy the development policies so successfully applied by East Asian countries before they joined the WTO. Under WTO rules export subsidies are not allowed, nor sequencing of appropriate measures on the way to full trade liberalisation. Industrial imitation is neither allowed. As noted, only the poorest nations are exempt from these restrictions.

Apart from the restrictions just mentioned, WTO's Agreement on TRIPS impairs the possibility for developing countries to copy protected technologies used by industrial countries. True, large countries such as China and India stand to benefit from these rights, but this does not apply to smaller developing countries that may see their ability to educate restricted (because of copy rights); the same applies to the provision of public health services to their citizens (given patent rights on expensive drugs).

Regional Trade Agreements

There are many more regional trade agreements than global trade agreements. The WTO listed over 100 regional agreements, whether they are customs unions, free trade agreements; whether they are between developing countries, or between developing and industrialised countries.

A customs union applies free trade between the members while applying a common external tariff. A free trade area slashes tariffs between the members but it does not apply a common external tariff. So, the member countries are free to apply their own tariffs for imported goods from without the free trade zone, thus allowing each individual member to benefit from the cheapest imports.

Arguably, the best-known—and most spectacular—regional agreement is the European Union (EU). By all standards, the EU is a remarkable success, taking into consideration Europe's dismal political and economic beggar-thy-neighbour history before WWII. The North American Free Trade Area (NAFTA) between the US, Canada and Mexico was another well-known free trade agreement. Its successor, the United States-Mexico-Canada Agreement (USMCA), may be undermined by the Trump Administration's hostile attitude towards Mexico, and to free trade at large. Although developing countries are involved in quite a few regional trade agreements, the total trade involved is relatively small: almost 50% of all trade among regional trade partners involves the EU; another 13% involves NAFTA.

In 1975, the European Economic Community (now European Union) signed an agreement with initially 46, and now 77, African, Caribbean, and Pacific (ACP) countries. It provided free access to the EU market for all ACP's manufactured goods and 90% of their agricultural exports. But this was not all. A Stabex Scheme was also concluded to stabilise the foreign exchange earnings of twelve important commodities. In 2000, Stabex was abolished and replaced by financial support from the European Development Fund (EDF). EU's assistance to ACP countries is now channeled through EDF.

How Developing Countries Fared

Emerging economies, applying what the Hekscher-Ohlin Theorem suggested, were benefitting from the lowering of trade barriers. As a consequence, the composition of their exports changed from primary products to (semi) manufactured goods. Some 24 developing countries—home to 3 billion people—had doubled their ratio of trade to income over the period 1980–2000.[44] Not surprisingly, their average annual growth rate rose from 3% in the 1970s to 5% during the last decade of the past century. As noted, emerging economies now play a prominent role in international trade, to the detriment of industrial economies.[45] SSA's achievements were disappointing: in 2013, SSA's market share of world manufactured exports was only 1.1%.[46]

International trade of industrialised and developing countries together now consists of primary products and (semi) manufactured goods. A fairly recent development is that, instead of building the whole supply chain, developing countries join international production chains to become competitive in one particular segment of that chain. When successful in the attempt, more jobs and higher incomes are being created.

The not so good news is that other developing countries traded less than they did around the end of the 1970s—they are falling behind. But it is wrong to blame globalisation for their disappointing performance. These countries failed to seize the opportunities that globalisation provided (unlike successful developing countries). Mancur Olson, for example, argued:

> Sometimes the shortcomings of the economic policies and institutions of poor countries make foreign investors and foreign firms unwelcome, or provoke the flight of locally owned capital, or make lending to these countries exceedingly risky. Whether the institutional and policy shortcomings of a country keep capital from having the productivity appropriate to its scarcity or discourage the investments and lending that would equalize the marginal product of capital across countries, they keep it from achieving its potential.[47]

Some time ago, the World Bank published a report entitled *Global Economic Prospects and the Developing Countries.*[48] Its message was that if global trade liberalisation were to continue, it would offer great opportunities for developing countries. According to the report, by 2015 world income would be $355 billion higher with merchandise trade liberalisation, of which developing countries would annually gain $184 billion.

Not everybody agreed. Rodrik argues that the report exaggerated the possible benefits.[49] He proposes that developing countries' policymakers rather focus on the fundamentals of economic growth: investment, macroeconomic stability, human resources development, plus good governance, and not let international economic integration dominate their thinking.

Rodrik confirms my own experience when I was posted at the Netherlands Embassy in la Paz, Bolivia, and, later, at the Netherlands Embassy in Lusaka, Zambia. Bolivia forms an integral part of three regional trade agreements. Despite these agreements, in 2017 Bolivia was still a raw materials exporter: fuels, ores, and gems accounted for 71.3% of Bolivia's total export. Zambia has not done any better than Bolivia. Zambia is a member of four regional trade agreements and one trade agreement with the EU. Like Bolivia, Zambia has not been able to diversify its exports. In 2017, copper still accounted for 75.7% of Zambia's total export.

Since 2008, the weight of developing and emerging economies in the global economy tipped over the 50% mark (expressed in PPP terms) for the first time.[50] During the second decade of this century, world economic growth and trade slowed down, caused by the negative effects of the Great Recession and China's gradual transformation from a manufacturing and export-led economy to one based on services and domestic consumption. Nonetheless, China and India, both having a huge domestic market, are attractive export markets for developing countries. However, international trade and world economic growth may be affected by various ongoing international trade disputes and Brexit.

Regarding poverty, in 2005, Branko Milanovic took a sample of 321 household income surveys from 95 countries, covering 90% of the entire world's population. He concluded that: (1) increased openness reduces the income share of the bottom six deciles, and (2) the adverse effect of openness on inequality is greater the lower a country's per capita income. However, Milanovic's conclusions were not all bad news for the poor: at an income per capita of about $7500.- the poor start to benefit relative to the rich.[51] Martin Ravallion, another authority on poverty analysis, concludes not in a reassuring manner: '.... based on the data available from cross-country comparison, it is hard to maintain the view that expanding trade, in general, is a powerful force for poverty reduction in developing countries.'[52]

Milanovic adjusted his 2005 insights in 2016 when his celebrated book *Global Inequality* came out. Regarding the impact on the poor, Milanovic concludes that the great winners have been the Asian poor and middle classes; the great losers, the lower middle classes of the rich world.[53]

In March 2018 Valentin Lang and Marina Mendes Tavares published an IMF Working Paper entitled *The Distribution of Gains from Globalization*.[54] They observe that many developing countries have experienced periods of strong economic growth and poverty reduction as they integrated their economies with the rest of the world. Regarding income inequality, a subsample of developing countries indicated that the gains from globalisation also reached the bottom of the income distribution and, thus, reduced poverty there. The authors conclude, after having analysed the effects on the various income deciles, that there is evidence for a poverty-reducing effect in developing countries and no evidence for income losses in absolute terms for any decile. This conclusion supports the view that globalisation helps reduce poverty in developing countries. Their findings also suggest that that there was an important role played by domestic policies aimed at realising more inclusive gains from globalisation.[55]

How to Ward Off Protectionism

Until not too long ago, protectionism was a dirty word, but it no longer seems to be. A 2007 *PEW Survey of Global Attitudes* observes that enthusiasm for further opening of the global economy is flagging in many industrialised countries and in some developing countries. Meanwhile, two huge regional trade deals in the making: the Transatlantic Trade and Investment Partnership (TTIP) and the Transpacific Partnership (TPP) have been shelved.[56] New bilateral and regional trade deals may be in the offing, thereby further undermining the international trade regime.

If a wave of protectionism can be staved off, in particular China and India could act as *the* engines of growth for developing countries exporting to these economic powerhouses. But more can be done to allow developing countries to benefit from international trade. For example, WTO rules preventing developing countries from diversifying their economies could be scrapped. Then, there is the phenomenon of *tariff-escalation* as applied by industrialised countries, meaning that processed raw materials, such as cocoa, tea, and coffee, are charged far higher tariffs than those for unprocessed raw materials. Mitigating or scrapping them would also help.

Safeguards are temporary tariffs to allow an industry time to make adjustments to better withstand competition from importers. Dumping duties are supposed to be applied to stop unfair trade practices or selling goods below their cost price. These duties can be used to ban imports and, at the same time, protect local manufacturers.[57]

Technical barriers limit competitive imports. The application of the rules of origin is yet another possibility to keep foreign competitors out. Joseph Stiglitz cites the example of America using rules of origin to promote its own exports: '...countries that make shirts using American cotton are given preferences which those who use the least expensive cotton are not.'[58] Doing away with technical barriers and rules of origin would benefit developing countries now banned from exporting their goods.

Particularly notorious are agricultural subsidies applied by the European Union, Japan, and America. Subsidised agricultural surpluses were dumped on the international market, crowding out developing countries' exports. For example, America spends $3.3 billion annually to subsidise 25,000 American cotton farmers, to the detriment of 10 million cotton farmers in Burkina Faso, Mali, Chad, and Benin. Protection is also given to many low-value manufactured goods in which developing countries have a comparative advantage, particularly in a wide range of textile goods.[59]

In sum, the world trade system works in many ways against the trade interests of poor developing countries.

Rodrik, Stiglitz and other world-class economists propose a carefully managed freeing up of the international labour market. Rodrik estimates that the gains to be made would outstrip any other proposal, including the entire package of trade measures as proposed under the Doha Round negotiations.[60] Milanovic argues: 'In the long run the antimigration battle cannot be won if globalization continues. A much better alternative would be to help reduce differences in average income levels between countries. In that case, migratory pressures would subside, and the world would, from the point of view of the standard of living, become a much more homogeneous place, not threatening the continuation of globalization.'[61]

Finally, the downsides of globalisation should be better addressed by governments of affected countries, through financial support to those who lost their jobs, providing retraining programs, promoting labour mobility, and employment creating businesses.

1.3 Conclusions

What conclusions can be drawn? Trade liberalisation and globalisation are both manifestations of the post-WWII spirit of multilateralism, contributing to many countries' economic growth and welfare. Industrialised countries and emerging economies benefitted most, poor developing countries least. Trade liberalisation and globalisation contributed to the reduction of poverty in many developing countries, but not in all.

A converging process of global incomes is ongoing; this is to a large extent explained by China's and India's phenomenal economic growth over the past few decades. This converging process may well have geopolitical and economic ramifications. Global inequality of incomes between individuals is increasingly driven by within-country inequality and decreasingly by between-country inequality.

International trade helped to lower the price of consumer and investment goods. Jobs were created in emerging economies whose industries benefited from enlarged international markets and transfer of technological knowledge. However, industrialised countries suffered from job losses, resulting from a loss of international competitiveness, but also from labour-saving technological advances. Once these negative effects became visible, it triggered a call for protectionism, but also for the need to address growing inequality within affected countries.

The composition of export products, in particular of emerging economies, changed from primary products, via labour-intensive manufactures, to high-tech exports, triggering high economic growth, greater total factor productivity, and an increase in income per capita. However, even when markets of industrialised countries opened up to developing countries' exports, in many instances this did not result in the transformation of their export package. In order to achieve sustained economic growth, developing countries better focus on the fundamentals of economic growth, i.e., investment, macroeconomic stability, human resources development, and good governance.

During the early 1960s, favourable trade relations with developing countries were considered by developed countries and multilateral institutions. UNCTAD offered the most promising forum for developing countries' trade and development interests. However, UNCTAD's achievements have been limited. As for trade relations, industrialised countries have not been generous to developing countries, as they are principally dictated by the former's financial interests. Industrialised countries continue to subsidise their agriculture and cotton production, thereby banning competition from farmers in developing countries.

If a wave of protectionism can be prevented, trade with China and India can become the engine of growth for developing countries. More can be done to allow developing countries to benefit from lowering tariffs. Other hindrances, such as WTO rules that prevent developing countries from diversifying their economies and tariff-escalation, could be mitigated or scrapped altogether.

Carefully managed freeing up of labour migration from poor to industrialised countries would help filling jobs that, given the ageing populations in the latter, would otherwise not be filled. It would also improve migrants' incomes, as well as their home countries' economic growth through remittances.

Notes

1. Rosling, H., Rosling, O. and Rosling-Rönnlund, A. (2018) *Factfulness; Ten Reasons We're Wrong About the World- and Why Things Are Better Than You Think*. London: Sceptre.
2. Thirlwall, A. and Pacheco-López, P. (2017) *Economics of Development*; Tenth Edition. London: Palgrave Macmillan, 38–39.
3. During the first lecture, Dani Rodrik always asks his graduate students: Would you rather be rich in a poor country or poor in a rich country? The standard answer is: Rich in a poor country. Wrong!, says Rodrik. The average poor person in a rich country still earns three times more than the average rich person in a poor country. And disparities in other aspects of well-being, like infant mortality, go the same way. Source: Rodrik, D. (2011) *The Globalization Paradox; Democracy and the Future of the World Economy*. New York: W.W. Norton, 135–136. Branko Milanovic observes: 'Today, it is much more important, globally speaking, whether you are lucky enough to be born in a rich country than whether the income

class to which you belong in a rich country is high, medium, or low'. Source: Milanovic, B. (2011) *The Haves and Have-Nots; A Brief and Idiosyncratic History of Global Inequality*. New York: Basic Books, 113.

4. Ibid., 209–210.
5. Production (or output) growth is created by growth in capital, labour, and technological progress. An example: suppose capital growth is 10, labour also grows by 10 units, and the growth of output is 12; then TFP is 2. Angus Maddison observed that one cannot judge the economic performance of nations only by the yardstick of per capita GDP, total factor productivity provides a strong indication thereof as well. Source: Maddison, A. (1995) *Monitoring the World Economy 1880–1992*. Paris: OECD, 26.
6. *Economics of Development*, 145.
7. There is a new wave of deindustrialisation ongoing. It can be observed that labour absorption capacity of the manufacturing sector is shrinking over time and that the point of beginning deindustrialisation is moving to earlier stages of the development process. Dani Rodrik coined this phenomenon premature deindustrialisation.
8. Maçães, B. (2018) *The Dawn of Eurasia; On the Trail of the New World Order*. London: Allen Lane, 5.
9. 'The rate of progress [of TFP; PdH] accelerated further in 1950–1973. Thus there was a 60-year boom in technical potential which was to be of tremendous significance for the performance of the world economy in the twentieth century.' Source: *Monitoring the World Economy 1820–1992*, 71.
10. Ibid., 73.
11. Over the years, on average only around 0.3% was in fact spent.
12. Deepak Lal and Hla Myint argue that cyclical instability is unlikely to be harmful for growth, but if for some reason there is a fiscally induced inflationary crisis during these cycles there could well be damaging effects on growth performance. Source: Lal, D. and Myint, H. (1996) *The Political Economy of Poverty, Equity, and Growth*. Oxford: Oxford University Press, 222. On page 226, the authors add that there appears to be a link between increasing public indebtedness, rises in money supply, and accelerating inflation in countries that suffer from a growth collapse.
13. Gold, D. *Peace Dividends and Development; Retrospectives and Prospects*. Newark: Rutgers University, (2001), 3–4.
14. In September 1999, the IMF established the Poverty Reduction and Growth Facility (PRGF) to make the objectives of poverty reduction and growth more central to lending operations to poorest member countries.
15. Under the topping up scheme, countries that unexpectedly suffered economic setbacks, due to external factors, such as rising interest rates or falling commodity prices, were eligible for increased debt forgiveness above the decision-point level.

16. Luce, E. (2017) *The Retreat of Western Liberalism*. London: Little Brown, 83.
17. *Perspective on Global Development; Rethinking Development Strategies*. Paris: OECD, 2018, 1.
18. *Economics of Development*, 20.
19. Hausmann, R., Pritchett, L., Rodrik, D. Growth Accelerations. Cambridge: *NBER Working Paper Series 10566*, June 2004.
20. Maddison, A. (2006) *The World Economy; Volume I: A Millennium Perspective. Volume 2: Historical Statistics*. Paris: OECD, 19.
21. Little, I. (1982) *Economic Development; Theory, Policy, and International Relations*. New York: Basic Books, 271.
22. Easterly, W. (2002) *The Elusive Quest for Growth; Economists' Adventures and Misadventures in the Tropics*. Cambridge: The MIT Press, 60.
23. Milanovic, B. (2016) *Global Inequality; a New Approach for the Age of Globalization*. Cambridge: The Belknap Press.
24. Ibid., 123.
25. 'Since these countries started as very poor, their high growth was globally equalizing. A lot of their citizens were brought closer to the income levels enjoyed by Europeans and Americans. .....Moreover, the recent strong acceleration of growth in India has meant that the world now has two strong 'engines' (China and India) of downward pressure on population-weighted intercountry inequality'. Source: *The Haves and Have-Nots*, 101.
26. Free Exchange. In: *The Economist*, 3 August 2019, 64.
27. *The Retreat of Western Liberalism*, 21.
28. Bloomberg reports that in 2017 the world's richest 500 people saw their wealth increased by 23% ($1000 billion). In January 2017, Oxfam calculated the wealth of the poorest half of the world's population. It amounted to $400 billion, which is less than half of the *increase* in wealth of the richest 500 people. One conclusion is unavoidable: the international economic system has not brought about a more equitable income and wealth distribution in the world. This development may become politically unsustainable, as Confucius once observed: 'Inequity is worse than scarcity'. However, taxing the wealthy is not necessarily the most appropriate reaction to the challenge, since the revenues are not that impressive. For example, Switzerland's revenue from its wealth tax is the equivalent of 1% of its GDP. In addition, there are problems regarding the proper estimation of wealth; there is tax avoidance, and wealth can be stowed away in an overseas tax haven. *The Economist* of 6 July 2019 observes: 'Most of the rise in the share of the income of the top 1% of households since the 1970s has resulted from growing disparities between winners and losers in the labour market, not growing income from wealth.... A wealth tax will not solve the inequalities that are most plainly visible: those caused by the growing

dearth of opportunity for people without college degrees and without expensive houses near successful cities', 11. Developing countries can introduce other measures, such as a fair, progressive income tax regime and an effective tax collection system. A part of the ensuing additional revenues can be invested in easing access to secondary and higher education by poorer sections of society, and in financing social safety nets for the poorest.
29. *Economics of Development*, 74.
30. Dollar, D., Kraay, A. (2000) *Growth is Good for the Poor*. Washington: World Bank.
31. *Economics of Development*, 75.
32. Garrett, G. Globalization's Missing Middle. In *Foreign Affairs*. Vol. 83 No. 6. November–December 2004, 89.
33. Lin, J. (2015) *Demystifying the Chinese Economy*. Cambridge: Cambridge University Press, 253.
34. Source: The Fund for Peace's *2018 Fragile States Index*. The numbers mentioned represent fragile or failed states scoring between 100 and 80 points.
35. Of the 30 low-income countries, 25 are SSA countries, 2 Asian countries, 2 from Oceania, and 1 Latin American country. Regarding lower middle-income countries: 11 are from SSA, 6 are Asian and 3 Oceanian countries, as well as 1 from the Middle East.
36. Ghani, A. and Lockhart, C. (2008) *Fixing Failed States; A Framework for Rebuilding a Fractured World*. Oxford: Oxford University Press.
37. Meier, G. (2001) The Old Generation of Development Economists and the New. In *Frontiers of Development Economics*. Ed: Meier, G. and Stiglitz, J. New York: Oxford University Press. Other authors proposed different distinctions. For example, Little distinguished in *Economic Development* structuralism from neoclassical economics. He wrote on page 19: 'Chenery does not hesitate to say that "the initial set of structural hypotheses was formulated in the 1950s by writers such as Paul Rosenstein Rodan, Ragnar Nurkse, W. Arthur Lewis, Paul [sic] Prebisch, Hans Singer and Gunnar Myrdal." Little added on page 20: 'The structuralist sees the world as inflexible. Change is inhibited by obstacles, bottlenecks, and constraints.'
38. In *From Keynes to Piketty* (2016), I included a summary of Karl Polanyi's classic *The Great Transformation* (1944). Polanyi (1886–1964) was an anthropological economist. He developed the Substantivist school of thought. Source: De Haan, P. (2016) *From Keynes to Piketty; The Century that Shook up Economics*. London: Palgrave Macmillan, 164–172.
39. The repeal of the Corn Laws in England is a telling example. David Ricardo campaigned for the repeal of the Corn Laws in which he, and others with him, was successful in 1846 when they were indeed repealed. Industrialists benefitted from them to the detriment of the landed gentry.

40. For example, under its standard GSP system, the EU imported Euros 31.6 billion from 23 beneficiary low-income and lower middle-income countries in 2016.
41. *Economics of Development*, 519.
42. These poorest developing countries enjoy the freedom to undertake policies that limit access to their markets or provide support to domestic producers or exporters in ways which are not allowed to other members, and they are provided with more time to meet their obligations or commitments under the WTO agreements. By the way, Michalopoulos rightly wonders why countries like Singapore and China, registered as developing countries by the WTO, would really need preferential treatment for their exports to penetrate developed country markets. Source: Michalopoulos, C. (2017) *Aid, Trade and Development; 50 Years of Globalization*. London: Palgrave Macmillan, 135.
43. Ibid., 137.
44. Globalization, Growth and Poverty; Building an Inclusive World Economy. Washington: *World Bank Policy Research Report*, January 2002, 5.
45. In 1980, the US represented 22% of the world economy. To date this percentage is down to 15%. In 1980, all traditional industrial economies contributed 60% of the world's GDP. Now they contribute around 30%.
46. UNIDO's *Industrial Development Report* 2018.
47. Olson, M. Big Bills Left on the Sidewalk: Why Some Nations are Rich, and Others Poor. In *The Journal of Economic Perspectives*, Vol. 10, No. 2 (Spring, 1996), 15.
48. *Global Economic Prospects and the Developing Countries*. Washington: World Bank; 2002.
49. Rodrik, D. (1998) *The New Global Economy: Making Openness Work*. Policy Essay No. 24. Baltimore: Johns Hopkins University Press.
50. *Perspective on Global Development; Rethinking Development Strategies*. Paris: OECD, 2018, 1.
51. Milanovic, B. (2005) Can We Discern the Effects of Globalization on Income Distribution? In *World Bank Economic Review*, 19(1): 21–44.
52. Ravallion, M. (2006) Looking Beyond Averages in the Trade and Poverty Debate. In *World Development*, 34 (8): 1374–1392.
53. *Global Inequality*, 20.
54. Lang, V., Mendes Tavares, M. (2018) The Distribution of Gains from Globalization. *IMF Working Paper*, WP/18/54.
55. Ibid., 38. However, Lang and Mendes warn that the results of the regressions undertaken should be interpreted with caution, among others, because they are based on a dataset that had not been subjected to scholarly scrutiny.

56. As for TPP, China is pushing the Regional Comprehensive Economic Partnership as an alternative to TPP.
57. Dumping is not only applied by industrial countries; it is applied by developing countries as well.
58. Stiglitz, J. (2006) *Making Globalization Work*. New York: W.W. Norton, 96.
59. *Economics of Development*, 518.
60. On p. 268 of *The Globalization Paradox*, Rodrik proposes a temporary work visa scheme of rich countries that would expand their labour force by less than 3%. Skilled and unskilled workers from developing countries would be allowed to work in rich countries for a limited period, say, 5 years. This would produce an estimated gain of $360 billion annually for the world economy. In addition, Michael Clemens of the Centre for Global Development estimates that if everyone who wanted to emigrate were able to do so, global GDP would double.
61. *The Haves and Have-Nots*, 163–164.

References

De Haan, P. (2016). *From Keynes to Piketty; The Century That Shook Up Economics*. London: Palgrave Macmillan.

Easterly, W. (2002). *The Elusive Quest for Growth; Economists' Adventures and Misadventures in the Tropics*. Cambridge: The MIT Press.

Free Exchange. (2019, August 3). *The Economist*.

Fund for Peace. (2018). *Fragile States Index*. Washington: The Fund for Peace.

Garrett, G. (2004). Globalization's Missing Middle. *Foreign Affairs, 83*(6), 84.

Ghani, A., & Lockhart, C. (2008). *Fixing Failed States; A Framework for Rebuilding a Fractured World*. Oxford: Oxford University Press.

Gold, D. (2001). *Peace Dividends and Development; Retrospectives and Prospects*. Newark: Rutgers University.

Hausmann, R., Pritchett, L., & Rodrik, D. (June 2004). *Growth Accelerations*. NBER Working Paper Series 10566. Cambridge: National Bureau of Economic Research.

Lal, D., & Myint, H. (1996). *The Political Economy of Poverty, Equity, and Growth*. Oxford: Oxford University Press.

Lang, V., & Mendes Tavares, M. (2018). *The Distribution of Gains from Globalization*. IMF Working Paper, WP/18/54. Washington: International Monetary Fund.

Lin, J. (2015). *Demystifying the Chinese Economy*. Cambridge: Cambridge University Press.

Little, I. (1982). *Economic Development; Theory, Policy, and International Relations*. New York: Basic Books.

Luce, E. (2017). *The Retreat of Western Liberalism*. London: Little Brown.
Maçães, B. (2018). *The Dawn of Eurasia; On the Trail of the New World Order*. London: Allen Lane.
Maddison, A. (1995). *Monitoring the World Economy 1880–1992*. Paris: OECD.
Maddison, A. (2006). *The World Economy; Volume I: A Millennium Perspective. Volume 2: Historical Statistics*. Paris: OECD.
Meier, G. (2001). The Old Generation of Development Economists and the New. In G. Meier & J. Stiglitz (Eds.), *Frontiers of Development Economics*. New York: Oxford University Press.
Michalopoulos, C. (2017). *Aid, Trade and Development; 50 Years of Globalization*. London: Palgrave Macmillan.
Milanovic, B. (2011). *The Haves and Have-Nots; A Brief and Idiosyncratic History of Global Inequality*. New York: Basic Books.
Milanovic, B. (2016). *Global Inequality; A New Approach for the Age of Globalization*. Cambridge: The Belknap Press.
OECD. (2018). *Perspective on Global Development; Rethinking Development Strategies*. Paris: OECD.
Olson, M. (1996). Big Bills Left on the Sidewalk: Why Some Nations are Rich, and Others Poor. *The Journal of Economic Perspectives, 10*(2), 3–24.
Ravallion, M. (2006). Looking Beyond Averages in the Trade and Poverty Debate. *World Development, 34*(8), 1374–1392.
Rodrik, D. (1998). *The New Global Economy: Making Openness Work*. Policy Essay No. 24. Baltimore: Johns Hopkins University Press.
Rodrik, D. (2011). *The Globalization Paradox; Democracy and the Future of the World Economy*. New York: W.W. Norton.
Rosling, H., Rosling, O., & Rosling-Rönnlund, A. (2018). *Factfulness; Ten Reasons We're Wrong About the World – And Why Things Are Better Than You Think*. London: Sceptre.
Stiglitz, J. (2006). *Making Globalization Work*. New York: W.W. Norton.
Thirlwall, A., & Pacheco-López, P. (2017). *Economics of Development* (10th ed.). London: Palgrave Macmillan.
UNIDO. (2018). *Industrial Development Report*.
World Bank. (2000). Dollar, D., & Kraay, A. *Growth Is Good for the Poor*. Washington: World Bank.
World Bank. (2002a). *Global Economic Prospects and the Developing Countries*. Washington: World Bank.
World Bank. (2002b). *Globalization, Growth and Poverty; Building an Inclusive World Economy*. World Bank Policy Research Report. Washington: World Bank.
World Bank. (2005). Milanovic, B. Can We Discern the Effects of Globalization on Income Distribution? *World Bank Economic Review, 19*(1), 21–44.

CHAPTER 2

Whatever Happened to the Third World

2.1 Introduction

Branko Milanovic once observed that never in the history of the world have the incomes of so many people risen by so much over a prolonged period of time. The entire world's average income approaches that of Brazil, or that of the United States in 1941.

This is what Deirdre McCloskey, Emerita Professor of economics and economic history at the University of Illinois at Chicago, observed:

> In 50 years if things go as they have since 1800, the terribly poor will have become adequately nourished. Slaves and women will be largely free. The environment will be improving. And the ordinary person worldwide will have become bourgeois.... Nowadays, although an age of widely circulating tales of impending catastrophe, there are many more reasons to be optimistic about our future.[1]

She writes about inspiring historical economic developments; however, she does so in average terms. If we break them down, a more nuanced picture emerges—one of economically successful countries, but also one of less successful middle-income countries, and of low-income countries that have not done well.

After the end of World War II (WWII), most of the newly independent countries were dirt poor. Spectacular economic development ever since (who would have predicted it 70 years ago?) resulted in significant changes

P. de Haan, *Whatever Happened to the Third World?*,
https://doi.org/10.1007/978-3-030-39613-8_2

in the global economy. For example, in 2009 approximately 75% of global GDP growth was generated by emerging economies and developing countries. Looking at the industrial sector, the share of developed countries in global manufacturing value added (MVA) dropped from 78% (2000) to about 65% (2013), while that of all emerging economies and developing countries put together, increased from 22% to 35%—with the caveat that this is overwhelmingly due to China's spectacular rise, whose share alone surged from 7% to 18% over the same period.

In 2016, 70% of the world's population lived in middle-income countries, and less than 10% in low-income countries. However, the incidence of extreme poverty is considerably higher among low-income countries as a whole (47.2%), compared with lower middle-income countries (18.7%), let alone compared with upper middle-income countries (5.4%).[2] The World Bank estimates that the percentage of the world's extreme poor will probably fall from 10% in 2015 to 8.6% in 2018. The bad news, however, is that extreme poverty has become harder to counter as a result of rapid population increase in sub-Saharan Africa (SSA). Ongoing wars in Syria and Yemen resulted in an almost doubling of the number of extreme poor there. Venezuela is not doing any better; the number of extremely poor Venezuelans is rising rapidly.

All in all, what we are witnessing is a process of differentiation between developing countries. A growing number of them are rapidly emerging as strong and dynamic economies, while the number of low-income countries is shrinking. It is worrying that some former middle-income and low-income countries are deteriorating into fragile or failed states.

Following Japan's example, in the 1960s and 1970s, the four Asian Tigers Hong Kong, Singapore, South Korea, and Taiwan, pulled away from other Third World countries. Quite a few others followed in their footsteps. China is the most telling example. Towards the end of 1978, the Chinese leader Deng Xiaoping was able to introduce economic reforms. Since then, China's economic growth was simply phenomenal. In the early 1990s, India opened its economy, after which the country achieved high and sustained economic growth figures. Together with Brazil, Russia, and South Africa, the BRICS countries are now important global economic and political actors. In their slipstream, new groups of countries are emerging, such as the 'Next-11': Bangladesh, Egypt, Indonesia, Iran, Mexico, Nigeria, Pakistan, the Philippines, Turkey, South Korea and Vietnam.

Between the increasing number of fast growers and the decreasing number of low-income countries, there is a fairly steady group of middle-income countries that have difficulties in transiting to high-income status. They seem to be hindered in their development by the middle-income trap.

There are still 34 poor low-income countries; most of them (26) are to be found in SSA. And there is a growing number of fragile and failed states, in which central government is so weak or ineffective that it has little control over much of its territory. It cannot provide public services. There is widespread corruption and criminality, refugees and involuntary movement of populations abound, and the economy is going down the drain.

2.2 The Evolution of the Third World in Figures

Legendary economist, Rudiger Dornbusch, once told his students at the Massachusetts Institute of Technology (MIT) that whenever he visited a county his hosts always said that 'here it is different.' Dornbusch then told his students that it never was. I believe that in one sense Dornbusch was right, but in another he was wrong. I will show you the economic evolution of the developing world. In doing so, I group them in different categories of countries: low-income, middle-income, and high-income countries, suggesting that countries in the same category are similar, as Dornbusch suggested to his students. Yet, when his hosts said that 'here it is different', they were also right. After all, each country has its unique history, culture, social values, what have you. Both aspects,—the similarity among countries' economic records, and their cultural, political and social differences—are, I hope, duly dealt with in this chapter.

Over the past half century, developing countries' real per capita income grew at an average rate of 2.1% per year. At first glance, this percentage seems not very high, but it is higher than what developed countries achieved in their early growth trajectory. For example, from 1864 to 1914, America's economy grew on average 1.8% per year.

Based on Gross National Income (GNI) per capita levels, the World Bank applies the following classification of countries: low-income countries, lower middle-income countries, upper middle-income countries, and high-income countries.[3] The 2018 World Bank countries classification is as follows:

- 34 countries belong to the low-income group, earning up to $995 Gross National Income (GNI) per capita in 2017;
- 47 countries constitute the lower middle-income category, earning between $996 and $3895.-;

- 56 countries are classified as upper middle-income countries ($3896.- –$12,055.- per capita); and
- 81 countries are high-income countries (> $12,056.- per capita).[4]

Based on the World Bank countries classification, developments over the period 1978–2018 are presented in Fig. 2.1. The number of countries and territories in the annual World Development Reports increased quite substantially in the course of time. The 1978 list includes 125 countries, while the number of countries and territories in the 2018 list had increased to 218. Consequently, to establish trends over time, I applied percentage changes rather than absolute numbers (Fig. 2.2).

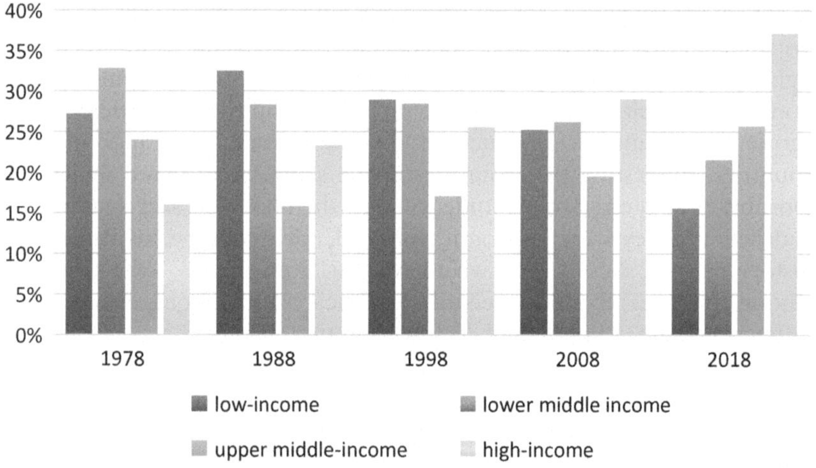

Fig. 2.1 Countries classification in percentages 1978–2018. (Source: World Development Reports 1978–2018. The 1978 World Development Report (WDR) also includes two categories: (i) capital surplus oil exporters (3) and (ii) centrally planned economies (11). I included the 3 surplus oil exporters in the industrialised (high-income) group. As for the 11 centrally planned economies, given their respective income levels, I included 5 of them in the lower middle-income and 5 in the upper middle-income group. Number 11, the DDR, is included in the high-income group)

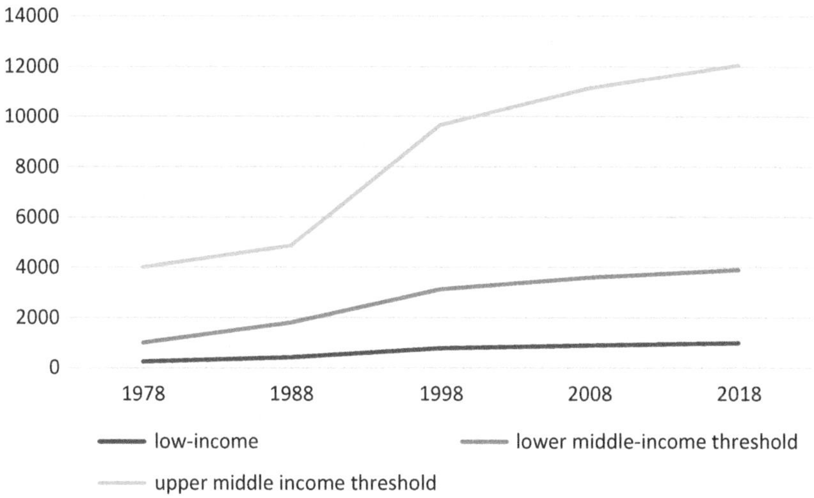

Fig. 2.2 Countries classification thresholds and average GNI per capita 1978–2018. (Source: World Development Reports 1978–2018). The 1988 WDR distinguishes between lower middle-income and upper middle-income countries. However, the report does not provide a threshold figure for the latter category. I chose $1799.- as the threshold for upper middle-income countries. A further operational classification used by the World Bank is the list of countries in Fragile and Conflict Affected Situations

The countries classification is being used by some developing countries in setting development goals. For example, Ghana set a goal of reaching middle-income status by 2015 (the goal was indeed reached). Bangladesh set its goal of graduating to a middle-income country by 2021. These are worthwhile goals, but they can also lead to disappointments and frustration, since not all development is necessarily upwards. As mentioned in Chap. 1, many developing countries experience ups and downs in their respective growth trajectories.

From 2002 to 2016, some countries slipped from high-income to upper-middle income, and then back again to high-income status, such as Antigua and Barbuda, Barbados, Hungary, Malta, and Latvia. Or from upper middle-income to lower middle-income status, and back to upper middle-income country status (Albania, Turkey, and Fiji). Or from lower middle-income to low-income, and then back to lower middle-income status (Mauretania, Solomon Islands, South

(continued)

(continued)

Sudan). Equatorial Guinea is the odd-man out—the country started as a lower middle-income country, then fell back to a low-income status, but subsequently gained the upper middle-income classification, and then a high-income status, propelled by substantial natural resource discoveries.

GNI per capita valued annually in US dollars, using a three-year average exchange rate, does not measure welfare or success in the fight against poverty. Nonetheless, the authors of the Bank's *Policy Research Paper 7528* argue that GNI per capita is found to correlate closely, in terms of both values and rankings, with a number of accepted indicators of development outcomes such as secondary school enrolment, stunting, birth attended by midwives, and the poverty head count ratio.[5] The cut off points between each of the groups are fixed in real terms: they are adjusted each year in line with price inflation.

2.2.1 Trends

What do these Figures tell us? The following trends can be identified over the period 1978–2018:

- Global real income grew substantially for all income groups, thanks to sustained economic growth over the entire period. The increase was most impressive for the high-income countries.
- Sustained world economic growth has not left the erstwhile Third World untouched. On the contrary; as real incomes have risen, the number of low-income countries, as a percentage of the total number of countries, dropped from 27% in 1978 to 16% in 2018, while the percentage of high-income countries more than doubled from 16% in 1978 to 37% in 2018.
- The number of middle-income countries increased from 71 in 1978 to 103 in 2018. This seems to suggest an impressive increase. However, looking at percentages the picture is quite different. In 1978, 57% were middle-income countries. In 2018 the percentage of middle-income countries had fallen slightly to 48%.
- Until the 1990s, more than half of the world's poor lived in East Asia and the Pacific, and about fewer than 1 in 5 lived in SSA. Since then,

large former low-income countries, such as India and China, have moved upwards to a lower middle-income and upper middle-income status respectively. As a result, by 2015 over half of the world's poor lived in SSA, and just 6% in East Asia and Pacific.[6]

2.3 Trends in the Four Developing Regions

In Chap. 1, a general picture was sketched of how the developing world evolved in economic, political, and social terms, and how global political and economic developments influenced this evolution. After the above statistical analysis, it is time to present relevant political and economic developments in the four developing regions: Asia, Latin America, SSA, and the Middle East and North Africa.

The role of corruption is not dealt with in what follows. This does not mean that corruption would be irrelevant in matters of growth and development—far from it. Apart from corruption being immoral, it retards development, and corruption erodes the *mores* of running a government and of doing business. However, this does not imply that corruption would hinder *all* growth and development. For example, in 2005 Bangladesh was at the bottom of Transparency International's Corruption Perception Index. Today, Bangladesh's economy is booming. But on the other hand, think of the huge amounts of oil money embezzled by successive Nigerian governments, or of Brazil's ousted President Dilma Rousseff charged with administrative misconduct. Malaysia's former Prime Minister, Najib Razak, is charged with embezzling hundreds of millions of Euro's from 1MDB, a Malaysian investment fund. Many more examples can be given; the point, however, is that corruption is a universal phenomenon; it always negatively affects economic growth and development, but in most cases corruption is not the sole reason why a country is poor or economically stagnant.

2.3.1 Asia

Japan was the first Asian country to embark on an impressive modernisation development policy, which started after the Meji Restoration in 1868. With ups and downs, Japan's economy has been growing ever since, be it at very modest pace over the past few decades. After the end of WWII, Japan's total factor productivity performance was extraordinary favourable, a result of huge skill reserves and top-notch education and managerial experience. Japan's example greatly influenced the four Asian Tigers. More Asian countries repeated what their neighbours had achieved. Yet, Asia is also home to very poor countries. In inequality terms, Asia is the most heterogeneous of all regions; the region contains very populous countries like Bangladesh and Nepal with low-income levels. There are also Asian countries that are doing much better in terms of income, such as China, Malaysia, the four Asian Tigers, and, not least, Japan.

In 1985, I worked as part of a small NGO team that visited China on the invitation of the Chinese government to identify development projects we could possibly support. The main mode of transportation in Beijing was still the bicycle. People in the rural areas we visited were unfamiliar with price setting and the market mechanism. In 1978, when China had just embarked on its economic reform strategy, the country was still one of the world's poorest, with a per capita income of $210, equivalent to one-third of the average per capita income of SSA countries at the time.

Beijing is now one of the world's most car-congested and polluted cities. China is a middle-income country, with a per capita income of $7755.- in 2018. It overtook Japan in 2010 as the world's second largest exporter of merchandise.[7] The country is now the second economy in the world. China is expected to become the world's first economy, overtaking America, around the middle of this century. China's outstanding loans amount to more than $700 billion, which is more than double what the IMF and WB loan together.[8] Four Chinese banks lead the group of ten biggest banks in the world.

China has become an influential international investment—and a donor country to developing countries. It is no coincidence that China's *Belt and Road Initiative* connects many developing countries with China.

Some commentators argue that the *Washington Consensus* (see Chap. 5) is being eclipsed by the *Beijing Consensus.* This is a catchy statement, but what does it mean?

The term Beijing Consensus is not uniformly described. This is not surprising, as the term is not officially coined. Some interpret the Beijing Consensus as one free from a particular ideology, unlike the Washington Consensus, which is inspired by liberal philosophy and neoclassical economics.

The Beijing Consensus would not project the Chinese way of doing things in other countries, although China brings with it its political and economic model, stressing state capacity. Regarding support to developing countries, the term would imply emergency

(*continued*)

(continued)

support for countries and soft loans for those countries not having access to the international capital market. And no questions asked about human rights or about freedom of expression; in other words 'soulless pragmatism.'[9]

However, one should take into consideration that China is wooing leaders of developing countries. China took the initiative for the establishment of the *Asian Infrastructure Investment Bank* (AIIB), a competitor of the World Bank, with 57 founding members. Before that, China, Brazil, India, Russia, and South Africa established the *New Development Bank* based in Shanghai, with an initial capital of $50 billion. Its focus is on climate change, better governance, and new instruments suited to twenty-first century financial markets.

China is engaged in a huge and wide-ranging geopolitical project: the *Belt and Road Initiative*, a strategy of deep economic integration (and a suitable AIIB investment project), connecting China with, among others, the shipping port of Rotterdam, the Netherlands, and Madrid's central train station.[10] Train tracks of enormous length, and shipping routes across the Indian Ocean, through the Red Sea and Suez Canal, are being constructed and developed.[11]

The Belt and Road Initiative strives to lower the economic distance between China and sixty-five other countries. After all, China's future economic expansion can only be achieved, if the supply of raw materials is ensured, capital finds attractive investments, and China's underdeveloped central and western territories get a development shot in the arm.

China is manifesting itself clearly and increasingly on the world stage. What President Xi Jinping said in February 2017 during a national security seminar may clarify what the Beijing Consensus involves. For the first time, he argued that China should guide the world in shaping a new world order:

> The overall trend of world multipolarity, economic globalization, and democratization of international relations remains unchanged. We should guide the international community to jointly build a more just and reasonable new world order.[12]

(continued)

(continued)

Eight months later, Xi added that state-directed capitalism would offer a new option for other countries and nations who want to speed up their development while preserving their independence.[13] This was a bold statement, as never before Xi had suggested that China should be in the lead. Nonetheless, Xi's statement remains rather abstract and open-ended.

At the beginning of the 1990s India opened its economy. India's economic growth has been impressive ever since, although not quite as impressive as China's.[14] India is opposed to China's Belt and Road Initiative, fearing China's enhanced political and economic prominence in the region. While China is mainly exporting manufactured goods, India's principal export consists of skills and technology. India's economic policies are geared towards promoting investments of big companies, including the ones pulling out of China, and getting a grip on the $150 billion bad debts of its nationalised banks. The country's social policies are aimed at improving the lives of ordinary Indians, including the poor, through cash handouts to farmers and broadening of health insurance for the poor.[15] If successfully implemented India's future will be bright.

There are more Asian success stories, such as Vietnam. Just 20 years ago, Vietnam was among the poorest countries in the world. In 1990, its GDP per capita was less than US$100—significantly lower than Tanzania's at the time. But in 2013, Vietnam had a GDP per capita above US$1700.-. The country is now a lower middle-income country. Its economic success was mainly triggered by its growing industrial sector, which now accounts for 40% of Vietnam's GDP.

Other Asian countries also performed well, such as Indonesia, Malaysia, the Philippines, Sri Lanka, and Thailand. Former 'basket case' Bangladesh is growing at a very high rate indeed. According to the IMF, in 2016 Bangladesh's economy was the second fastest growing major economy, with a growth rate of 7.1%. More and more Bangladeshis can spend their incomes on luxury.[16]

Despite the variety of economic policy approaches, Maddison attempted to capture a few characteristics of an Asian development 'model'. Here they are: (i) after the end of colonial rule, national elites were capable of mounting very large increases in capital formation and education levels, (ii) the absence of large inequalities in income and wealth, making for greater socio-political coherence, (iii) the colonial drain was replaced by a net inflow of foreign capital and aid. Moreover, Asian countries were cautious in their foreign borrowing and their fiscal policies, (iv) after 1950, Asian countries benefited from buoyant world trade; (v) Asian countries have high labour inputs, with much longer working hours than in other parts of the world; and (vi) Asian countries achieved a large start-up bonus because they started far from the productivity frontier.[17]

Having shed their low-income status, these Asian countries belong to the so-called emerging economies. An intriguing question is, what factors played a role in Asia's rise after decolonisation? The success stories of South Korea and Singapore, described below, provide answers.

What Maddison overlooked was the fact that rapid agricultural growth in China, India, and Vietnam acted as the prescursor to the rise of their respective industrial sectors. In Asia, the Green Revolution was supported by government policies, triggering tripled and even quadrupled yields of crops such as wheat, rice and maize. Food remained cheap, which helped to keep wages low.

Surely, there are still low-income countries in Asia, but not that many. According to the 2018 World Bank countries classification list, Afghanistan, East Timor, North Korea, Nepal, and Tajikistan are low-income countries. In the past, the majority of the world's poorest people lived in Asia. Over the past forty years China has been able to lift 600 million poor people out of extreme poverty. India followed suit: 271 million Indians no longer live in dire poverty.

Human capital is groomed at schools, technical training facilities, colleges, and universities. The Organisation for Economic Cooperation and Development (OECD) undertakes every three years its Programme for International Student Assessment (PISA), a test of 15-year-old pupils around the world. The students are tested on their proficiency in science, reading, mathematics, and collaborative problem solving. The 2015 list of the ten best performing countries includes seven Asian countries/territories. Singapore topped the list.[18] Educators around the world envy Singapore's success and try to copy the country's approach, which consists of teacher training, tightly-focused lessons, and long-term educational planning by the government.

Of the world's twenty best-performing countries of the World Bank's 2018 Ease of Doing Business Ranking, five are Asian: Singapore (2), Hong Kong (4), South Korea (5), Taiwan (13), and Malaysia (15).

In conclusion, a combination of political leadership committed to growth and modernisation, talented entrepreneurs, a properly educated workforce, cautious fiscal and sound macroeconomic policies, a conducive business climate, and openness to the outside world, explain to a large extent why many Asian countries have been able to: (i) rapidly modernise their economies, promoted by sound economic policies; (ii) improve their citizens' income; (iii) eliminate poverty to a large extent; and (iv) offer high-quality education. Not all is well, surely, but what has been achieved in economic terms over the past four decades is truly impressive.

2.3.2 Latin America

From 2000 to 2006, I was posted at the Netherlands Embassy in La Paz, Bolivia,—then the poorest South American country (in 2018 it still was). The gap between rich and poor was wide; Bolivia's principal export products were raw materials, minerals, oil and gas.[19] If at the time a US-inspired coca eradication programme would not have been implemented, the illegal trade in coca leaves—the raw material for the production of cocaine—would have boosted Bolivia's GDP quite substantially. During the 1980s, Bolivia went through a grueling period of hyperinflation, but this had been brought under control. Indeed, Bolivia's monetary and fiscal situation was reasonably healthy. This did not apply to the political situation; it was volatile, to say the least. Over the period 2000–2006, one president died, and another fled the country; his successor was ousted shortly after, ushering in the leader of the *cocaleros*, Evo Morales, Bolivia's President from 2006 to November 2019. As I was finishing this chapter, Morales fled to Mexico, triggering violent protests.

Latin America is rich in fertile land and natural resources. But the region is also known for the large gap in income and wealth between rich and poor people.[20] Uruguay has the lowest inequality in the region; the highest inequality is to be found in Brazil and Bolivia.

> Latin American countries have tended to grow at broadly similar rates, no particular 'pumas' are in sight, and lowering inequality seems to be a Sisyphean task that many a government in Latin America has tried with very little success. Entrenched interests, large gaps in educational achievement, and racial divides all make such a reduction in inequality difficult to contemplate over the short to medium term.[21]

In 1959, Cuba's President Fulgencio Batista was ousted by Fidel Castro, who installed a socialist regime. This prompted America to pay more attention to Latin America. In 1961, The *Alliance for Progress* launched by President Kennedy, was presented as a substantial economic assistance programme. However, its hidden objective was to keep the region free from left-leaning regimes. This has not always been successful, as the region's recent history demonstrates. Castro's political philosophy was not successful in 'liberating' Latin America. Apart from the import-substitution development policy, some Latin American countries adopted development policies inspired by socialist principles, while others felt inclined, especially after economic crises, to resort to market-oriented policies.

From time to time, various Latin American countries are plagued by political and macroeconomic instability. The recurrence of financial crises and their effects on economic activity show that Latin America's history keeps repeating itself. The institutional make-up of most Latin American countries is built upon the institutions left behind by former colonisers, Spain and Portugal. Institutional economists would argue that Latin America's development demonstrates path dependency (see Chap. 6). Despite more than two centuries of independence, only Argentina, Chile, Panama, Puerto Rico, and Uruguay achieved a high-income status. All others are middle-income countries. By the year 2000, most of Latin America's export still consisted of raw materials; only Mexico and Brazil exported slightly more manufactures than raw materials.

After the Great Depression, most countries embarked on an import-substitution strategy, triggered by scarce import products.[22] After WWII, import substitution became a true Latin American doctrine, squarely integrated in Raúl Prebisch's trade theory (see Chap. 7). However, this inward-looking strategy was abandoned during the 1980s—Latin America's lost decade. Rodrik observes that over the period 1950–1980, the overall record of import-substituting industrialisation (ISI) was rather impressive.[23] For example, Brazil, Mexico, and scores of others experienced faster rates of economic growth under ISI than at any other time in their economic history. During these three decades, Latin America registered an average annual growth rate of more than 2.5% per capita.

In 1950, per capita real income in Latin America was three times higher than Asia's, and about half of that of advanced countries. Europe's total factor productivity grew fastest at the time, but it was closely followed by East Asia's and Latin America's. But at the beginning of the 1980s, total factor productivity growth in Latin America turned negative. What happened?

Argentina, at the time led by Juan Peron, defaulted in 1956. This prompted the establishment of the *Paris Club*, a group of officials from major creditor countries whose role is to come up with co-ordinated and sustainable solutions to the payment difficulties of debtor countries. Argentina's default proved to be the harbinger of more financial and monetary trouble. During the 1970s, Latin America was swamped with easily accessible petro-dollar loans. In particular countries led by autocratic governments, such as Mexico, Argentina, and Brazil, borrowed heavily from the international market. Other dictators followed suit, expecting that they could buy legitimacy from the population through debt-financed economic growth and the creation of more jobs. Continued expansionary monetary and fiscal policies led to financial disaster, exacerbated by the fact that many Latin American countries had delayed pursuing stabilisation programs. Although these expansionary policies led to strong economic growth in the first half of the 1970s, also triggered by favourable primary commodity export prices, they resulted in (hyper)inflation and a continuation of large current account deficits.[24]

In 1982, Mexico defaulted. Soon after, also Argentina and Brazil needed financial help from the International Monetary Fund (IMF), World Bank, and other international creditors. In short, Latin America experienced a lost decade, characterised by low or even negative economic growth, near-uncontrollable macroeconomic instability, two- or three-digit inflation, fiscal crises, and great distortions in resource allocation. Total factor productivity growth turned negative. Other developing regions also experienced lower economic growth, but not negative productivity growth. In sum, between 1981 and 1994, Latin America's economic performance was disastrous compared to the US and the rest of the world.[25]

After the lost decade, almost all Latin American countries drastically altered their development strategy, placing greater emphasis on market-friendly and export-oriented policies in line with the Washington Consensus philosophy. The role of the state changed, putting less emphasis on its role in the productive process and more on making institutions conducive to modernisation and growth.

The implementation of structural reform programmes implied a rather long period of relatively poor economic performance. How did this work out? As of the start of the new millennium, left-leaning populists were elected in countries like Argentina, Bolivia, Ecuador, Nicaragua, and Venezuela, reviving Peron's populist—and Castro's socialist legacies. This has not been beneficial for most countries involved: In Argentina the value of the peso, the country's currency, plunged; the economy shrank and inflation soared. In 2019, the country had to, once again, call in the IMF to provide a $57 billion loan. In Nicaragua a civil war is being waged, and Venezuela now is a failing state. Towards the end of 2019, there was popular unrest in Bolivia, Chile, Ecuador, and Colombia.

Brazil is the only Latin American country forming part of the BRICS. Much smaller economies, like Chile's and Uruguay's have been doing well, and so has Panama. As for Chile, during the Pinochet regime, market-friendly policies were introduced. The country's dependence on copper was mitigated by economic diversification. Wine became an important export product, as well as salmon and cherries.[26] From an economic achievement point of view, Chile is a model for other countries in the region. Nonetheless, in October 2019, Chileans demonstrated in huge numbers against inequality of income and wealth, and inadequate public services.

What about Latin America as a whole? IMF's 2019 growth projections for the region have fallen from the original 2% to 1.4%. Compared to projections for other developing continents, Latin America is falling behind. This is not a recent phenomenon; it has been going on for several decades. The gap between the region's average income per capita and that of the US is now wider than it was in 1950. Among the world's middle-income countries, Latin America is overrepresented (see Appendix 2). This suggests that the region's economies have encountered obstacles in transiting to a high-income country status; they suffer from the middle-income trap (see Appendix 2).

However, the region attracted foreign investors thanks to responsible fiscal policies (except in countries such as Venezuela, Brazil, and Argentina) coupled with market—and trade liberalisation, as well as an expanded network of international trade agreements. Before China appeared on the horizon as investor, the Brazilian Development Bank invested heavily in the region. To date, Chinese investments eclipse those of the World Bank, the International Development Bank, and the Development Bank of Latin America (CAF) put together.

Since 2005, the Chinese government lent an estimated $140 billion, of which 90% went to investments in Venezuela, Brazil, Argentina and Ecuador. This includes investments in the context of China's *One Belt One Road* initiative.[27] In addition, China's foreign direct investment (around

$110 billion from 2005 to 2018) has gone to Brazil, Peru, Argentina, more recently, Mexico.[28] Four major Chinese banks are operating in the region in partnership with international banks. In the end, the question is who is to benefit: China or Latin America? It depends on the quality of Latin America's domestic policies, its negotiation capabilities, and the transparency of the conditions obtained.

2.3.3 Sub-Saharan Africa

Economic growth and development is not only promoted by the right economic policies and an appropriate institutional framework; it also requires a variety of technical and managerial capabilities to get things done. To date, India has 130 and Brazil 168 scientists and engineers for every million inhabitants, but SSA avails of only around 35 scientists and engineers for every million inhabitants.[29] The intellectual, professional, and managerial base upon which SSA countries had to start and continue their development was simply too small.

The colonisation of SSA spanned a relatively short period of time: not more than 70 years. In 1957, Ghana was the first African country to gain independence. Many former French, British and (as of 1974), former Spanish and Portuguese colonies followed. For example, Nigeria and Zaïre gained independence in 1960, Tanzania in 1961, Kenya in 1963; Mozambique gained independence in 1974, and a year later Angola. In the 1950s, SSA countries began with a slightly higher GDP per capita than Asia's. But this advance was of short duration, as we shall see.

The new African leaders were in a jubilant mood; after all, they now could take charge of their countries' development, based on their own ideas, and not on those of their former colonisers. Moreover, Africa had a lot to offer by way of fertile lands and minerals that, during the early years of independence, were commanding good prices at international markets. Many young African countries, often one-party states, embarked on a state-led capital-intensive industrialisation drive, as suggested by first generation development economists and wholeheartedly embraced by African leaders, but not corrected by political opposition or a vocal civil society. Agriculture, which formed the basis of the typical SSA economy, and which is such an important sector in promoting broader economic growth, was neglected.[30] In many instances, farmers were exploited by government-run marketing boards; prices paid for their export crops were deliberately kept below the export price, in order to earn foreign exchange for the government. Food crops were also paid a pittance to keep food prices low in urban centres.

'As in China, these newly independent countries...began to pursue modernization guided by the then—mainstream theories, hoping to build up advanced capital-intensive industries on their agrarian base. The priority industries went against the countries' comparative advantages and were not viable in open, competitive markets. The establishment of those industries and their continued operation relied on government protection and subsidies through various distortions to the market system. Despite the tireless efforts of a generation or two, economies stagnated, social and political crises broke out, and the gap with the developed world in per capita income grew ever wider.'[31]

The result was disastrous; the typical SSA country had created badly managed state corporations, adding to the government's already accumulated deficits.[32] During the 1970s, two oil shocks worsened the situation. Oil imports became much more expensive, and the same applied to repayment of international loans caused by increased interest rates, and—confirming that a disaster never comes alone—demand for SSA's exports dropped, triggered by a recession in developed countries.

By the mid-1980s, around forty SSA countries were near-bankrupt. Many of them also registered negative economic growth—their economies shrank. Two-thirds of SSA's population lived in conditions of extreme poverty. Most of them were as poor, or even poorer, than they had been at the time of independence.[33] By 1992, SSA's per capita income was about the same as Western Europe achieved in 1820.[34] Structural reform, inspired by the Washington Consensus philosophy, was required to turn their troubled economy around, what amounted to two 'lost decades'. Further, these structural reforms did not help to improve the agricultural sector's productivity.

Much of the support in place for agriculture in Africa was dismantled in the 1970s by World Bank structural adjustment programmes; for example, subsidies for fertilizers and seeds, guaranteed prices for crops, and research and development—all the policies that supported Asia's so-called Green

Revolution in the 1960s, which tripled and quadrupled yields of crops such as wheat, rice and maize.[35]

In the early 1990s, the Cold War had ended. Kleptocratic and repressive regimes, such as Mobutu's Zaïre, lost support of Western donors.[36] There was talk of a peace dividend—meaning that poor countries would receive more aid based on what they needed rather than on their political allegiances as practiced during the Cold War days. Despite raised hopes of increased aid, SSA countries benefitted very little. During the 1990s, foreign direct investment in developing countries grew sevenfold, but Official Development Assistance (ODA) decreased in per capita terms and measured as a share of the receiving country GNP.[37]

Until not too long ago, Africa lagged behind other regions in economic growth and income per capita terms. In 2002, William Easterly analysed income differences between East Asia and Africa as explained by differences in policies and other factors. He concluded: 'Africa's higher government budget deficits, higher financial repression, and higher black market premium explain about half of the growth difference between East Asia and Africa over three decades. If policies truly cause growth, then Africa would have been $2000 richer per person if African economic policies had been at East Asian levels.'[38]

Since then, developments have improved. A remarkable number of SSA countries have achieved commendable economic growth figures. Over the period 2000–2007, two-thirds of their economies grew at more than 5.5% per year. One-third of them even managed to achieve 7% per year. These are impressive growth figures, particularly considering that some SSA countries do not include in official economic statistics what is happening in Africa's informal economies.[39] However, growth has yet to translate into more equitable income and wealth distribution. SSA remains one of the most unequal regions globally.

The Great Recession, which broke out in September 2008, did not harm SSA much. China continued buying SSA's export commodities. During the first decade of this century, trade (including arms) between China and SSA grew tenfold, reaching $115 billion. China established businesses, invested in SSA-based banks, and provided loans to African governments wanting to invest in infrastructure, such as roads, railways, and harbours.[40] China also became a prominent donor country.

China is not the only country taking an interest in SSA. From 2000 to 2016, more than 320 embassies were opened in Africa. Apart from China,

India, Turkey, Russia, Brazil, and Japan opened new embassies. Over the same period SSA's trade with Turkey and Indonesia has more than tripled, and it has quadrupled with Russia. In October 2019, Russian President Vladimir Putin invited forty African Heads of State to discuss closer cooperation between SSA and Russia.

It is telling that by 2006, SSA's three biggest trade partners were the US, China, and France. But in 2018, China came first, India second, and America only third. The US has cut its aid budget for SSA and announced a 10% reduction of its troops there. True, the biggest foreign direct investors are American, British, and French. However, Chinese investments, including those of state-backed companies, are rapidly catching up, closely followed by investors from Singapore and India. Some commentators talk of a new scramble for Africa.

During the first half of the second decade of this century, economic growth in most SSA countries, in spite of increased remittances,[41] slowed down. Dani Rodrik wonders on what exactly SSA's past growth was based. He would have expected that manufacturing would have explained part of it. However, SSA's manufacturing is rather stagnant. The growth came from productivity increase in the agricultural sector, and from remittances. Agricultural surplus labour was absorbed in the service sector. But this sector demonstrated negative labour productivity. Rodrik concludes that if productivity will not increase consistently, continued convergence with high-income countries may not happen.[42]

Zambia is an example of what happened in quite a few other SSA countries. It pained me to read about the country, where I worked and lived from 2006 to 2013. In those years, Zambia was doing quite well, achieving robust economic growth, enjoying political stability, and applying sound macroeconomic policies. One after another shopping mall opened in Lusaka, Zambia's capital. In 2005–2006, Zambia received debt forgiveness, but at the end of 2019, the country is on the verge of another financial crisis. Copper prices, the country's principal export product, dropped and economic growth slowed. The government borrowed and spent the funds on infrastructure, but also doubled the salaries of civil servants, instead of spending it on growth- and employment-generating investments. Public debt increased rapidly from 21% of GDP in 2011 to 59% in 2017. The IMF says that Zambia is one of the 18 SSA countries at risk of 'debt distress'.

Yet, there is room for some optimism. The World Bank's 2017 *Global Economic Prospects* report talked about a fragile recovery.[43] This observation is based upon modestly rising commodity prices, strengthened external demand, and the end of the drought in the eastern part of SSA. Inflation is gradually decelerating, although in some countries it remains high. Reforms to tackle macroeconomic imbalances are ongoing. On the downside, there is concern about political uncertainties in South Africa, SSA's largest economy, which negatively affects investments there. The report expresses concern about Angola and Nigeria; both countries are confronted with tight foreign exchange liquidity as a result of distortions in their foreign exchange markets. The economies of these three economic 'power houses'—(together they make up more than half of SSA's GDP) are stagnating, pulling down SSA's overall economic performance. The World Bank estimates that SSA's 2018 growth could reach 3.4%. This is the outcome of putting together the growth figures of SSA's laggards and star performers over 2017, such as Ethiopia (8.3%), Tanzania (7.2%), Côte-d'Ivoire (6.8%), Senegal (6.7%), and Ghana (6.1%). This average growth rate of 3.4% is not enough to reduce poverty.[44] Compared to the World Bank, the IMF is more optimistic: it reported that one-third of SSA countries can expect a GDP growth of more than 5% in 2019.

Africa's vast agricultural, minerals, and oil and gas potential has not been used to the fullest extent. Just two examples: (i) since 1960, Africa's food production has fallen by 10%; only 4% of SSA's cropland is irrigated, fertiliser use was only 10% of the world average; (ii) Africa's share of 2.7% of the world's economic output is a small fraction. Human development's potential is also insufficiently tapped. Although more than double the percentage in 2000, only 9% of SSA's young people undergo tertiary education (vocational colleges and universities); this is much lower than the percentage for South Asia (25%), let alone that for Latin America and the Caribbean (51%). Another potential is trade-related. Should the African Continental Free Trade Area agreement be ratified, it would take away non-tariff and tariff barriers, broaden the markets for SSA producers and consumers, especially those in many land-locked countries, and give the countries involved a stronger bargaining position in international trade negotiations.

At the start of this section, I wrote that committed African presidents promoted their countries' development, but it typically ended with their demise. A fresh modernisation injection is created by 'pockets of efficiency', despite adverse investment environments in many countries. Just one recent example out of many: Ethiopia's Horticulture Development Agency proved to be far more effective and customer-oriented than most other Ethiopian government agencies.[45] Ethiopia has more to offer. Building on its flagship rural safety net project, Ethiopia's Urban Productive Safety Net Project, launched in 2007, is designed to cater to urban poor; this is a firm step towards building a national social-security system. The programme provides training, temporary work, and small grants to those who want to start a business. Around 400,000 poor Ethiopians have benefitted so far. The government aims to reach out to 4.7 million Ethiopians in 1000 towns and cities. More of these social safety net programs are being implemented across Africa, amounting to 1.5% of GDP.

Is Africa no longer the 'hopeless continent'? Perhaps not, given satisfactory past growth rates, better schooling, better health, fewer poor, a rapidly expanding urban middle-income class, and better macroeconomic policies. Mobile phones, including mobile banking, are rapidly conquering SSA. However, over the past two decades too much of SSA's growth has been sustained by primary commodities. Diversification of SSA's economies, making them less dependent on sharp price fluctuations of export products, is still a far cry away.[46] Low productivity is another challenge. SSA has performed the least in total factor productivity compared to other regions of the world.[47] Apart from rampant corruption, and poor infrastructure (bad roads, shortage of power), doing business is not easy.[48] The quality of governance and institutions is unimpressive: property rights are not well protected, and transparency and accountability is lacking. SSA countries typically register poor scores in the Worldwide Governance Indicators.[49] SSA is home to the world's largest number of low-income countries and fragile and failed states (see Sect 2.4.3). If these weaknesses are redressed by a political leadership genuinely committed to development, SSA's future will be bright. SSA's young—and still growing—population may then no longer be a liability but in turn into a blessing (challenges include how to provide jobs for young labour-force entrants and quell illegal migration).

Richard Dowden argues that the three motors driving Africa's change are mobile phones, China, and the emergence of a new African middle class.[50] What Dowden said may be an oversimplification, but his message suggests that SSA is slowly turning the corner. The development wheel does not have to be reinvented, Asian countries demonstrated that it can be done.

2.3.4 *The Middle East and North Africa*

This region includes, apart from Israel, the 22 Arab League member-countries.[51] These are a wide variety of nations, ranging from rich oil-states to impoverished fragile states ravaged by conflicts and civil war. One overarching influence in the region's economic development is the price of oil. When the price of oil increases, oil-producing countries benefit, but the region's oil-importing countries suffer quite substantially, including the threat of instability, or even armed conflict.

Regarding rich oil states, a further distinction can be made: (i) the United Arab Emirates (UAE) and Qatar, (ii) Algeria, Libya, and Sudan, and (iii) Saudi Arabia. The Emirates and Qatar apply an open economy policy, attracting foreign direct investment, start-ups, intellectual and business talents. In addition, they invest in employment creation, education, and health. Consequently, the countries involved typically have better HDI scores.[52] Algeria, Libya, and Sudan attract less foreign direct investment and register lower HDI scores than the Emirates and Qatar. Saudi Arabia is by far the region's largest oil producer. The country's economy is still very much dependent on oil. Diversification, privatisation, and modernisation of the economy are in their infancy. The country's objective is to move away from the current rentier system, fuelled by the Kingdom's huge oil proceeds. As for investments in education and health, Saudi Arabia's HDI score is slightly below the ones of the Emirates and Qatar.

A few of the region's general characteristics, economic developments, and challenges can be discerned. During the 1980s, state-led development models based on import-substitution, made way for outward-looking models in pursuit of private sector development and international trade. The countries that had taken stabilisation measures during the 1980s and 1990s, had brought inflation and budget deficits under control. Nonetheless, after the economic slump in the 1980s, growth continued to stagnate and remained vulnerable to oil- and agricultural price fluctuations.[53] Over the period 1975–1998, economic trends presented a picture of decline, mirrored by a steady reduction in investment, yielding low productivity of physical capital. Labour productivity also declined. The World Bank estimated that the region's total factor productivity showed a steady decline of −0.2% per year. Inadequate access to quality education partly explains this downward trend. Adult literacy in the region was 62%, while the global average was 79%. The region's mean years of schooling was far below the level achieved in East Asia. The share of womens participation in GDP in the Arab region was on average 29%, while the percentage of women in all developing countries was 50%. In short, the Arab region's human capabilities, particularly those of women, represented an inadequately tapped asset.

Throughout the 1990s, exports from the region—over 70% of which consisted of oil and oil-related products—grew at 1.5% per year, far below the world average of 6%. Manufacturing exports had not increased. In addition, private capital flows lagged behind those of other regions. In 2002, important macro variables were still underperforming, such as employment, savings, productivity, and non-oil exports. As for employment, about 29% of the region's workforce was unemployed—the highest percentage in the developing world. The challenge of full employment was compounded by rapid population growth, adding six million labour-force entrants per year. Rapid population growth impinged upon GDP per capita growth. Over the period 1975–1998, the region's real annual per capita GDP growth was very slow indeed—around 0.5%—while the world's average increase was 1.3%, implying a relative deterioration in the average standard of living.

The Arab countries had the lowest level of dire poverty in the world, yet one out of every five people lived on less than $2 per day.[54] The good news is that inequality in these countries is relatively low; those at the bottom quintile of income distribution benefitted from migration and remittances. Traditional Islamic arrangements, such as *zakat* and *sadaqa*, also helped. This suggests that the impact of rapid economic growth on poverty would be quite effective.

The 2002 *Arab Human Development Report* (AHDR) argued that to improve developments, binding constraints—such as the lack of accountability, transparency, and integrity, as well as inadequately trained human resources—had to be overcome.

Although Arab population growth rates are declining, the demographic 'wave' they created in its young adult years, is adding to the swelling numbers of unemployed and frustrated youth.[55] Young men wishing to marry and create families, often cannot do so, because they cannot find a job, and thus cannot generate income and savings in order to pay for the wedding, housing, etc.[56] Not having bright prospects, they may feel attracted to the ideology of radicalised groups. The position of women has not improved since 2002. The 2016 AHDR underscores that female labour force participation is slightly less than 24%. As mentioned, the share of women in GDP in the Arab region is only about 29%, against 50% in all developing countries. The poverty rate is 31.6% among women, compared to only 19% among men.[57]

Since 2002, the number of armed conflicts and violent crises has risen, leading to regime change in some countries or to civil wars, in which millions of people are being killed or uprooted.[58] The ongoing conflict between Israel and Palestine is no longer front-page news, as it is being eclipsed by conflicts in Iraq, the Maghreb, Lebanon, Sudan, Syria, and Yemen. In some of these conflicts, major powers are involved, such as Iran, Saudi Arabia, Turkey, Russia, America, and the European Union. These conflicts boost military expenditures and destroy productive resources, capital, and labour.

Arab countries have entered the modern world, while maintaining a strong role of Islam in the public and private domain. The 2011 Arab Spring triggered the collapse of several Arab regimes, creating a political void without a clear political alternative and inviting various Islamist parties to step in.

Despite the reforms of the 1980s and 1990s, little has changed in economic terms. The state, while rolling back government employment, still plays the most prominent role in the economy. The 2016 AHDR argues that the typical Arab development model still depends on inefficient forms of intervention and redistribution, and that for its financing is heavily dependent on aid, remittances, and rents from oil revenues. The public sector either crowded out or manipulated the (weak) private sector or forged uncompetitive alliances.[59] Manufacturing has grown at a snail's pace. Unemployment, which at 29% is the highest in the world, remains the biggest challenge. Given the demographic wave, the region needs to create more than 60 million new jobs in the next decade to stabilise youth employment—a huge challenge. Ongoing decline in foreign direct investment and tourism is not helpful in this realm. The situation in Algeria, presented in the box below, illustrates the challenges.

> 'Algeria is one of Africa's largest oil and gas producers, but corruption and inefficient subsidies have squandered much of its wealth. Endless bureaucracy deterred foreign investment.
>
> Young people make up most of the population. One in four are jobless. Low oil prices have pinched the budget. Foreign reserves, though still a sizeable $65bn, are barely a third of what they were five years ago.'[60]

In 2017, average economic growth in the region was 1.4%. The 2017 World Bank's *Global Economic Prospects* expected economic growth to pick up to an average of 3% in 2018–2019, reflecting the positive impact of reforms and stabilisation policies, the increase in oil prices and external oil demand. However, some caution is called for, given the sluggish implementation of reforms, governments' tendency to apply pro-cyclical fiscal policies, rising debt levels, and, as noted, high unemployment among young men and women.[61] In ensuring a better economic outlook, a 2017 World Economic Forum report suggests the following: (i) transiting away from natural resources and diversifying the economy; (ii) increasing the role of the private sector and diminish the state's intervention in the market; (iii) ensuring that opportunities are available for the youth and its growing work force.

2.4 Categories of Countries

The Third World as we knew is gone. This does not mean that there will no longer be poor countries on the planet. They are still there, but—as we have shown—their number has fallen. One of the objectives of the Sustainable Development Goals is to end extreme poverty. Also encouraging is the growth in the number of high-income countries. Not so encouraging is the plight of middle-income countries, often bogged down by the middle-income trap. Another worrying development is that, since the beginning of this century, the number of fragile and failed states has increased.[62]

The story of South Korea's very rapid growth from a poor low-income to a high-income country, elaborated below, demonstrates how successful developing countries managed to do just that. In Appendix 1 to this chapter Singapore's exceptional development is described as well.

Regarding the fairly large group of middle-income countries, some may graduate to a high-income status; however, for the time being most of them are held back by the middle-income trap. They have been unable to compete in high value-added markets, dominated by high-income economies because their work forces are not sufficiently skilled and their institutional framework is not sophisticated enough. This is elaborated in Sect. 2.4.2.

Low-income countries encounter various traps in their attempt to shed poverty. Some low-income countries may graduate to a middle-income status. However, others will stay poor or, worse, join the ranks of fragile or failed states, as described in Sect. 2.4.3.

2.4.1 An Asian Success Story

The remarkable story of South Korea's rapid economic development, and the unorthodox policies applied, are vividly described by Ha-Joon Chang in *Bad Samaritans*.[63] The book is an elaboration of Chang's earlier book *Kicking Away the Ladder*, in which the author expressed strong, some would say controversial, opinions about development—what works and what does not.[64] The book's central theme is that developing countries should be given the opportunity to design and implement their own development policies, in particular the development of their industrial sector behind tariff walls, until these industries are mature enough to successfully compete in the international market. It is industrial development that enhances productivity, and in turn creates a country's prosperity. Below, a summary of *Bad Samaritans* is presented, interspersed with my comments.

Chang argues that, as he calls it, the 'International Development Policy Establishment' seems to forget how rich countries developed at the time. The author found inspiration for *Bad Samaritans* in his home country's spectacular economic growth. Over the past four decades, South Korea's per capita income grew around 14 times in purchasing power terms. Compare this to the United Kingdom—it took the UK 58 years to achieve the same result.[65]

The author explains South Korea's phenomenal growth in a nutshell: 'The secret of its success lays in a judicious mix of protection and open trade, with the areas of protection constantly changing as new infant industries were developed and old infant industries became internationally competitive.' This protectionist policy was applied by the United Kingdom and the United Sates during the development of their respective industrial sectors.[66] Chang brings Alexander Hamilton, America's first Treasury Secretary, to mind. In his 1791 *Report on the Subject of Manufactures*, Hamilton argued that the federal government should protect American industry until it was strong enough to compete with foreign companies. Hamilton's trade policy was firmly established by 1820 and lasted beyond The First World War. He was opposed to Adam Smith's free trade doctrine.[67]

(*continued*)

(continued)

When they were in catching-up positions, the NDCs [Now Developed Countries; PdH], protected infant industries, poached skilled workers and smuggled contraband machines from more developed countries, engaged in industrial espionage, and willfully violated patents and trademarks. However, once they joined the league of the most developed nations, they began to advocate free trade and prevent the outflow of skilled workers and technologies; they also became strong protectors of patents and trademarks. In this way, the poachers appear to have turned gamekeepers with disturbing regularity.[68]

This *infant industry* policy was implemented with considerable success by many newly independent poor countries during the early decades of their development. Over the period 1950–1970 their average annual growth rate was 3.0%.[69] For them, it was an upbeat Industrial Revolution period. However, in the 1970s this policy was replaced by *neo-liberal* policies pushed down the throat of Third World countries by the Bad Samaritans, i.e., the donor community, under the leadership of the International Monetary Fund and World Bank, later joined by the World Trade Organisation.[70] As a result of this dramatic policy change, Latin America's average annual growth rates fell from 3.1% in the 1960s and 1970s to 1.7% in the 1990s. SSA did even worse: many African countries registered negative per capita growth rates over the period 1980–2002.

Unfortunately, Chang does not explain why this dramatic policy change was forced upon these countries. Nowhere in his book is it mentioned why the initial state-led infant industry policy had to make way for open market neo-liberal policies. In fact, the affected countries were nearly bankrupt. Their government-subsidised industries had produced more *white elephants* than sellable products. In addition, their respective public sectors had become so bloated that governments' finances were inadequate to foot the bill. Their industrial sector was simply unable to contribute to the government budget. To make matters worse, raw material export income had dramatically fallen as a result of a recession in rich countries in the early 1970s.

(*continued*)

(continued)

The indebted countries had no choice but to request financial support from the international financial institutions and bilateral donors. And there were strings attached. These neo-liberal strings prevented the affected countries from further building up their industrial sector behind tariff walls. Instead, they had to implement *Washington Consensus* policies, packaged as Structural Adjustment Programmes (SAPs), including restrictive macroeconomic policy, opening up their markets for foreign products and investments, privatising state enterprises, and cutting governments' public sector to size. The population suffered, in particular the poor. Economic growth slowly recovered but at much lower rates than before.

Chang concludes that the countries implementing these SAPs were not given the time to properly develop and strengthen their industrial sectors to prepare them for the international market. It is not only a matter of erecting protective tariff walls behind which industries of an advanced technological level can be developed; but also, before this is achieved, a matter of promoting industries exporting relatively simple goods, such as textiles.

> The popular impression of Korea as a free-trade economy was created by its export success. But export success does not require free trade, as Japan and China have also shown. Korean exports in the earlier period—things like simple garments and cheap electronics—were all means to earn the hard currencies needed to pay for the advanced technologies and expensive machines that were necessary for the new, more difficult industries, which were protected through tariffs and subsidies.[71]

Chang did not consider the fact that SSA's internal markets were typically small. These markets simply generated insufficient demand for the products of protected infant industries. Moreover, most SSA countries are landlocked; high transportation costs hindered these countries' exports.

(*continued*)

(continued)

The way to get out of poverty, argues Chang, is through a process of more and more sophisticated industrialisation. Through the acquisition of ever more advanced technologies, the economy's productivity will be enhanced. Initially, developing countries will have to import foreign technology that has to be paid for. The foreign currency needed will have to be generated by either the country's exports of relatively simple industrial products, such as garments, or by foreign aid.

Chang does not address foreign aid's role in South Korea's spectacular development. *Bad Samaritans* suggests that South Korea's development was home-grown. But aid also played a part in the process. For example, David Steinberg argues that in the 1950s, US aid to South Korea, through military training and assisting a massive expansion of education, provided the foundation for South Korea's impressive growth rates in the 1960s and beyond.[72] America promoted South Korea's land reform process, which played a vital role in the country's rapid economic development and in significantly reducing poverty.[73]

South Korea is one of the four Asian Tigers, having applied a set of unorthodox economic policies that catapulted the country to a high-income status in a very short time. In the preface of this book, I quoted the *Growth Report's* six secrets of success: (i) commitment to growth in combination with effective governance; (ii) high saving and investment rates; (iii) fast export growth; (iv) macroeconomic stability; (v) knowledge and technology import; and (vi) market-friendly policies. *Bad Samaritans* does not touch upon all of them, but the fact that South Korea's leadership demonstrated a commitment to growth, comes through loud and clear. The same applies to fast export growth and knowledge and technology import. Market-friendly policies were established once South Korea's industries had the time to mature behind protective walls, before successfully entering the international market.

In Appendix 1 Singapore's rapid economic development is described. Singapore's success coincide with all of the Growth Report's six secrets of success.

2.4.2 The Middle-Income Trap

There are various descriptions of the middle-income trap. I found a succinct one in an IMF Working Paper: 'The 'middle-income trap' is the phenomenon of hitherto rapidly growing economies stagnating at middle-income levels and failing to graduate into the ranks of high-income countries.'[74] Most growth models assume a smooth convergence path. As presented in Chap. 1 (see Sect. 1.2), such a gradual path is not happening in the real world—there are growth accelerations, followed by growth slowdowns, stagnation, or even negative growth, after which economic growth may pick up again.

Since the 1980s (when globalisation picked up again) the world's poor countries did well: during the 1980s and 1990s their real per capita income increased by more than 160%. This miracle was not spurred by agricultural export; rather, it was large-scale standardised manufactured goods that contributed to the increase of per capita incomes. In contrast, middle-income countries—almost all Latin American countries, former Soviet republics, and much of the Middle East—did not do so well. Over the same period, their real per capita incomes grew by less than 20%.

In 2004, Geoffrey Garrett published *Globalization's Missing Middle*.[75] Garrett argues that middle-income countries have not done nearly as well under globalised markets as either richer or even poorer countries. For example, middle-income countries, such as Mexico and Poland, would like to compete with Japan and Germany in the American market for high-value goods and services. The problem is that their respective workforce is not skilled enough. As a result, they—and other middle-income countries for that matter—are forced into unwinnable battles with China for a market share in simple manufacturing and, increasingly, with India, for low-wage service-sector exports.[76] Garrett's advice is to give people in these middle-income countries access to education and training that can transform them into successful knowledge workers. In addition, to shoulder effective financial systems, and promote good governance, these countries need institutional reforms in government, banking, and law to protect property-rights.

Lin provides another explanation: 'After World War II many Latin American countries carried out the 'secondary import substitution' strategy to develop some capital-intensive industries.... Not surprisingly, it resulted in inadequate employment, an unfair distribution of wealth, and a mushrooming of slums. Under the pressure of unemployment and social tension, those countries resorted to so-called democratic politics. The politicians offered temporary social welfare policies to the electorate. But it produced the Latin American middle-income trap, featuring stagnation, failure to narrow the income gap with advanced countries, periodic financial turmoil, and economic crises.'[77]

Slowdowns
The IMF Working Paper's authors present a comparative analysis of successful East Asian economies and stagnating Latin American economies having reached the level of $3000.- per capita. GDP growth is created by physical capital, human capital, the expansion of the working age population, and total factor productivity growth. After having analysed a number of Latin American countries in the 1980s, Aiyar et al. note that steep falls in their respective total factor productivity (TFP) growth rates explain to a large extent growth slowdowns, although lower physical capital growth played a part as well. By contrast: '...the success stories of East Asia (and much more recently China and India) are underpinned by robust TFP growth.'[78] A comparison between Latin American and Asian middle-income countries is presented in Appendix 2.

Dissenters
As is often the case in economics, there are dissenting views; this also applies to the middle-income trap. For example, Fernando Gabriel and David Rosenblatt beg to differ. They present their findings in a paper entitled *Middle-Income Traps; A Conceptual and Empirical Study.*[79] The authors argue that there is little support for the idea of a middle-income trap. They question whether the alleged inability of countries to progress from middle-income country (MIC) to high-income status (HIC) implies that there is a trap. Given the fact that there have only been some 200 years of modern economic history, the authors analyse the evolution of MICs across time, while asking what a reasonable timeframe would be to graduate to a high-income status.

To answer this question, they analysed the transition of 125 countries in ten-year periods from 1950 to 2008.[80] The authors conclude that that there is little to no evidence of the existence of a middle-income trap. The upper middle-income to high-income transitions appear to be as likely as lower middle-income to upper middle-income transitions. Regarding the expected time it takes to move from upper middle-income to high-income status, the authors find very little evidence supporting the claim that it takes longer to make this transition than the transition from lower middle-income to upper middle-income.[81]

At the beginning of their paper the authors note that modern economic history is only 200 years old, and 200 years is a short time span for convergence to occur. History demonstrates that transition states have taken a long time to converge. Therefore, it may be a misnomer, the authors argue, to consider growth slowdowns to be a trap, because in some cases these states have simply represented a slower convergence path. Their growth patterns also do not conform to one clear pattern that can be easily characterised as a trap.[82]

Alternative Approaches

Tilman Altenberg and Wilfried Lütkenhorst (A&L) analyse the challenges involved from the point of view of the role of industrialisation.[83] A&L argue that economic growth and shedding poverty is about productivity. At early stages of development, the size of the productivity gap between rich and poor countries, the lack of entrepreneurial competences, and market failures call for a particularly interventionist role of industrial policy. This is because the role of industry in an economy, in particular manufacturing, is to promote productivity. In many developing countries market transactions are embedded in many non-market customs and rules that hamper efficient resource allocation. For all these reasons, the productivity gap separating today's developing countries from the top industrial countries is much larger than the gap that the now developed industrial latecomers had to overcome in the nineteenth century to catch up with Britain and other frontrunners. The authors then arrive at the middle-income trap:

> At higher income levels, the sources and drivers of growth differ from those that enable a country to move out of conditions of poverty. Competitive pressures are intensifying: not yet able to fully compete with more sophisticated producers in mature industrial economies, and no longer able to compete against low-cost producers from poorer countries, such a precarious 'sandwich' position can stifle and ultimately trap further development efforts.[84]

The key question for middle-income countries seeking to overcome the middle-income trap is how to move from a low-cost to a knowledge-based economy. Quite a lot is required: achieving higher levels of technology, promoting innovation, strengthening specialised technical skills, developing financial markets, promoting property rights protection, strengthening accountability and transparency, and curbing corruption. Each country will follow its own evolutionary path, in which not necessarily all requirements will have to be fulfilled.

As elaborated in Chap. 4, during the early days of developing countries' economic development, state-led industrialisation was popular, but not for long.

> Many developing countries have followed the respective ideological mainstream, adopting radical policy changes. In the 1950s and 1970s most developing country governments (especially in Africa, Latin America, and South Asia) intervened in markets with the aim of building national industries. The late 1980s and 1990s witnessed the dismantling of protective trade policies and selective economic promotion under the hegemony of neo-liberal orthodoxy.[85]

A&L conclude that the most serious error of past industrial policies was to focus on building physical industrial infrastructure rather than creating a competitive environment and nurturing innovative entrepreneurship and institutional learning. More advanced international competitors have already established long-term relationships with suppliers and customers. They can tap into a pool of staff equipped with relevant skills. And they had the time to grow and thus benefit from economies of scale. Given these drawbacks for countries that want to move up the ladder, what can be done?

A&L suggest analysing what drives global production networks and value chains, and identifying ways of insertion that would enhance their productivity. To date, more than half of the trade in goods and almost three quarters of the trade in services are generated by so-called intermediate inputs; i.e., products not intended for final consumers but as inputs for further processing. Another possibility is to develop so-called niche markets; Chile did this with commercial salmon farming and cherry cultivation, and India with IT-enabled services.[86]

Skipping Industrialisation

Given the hindrances facing middle-income countries—and the superior competitiveness of Asian countries—in transiting to high-income status, some analysts wonder whether it would not be better to skip industrialisation and move directly to the development of the service sector. Does this proposal make sense?

Chang is no supporter of this idea. He says: 'As for the idea that developing countries can largely skip industrialization and enter the post-industrial phase directly, it is a fantasy. Their limited scope for productivity growth makes services a poor engine of growth. The low tradability of services means that a more service-based economy will have a lower ability to export.'[87]

The Growth Report deals with the question in a wider, more evolutionary, perspective. This is what the report suggests:

> Increasingly, growth must spring from knowledge, innovation, and a deeper stock of physical and human capital. Services also assume a more prominent role in the economic mix. The growth strategies that served an economy well at lower levels cease to apply. Instead of providing targeted support to labor-intensive sectors, governments must expand higher education to support the growing service sector of the economy. Skills must be upgraded across the spectrum of employment. Otherwise the disappearance of unskilled manufacturing jobs will leave the less skilled and less educated part of the population stranded without good employment options.[88]

2.4.3 Low-Income Countries and Failed States

Sir Paul Collier was once invited by the government of the Central African Republic, a dirt poor landlocked SSA country, to advise the government about what to do to get development going. When advising developing countries' governments, Collier had the habit of first asking them which country they wished to be like in twenty years' time. After the government ministers of the Central African Republic had discussed the question at some length, the answer was Burkina Faso: another landlocked poor country. This answer suggested that the ministers did not have high hopes for their country's growth potential.[89] Being landlocked with bad neighbours, is one of the four traps identified by Collier that prevent poor countries from developing. The other three are the conflict trap, the natural resources trap, and the bad governance trap.[90] While some poor countries managed to develop, growing themselves out of the 'danger zone', the economies of countries caught in one of these traps fell behind; some even fall apart. Collier calculated that a billion people live in these countries; hence the title of his celebrated book, *The Bottom Billion*.[91] These typically small countries are characterised by low income, slow or negative economic growth, and dependent on primary commodity exports.

Collier introduced the term failing states.[92] He observes that poor countries with weak states stand a great chance of being caught in a conflict trap, and are prone to civil war or coups d'état. Collier argues that poverty is a strong factor in armed conflicts—much more than, for example, income inequality or ethnic differences. In addition, dependency on primary commodity exports, such as oil and diamonds, increases the risk of civil war. The author estimates that civil war tends to reduce growth by around 2.3% per year: the typical seven-year war leaves a country around 15 percent poorer than it would have been otherwise.

> Wars and coups keep low-income countries from growing and hence keep them dependent upon exports of primary commodities. Because they stay poor, stagnant, and dependent upon primary commodities they are prone to wars and coups. Wars and coups feed on themselves in other ways that make history repeat itself.[93]

Regarding the natural resource trap, not only poor countries but also some middle-income countries are caught in this trap. However, for poor countries natural resources loom large because their economies are small, and resource wealth takes away incentives to diversify exports. A wealth of natural resources breeds autocracy, patronage, blocks restraints such as accountability, and promotes unproductive investments.[94]

Many SSA countries are landlocked. Around 30% of SSA's population lives in landlocked and resource-scare countries. This is not helpful, especially when their neighbours present challenges, as neighbouring countries are important for the transportation of a landlocked country's export products. When these neighbours have bad roads and congested ports, this worsens a landlocked country's competitiveness.

There are positive or negative spill-over effects as well. Globally speaking, if a country's good neighbour grows by an additional 1%, the country grows by an additional 0.4%. For landlocked countries with good neighbours, the percentage is 0.7%. But for African landlocked countries, typically having bad neighbours, it is only 0.2%. Collier has not come across an example of a landlocked, resource-scarce country with bad neighbours that had made it to middle-income status. The normal condition for a failing state is to be stuck, as bad policies and bad governance are persistent.

However, Collier observes that not all low-income countries that fall below the cut off line are failing states.

Bad neighbours are one drawback, bad governance in a small country is another. Take corruption. It impedes development, but it matters more in small countries with few opportunities than in large ones with better opportunities. For example, Bangladesh and Chad ranked lowest on the 2005 Transparency International Perception Index list. Yet, this did not prevent Bangladesh from adopting fairly sensible economic policies, and promoting the export of labour-intensive manufactured goods and services. Collier explains that partly due to export processing zones providing islands of better governance; in other words, the government of Bangladesh managed to keep its corrupt governance from choking off export activity.[95] By contrast, Chad is a small country; it has no scope for exports. Chad is an aid receiver and it has oil. What can be done? From the proceeds, the government could provide better public services. However, due to corruption, 99% of the funds intended for health clinics never reached them. The conclusion is clear: bad governance mattered in Chad more than in Bangladesh because the former's only option was for government to provide services, and corruption had closed off this option.

Since 2005, the Fund for Peace has published its annual *Fragile Sates Index*, which applies twelve social, economic, and political indicators to rank the position of states in the Index.[96] According to the Fund for Peace, a fragile state has several attributes. Common indicators include a state whose central government is so weak or ineffective that it has little practical control over much of its territory; it cannot provide public services; there is widespread corruption and criminality; refugees and involuntary movement of populations abound; and the economy is going down the drain.

The Fund for Peace's 2019 Index ranks 178 countries ranging from 'very high alert' to 'very sustainable.' The Fund casts its net very wide indeed. In 2019, the very high alert states were Yemen, Somalia, South Sudan, Syria, and the Democratic Republic of Congo. Next in line were the following 'high alert' states: The Central African Republic, Chad, Sudan, and Afghanistan. Together, these nine countries constitute 'hard core' failed states, so to speak. At the other end of the scale we find the 'very sustainable' states: Canada, Iceland, Australia, Denmark, Switzerland, Norway, and Finland. In between, there are 22 states falling in the 'alert' category. Then, 29 'high warning' countries, led by Venezuela down to Tanzania, after which 35 'elevated warning' states are listed, starting with

Lesotho and ending with Tunisia. The remainder of the listed countries is on the safe side; they belong to the 'stable', 'more stable', or 'very stable' categories. The very best scoring countries find themselves in the 'sustainable' and 'very sustainable' categories.

Damage Done

Collier observes that civil war tends to reduce growth by around 2.3% per year. Thirlwall and Pacheco-López estimate that failed states now contain approximately 1.5 billion people or 20% of the world's population. They account for 30% of people living on less than $1.90 per day; poverty rates in these countries are over 20% higher than in other low-income countries.[97] Some studies estimate that by 2030, 85% of extremely poor people will live in fragile states. The World Bank calculates that civil conflict costs the average developing country approximately 30 years of GDP growth. These costs include not only damage done to a country's infrastructure, lost human lives and capital, and foregone income from tourism, but also reduced domestic and foreign investment, reduced government income and thus an inability to invest in education and health services.

One of Collier's messages is that in particular poverty breeds state failure. While low income may not be the only characteristic of a failed state, it nevertheless is a very important one. To test this observation, I have taken the 59 worst scoring states in the 2019 *Fragile States Index*, and compared them with the 2018 World Bank countries classification. Of these 59 worst scoring states, 30 were low-income countries, while 21 belonged to the lower middle-income group. The result: 86.4% of the worst scoring states are low-income or lower middle-income countries.[98]

What Can Be Done?

Collier argues that fragile states entangled in a conflict or coup trap cannot break the trap by themselves. They need help. The question then is who is to help and what *can* be done? Myles Wickstead suggests that bilateral aid should increasingly focus on these countries:

> This is for a number of reasons. First, there is a strong humanitarian motivation to help; many innocent and vulnerable people inevitably get caught up in what is in effect a low-level but ongoing emergency situation, and it is right to give them whatever support is feasible. Second, it is estimated that by 2030 around three-quarters of the world's poorest people will live in

> failed and fragile states (largely in Africa). Third—and as has become very evident in recent years—armed and violent groups (many of them now operating in the name of religion) are able to use dysfunctional states as a base; and in any event, conflict and insurrection rarely stop precisely at national borders.... Finally, fragile states are in other respects too weak links in the global system; addressing health pandemics or the trade in illegal drugs also requires global participation.[99]

This quotation prompts the question why bilateral donors in particular should focus on these countries? Bilateral donors have the capacity and knowledge, argues Wickstead, to focus on countries coping with particularly difficult problems. They have the necessary staying power and can provide the types of aid that are required—they are in the business of structural development. He also presents a moral argument: '...the international community must continue to support if it is to put its hand on its heart and say that it remains determined to deliver on its promise that no-one should be left behind.'[100] There is also the argument that it could prevent terrorist groups from operating in states without a central authority. Finally, failed states impose so-called negative externalities on the rest of the world, such as refugees who are displaced by war, economic migrants in search of jobs in stable countries, and drug—and human trafficking.

Based upon the World Bank's *Harmonized List of Fragile Situations*[101] the Bank established a Low-Income Countries Under Stress Fund. The objective of this fund is to assist low-income countries under stress to implement reforms necessary for re-engagement with the international community and to address urgent social needs, such as HIV/AIDS. It is the UK government's intention to spend one-half of its bilateral aid budget on 20 or more countries, mainly in Africa, where the state has virtually collapsed.[102] With the help of the international community, some countries, such as Rwanda, have been able to leave their civil war behind them.

It is important to analyse what the underlying causes would have been why a particular state slid backwards into a situation of near anarchy. In other words, a one-size-fits-all approach, typically focused on strengthening the state's capacity, may not be the appropriate one.

In *Fixing Failed States*, Ashraf Ghani and Clare Lockhart introduce the notion of a sovereignty gap between de jure state sovereignty and de facto capabilities of states to serve their population and act as responsible member of the international community.[103] The authors argue that outdated one-size-fits-all solutions, involving lots of aid monies, have not brought about the intended results. Constant humanitarian interventions cost billions of dollars to maintain, yet they do not prevent conflict from re-emerging and do not leave capable states in their wake. Instead, a state-building path would enable both humanitarian actors and international military forces to exit more quickly, once deployed.

There is little understanding, the authors argue, of the long-term commitment that is required to redress state failure. The key lies in examining what successful states did to become sustainable sovereign states. After all, there are examples of countries that have transitioned from poverty and instability to prosperity and security. The authors present a strategic framework to define the functions of the state, design the organisational structure necessary for the performance of these functions, and aligning actors to the goal of state building. The central idea is the understanding of the state as a dynamic, citizen-oriented mechanism that is necessary for the creation of a legitimate economic, social, and political order. The authors' inspiration was the 'reversed history' that countries like Singapore and Ireland achieved in creating effective states despite significant challenges they encountered on the way.

Appendix 1: Lee Kuan Yew's Singapore

Introduction

Singapore pulled itself out of its Third World status into a sophisticated First World country. This can be mainly attributed to the exceptional talents of Singapore's first Prime Minister Lee Kuan Yew.

When I told my daughter that I was writing about Singapore's phenomenal economic success, she said that she had visited Singapore during her trip across Asia. She found it a very pleasant place to stay: 'It was so nice to visit a clean and green city and a clean guest house where all appliances worked. After having stayed in filthy back packer lodges in other Asian countries, I really needed it'. This is exactly what Lee Kuan Yew wanted to offer tourists. He understood that Singapore had to provide better and cleaner services if it wanted to attract tourists who would create a lot of employment for Singapore's citizens. He was very successful in this endeavour (Singapore receives more than three million tourists annually) as in many other undertakings.

In 2000, after his retirement from government, Lee published his memoirs.[104] The author explains how Singapore achieved its impressive economic development. But Lee also explained why and how Singapore prioritised education, reflective of the new endogenous growth theory (see Chap. 5) which underscores the growth potential of human development. Singapore also developed its own social security system, including subsidised housing, health insurance, and old-age pension. Corruption did not get much chance in Singapore, as Lee elaborately explained. In short, Singapore may not have been a typical Third World country, yet how it managed to become a First World country, explained by Lee in broader than only economic terms, makes fascinating reading. Most of what is described below is based on his book.

Success Factors

Singapore's rapid economic development demonstrates that a developing country can achieve it, provided the country is inspired and directed by 'superior intelligence, discipline, and ingenuity', as Henry Kissinger wrote in his preface to Lee's book. Singapore's annual per capita income had grown from $1000.- in 1965 to around $30,000.- in 2000. This is an embarrassing reminder for many SSA countries whose respective per capita incomes have not grown much since they gained independence. While many African countries suffer from a natural resource curse, one could say that Singapore benefitted from not having natural resources.

What are Singapore's success factors? What exactly have Singapore's growth ingredients been, when considering that Singapore has a relatively small population of mixed Chinese, Indian, and Malay composition. Its main advantage is its location. Singapore's South East Asian's central location and its natural harbour made the British decide that the city would serve as the empire's entrepôt for that region. Another vital asset is Singapore's human resources, as we shall see.

The year 1965, when Singapore gained its independence, was not a glorious year. On the contrary, it probably was the most difficult year for Cambridge-educated Prime Minister (Harry) Lee Kuan Yew and his team of ministers. Having been ejected from the federation,[105] they were on their own. A communist uprising was imminent, Singapore was totally dependent on Malaysia for its water supply, and Indonesia's Confrontation policy threatened Singapore's very existence. But as the Chinese saying goes 'the sparrow though small has all five organs'. This is how Lee characterised Singapore's plight:

> To survive, we had to be better organized and more efficient and competitive than the rest of the region or there was no reason for our role as a nodal point between advanced and the developing countries.... The story of Singapore's progress is a reflection of the advance of the industrial countries—their inventions, technology, enterprise, and drive.[106]

The young government's first priority was to ensure internal and external security. The British still protected Singapore's borders, but by 1971, they would withdraw their forces. So time was not on Singapore's side to establish its own defence force. Young people were recruited and foreign senior officers were hired to train military personnel. By 1990, Singapore had a respected and professional force, operating modern defence systems, capable of defending Singapore's independence.

From an economic point of view, Singapore's prime goal was industrialisation; it was the only way to survive. Singapore implemented the principal advice of the first generation of development economists (see Chap. 4). A Dutchman played a crucial role in Singapore's industrialisation process. In September 1960, Dr. Albert Winsemius led a United Nations Development Programme (UNDP) mission to Singapore to advise on industrial development. He would continue to advise the government, in particular Lee himself and the minister of finance, for the next 23 years. Lee observed that there was a 'congruence of the Calvinistic and Confusion philosophy of life' between him and Winsemius.[107]

The first report of Winsemius included two essential preconditions for Singapore's success. The first one was to eliminate the communists who made any industrial progress impossible because of their destabilising influence. The second precondition may have been somewhat puzzling at first sight: to keep Raffles statue were it was.[108] Leaving it were it was would be a symbol of public acceptance of the British heritage, and would not shy away necessary American and European technical, managerial, entrepreneurial, and marketing know-how. The Winsemius report was a welcome one, since the government badly needed to attract businesses and foreign companies to invest in Singapore, in order to create jobs for the many unemployed. Singapore benefitted from the technical advice of top-notch experts. This must have inspired Lee's thinking about development cooperation. He argued that Singapore always preferred to give aid in the form of training and technical assistance, but not in grants which could be misused.[109]

The government invested in the necessary infrastructure, such as roads, electricity, water- and sewage systems. In parallel, the Singapore Tourist Promotion Board was established, to promote this labour-intensive industry. In 1961, the Economic Development Board (EDB) was created to facilitate industrial development and to create jobs. The government provided economic protection for locally assembled cars, refrigerators, air conditioners, TV-sets, and other appliances in the hope that in future their full production would be located in Singapore. Gradually, protective tariffs were removed.

The government managed to attract Hong Kong-based and Taiwanese producers of toys, textiles, and garments to build factories in Singapore. The government took the lead in starting new industries such as steel mills (National Iron and Steel Mills), service industries such as Neptune Oriental Lines, Singapore International Airlines, and the high-tech company Singapore Technologies.

State monopolies, such as the Port Authority and Singapore Telecom, have gradually been turned into separate entities, free from ministerial control, so that they could be managed as efficient, profitable, competitive companies. Former Royal Air Force Changi air base, was transformed into Changi International Airport, providing top-of-the-bill airport services.

The authorities promoted good labour relations, provided fiscal incentives, and facilitated exports. Multinationals such as Texas Instruments, Hewlett-Packard, and General Electric established factories in Singapore. In the late 1970s, oil refineries of the 'usual oil-producing suspects', such as Shell, Mobil, Esso, and BP, started to expand their respective capacities into petrochemicals. Lee proudly mentioned that by the 1990s, Singapore had become the world's third largest oil-refining center after Houston and Rotterdam, and the third largest oil trading centre after New York and London.[110] Equally important, sound macroeconomic policies were designed, consisting of the simple rule of not spending more than collected in revenues, except in times of recession.

Employment and Education

Towards the end of the 1970s the unemployment problem had been solved thanks to many investments by Singaporean and foreign firms. The next challenge was skill-upgrading of Singaporeans to meet more demanding international technical and managerial standards. Lee wanted to create a 'First World oasis in a Third World region.' This implied that Singaporeans had to be trained to, indeed, enable them to provide First World standard services.

Singapore invited French, Japanese, German, and Dutch companies to establish their own training centers with their own instructors to train Singaporean technicians. Some were joint-ventures with corporations such as Philips (Dutch), Rollei (German), and Tata (Indian).

Pasir Panjang's former military complex was transformed into Singapore's National University campus, catering to 26,000 students. Singapore's top scholars were chosen from the best of each year's crop of students and sent to the best universities in Britain, Canada, Australia, New Zealand, Germany, France, Italy, and Japan. Once Singapore could afford the costly American tuition fees, American universities were added to the list. Singapore became the first Asian country to break into the top-10 international higher education systems.

Since Singapore could not count on its own hinterland (i.e., Malaysia), nor on Indonesia because of its aggressive confrontation policy, the city-state needed to look further afield to America, Europe, and Japan to induce manufacturers of these countries to produce in Singapore.[111] Lee himself, acting like a true entrepreneur, attracted foreign businesses to come to Singapore. He described his first official visit to America in October 1967 as follows:

> I recounted to 50 businesspeople at a luncheon in Chicago how Singapore had grown from a village of 120 fishermen in 1819 to become a metropolis of 2 million. This was because its philosophy was to provide goods and services 'cheaper and better than anyone else, or perish.' They responded well because I was not putting my hand out for aid, which they had come to expect of leaders from newly independent countries. I noted their favorable reaction to my 'no begging bowl' approach.[112]

American business people looked for political, economic, and financial stability, as well as sound labour relations. Singapore was able to provide both. Red tape was limited to a minimum through the creation of a one-stop agency, relieving interested foreign investors from having to go from one ministry to another agency to obtain the necessary permits.

Anticorruption

Corruption, a notorious phenomenon in the region, was brought under control. This was achieved by paying the meritocratic civil service and cabinet ministers well—matching salaries paid in the private sector. The country's top leadership was beyond reproach. The government enacted an anticorruption law combined with a strong enforcement system. The Corrupt Practices Investigation Bureau was instructed to go after the so-called 'big fish' in the high echelons of society. As regards 'smaller fry', procedures were simplified and discretion was removed by having widely published guidelines.

Voting is compulsory in Singapore. The country had avoided the use of money to win elections.[113] Singapore scores consistently high on Transparency International's (TI) Corruption Perception Index. In 2018, Singapore occupied slot 3 on TI's list, together with Finland.

Former French President Valéry Giscard D'Estaing once asked Lee why Singapore did develop and not the other developing countries. Lee wrote the following:

> I could only tell him what I thought where the primary reasons: first, stability and cohesion in society; second, a cultural drive to achieve and a thrifty, hardworking people always investing in the future, with high savings for a rainy day and for the next generation; third, a great reverence for education and knowledge.[114]

Lee added that Giscard was not satisfied that this was the complete answer.

Welfare

Singapore is by all standards a rich country. Does it have a comparable welfare system as other advanced countries had introduced in the course of their economic development? The short answer is: no. Singapore developed its own system. The basic philosophy behind it is as follows: 'To even out the extreme results of free-market competition, we had to redistribute the national income through subsidies on things that improved the earning power of citizens such as education. Housing and public health were also obviously desirable.'[115]

Singapore's Housing and Development Board launched a home-ownership scheme, which consisted of low-cost housing for workers. At the time, the British had introduced a Central Provident Fund (CPF) as a simple saving scheme for retirement. This proved to be inadequate. The government allowed that workers' accumulated savings could be used by them for the down payment of their house. In 1996, there were already 70,000 home owners among the workers. Today, more than 80% of Singaporeans live in government-built flats, with 95% owning their homes.

The British National Health Service was a failure, Lee observed, while American-style health insurance schemes were expensive, triggering wasteful and extravagant treatments. So, what would be a better, yet fair, system? The government calculated that 6%–8% of a person's CPF contribution was sufficient to co-pay medical expenses for a family. Medisave was introduced charging 6% of a worker's wages to cover part of the medical costs of the worker, his spouse, children, parents and grandparents. Later, Medishield was added; an optional insurance against the costs of catastrophic illnesses.

What pension scheme was established? Again, CPF was the appropriate vehicle. All workers accumulated their own savings in the CPF for their old age. CPF was allowed to use these savings to invest in, for example, public utilities such as the Singapore Bus Service or Singapore Telecom. In addition, workers' home ownership added to their assets, which could be capitalised when the time had come. Lee concluded: 'The CPF has provided workers with a comprehensive self-financing social security fund equal to any old-age pension system or entitlement program, without shifting the burden to the next generation of workers. It is fairer and sounder to have each generation pay for itself and each person for his own pension fund.'[116]

Democracy and Development

Directly, and between the lines, Lee time and again emphasised that Singapore's political system is a democratic one. Lee's simple philosophy was that if a party delivers the goods to the electorate in a satisfactory manner (and every time better), the party will be re-elected.[117] And this is what happened in Singapore. His party, the Singapore Action Party (PAP) is by far the largest party in Singapore's parliament. Yet, Lee is sometimes portrayed as a (benevolent) dictator. Strictly speaking, this is incorrect, as he was accountable for his deeds to Parliament. In a speech to the 18th Philippine Business Conference Lee said: 'I do not believe democracy necessarily leads to development. I believe what a country needs to develop is discipline more than democracy.'[118]

Some measures taken by Lee and his colleagues in Cabinet encroached on the liberty of individuals. For example, in the early 1970s men wearing long hair were not tolerated. A liberal-minded person would say that a man's hair length is none of government's business. Firecrackers were banned; a tough decision, considering that the majority of Singaporeans is of Chinese origin. The best-known example, is Singapore's chewing gum ban.

Although none of these examples are major issues, the question is whether Singapore's strict attitude, as developed by the Lee Administration would survive. In other words, would this system be sustainable? In 1995, Harvard political science professor Samuel Huntington, author of *The Clash of Civilizations*, compared Taiwan with Singapore: 'The freedom and creativity that President Lee has introduced here in Taiwan will survive him. The honesty and efficiency that Senior Minister Lee has brought to Singapore are likely to follow him to his grave.'[119] Huntington was wrong. Lee stepped down as Prime Minister in 1990. He continued as Senior Minister in the Cabinet from which he retired in 2000. In 1990, Goh Chok Tong succeeded Lee. In 2004, Hsien Loong, Lee's son, succeeded Goh.

Lee died in 2015. Singapore is still going strong. Its economic performance, although registering lower growth figures than in the past, is as solid as ever. In 2018, Singapore's per capita income was $65,627.- and its growth rate was 3.28%. Singapore's ranking on TI's Corruption Perception Index was even better than it was during Lee's time. PAP lost some support in recent elections to opposition parties, yet, PAP is still the largest political party in Singapore's parliament. Singaporeans have shown an increasing willingness to speak up, and may, in future, be ready to challenge the government-knows-best philosophy of their rulers.

Appendix 2: The Middle-Income Trap in Figures

Latin American countries are typically portrayed as victims of the middle-income trap. Latin America is home to what Angus Maddison calls 'faltering economies'.[120] These economies have been falling behind instead of catching up. I would add: they are stuck in the middle, between low-income and high-income countries. A few Asian countries also belong to the group of faltering economies.

I compared the Latin American middle income-countries in the Wold Development Report list of 1978 with Latin American middle-income countries included in the 2018 World Development Report. The same was done for Asian countries. The result is reflected in Table 2.1.

Out of 18 Latin American middle income-countries in 1978, 14 of them (77.7%) had not been able to shed their middle-income status in 2018. Four Latin American countries have done better; in 2018 they had transitioned into high-income countries. However, Venezuela has done worse—although still classified as a middle-income country—the country is in fact a failed state.

Table 2.1 Latin American and Asian middle-income countries compared 1978–2018

Latin American middle-income countries	*Latin American middle-income countries*	*Asian middle-income countries*	*Asian middle-income countries*
1978	*2018*	*1978*	*2018*
Bolivia	Bolivia	Thailand	Thailand
Honduras	Honduras	Philippines	Philippines
El Salvador	El Salvador	Korea Rep.	(high income)
Colombia	Colombia	Malaysia	Malaysia
Guatemala	Guatemala	Taiwan	(high income)
Ecuador	Ecuador	Iraq	Iraq
Paraguay	Paraguay	Iran	Iran
Nicaragua	Nicaragua	Singapore	(high income)
Dominican Republic	Dominican Republic	Hong Kong	(high income)
Peru	Peru		
Costa Rica	Costa Rica		
Chile	(high income)-		
Mexico	Mexico		
Brazil	Brazil		
Panama	(high income)		
Uruguay	(high income)		
Argentina	(high income)		
Venezuela	Venezuela		
Total 18	**Total 14**	**Total 9**	**Total 5**

Source: World Development Reports 1978, 2018

The picture for Asia is different. In 1978, the World Bank list included 9 Asian middle-income countries. In 2018, five of them (55.5%) were still middle income countries, while four Asian countries had transitioned into high-income countries.

Now, why are Latin American countries doing worse? We have seen above that Garrett's advice was to give people in middle-income countries access to education and training that could transform them into successful knowledge workers, to fill up the shortage. In addition, these countries would need institutional reforms in government, banking, and law to protect property-rights, to shoulder effective financial systems, and promote good governance.

Maddison added a monetary and financial explanation. He observed that Latin American countries (with the exception of Chile after 1973) had not followed IMF's advice of fiscal and monetary rectitude, resulting in high inflation rates which proved to be difficult to control. Many countries over-borrowed, while international interest rates went up. Between 1973 and 1982, Latin America's international debt increased seven-fold. Mexico defaulted in 1982; other countries followed. Private lending stopped, capital flight ensued. There was a massive need for retrenchment in economies on the verge of hyperinflation and fiscal crisis. In most countries resource allocation was distorted by subsidies, controls, widespread commitments to government enterprise, and detailed inteventionism.[121] After 1990, economic growth revived but the process was interrupted by contagious episodes of capital flight. On page 154 of *The world Economy*, Maddison mentioned that for 1980–1999 as a whole, per capita income in Latin America had risen by less than 0.3% per year compared with over 2.5% from 1950 to1980. A growth rate of 0.3% implies an income doubling over 250 years.

The four Asian countries that had transitioned into high-income countries, applied most, if not all, of the six secrets of success, as identified by *The Growth Report*.

Notes

1. McCloskey, D. (2010) *Bourgeois Dignity; Why Economics Can't Explain The Modern World*. Chicago: The University of Chicago Press, 3.
2. The World Bank's Classification of Countries by Income. *Policy Research Working Paper 7528*, 12 January 2016.

3. As of 1978, the World Bank introduced a simple countries classification: low-income countries (LICs) and middle-income countries (MICs), industrialised countries, capital-surplus oil exporters and centrally planned economies, using Gross National Income (GNI) per capita. From 1983 onwards, the middle-income classification was divided in two-sub categories: lower middle-income and upper middle-income countries. As of 1989, a high-income threshold was introduced to include high income countries (HICs). Since then, the classification has not changed.
4. In their Data Blog of 12 January 2016, Neil Fanton and Umar Serajuddin argue that: 'Our general finding is that using fixed thresholds that are held constant over time, adjusting only for price inflation, provides an absolute method of assessing change that many still find appealing. …GNI per capita also continues to be a reasonable choice for a classifying variable. While clearly not perfect, GNI correlates well with several other indicators commonly used to assess the progress of countries.'
5. *Policy Research Working Paper 7528*, 16.
6. *World Development Indicators*, 9 August 2018.The document also mentions that in East Asia and the Pacific, slower population growth and rapid declines in poverty rates have reduced the number of poor from more than one billion in 1981 to just above 45 million in 2015. It is projected, assuming no changes in economic policies nor in average annual growth, that by 2030, 86% of extreme poor people will live in SSA.
7. Lin, J. (2012) *Demystifying the Chinese Economy*. Cambridge: Cambridge University Press, 2.
8. *The Economist* reported on 13 July 2019 that: '…50 biggest recipients now have debts with China worth about 17% of their GDP on average, up from 1% in 2005. Strikingly, many were granted debt relief by wealthy creditors in the early 2000s after a wave of defaults. But thanks to China's largesse they are now on track to reach the same levels of debt that they had before the crisis.', 64.
9. Maçães, B. (2018) *The Dawn of Eurasia; On the trail of the New World Order*. London: Allen Lane, 7.
10. In early September 2019, the world's largest container ship docked for the first time at the port of Rotterdam. She started her journey in Tianjin in Northern China, and docked at different ports on the way. 47,500 automobiles were unloaded, together with 386 million pairs of shoes; a highly efficient, relatively cheap and environment-friendly way of transporting products.
11. Djibouti is by all standards a small African country, populated by barely 1 million citizens, bordering the Red Sea. China is investing heavily in the country, since it is projected to be a 'staging post' on China's Belt and Road Initiative, as *The Economist* reported on 21 July 2018. China has

lent Djibouti $1.4 billion (75% of Djibouti's GDP). In 2015, Djibouti was Africa's fifth-biggest recipient of Chinese credit. At the end of 2016, China owned 82% of Djibouti's external debt which could undermine Djibouti's sovereignty.

12. *The Dawn of Eurasia*, 127.
13. Rush Doshi. Xi Jinping Just made It Clear Where China's Foreign Policy Is Headed. In *Washington Post*, 25 October 2017.
14. There are doubts about India's growth figures. Some analysts reckon that the country's average annual growth would be around 4.5%, rather than the official 7% as presented by the government.
15. Meanwhile, close to 100 million toilets have been constructed to boost public health and eliminate 'open defecation', which—to my horror—I have seen when passing by Bombay's slums *en route* to Surat.
16. For example, in 2000 just 300,000 Bangladeshis went on holidays within the country; in 2007 seven million could afford a vacation in Bangladesh.
17. Maddison, A. (1995) *Monitoring the World Economy 1880–1992*. Paris: OECD, 77–78.
18. Singapore, Japan, Taiwan, Macao, Vietnam, Hong Kong, and China (represented by four very large cities).
19. In 2017, fuels, ores, and gems still accounted for 71.3% of Bolivia's total export.
20. Branko Milanovic observes that if one were to rank regions by how unequal the countries in each of them are, one could say that the top belongs to Latin America, closely followed by Africa, then Asia, and the least unequal are the rich countries and the post-communist nations. Source: *The Haves and Have-Nots*; 31.
21. Ibid., 185.
22. Hofman, A (2000) *The Economic Development of Latin America in the Twentieth Century*. Cheltenham: Edward Elgar, 11.
23. Rodrik, D. (2011) *The Globalization Paradox*. New York: W.W Norton 169.
24. *The Economic Development of Latin America in the Twentieth Century*, 133.
25. Ibid., 127. Hofman observes that regarding Latin America's GDP per capita, it remained almost stable relative to America during the first 80 years of the twentieth century, but deteriorated steadily during the lost decade of the 1980s.
26. Cherry production benefitted from a combination of a free trade agreement with China, and top-notch Chilean entrepreneurship. In 2018, Chile exported $1.1 billion worth of cherries to China; the equivalent of two-thirds of Chile's wine export.
27. China is becoming more strict in its lending conditions. It issued official guidelines, reflective of its concern about corruption and borrowers'

environmental and social policies. Instead of the earlier touch-and-go policy, China now demonstrates a longer term interest in its investments. For example, Latin American ports are no longer only constructed by Chinese companies; the ports' management now also forms part of the deal.

28. Initially, Chinese investments went to extractive industries; however, currently more than half of them are invested in service-oriented activities, and in activities reflective of the changing tastes of Chinese consumers, such as Chilean vineyards and cherries production facilities, plus meat packaging plants in Uruguay.
29. China, by the way, can boast of a larger number: 450. Europe benefits from 2500 scientists and engineers for every million inhabitants. America is topping the list with 4000 of them.
30. This did not apply to Cameroon, Cote d'Ivoire, Kenya, Malawi, and Swaziland. The agricultural sector was well managed in these countries.
31. *Demystifying the Chinese Economy*, xv.
32. Maddison added another cause of SSA's financial difficulties: 'China, the USSR, Cuba, and East European countries supplied economic and military aid to countries viewed as proxies in a world-wide conflict of interest. Western countries were strongly influenced by this competitive situation. They were less fastidious in allocating aid than they might otherwise have been. As a result Africa accumulated large foreign debts which had a meagre development pay-off.' Source: *Monitoring The World Economy*, 56.
33. Meredith, M. (2014) *The Fortunes of Africa; A 5000-Year History of Wealth, Greed, and Endeavour*. New York: Simon & Schuster, 621.
34. Maddison, A. (1995) *Monitoring the World Economy 1880–1992*. Paris: OECD, 22.
35. Thirlwall, A., Pacheco-López, P. (2017) *Economics of Development*. Tenth Edition. London: Palgrave Macmillan, 152.
36. Mobutu funnelled huge sums abroad to buy luxury houses, office blocks, and grand estates in Belgium, France, Switzerland, Spain, Portugal, Italy and other countries, as Meredith reports in *The Fortunes of Africa*. An 2003 African Union report estimated that corruption cost Africa $148 billion per year—more than one-quarter of Africa's entire GDP.
37. Gold, D. *Peace Dividends and Development; Retrospectives and Prospects*. Newark: Rutgers University, (2001), 3–4.
38. Easterly, W. (2002) *The Elusive Quest for Growth; Economists' Adventures and Misadventures in the Tropics*. Cambridge: MIT Press, 237.
39. For example, it is estimated that in 2016 Uganda's informal exports, worth some $419 million, are equivalent to 17% of recorded trade. It is further estimated that perhaps between 30% and 40% of trade in Southern

Africa is informal. In Benin, informal transit trade to Nigeria may account for a fifth of its GDP. Source: *The Economist*, 1 September, 2018, 58.

40. *The Economist* of 29 June 2019 reports that China appears to become more strict with lending to African governments. During a recent visit to Beijing, Kenya's President, Uhuru Kenyatta, was given to understand that Kenya would not get an expected additional $3.5 billion loan to complete its ambitious railway project. China now doubts the project's economic viability, including Kenya's ability to repay the loan. Beijing also raised questions about corruption. The article ended by noting that 'China's shift closer to Western lending standards is a step in the right direction.', 34.
41. Remittances to SSA grew almost 10% to $46 billion in 2018, supported by strong economic conditions in high-income economies. Source: World Bank, Migration and Development Brief 31.
42. Rodrik, D. *Growth without Industrialization?* Project Syndicate, 10 October 2017.
43. World Bank Flagship Report (2017) *Global Economic Prospects.* Washington: World Bank.
44. SSA's rapid population growth dampens any increase in per capita income. By 2025 the UN predicts that there will be more Africans than Chinese people.
45. Altenburg, T., Lűtkenhorst, W. (2017) *Industrial Policy in Developing Countries.* Cheltenham: Edward Elgar, 97.
46. 'Manufacturing in Africa is only for the brave. In Nigeria it makes up about 10% of GDP.... In South Africa...it accounts for 13% of GDP, down from a fifth in 1990.... Between 1970 and 2013, Africa's share of global manufacturing output fell from 3% to 2%.' Source: The 1.2 Billion Opportunity. In *The Economist*, 6 April, 2016, 6.
47. Hussain, A. (2016) Understanding the Total Factor Productivity Shortfall in Sub-Saharan Africa. *The Horn Economic and Social Policy Institute; Working Paper 02/16*, 2. On page 15 the author concludes: 'Thus, there is substantial room to improve TFP in SSA by improving its institutional quality, reducing its restrictive trade policy and mitigating the effect of its predominantly tropical nature and being landlocked.'
48. Mauritius and Rwanda score well below slot number 30; all other SSA countries score much worse. 'Sovereign-wealth funds are desperate to invest in long-term projects, but cannot find nearly enough opportunities for reasonably safe investments to soak up the available capital.' Source: *The 1.2 Billion Opportunity*, 11.
49. The indicators are: voice and accountability, political stability and absence of violence, government effectiveness, regulatory quality, rule of law, and control of corruption.

50. Dowden, R. (2008) *Africa; Altered States, Ordinary Miracles*. London: Portobello Books, 516.
51. Algeria, Bahrein, Comoros, Djibouti, Egypt, Iraq, Jordan, Kuwait, Lebanon, Libya, Mauretania, Morocco, Oman, Palestine, Qatar, Saudi Arabia, Somalia, Sudan, Syria, Tunisia, the United Arab Emirates, and Yemen.
52. On the 2019 Human Development Index, the Emirates occupied 34th, and Qatar 37th place. Regarding the second group, Algeria occupied place 86, Libya 108, and Sudan 167. Finally, Saudi Arabia occupied 39th place.
53. *Arab Human Development Report 2002, Creating Opportunities for Future Generations*. New York: UNDP, 4.
54. Ibid., 5.
55. 'Many settle for informal work at low wages...Between 2000 and 2005, for example, three-fourth of new labour-market entrants in Egypt were employed in the informal sector...Similarly, over 2001–2007, 69 percent of the new jobs in Syria were informal.' Source: *Arab Human Development Report 2016; Youth and the Prospects for Human Development in a Changing Reality*, 32.
56. The 2016 AHDR observes in this respect: 'Youth also face large entry barriers to jobs, marriage and housing, where older groups enjoy privileges, largely acquired under public programmes during the oil booms.', 32. On page 36, the report also suggests that a sense of exclusion and lack of opportunities for these young men may politically radicalise them.
57. Ibid., 33.
58. In 2014, 41% of the world's displaced population were represented by the Arab region. Some 98% of displaced people from the region originate from conflict-ridden Iraq, Lebanon, Palestine, Somalia, Sudan, Syria, and Yemen.
59. *Arab Human Development Report 2016*, 29.
60. *The Economist*, 31 August 2019.
61. One has to take into consideration that with only one newly registered firm per 1000 working age adults, the countries in the region are among the ones with the lowest level of entrepreneurship in the world.
62. *The Failed Sates Index 2005* mentions that a report commissioned by the CIA had put the number of failing states at about 20. The World Bank had identified about 30 'low-income countries under stress'. The *2019 Failed States Index* includes many more states in various stages of disrepair.
63. Chang, H.-J. (2008) *Bad Samaritans; The Myth of Free Trade and the Secret History of Capitalism*. New York: Bloomsbury Press.
64. Chang, H.-J. (2002) *Kicking Away the Ladder; Development Strategy in Historical Perspective*. London: Anthem Press. The book criticises the

International Development Policy Establishment (IDPE)) for recommending the wrong neo-liberal *one-size-fits-all* policies to developing countries. What this IDPE considers as 'bad' policies, are in fact not so, argues Chang. Instead, the IDPE should allow developing countries to adopt policies and institutions that are more suitable to their stage of development and to other conditions they experience, which enables them to grow faster.

65. The author presents the following comparison on page 3: In 1961, eight years after the end of South Korea's war with North Korea, the average South Korean earned $82 per year. This was less than half the average Ghanaian citizen's annual income of $179. In 2004, South Korea's per capita income was $22,900. Ghana's per capita income in that same year was $2080. (Both countries' per capita income was on PPP basis).
66. This also applied to Japan when, in the second half of the nineteenth century, the Minister of Industry in the Meji government, Okubo Toshimichi, recognised the need for protection and state-led industrialisation as a precondition for catching up with the West.
67. Despite the fact that Adam Smith advised the Americans not to develop manufacturing. Smith wrote that any attempt to stop the importation of European manufactures would obstruct rather than promote the progress of their country towards real wealth and greatness.
68. *Kicking Away the Ladder*, 64.
69. Maddison mentioned 2.1% per capita income growth for these countries over the same period.
70. Obviously the Bad Samaritans are the antipode of the biblical Good Samaritan, who helped a person who had been robbed by highwaymen, despite the fact that Samaritans were known for taking advantage of those in difficulties.
71. *Bad Samaritans*, 14–15.
72. Steinberg, D. (1985) Foreign Aid and the Development of the Republic of Korea: The Effectiveness of Concessional Assistance. In *AID Evaluation Special Study No. 42*. Washington: USAID.
73. In Korea, land reform occurred in two stages. The first, initiated by U.S. forces in 1947, distributed the land confiscated from the Japanese at the end of World War II to the tillers and put a ceiling on rents of other land. The second, begun in 1950 and completed after the Korean War, was undertaken by the Korean government after a lengthy debate in the legislature. The government took over landlord properties, paid the latter nominal compensation, and distributed the land to 900,000 tenants, effectively eliminating tenancy. Source: *The East Asian Miracle*, 161.
74. Aiyar, S., Duval, R., Puy, D., Zhang, L. (March 2013) Growth Slowdowns and the Middle-Income Trap. *IMF Working Paper*, WP/13/71, 1.

Another interesting paper on growth slowdowns is *Growth Slowdowns Redux*, by Barry Eichengreen, Dongyuan Park, and Kwanho Shin. (April 2013). They define a growth slowdown episode as one in which three conditions are satisfied: (i) growth in the preceding period is greater than or equal to 3.5 percent per annum; (ii) the difference in growth between the current and preceding period is greater than or equal to 2 percentage points per annum; and (iii) the country's per capita income exceeds $10,000 in 2005 constant international prices. Hence the country focus of this paper is narrower than in IMF's paper.

75. Garrett, G. Globalization's Missing Middle. In *Foreign Affairs*. Vol. 83 No. 6. November–December 2004.
76. Ibid., 85.
77. *Demystifying the Chinese Economy*, 253.
78. *Growth Slowdowns and the Middle-Income Trap*, 7.
79. Gabriel, F., Rosenblatt, D. Middle-Income Traps; A Conceptual and Empirical Study. *Policy Research Working Paper* 6594. Washington: World Bank. September 2013.
80. Countries were divided in five relative income groups. The authors observe that the selection of the relative income intervals along with the choice of the period intervals, plays a fundamental role in determining the elements of the transition probability matrix.
81. *Middle-Income Traps*, 16.
82. Ibid., 25.
83. Altenburg, T., Lűtkenhorst, W. (2017) *Industrial Policy in Developing Countries*. Cheltenham: Edward Elgar, 81.
84. *Industrial Policy in Developing Countries*, 146.
85. Ibid., 40.
86. Ibid., 68.
87. Chang, H.-J. (2010) *23 Things They Don't Tell You About Capitalism*. London: Penguin Books, 89.
88. *The Growth Report; Strategies for Sustained Growth and Inclusive Development*. Washington: World Bank (2008), 9.
89. A few months after Collier's visit there was a coup, confirming that poor countries like the Central African Republic can easily get caught in the conflict trap.
90. One might think that Collier had forgotten to include the poverty trap. This was not the case as the author rightly argued that in the beginning of human development all countries were poor, and yet most of them, sooner or later, grew in economic terms.
91. Collier, P. (2007) *The Bottom Billion*. Oxford: Oxford University Press.
92. The author used the World Bank's Country Policy and Institutional Assessment Index. The scoring system rates 20 aspects of governance and

policy on a six-point scale. Collier applied a low cut off to define the really bad. The countries below the cut-off point are *failing states*; they are failing their citizens, and they are failing to grow. Ibid., 67–68.

93. *The Bottom Billion*, 37.
94. As for restraints, Collier has this to say: 'So, if resource riches are so bad for restraints, how come Norway has them? Well, it got them before it got its oil. Not only is growth good in itself, but it feeds back upon the rules of the political game. Political restraints are promoted by a higher level of per capita income. Economic development gradually induces healthy institutional change. Norway has nothing special by way of restraints—it just has the sort of rules that are normal for its level of development.' Ibid., 51.
95. Ibid., 65.
96. Each country is given a score up to ten for a dozen political, military, social, and economic indicators. These include demographic pressures, refugee numbers, economic growth, high economic inequality, human rights abuses, external intervention, and the legitimacy of its government. The more unstable a country, the higher its total score, which ranges between100–120 (very high alert) to 0–10 (very sustainable).
97. *Economics of Development*, 267.
98. Of the 30 low-income countries, 25 are African countries, 2 Asian countries, 1 Latin American country, and 2 from Oceania. Regarding lower middle-income countries: 11 are African, 6 Asian, and 3 Oceanian countries, as well as 1 from the Middle East.
99. Wickstead, M. (2015) *Aid and Development*. Oxford: Oxford University Press, 91.
100. Ibid., 93.
101. The Bank's first list was compiled in 2006, and has since gone through a series of changes in terms of classification from the Low Income Countries Under Stress List (2006–2009), to the Fragile States List (2010) to the, now, Harmonized List of Fragile Situations.
102. *Economics of Development*, 268.
103. Ghani, A., Lockhart, C (2008) *Fixing Failed States; A Framework for Rebuilding a Fractured World*. Oxford: Oxford University Press.
104. Lee Kuan Yew (2000) *From Third World to First; the Singapore Story 1965–2000*. New York: Harper Collins Publishers.
105. Malaysia applied a policy to advance the position of the Malay population, while Singapore insisted on equal opportunities for all ethnic groups.
106. Ibid., 688–689.
107. Ibid., 61.
108. Samford Raffles had established Singapore in 1819, then a small fishermen's village.

109. Ibid., 526.
110. Ibid., 68.
111. Lee refuted the '*dependencia*' school of thought which argued that multinational corporations continued colonial patterns of exploitation that left the developing countries selling raw materials to and buying consumer goods from the advanced countries. Lee wrote on page 58 that Third World leaders believed this theory of neocolonialist exploitation, but he and his cabinet ministers had a real problem to solve and could not afford to be conscribed by any theory or dogma.
112. Ibid., 56.
113. Ibid., 165.
114. Ibid., 426.
115. Ibid., 96.
116. Ibid., 105.
117. In his own words: 'We got them to vote for us again and again by providing jobs, building schools, hospitals, community centers, and most important of all, homes which they owned.', 165–166.
118. Ibid., 304.
119. Ibid., 493.
120. Maddison, A. (2006) *The World Economy; Volume 1: A Millennial Perspective. Volume 2: Historical Statistics.* Paris: OECD, 25.
121. *The World Economy*, 151.

References

Aiyar, S., Duval, R., Puy, D., & Zhang, L. (2013, March). *Growth Slowdowns and the Middle-Income Trap.* IMF Working Paper, WP/13/71.

Altenburg, T., & Lűtkenhorst, W. (2017). *Industrial Policy in Developing Countries.* Cheltenham: Edward Elgar.

Arab Human Development Report. (2002). *Creating Opportunities for Future Generations.* New York: UNDP.

Arab Human Development Report. (2016). *Youth and the Prospects for Human Development in a Changing Reality.* New York: UNDP.

Chang, H.-J. (2002). *Kicking Away the Ladder; Development Strategy in Historical Perspective.* London: Anthem Press.

Chang, H.-J. (2008). *Bad Samaritans; The Myth of Free Trade and the Secret History of Capitalism.* New York: Bloomsbury Press.

Chang, H.-J. (2010). *23 Things They Don't Tell You About Capitalism.* London: Penguin Books.

Collier, P. (2007). *The Bottom Billion.* Oxford: Oxford University Press.

Dowden, R. (2008). *Africa; Altered States, Ordinary Miracles.* London: Portobello Books.

Easterly, W. (2002). *The Elusive Quest for Growth; Economists' Adventures and Misadventures in the Tropics*. Cambridge: MIT Press.
Eichengreen, B., Park, D., & Shin, K. (2013, April). *Growth Slowdowns Redux*. Manila: Asian Development Bank.
Gabriel, F., & Rosenblatt, D. (2013, September). *Middle-Income Traps; A Conceptual and Empirical Study*. Policy Research Working Paper 6594. Washington: World Bank.
Garrett, G. (2004, November–December). Globalization's Missing Middle. *Foreign Affairs, 83*(6), 84–96.
Ghani, A., & Lockhart, C. (2008). *Fixing Failed States; A Framework for Rebuilding a Fractured World*. Oxford: Oxford University Press.
Gold, D. (2001). *Peace Dividends and Development; Retrospectives and Prospects*. Newark: Rutgers University.
Hofman, A. (2000). *The Economic Development of Latin America in the Twentieth Century*. Cheltenham: Edward Elgar.
Hussain, A. (2016). *Understanding the Total Factor Productivity Shortfall in Sub-Saharan Africa*. The Horn Economic and Social Policy Institute; Working Paper 02/16.
Lee, K. Y. (2000). *From Third World to First; the Singapore Story 1965–2000*. New York: Harper Collins Publishers.
Lin, J. (2012). *Demystifying the Chinese Economy*. Cambridge: Cambridge University Press.
Maçães, B. (2018). *The Dawn of Eurasia; On the Trail of the New World Order*. London: Allen Lane.
Maddison, A. (1995). *Monitoring the World Economy 1880–1992*. Paris: OECD.
McCloskey, D. (2010). *Bourgeois Dignity; Why Economics Can't Explain The Modern World*. Chicago: The University of Chicago Press.
Meredith, M. (2014). *The Fortunes of Africa; A 5000-Year History of Wealth, Greed, and Endeavour*. New York: Simon & Schuster.
Milanovic, B. (2011). *The Haves and Have-Nots; A Brief and Idiosyncratic History of Global Inequality*. New York: Basic Books.
Rodrik, D. (2011). *The Globalization Paradox; Democracy and the Future of the World Economy*. New York: W.W. Norton.
Rodrik, D. (2017, October). *Growth Without Industrialization?* Project Syndicate, 10.
Steinberg, D. (1985). *Foreign Aid and the Development of the Republic of Korea: The Effectiveness of Concessional Assistance*. USAID AID Evaluation Special Study No. 42. Washington: USAID.
The 1.2 Billion Opportunity. (2016). *The Economist*, April 6.
The East Asian Miracle; Economic Growth and Public Policy. (1993). New York: Oxford University Press.
The Failed Sates Index 2005. Washington: The Fund for Peace.

The Failed States Index 2019. Washington: The Fund for Peace.
The Growth Report; Strategies for Sustained Growth and Inclusive Development. (2008). Washington: World Bank.
Thirlwall, A., & Pacheco-López, P. (2017). *Economics of Development* (10th ed.). London: Palgrave Macmillan.
Wickstead, M. (2015). *Aid and Development*. Oxford: Oxford University Press.
World Bank. (1978). *World Development Report 1978*. Washington: World Bank.
World Bank. (2016, January). *World Bank's Classification of Countries by Income*. Policy Research Working Paper 7528. Washington: World Bank.
World Bank. (2017). *Flagship Report Global Economic Prospects*. Washington: World Bank.
World Bank. (2018, August 9). *World Development Indicators*. Washington: World Bank.
World Bank. (2019, April). Migration and Development Brief 31.

CHAPTER 3

What Preceded Development Economics

3.1 Introduction

The central theme of development economics is growth; more precisely, what would the sources be that promote economic growth of poor countries. This does not suggest that economic growth would be a subject studied by development economists only. Questions about economic growth had already been dealt with by Adam Smith (1723–1790) and other classical economists.

Smith presented an optimistic growth theory based upon the division of labour, resulting in increasing returns and economic growth. However, other classical economists sketched a gloomy picture, such as Thomas Malthus (1766–1834), who predicted that population growth would eclipse the supply of food, as the agricultural sector suffered from diminishing returns. In other words, there was insufficient food for the growing population. David Ricardo (1772–1823) was another pessimist; he agreed with Malthus that agriculture suffered from diminishing returns, which in turn would result in a reduction of the industrial sector's profit rate. The end result would be a stationary state. Ricardo's projection was not as dismal as the one of Karl Marx (1818–1883). He developed his theory while the Industrial Revolution was in full swing. He predicted that capitalism would collapse. In essence, Marx's reasoning was the following. As a result of fierce competition between capitalists, profit rates would decline and '*verelendung*' (immiserisation) of the exploited workers would lead to revolution.

P. de Haan, *Whatever Happened to the Third World?*,
https://doi.org/10.1007/978-3-030-39613-8_3

During the time of the classical economists, most countries were poor; there was not much sustained economic growth per capita. Angus Maddison (1926–2010) observed that from the year 1000 to 1820 the advance in per capita income was a slow crawl—the world average rose about 50 percent. Most of the growth went to accommodate a fourfold increase in population.[1] However, this more or less stationary situation started to change with the onset of the Industrial Revolution. Once the Industrial Revolution got well underway, the gap in wealth between industrialising countries (mainly Western European countries, including—somewhat later—Western offshoots (North America, Australia, and New Zealand), and all other countries started to widen.

Around the beginning of the twentieth century, some colonial powers felt that their colonies should no longer be treated as providers of valuable raw materials only. The idea dawned that the citizenry of the colonies deserved to be educated and should receive health services, in order to provide the skilled labour needed for the colonies' future development. One of these colonial powers was France, introducing its *mission civilisatric*. Another one was the Unite Kingdom, conscious of the 'white man's burden'. In the Netherlands it was also felt that something had to be done to counter its extractive colonial policies. Around 1900, the Netherlands' government introduced its so-called *ethical policy* for the Netherlands East Indies. The philosophy behind this policy was to prepare the Indonesian population for economic and political independence. Besides investment in roads, irrigation, agricultural extension, and rural credit, education was one of this policy's cornerstones. However, the implementation was not very impressive, to say the least. By 1930, still around 90% of the Indonesian population was illiterate. During the 1940s, achievements in education were a bit better: around 40% of the Indonesian children attended primary school. Nonetheless, during the period 1900–1940, only 23,000 Indonesians completed secondary school; a grossly insufficient number to take over middle-management government jobs after independence. The reasons for this poor performance were financial and political. As regards funding, this was persistently insufficient. And regarding the political aspect, educating a colony's population promotes ideas about freedom and independence. In Indonesia this was not different. The educated Indonesian elite successfully led Indonesia's struggle for independence.

At the time, this politically-inspired emancipatory intention coincided with an emerging scholarly interest in the economic development of colonies and other poor tropical countries. The insights developed by scholars, often geographers, now appear to be rather basic and, here and there, politically incorrect. Development economics, as a sub-discipline of economics, evolved after the end of WWII, when a whole range of colonies gained independence. Quite a few, but not all, of these former colonies were typically poor, agrarian, and overpopulated.

3.2 What Scholars Thought About Development Before World War II

The question why colonies and other poor countries were underdeveloped was analysed from different vantage points. Geographers presented theories explaining which geographical locations and climates were favourable for development and which ones were not. Economists focused on the economic *dualistic* nature of colonies and other underdeveloped countries.

Now, to give an idea of what geographers proposed, the analysis of Ellsworth Huntington, professor of geography at Yale University, is illustrative. Huntington was a representative of the *geographic determinism* school of thought that attempted to establish correlations between climate, soil, landforms, and social, political, and cultural phenomena. His *Civilization and Climate* is a classic.[2] Although Huntington's views have been refuted because of their scientific and political incorrectness, much later economic geography regained prominence as an explanatory factor of prosperity or poverty, elaborated in Chap. 6.

An early representative of *dualism* is Julius Herman Boeke, professor of tropical-colonial economics at Leiden University in the Netherlands. He denied that the tenets of mainstream economics were applicable to tropical-colonial conditions. He argued that there was a need for a separate theoretical approach to the specific conditions of colonised and underdeveloped territories. Boeke's ideas are not widely known because most of his publications were in Dutch. Only later in life he published a few works in English, such as *The Evolution of the Netherlands Indies Economy*.[3] The term *dualism* lives on in development economics, be it in a different meaning than understood by Boeke.

3.3 Civilisation and Climate

While Huntington's theory has been refuted and discredited for its scientific and political incorrectness, it is interesting to take a closer look at what he had to say, to appreciate his hypothesis.

Huntington argued that a particular kind of climate (i.e., a temperate climate) is necessary for the development of a high civilisation. While acknowledging that man can live in any region where he can obtain food, his physical and mental energy and his moral character reach their highest development only in a few strictly limited areas. In a nutshell, Huntington's hypothesis is this:

> Today a certain peculiar type of climate prevails wherever civilization is high. In the past the same type seems to have prevailed wherever a great civilization arose. Therefore, such a climate seems a necessary condition of great progress.[4]

Huntington published *Civilization and Climate* in 1915. Some of his texts would now be considered racist. For example, the author observed that in the tropics most people lived in the open air, which led to a devaluation of moral standards, so much so that their thoughts and energy were largely swallowed up in matters of sex.

Much more important is the scanty dress of the women, and its character which calls attention to their sex. Livingstone [the explorer/missionary; PdH] speaks with disgust of the way in which his carriers, hour after hour, discussed the breasts of the half-naked women whom they met.[5]

The author admitted that climate is not the only—let alone the most important—cause of civilisation; it is one of several. Yet, each civilisation is conditioned by the degree of energy possessed by a society. If a race lacks energy, no amount of excellence along other lines will place it in first rank. Civilisation seems to make great progress only where a stimulating climate exists. A high civilisation promotes growth and it is fruitful in new ideas, only where the climate gives men energy. Huntington concluded: 'The climate of many countries seems to be one of the greatest reasons why idleness, dishonesty, immorality, stupidity, and weakness of will prevail. If we can conquer climate, the whole world will become stronger and nobler.'[6]

Huntington scored the North-East coast of the United States (where he lived) as a territory with a 'very high' civilisation, together with the

South-Western part of California, Great Britain, large stretches of Western Europe, the South-Eastern coast of Australia and New Zealand. As for the rest of the world, only the areas around Buenos Aires and Cape Town, as well as Japan scored 'high'. All other territories scored from 'medium' to 'very low'.

Variability in temperatures between countries did not only stimulate or retard mental and physical activity, Huntington also analysed piecework records from Connecticut factories. He claimed that he found evidence that people worked harder when the barometric pressure varied over the course of day. With charts, graphs and tables, the author claimed his factory productivity figures supported the idea that a stimulating climate drove the development of superior 'racial character' and the advance of civilisation.

In 1914, Huntington's initial findings were published in a series of three articles in *Harper's Magazine*. Even then, the articles triggered angry letters to the Editor from Southern gentlemen, inquiries from medical men, and psychologists.[7] After *Civilization and Climate* came out a year later, Huntington's theory came under fire because of the shaky basis for his insights, his overemphasis on climatic influence, and his racial prejudice. For example, Huntington's biographer, Geoffrey Martin, quotes the reaction of William Jackson Humphreys of America's Weather Bureau. Humphreys wrote about Huntington's insights: '...its broader conceptions are mere fantasies, while its details show little regard for facts and none for physics...it is as far from being scientific as *Alice in Wonderland*.'[8] The role of technology, so crucial in explaining sustained economic growth since the Industrial Revolution, was not properly dealt with. Huntington does refer to innovation in the field of technology as linked to climate, but he is silent about the ease of its dissemination; after all, technological progress has had, and continues to have, global impact. Nico Stehr and Hans von Storch conclude as follows: 'Although the discussion on the impact of climate on societies did not cease abruptly in social science, it ultimately was discredited and....vanished almost without any trace as a largely compromised and widely discredited line of inquiry.'[9]

Meanwhile, climatic determinism had already lost its prominent position to cultural anthropology, as developed by Franz Boas, Margaret Mead, and Ruth Benedict. Cultural anthropology underscores that culture has to be appreciated and studied in its own right, rather than as a result of the physical environment.

Nowadays climate plays a less prominent role in the development process. And nature is no longer viewed as a regular, static entity and, therefore, climate is no longer seen as resting in a state of fixed equilibrium. Discoveries in the medical science helped to eradicate tropical diseases. Technical devices, among them air conditioning, limit climate's influence on people's productivity. No longer climate is a defining force in development; a favourable institutional framework, sensible economic policies, a healthy and educated population, and a conducive business environment; all these factors, and others, constitute the basis upon which economies can thrive.

As for climate proper, more than a century after the publication of *Civilization and Climate*, climate change is now a major global concern.[10] Hopefully the *Climate Agreement*, concluded in Paris in December 2015, and—before that—the adoption on 27 September 2015 by the General Assembly of the United Nations' 17 Sustainable Development Goals will help to repair the damage done.

3.4 Dualism

Boeke denied that classical economics was applicable to tropical-colonial conditions. He studied the situation in the Netherlands East Indies where the native population lived side by side with foreigners, resulting in a clash, as he perceived it, between two heterogeneous stages of development. He observed that there was no sense of solidarity between the native population and foreigners, but one of ruling and being ruled.

Boeke argued that colonial economics is different in its assumptions and approach from those of classical economic theory:

1. Because much that is axiomatic in the abstract-theoretical or deductive method must be recognized as non-existent in the economic mentality of the Natives.
2. Because even in case it might be possible to accept a certain measure of economic inclination, the economic problems coming to the fore in a colonial society are so specific in nature that there is little scope for applying the principles derived from Western conditions to any great extent.[11]

The basis for this fundamental insight is the distinction Boeke made between economic and social needs. He observed that there was a force in

Western countries that was unifying and promoting economic growth. That force was capitalism. He wondered why capitalism had not exerted a similar effect in Eastern societies.

Western capitalism did not find in Eastern society the institutions ready to take charge of propagating its principles and achievements, but had to send out its own representatives for the purpose. As a consequence came the settlements which, woven around the periphery of southern eastern Asia like a wreath, have brought the 'colonial'; element in the eastern economy, importing a new dualism of an economic type.[12]

Boeke concluded that this dualism would be permanent, unless a development comparable to the evolution of capitalist countries would lead to social mobility of the lower strata of society, like Japan had undergone. In short, dualistic economies are to be found in territories where capitalism has not acted as a force in promoting technological and economic development of the masses, and where –as a result—a predominantly agrarian population has economically stagnated and where Malthus' law rules.

Now, the million dollar question is whether the indigenous population would be able to free itself from the economic shackles of colonial forces and participate in the economy on their own terms. Another question was whether the colonial power would promote their liberation and their economic improvement. We know the answers to these questions; but what were Boeke's answers at the time? He observed that in Indonesia, and in a number of other Asian territories, dualism was not a temporary phenomenon but an essential—and lasting—characteristic of their economic structure. He referred to India's *panchayat* legislation, intended to restore the former village administration with limited rights of self-government and taxation. In his view, these rights and taxation are relevant, as they accept the existing dualism and intend to mitigate its disadvantages by strengthening village life.

Agricultural life in Indonesia involved periodic unemployment. The seasonally unemployed used to work in, for example, the production of handicrafts. However, these types of sideline employment opportunities were increasingly decreasing under the influence of Western capitalism. So, more and more people depended on agricultural activities for their livelihood, leading to their impoverishment. In a village economy, economic laws are overshadowed by social laws prescribed by religion, custom, and tradition. If an economic policy is to be acceptable to the village economy, it must be embedded in the local religious and ethical context. Boeke's firm opinion was that the gap between the economic structure of high capitalism and that of a non-capitalistic village community will not be closed. The indigenous element 'does not correspond to Western economic laws.'[13] This indigenous element in economic terms is represented by an inverse elasticity of supply; i.e., the higher the price the smaller the supply. In other words, a high price for a product would not induce the producer to produce more.[14]

3.5 The Role of Geography Revisited

While climate is one aspect of economic geography, location is another. A territory's location constitutes one of the factors that explains its economic growth or stagnation.

Economic geography deals, among others, with spatial concentration. 54% of world GDP is produced on only 10% of its land area. Even this calculation understates concentration, because it assumes that economic activity is evenly spread across the map within each nation. But this is not so. For instance, within the United States, 2% of the land area produces 50% of America's GDP, reflecting cities' dominant contribution to production.[15]

Regarding location, Paul Krugman gave economic geography a shot in the arm. In 2008, Krugman was awarded the Nobel Prize in Economics for his contributions to economic geography.

He analysed regional and international factor mobility, in the context of an international trade model. In a nutshell, Krugman argues as follows. The production of manufactured goods will concentrate in the location where there is a large market. This will be reinforced by the notion that it is more desirable to live and produce near a concentration of manufacturing production because it is less expensive to buy the goods that this location provides. However, if transportation costs continue to fall, the importance of being close to markets and suppliers will decline. Peripheral countries offer potential producers the advantage of lower wages. At some point the decline in transportation costs will be sufficient that the lower wage rate in the periphery more than offsets the disadvantage of being remote from markets and supplies. At this point manufacturing will have an incentive to move out from the core to the periphery again, eventually resulting in the convergence of wage rates. Krugman's insights in the domain of new economic geography are presented in more detail in Chap. 6.

In 1997, Jared Diamond published a bestseller entitled *Guns, Germs and Steel; a Short History of Everybody for the Last 13,000 Years.*[16] In this monumental work, Diamond describes how geography and biogeography together moulded the respective developments of Europeans, Asians, sub-Saharan Africans, and aboriginal Australians. He argues that Eurasia forms a very large territory, whose axis stretches from West to East, providing similar climatic conditions for promoting the relative rapid spread of agricultural practices and related technological inventions throughout the region. Comparing this with Africa and the America's, their axis runs vertically from North to South, thus encompassing varying climatic conditions, including tropical ones, which limit the spread of crops that thrive in cooler climates.

Jeffrey Sachs argues that geography plays an important part in explaining development through its impact on the public health environment, and on transport costs.[17] In his paper, Sachs presents arguments against the proposition that institutions constitute *the* explanatory factor for economic growth (see Chap. 6).

There is now a wider recognition of the role played by geography in the development process. Dani Rodrik, Arvind Subramaniam and Francesco Trebbi found that distance from the equator is a significant (positive) contributor to institutional quality.[18] Rodrik concludes that even if geography and endowments do not exert an important independent impact on incomes, they may have a significant indirect impact through institutions.[19]

3.6 Dualism Lives On

Boeke is remembered for his discovery of the dualistic nature of colonial economies, which helped to better understand the positive and negative economic incentives obtaining within these economies. His insights have been taken on board by development economists. Some of them are briefly presented below.

Arthur Lewis (1915–1991) presented a dual economy which assumed a backward sector, usually identified with non-capitalist subsistence agriculture, and a modern capitalist sector. The backward sector was suffering from population pressure, in that the maximum amount of labour that could be productively employed was supplied by too many people. In other words, a situation of underemployment existed, in which the marginal product of labour was zero or even negative.

Lewis argued that these underemployed workers could supply the modern sector with a sheer unlimited supply of labour at a wage just above the subsistence level. Since the wages in the modern sector are to a large extent based on the wages paid in the subsistence sector, it was in the capitalists' interest to keep the subsistence sector wages low. The transfer of surplus labour to the modern sector would come to an end once there was no more surplus labour to be transferred. More on Lewis's insights are presented in Chap. 4.

Lewis was a prominent representative of the first generation of development economists. They developed, in Paul Krugman's words, a high development theory.[20] Krugman argues that these economists had a core preoccupation with the difference between modern sectors that were presumed to be characterised by economies of scale, and traditional sectors that were not. In other words, the distinction that Boeke made much earlier, constitutes an integral part of this high development theory.

Hla Myint (1920–2017) also recognised the relevance of the concept of dualistic economies, be it from a different vantage point. In *Organizational Dualism and Economic Development*, Myint pays attention to the dualistic nature of the economies of developing countries. Myint argued that dualism is a phenomenon of an underdeveloped organisational framework, characterised by the incomplete development of the market network and of an immature administrative and fiscal system of the government.[21]

Ian Little (1918–2012) devoted an entire chapter of *Economic Development* to the dual economy, in which he correctly refers to Boeke's views on the matter:

> The distinction between capitalism and the 'subsistence economy' (to use a later phrase) is virtually the same as that stressed by W.A. Lewis a decade later in his fecund article 'Economic Development with Unlimited Supply of Labour'. But Boeke was far from tracing the potential path of development that might result from the interaction of these two sectors in the manner of Nurkse, Lewis, and many other followers. In particular, he had no concept of surplus labor and subscribed to the 'colonial' view of a backward-rising labor supply curve.[22]

In a situation where the employer is inspired by the need or desire to sustain a certain number of employees, rather than to maximise profit, Little concluded that duality could be defined in different ways. He chose the following definition: 'But a useful analytic institutional definition would seem to be that an economy is dualistic when a significant part of it operates under

> such a paternalistic or quasi-feudalist regime, while another significant part operates under a system of wage employment—which may be capitalist or socialist (if state capitalism is regarded as a variety of socialism).'[23]

Deepak Lal and Myint also recognise dualism in developing economies. For example, they observe that Peru shares with other Latin American countries the problem of dualism between the modern sector and the urban informal sector. In Peru's case this dualism is aggravated by the existence of a large indigenous Indian population in the traditional sector which has been bypassed by the expansion of primary exports from the modern sector.[24]

Thirlwall and Pacheco-López describe the role of capital intensity in perpetuating the dualistic nature of a particular economy:

> First, relatively fixed technical coefficients (that is, low elasticity of substitution between factors) means that labour can be absorbed from agriculture into industry only as fast as the growth of capital, and, second, capital intensity itself will restrict employment opportunities in the industrial sector, contributing to urban unemployment and perpetuating underdevelopment in the rural sector.[25]

In *Limited Access Orders in the Developing World*, Douglass North et al. introduce the phenomena of limited access order societies (LAOS) and open access societies (OAS.)[26] The authors observe that many LAOS have dualistic economies with a domestic economy governed by domestic rules and institutions on the one hand, and international enclaves run by OAS rules and institutions on the other. LAOS elites gain from this duality as it gives them the opportunity to prosper without having to bother about the development of their domestic economy.

Notes

1. Maddison, A. (2001) *The World Economy; A Millennium Perspective*. Paris: OECD, 17.
2. Huntington, E. (1915) *Civilization and Climate*. New Haven: Yale University Press.
3. Boeke, H. (1946) *The Evolution of the Netherlands Indies Economy*. New York: Netherlands and Netherlands Indies Council, Institute of Pacific Studies.
4. *Civilization and Climate*, 9.

5. Ibid., 46–47. I lived six years in Zambia during which time I noticed that Zambian men are more attracted to Zambian ladies' behinds than to their breasts. I wondered whether since Livingstone's days this attraction had shifted from breasts to behinds. However, it is possible that Livingstone did not sufficiently understand the language spoken by his carriers. By the way, Livingstone condemned the slave trade in East Africa.
6. Ibid., 294.
7. Martin, G. (1973) *Ellsworth Huntington; His Life and Thought*. Hamden: The Shoe String Press, 114.
8. Ibid., 105.
9. Stehr, N. and Von Storch, H. *Climate Determines: an Anatomy of a Disbanded Line of Research*. (October 1998), 19.
10. Huntington had this to say about climate change: 'In a thousand years.... no highly favourable region may exist upon the globe, and the human race may be thrown back into the dull, lethargic state of our present tropical races.'
11. Van Marle, A., Ed. (1961) The Theory of Dualism. In *The Concept of Dualism in Theory and Practice*. The Hague: W. van Hoeve Publishers Ltd, 11.
12. Ibid., 172–173.
13. Van Marle, A. Introduction. In *Indonesian Economics; the Concept of Dualism in Theory and Practice*, 19.
14. Kate Raworth applauds a comparable attitude in *Doughnut Economics*, citing an example of a traditional society that lived by the principle of sufficiency, such as the Cree in northern Manitoba, whose response to European traders, who offered them higher prices for their furs, was to bring fewer furs to the Europeans' trading post. Source: Raworth, K. (2017) *Doughnut Economics; Seven Ways to Think Like a 21st Century Economist*. London: Random House Business Books, 282.
15. Easterly, W. (2001) *The Elusive Quest for Growth; Economists' Adventures and Misadventures in the Tropics*. Cambridge: The MIT Press, 165.
16. Diamond, J. (1997) *Guns, Germs and Steel; a Short History of Everybody for the Last 13,000 Years*. London: Jonathan Cape.
17. Sachs, J. (2003) Institutions Don't Rule: Direct Effects of Geography on Per Capita Income. *NBER Working Paper No. 9490*. Boston: National Bureau of Economic Research.
18. Rodrik, D., Subramanian, A., Trebbi, R. (2004) Institutions Rule: The Primacy of Institutions over Geography and Integration in Economic Development. In *Journal of Economic Growth* 9.2: 131–165.
19. Rodrik, D. (2007) *One Economics, Many Recipes; Globalization, Institutions, and Economic Growth*. Princeton: Princeton University Press, 187.

20. Krugman, P. (1993) Towards a Counter-Counterrevolution in Development Theory. In *Proceedings of the World Bank Annual Conference on Development Economics 1992*. Washington: World Bank.
21. Myint, H. (1985) Organizational Dualism and Economic Development. In *Asian Development Review* 3 (1), 25–42.
22. Little, I. (1982) *Economic Development; Theory, Policy, and International Relations*. New York: Basic Books, 86–87.
23. Ibid., 95.
24. Lal, D., Myint, H. (1996) *The Political Economy of Poverty, Equity, and Growth*. Oxford: Clarendon Press, 209.
25. Thirlwall, A., Pacheco-López, P. (2017) *Economics of Development*. Tenth Edition. London: Palgrave Macmillan, 285.
26. North, D. et al. (2007) Limited Access Orders in the Developing World: A New Approach to the Problem of Development. In: *World Bank Working Paper 4359*. Washington: World Bank.

References

Boeke, H. (1946). *The Evolution of the Netherlands Indies Economy*. New York: Netherlands and Netherlands Indies Council, Institute of Pacific Studies.

Diamond, J. (1997). *Guns, Germs and Steel: A Short History of Everybody for the Last 13,000 Years*. London: Jonathan Cape.

Easterly, W. (2001). *The Elusive Quest for Growth: Economists' Adventures and Misadventures in the Tropics*. Cambridge: The MIT Press.

Huntington, E. (1915). *Civilization and Climate*. New Haven: Yale University Press.

Krugman, P. (1993). Towards a Counter-Counterrevolution in Development Theory. In *Proceedings of the World Bank Annual Conference on Development Economics 1992*. Washington: World Bank.

Lal, D., & Myint, H. (1996). *The Political Economy of Poverty, Equity, and Growth*. Oxford: Clarendon Press.

Little, I. (1982). *Economic Development: Theory, Policy, and International Relations*. New York: Basic Books.

Maddison, A. (2001). *The World Economy: A Millennium Perspective*. Paris: OECD.

Martin, G. (1973). *Ellsworth Huntington: His Life and Thought*. Hamden: The Shoe String Press.

Myint, H. (1985). Organizational Dualism and Economic Development. *Asian Development Review, 3*(1), 25.

North, D., et al. (2007). *Limited Access Orders in the Developing World: A New Approach to the Problem of Development*. World Bank Working Paper 4359, World Bank, Washington.

Raworth, K. (2017). *Doughnut Economics: Seven Ways to Think Like a 21st Century Economist*. London: Random House Business Books.
Rodrik, D. (2007). *One Economics, Many Recipes: Globalization, Institutions, and Economic Growth*. Princeton: Princeton University Press.
Rodrik, D., Subramanian, A., & Trebbi, R. (2004). Institutions Rule: The Primacy of Institutions over Geography and Integration in Economic Development. *Journal of Economic Growth, 9*(2), 131–165.
Sachs, J. (2003). *Institutions Don't Rule: Direct Effects of Geography on Per Capita Income*. NBER Working Paper No. 9490, National Bureau of Economic Research, Boston.
Stehr, N., & Von Storch, H. (October 1998). *Climate Determines: An Anatomy of a Disbanded Line of Research*. Unpublished.
Thirlwall, A., & Pacheco-López, P. (2017). *Economics of Development* (10th ed.). London: Palgrave Macmillan.
Van Marle, A. (1961a). The Theory of Dualism. In *Indonesian Economics: The Concept of Dualism in Theory and Practice*. The Hague: W. van Hoeve Publishers Ltd.
Van Marle, A. (1961b). Introduction. In *Indonesian Economics: The Concept of Dualism in Theory and Practice*. The Hague: W. van Hoeve Publishers Ltd.

CHAPTER 4

The First Generation of Development Economists

4.1 Introduction

The heyday of development economics started after the end of World War II (WWII). Before the war, there was not much attention for the social and economic development of colonies and other poor tropical countries. After WWII, prompted by a decolonisation wave, development economists proposed approaches suggesting that economic development of newly independent countries would put them on the path of balanced growth promoted by capital accumulation through a 'big push'.

It is a pleasure to read the works of these early development economists as they radiate optimism, suggesting that economic development of poor countries could be achieved! That is, provided a strong state would lead the process, since a reliable price system had not yet developed in these young countries. It was assumed that markets were too weak to perform their allocative function. Another assumption was that foreign aid would help to get the development process going.

The first generation consisted of economists such as Arthur Lewis (1915–1991) who elaborated the movement of abundant labour from the agricultural to the industrial sector, and Walt Rostow (1916–2003) who presented his linear stages of growth model. Paul Rosenstein-Rodan (1902–1985) found his big-push inspiration in the study of industrialisation processes in Eastern and Southeast Europe. A balanced growth strategy for underdeveloped countries was proposed by Ragnar Nurkse (1907–1959), who said that balanced growth would break the vicious

P. de Haan, *Whatever Happened to the Third World?*,
https://doi.org/10.1007/978-3-030-39613-8_4

circle of poverty and thus the inability to save and invest. Simon Kuznets (1901–1985) is another formidable representative of the first generation. He analysed the dynamics of structural change and its effects on the distribution of income and wealth. Hollis Chenery (1918–1994) introduced the two-gap model; both had to be overcome to promote economic growth.

This generation provided the theoretical and historical basis upon which younger generations built their insights and models. The first generation also emphasised the role of basic economic notions, such as the interplay between saving and investment, marginal productivity of capital and labour; relevant to any development process. The economists involved introduced new economic terms that live on.[1] What this generation also shared was the need of a structural transformation of low productivity activities in agriculture, petty trade, and the like, to high productivity specialised manufacturing. The urgency of this transformation was prompted by widespread poverty of rapidly increasing populations wishing to catch up with developed countries. After all, the industrialisation process of developed countries had resulted in productivity growth, and higher per capita incomes.

As newly independent countries' saving rates were inadequate, massive capital investments were called for, among others to be funded by foreign aid.[2] Capital investment would bring high returns, as the potential for productivity increase was high in developing countries. Developed countries already had a lot of capital invested which implied less potential for additional productivity gains.

The relationship between industrial growth, the growth of productivity, and income growth—together resulting in structural change—is succinctly captured by Nicholas Kaldor's three growth laws, named after Sir Nicholas Kaldor (1908–1986). Now, what do these growth laws consist of? The first one says that there is a strong positive correlation between the growth of manufacturing output and GDP growth. The second law says that there also exists a strong positive correlation between the growth of manufacturing output and productivity growth of manufacturing. Then, there is a strong positive relationship between growth of manufacturing output and growth of productivity *outside* manufacturing; this is Kaldor's third growth law.

However, this is not the whole story about Kaldor's growth laws. Suppose the possibility to absorb labour from the sector with diminishing returns dries up, what will happen? The answer is simple: further GDP growth will slow down. Then, there is the important question of what

A UNIDO *Policy Brief* provides an example of Kaldor's growth laws. After 1978, China introduced sweeping economic reforms, which to a large extent explain China's phenomenal economic growth and rapid structural change in a period spanning only three decades. The traditional agricultural sector, in which 70% of the total Chinese workforce was employed, declined in importance, while the industrial sector grew rapidly, resulting in higher value-added. As a result, in 2009 only 38% of the workforce was still engaged in agriculture, while the industrial sector's labour force had expanded from 17% to 28%. The government and service sector absorbed the remainder of the workforce. The Policy Brief concludes that China is an economic powerhouse, as a result of its planned structural change, spurred by economic reforms, liberalised foreign trade, and high domestic and foreign investment in its industrial sector.[3]

triggers the growth of the industrial sector? Initially, demand has to come from the agricultural sector, being the economy's largest sector. Irma Adelman (1930–2017) argued that agricultural demand can indeed be a major stimulus to industrialisation.[4] However, in a later development stage it will have to be foreign demand. The internal market is typically too small to create economies of scale. So, export markets will have to be developed. The most successful developing countries are all export-led growth countries. This may boost the exporting economy even more, creating a predicament for other developing countries. After all, how can they ever become a serious competitor in international trade, or are they going to remain a so-called peripheral country?

The collapse of world trade during the *Interbellum* (1918–1939), and in particular the collapse of commodity prices, resulted in pessimism about the export prospects of Third World countries. To lift developing countries out of poverty, and lessen their dependency on agricultural and mineral export products, industrialisation through capital accumulation was the answer. Where the traditional agricultural and mineral export sector fell short of feeding development, the first generation was confident that active and wide-ranging government intervention would act as an engine of growth. Hence a combination of external pessimism and internal optimism constituted the characteristic mood at the time. As we shall see, optimism about assumed effective government intervention was unjustified.

4.2 The Main Characteristics of the First Generation's Proposals

4.2.1 *The Role of Government*

Where does the initial confidence in government's principal developmental role come from? The optimistic post-WWII mood, the successful implementation of the Marshall Plan, and the government-led rapid economic development of the Soviet-Union explain this confidence. Moreover, the Great Depression (of which export-oriented colonies had suffered a lot) was countered by government actions such as the *New Deal* in America.

First generation development models applied macroeconomic Keynesian-inspired *aggregate* notions: total saving, total investment, total demand, full employment, what have you.[5] Narrowing the gap between rich and poor countries could be done by applying a *one-size-fits-all* near-mechanistic development model, inspired by developed countries' past growth trajectories. This process could thus benefit from the lessons learnt by industrialised countries.

These models required strong state action. The government of a developmental state was to promote capital accumulation, utilise reserves of surplus labor, undertake policies of deliberate industrialisation, relax foreign exchange constraints through import-substitution, and coordinate the allocation of resources through programming and planning.[6] These aggregate models suggested that government promote the necessary transformation from a predominantly agriculture-based economy to an industrialised one through capital formation.

4.2.2 *Development Planning*

Any government that consciously intervenes in the economy with some end in view may be seen as planning.[7] It was widely felt that—given their overriding role—governments of developing countries needed to plan their activities to promote economic development. Planning is typically done by economists and econometrists with inputs from sectoral experts Development planning, consisting of assumptions, predictions, and targets became popular—planning was regarded as *the* means to engineer economic development. Government investments would be the 'development lever' through the extension of the public sector and through wide-ranging government policies.

The most essential feature of a comprehensive development plan, observed Little, was the attempt to allocate investment with a view to altering the structure of the economy.[8] Planning of the economy was an established phenomenon in socialist countries, where the allocative role of the market was replaced by centrally planned economic activities.

Inspired by the success of the Marshall Plan and President Kennedy's *Alliance for Progress*, the World Bank asked developing countries to come up with development plans in order to qualify for aid. The Harrod-Domar model (elaborated below) came in handy because it enabled planners to estimate the country's saving and capital requirements to achieve economic growth. Once a country would have set its economic growth rate, planners could figure out what the country's saving rate should be to meet the growth target.[9] Specific projects were to be planned by ministries or other public bodies. For example, sectoral planning of agricultural projects was the responsibility of the ministry of agriculture.

However, a paradoxical situation emerged: on the one hand developing countries needed to plan their development, but on the other they lacked the means and the human capital, including the tools to design and undertake the planning tasks ahead. Little rightly observed: 'The implied claim that central planners can correctly estimate demands is breathtaking: experience has shown that their errors are monumental.'[10] And Lewis wondered:

> Why then do backward countries take more readily to planning? Because their needs are obviously much greater. And it is also this that enables them to carry it through in spite of error and incompetence. For, if the people are on their side, nationalistic, conscious of their backwardness, and anxious to progress, they willingly bear great hardships and tolerate many mistakes, and they throw themselves with enthusiasm into the job of regenerating their country.[11]

By the 1970s, the inadequacies of development planning were exposed. In *Development Planning*, Jan Tinbergen (1903–1994) had emphasised that foreign trade should not be neglected as a potential source of any tradable input or final product, nor as an outlet for any locally-produced goods.[12] However, this aspect was often neglected in development plans. And Arnold Harberger (1900–1995) argued: '...the growth process is the outcome of a huge number of different decisions, at levels which at least include the work site, the plant, the firm, the labour union, and the various layers of government, and if these decisions cover the whole range of problems..., it follows quite directly that there are many, many ways in which governmental actions can and will impinge on the growth process.'[13] In other words, planning an economy is quite a challenge, to put it mildly.

4.2.3 *Balanced and Unbalanced Growth*

Balanced growth proponents underscored the need for government to plan individual investments, given the fact that, as noted, the price system in developing countries could not yet properly perform its function. There was, however, another prominent economist who proposed the opposite: unbalanced growth. He argued that imbalances created incentives and helped to economise on the decision-making process. This is what Albert Hirschman (1915–2012) argued in *The Strategy of Economic Development.*[14] He dismissed obstacles to development such as limited savings. Instead, creative tensions stemming from unbalanced growth would attract savings and entrepreneurship to sectors characterised by excess demand. Government was supposed to promote growth in those sectors and regions with high backward and forward linkages which generated most creative tension. Spatial imbalances were necessary, argued Hirschman, to exploit agglomeration economies, thereby contributing to higher productivity and higher incomes. So, no economy-wide 'big push'; instead, focus on a few strategic industries, advised Hirschman, as their progress will induce progress in other sectors.

4.2.4 *The Crucial Role of Savings*

On the subject of aggregate savings, first-generation development economists noted that developing countries' saving rate (typically around 5%) was simply too small for the investments required. A higher saving rate was needed to finance investments in the industrial sector, in order to increase a country's productivity and per capita income, which in turn would generate more savings.

Lewis, for example, argued that economic development's central problem is to understand the process by which a community—previously saving and investing 4–5% of its national income—converts itself into an economy where voluntary saving is running at 12% to 15% of national income, or even more. Ragnar Nurkse observed that *the* general economic problem was to direct as much as possible of the increment in real income into saving, and to allow as little as possible to go into an increase in consumption. There was thus a *financing gap* to be filled by foreign loans or external grant aid to break the vicious circle of poverty.

4.2.5 *Foreign Aid*

Foreign aid could help with the necessary importation of capital goods and services. Aid included technical as well as financial assistance until such time that recipient countries could finance and manage their own development. For example, Rostow argued that technical assistance, soft loans, and grants could be helpful in the development process. Rosenstein-Rodan's big-push implied heavy sacrifices in consumption; hence his strong plea for foreign aid to finance part of the investments required in the big-push, so that domestic consumption would not have to be limited too much. Balanced growth proponents assumed that, although there was enough potential of an international supply of industrial investments, there was a shortage of domestic savings to pay for them. Financial aid could fill up this shortage.

4.2.6 *Almighty Government?*

Original enthusiasm about the government's role in the development process gradually evaporated, making way for concern. Governments' limitations in its planning and implementation capacities were more and more exposed. Moreover, as Friedrich Hayek had noted, planning was unfeasible because the market-based price mechanism was essential in the efficient allocation of resources. Hayek compared the price system with a system of telecommunications. Distortions of this system, for example caused by inflation or wage and price controls, give the wrong signals. Prices will no longer reflect the most efficient modes of production.[15] In short, development planning became discredited, not in the least as in the 1970s and 1980s growth figures of many developing countries started a downward slide. Meanwhile, Southeast Asian countries, having had an open eye for the guiding role of market prices, and the importance of investing in viable labour-intensive export industries, became much more successful.

There was also an ideological dimension of government's prominent developmental role. For example, Deepak Lal and Hla Myint (1920–2017) argued that among the élites in the Third World there was a lot of envy and resentment about having been excluded from positions of power during pre-independence days, during which a transition process was already underway. The resulting strong nationalist sentiment, including its economic dimension, was a natural response in most societies moving from the cultural homogeneity of traditional immobile agricultural societies to modern mobile societies. This social mobility was propelled by the process of industrialisation. In addition, apart from adding to their national prestige, most Third World governments found that their limited industrial base was the major weakness in their dealings with the West. It is not surprising that the principal Third World ideology consisted of a form of nationalism associated with some combination of the productivist and distributivist versions of the state, viewed as an enterprise association.[16]

A concern was whether the industrialisation process could proceed fast enough to eventually close the gap between rich and poor countries, while neo-Marxist development economists' concern was that the gap between rich and poor countries would only widen (see Sect. 4.7).

4.3 The Harrod-Domar Model

Roy Harrod (1900–1978) and Evsey Domar (1914–1997) each developed a growth model, which were basically similar. In the early years, the Harrod-Domar model was widely applied by development economists and planners alike.

Now, what is it that triggers economic growth? The rate of saving and investment both play an important explanatory role in the model. The engine of growth is equal to the ratio of investment to GDP plus the productivity of investment. The model's principal assumption is that the capital-output ratio is constant. This assumption left no space for other factors that would influence economic growth. Nor could it explain why some countries save and invest more than others, and what would cause differences in productivity between them.

The model was originally formulated for recession conditions of an industrial economy's mature phase. Harrod, a British economist, took Keynes's static equilibrium (of income and output) analysis as the starting point to arrive at his dynamic growth model. Harrod asked what the growth rate of income should be to invite investment to such a level that it was equal to the rate of saving, to make sure that there be a moving equilibrium in a growing economy.

This moving equilibrium is achieved through the warranted growth rate. What is this warranted growth rate? Harrod defined it as that rate of growth which, if it occurs, will leave all parties satisfied that they have produced neither more nor less than the right amount. In other words, it will put them into a frame of mind which will cause them to give such orders as will maintain the same rate of growth.[17] Apart from the warranted growth rate, Harrod also distinguished the natural growth rate which is composed of the growth of the potential labour force and the growth of potential labour productivity.

American economist Evsey Domar arrived at the same insights. He argued that investment not only increases demand through the multiplier (a Keynesian term), but investment also increases supply since it expands capacity. He wondered what he growth rate of demand should be in order to maintain full use of the rising productive capacity resulting from capital accumulation. Since consumer demand cannot supply the entire market for additional output, investment must grow in order to use the new capacity added by the previous period's investment. Thirlwall and Pacheco-López provide an example how Harrod-Domar could be applied in a developing country situation:

> In most developing countries the natural growth rate exceeds the warranted rate. If the population growth is, say, 2% and labour productivity is growing at 3%, this gives a rate of growth of the labour force in efficiency units of 5%. If the net savings ratio is, say, 9%, and the required incremental capital-output ratio is 3, this gives a warranted growth rate of 3%. This has two main consequences. First, it means that the effective labour force is growing faster than capital accumulation, which is part of the explanation for growing unemployment in developing countries. Second, it implies plans to invest greater than plans to save, and therefore inflationary pressure. If gn = 5% [natural growth rate; PdH] and cr = 3 [required extra capital to invest; PdH], there will be profitable investment opportunities for 15% saving, whereas actual saving is only 9%.[18]

The model demonstrated, among others, that poor countries remained poor because they weren't able to invest, given their low average saving rate, resulting in a financing gap. Although, as noted, the Harrod-Domar model was based on the analysis of developed economies, it was nonetheless applied to developing countries to estimate the saving and capital requirements with the objectives to correct disbalances and to achieve sustained growth.[19]

4.4 The First Generation in More Detail

4.4.1 Paul Rosenstein-Rodan

Arguably, the earliest representative of the first generation is Paul Rosenstein-Rodan, whose 1943 article *Problems of Industrialisation in Eastern and South-Eastern Europe* is a classic.[20]

This article is about industrial development in depressed geographical areas. Large industrialisation would help to improve employment and incomes in these areas. Although the author uses Eastern and Southeastern Europe as an example, his *big push* approach could also be applied to other depressed areas, such as the Far East, characterised by an agrarian excess population. The workers involved could be employed either through emigration or by way of capital investment in their own country. Emigration would pose so many difficulties that it would not be feasible on a large scale. Hence, the best way forward, argued the author, is industrialisation, sufficiently large to reach an optimum size of the industrial enterprises.

Two models of industrialisation can be considered: (a) the Russian model, aiming at self-sufficiency, without international investment, or (b) industrialisation based on substantial international investment, opening up to the world economy. The Soviet approach would result in a slow process since the required capital must be supplied internally at the expense of local consumption, and it would lead to an isolated unit in the world economy. The second alternative is better. The industrialisation process could be done much quicker; consumers would suffer less (given the availability of international lending); unemployed workers could find employment in labour-intensive industries; and heavy industries in developed countries could supply all the needed investment. Finally, international political stability would be enhanced through the employment of agrarian excess population.

Rosenstein-Rodan understood that his big push proposal was a tremendous task without historical precedent. In the past, investments were financed from profits made. There were other reasons for the fact that so far no such comprehensive scheme was implemented. In the past technical progress was the main driving force, while industrialisation in depressed areas implied the application of given technical knowledge. The increase in overhead costs and fixed capital would add to the risk of capital losses. And political risks are greater than they were in the past. In response, state supervision and state guarantees could lower these risks. Therefore, state supervision and guarantees constitute a vital precondition for a very large industrial investment scheme.

Now, what would be involved in pulling such a wide-ranging scheme off? First of all, training of the agricultural labour force was required, so that the trained workers can be employed as industrial workers. This cannot be done by private firms; it would simply be unaffordable. Again, the state was to play a role—the necessary investments should be counted as capital investment by the state.

The most important aspect of planned large-scale industrialisation is complementarity of different industries. This would create its own additional market. Such a complementary industrial system obviously reduces the risk of not being able to sell. More external economies are created when a sufficiently large number of new industries is established. They then become internal profit centres from which dividends can be paid. Based on the pre-WWII experience, private investors will initially not be willing to invest.

The alternative is for governments in creditor countries to guarantee the loans, or to lend the funds themselves.... The availability of foreign funds, foreign technical assistance and foreign machinery, however, will transform the process of national development from one which would threaten to disrupt international economic relations and trade to one which can make a key contribution to the expansion of world income and the reorganization of world trade.[21]

Once the marginal propensity to save exceeds the average savings rate, domestic savings will be sufficient to finance the desired economic growth rate without foreign aid. To make the entire enterprise self-liquidating, a part of the industries will have to be export industries, for example in the domain of processed food and light industrial products. The exports will have to be sold in creditor countries. These exports represent the main part of the developing countries' share in the world expansion. Although the income elasticity of rich countries may not be very high regarding imports, yet, there may be one good for which this elasticity is high: leisure. This does not require the import of material goods; the importing rich countries may have to accept a part of their share in economic expansion in the form of more leisure; i.e., limiting the work week to 40 hours, while Eastern Europe would maintain a 48-hour work week.

4.4.2 Ragnar Nurkse

Ragnar Nurkse's name is associated with the term balanced growth. In *Problems of Capital Formation in Underdeveloped Countries*, Nurkse elaborates his balanced growth proposal.[22]

This book is an attempt to use economic theory to clarify some of the basic conditions for progress in poor countries, typically under-equipped with capital. Nurkse focuses the attention on the accumulation of material capital to increase production's efficacy. He assumed that there is a large fund of technical knowledge available in the world which can be utilised by underdeveloped countries, provided financial resources are available.

The small size of the domestic market and low capital intensity hinder development. The question is: how to remove them? This can be done by boosting productivity. And productivity depends to a large extent on the degree of capital intensity of production. This is what Nurkse writes about overcoming the observed vicious circle, resonating Rosenstein-Rodan's complementarity idea:

> Here is an escape from the deadlock; here the result is an overall enlargement of the market. People working with more and better tools in a number of complementary projects become each-others' customers. Most industries catering for mass consumption are complementary in the sense that they provide a market for, and thus support, each other. This basic complementarity stems ... from the diversity of human wants. The case for 'balanced growth' rests on the need for a 'balanced diet'.[23]

Nurkse refers to *Say's Law*—each supply creates its own demand. However, with a given labour force, techniques, and natural resources, it is only with the infusion of more capital that production can be increased. But why would anybody wish to invest? Nurkse brings to mind Schumpeter's creative entrepreneurs who took a risk, as they had faith in seeing the potential market. But this is not applicable to underdeveloped countries.[24] There, investments have to be organised to some extent. Take Japan: its early industrial development was promoted by the state.

Capital investment creates an essential basis for expanding a country's international trade. Underdeveloped countries should not push export of primary products that are prone to inelastic demand. Their economic growth must come from increased production for the domestic market. Now, as productivity increases—and the domestic market expands—the volume of external trade will grow. Nurkse anticipated that underdeveloped countries' balanced growth would create a healthy foundation for their inclusion in international trade.

There are overpopulated and underpopulated countries. The former suffer from disguised unemployment. Taking away people from the agricultural sector, without negatively affecting output, and having them produce something in another sector, adds to the country's income. Transferring labour from low productivity agriculture to high productivity industry can only take place if additional capital is invested. This can be done by increasing the agricultural sector's productivity, since a more productive agricultural sector produces more savings from which industrial capital investments can be paid. After all, the Industrial Revolution was not possible without the preceding agricultural revolution. In sparsely populated countries, a productivity boost in agriculture is a prerequisite for capital formation in the industrial sector.[25]

Private investment alone cannot finance underdeveloped countries' development. So far, most foreign investment went into extracting industries working mainly for export to developed countries. The lack of public overhead capital did not invite foreign direct investment. What about other financing means? Japan comes to mind: its land tax was a formidable source of domestic finance during the early part of its industrial development. Japan attracted considerable amounts of foreign direct investment, but only after the government had invested large sums in the country's infrastructure. By that time, the market had grown, public infrastructure facilities were in place, creating an attractive environment for foreign investors.

Can foreign aid relieve the shortage of capital? It depends, says Nurkse. Aid may trigger higher local consumption. If aid is to be invested in capital formation, the absorptive capacity of the receiving country may be a limiting factor. As for the allocation of available domestic and foreign resources, comprehensive planning is key, ensuring that top priority is given to capital formation.

When the prices of export products of underdeveloped countries increase, it is possible to import larger quantities of capital goods. Now, if their export prices continue to rise, it would give them the added resources to invest in capital formation; no outside help would then be needed. But will it work? Again, income will increase inducing the population to consume more on domestic and imported goods. Domestic prices will go up, triggering inflation. The tendency to import will rise as well. Increased imports will probably not consist of capital goods. Only when the government will tax away the increased income, the importation of capital goods can be secured.

Three questions arise: (a) can import restrictions help by increasing the incentive to invest; (b) can the supply of capital be enlarged through foreign trade; and (c) can capital formation be increased by restricting imports of consumer goods? Regarding import restrictions, the infant industry argument comes to mind. Such a policy may help; however, if protection were all that was needed for economic development, the problem would have been solved already. Tariff protection is insufficient to promote economic growth. Industry protection overlooks the challenge of capital supply; after all, infant industry creation must precede infant industry protection. Foreign capital will only be invested in strong industries, protected by tariff walls. Foreign capital has so far gone to export industries (such as mining) rather than in industries producing for the domestic market. Foreign trade can generate funds to obtain capital goods from advanced countries. Restricting the importation of (luxury) consumer goods facilitates the importation of capital goods.

What happens to the domestic flow of money income and to the balance between saving and investment? It depends on what people do with that part of their income which they used to spend on imported consumption goods. Suppose they save that part. This saving will pay for the imported capital goods and, thus, adds to the rate of capital formation. But suppose that part will be partly spent on domestic consumer goods. This leaves room for the importation of some capital goods, funded by domestic credit. The increased demand for local consumption goods will drive out the domestic production of capital goods; total net capital formation will then not increase. In addition, inflation will lead to a misdirection of resources through a failure to replace inventories and fixed equipment. So, limiting foreign trade will probably not lead to more domestic capital formation. It is essential to extract more saving out of the national income. This is best done by compulsory saving through public finance. If this cannot be done, an increase in domestic capital formation is not possible.

In essence, capital is created at home; domestic action is essential for the effective use of external contributions (including grant aid) and domestic resources. As development takes off, the capital accumulated will itself help to produce an increase in real income, which is to be ploughed back into the country's capital stock. The challenge is to maximise the marginal saving ratio. In fact, the marginal propensity to save is *the* crucial determinant of growth. In sum, the challenge is to direct as much as possible of the increment in real income into saving, and to allow as little as possible of it to go into an increase in consumption.

Governments of underdeveloped countries have the task to invest in essential public works. This makes for a lumpy process. As Hans Singer noted, the problem is not marginal productivity of capital, but one of structural change and all-round growth. This provides a skeleton structure into which the economy must be encouraged to grow through less lumpy and more widely diffused investments of capital through entrepreneurs. There may be other ways in which capital enters into the social culture of an underdeveloped country, but opportunity for private investment may be the most effective one.

4.4.3 William Arthur Lewis

William Arthur Lewis is one of the 'founding fathers' of development economics. *Economic Development with Unlimited Supplies of Labour* is arguably Lewis's most influential contribution to development economics.[26]

It is a brilliant, elegantly composed text. Written in the classical tradition, it is based on the assumption of the availability of an unlimited supply of labour at subsistence wages. Production would grow through capital formation. This was the case for Europe and America, but not—as Lewis noted—for large parts of Asia where there was indeed an unlimited supply of labour, where economic growth could not be taken for granted.

The purpose of Lewis's essay was to demonstrate what can be made of the classical framework in solving problems of distribution, accumulation, and growth; first in a closed and, subsequently, in an open economy. He had in mind underdeveloped economies plagued by a huge surplus of labour where the marginal productivity of labour was negligible, zero, or even negative. This disguised unemployment was to be found in agriculture, but also in the entire informal sector. Hence in an over-populated economy an enormous expansion of new industries and new employment opportunities could be created without any shortage of unskilled labour.

In a closed economy, the supply of labour is 'unlimited' so long as this supply, at subsistence level wages, exceeds the demand for labour. The real development bottlenecks are capital and natural resources. Capital will be invested up to the point where the marginal productivity of labour equals the current wage. Obviously, as more capital becomes available more workers can be employed coming from the subsistence sector, and their output per head will rise. The migration of labour from agriculture to manufacturing, and the corresponding structural transformation of the economy is *the* engine of growth and economic development.

It is in the interest of capitalists to keep wages low. This level depends on the earnings in the subsistence sector. Lewis observed that capitalists will almost never do anything to help make the subsistence sector more productive. The record of every imperial power in Africa in modern times, argued Lewis, is one of impoverishing the subsistence economy, either by taking away people's land, by demanding forced labour in the capitalist sector, or by imposing taxes to drive people to work for capitalist employers.

In so far as the capitalist surplus is reinvested, the capitalist sector grows, absorbing more labour from the subsistence sector, until the labour surplus disappears. Growth of technical knowledge is very important, as it results in a rise in wages and so reduces the capitalist surplus. Inside the capitalist sector knowledge and capital work together; they result in labour—or capital saving production processes. However, in economies where techniques are stagnant, savings are not reinvested to increase productivity; they are used to build pyramids, churches, and the like.

Economic development's central problem is to understand the process by which a community which was previously saving and investing 4–5% of its national income, converts itself into an economy where voluntary saving is running at 12–15% of national income. The essence of economic development is rapid capital accumulation. One cannot explain any 'industrial' revolution until one can explain why saving increased relatively to national income.

Why do people save more? It is because they have more to save. Nearly all saving is done by people who receive profits from rents. Throughout the expansion phase, subsistence incomes remain constant since labour can yield up to the growing capitalist sector without reducing subsistence output. Therefore, the growth process increases the capitalist surplus, but also the capitalist employees' income. Now, if one asks why underdeveloped countries save so little? The answer is not that that they are poor, but because their capitalist sector is so small. So, if their capitalist sector would be larger, profits would be larger and savings and investments would be larger as well.

As for income inequality, the capitalist sector contributes to its increase. But inequality of incomes in itself does not automatically imply a high level of saving. Only if inequality goes together with profits, this favours capital formation. Capitalists also create capital out of an increase in the money supply (read: bank credit). In the classical model capital formation goes up, but consumer goods output will not be immediately affected. Prices will rise though, since labour is paid out of new money, while the volume of consumer goods is lagging behind. This inflationary process does not go on forever; it stops when voluntary savings increase to a level where they are equal to the inflated level of investment.

If unlimited labour is available at a constant real wage rate, the capitalist surplus will rise continuously, and annual investment will be a rising proportion of national income. The process will stop when capital accumulation has caught up with population, so that there is no longer surplus labour. But it may stop *before* that situation is reached. Various circumstances may explain this, ranging from the possibility that the subsistence sector may become more productive (triggering an increase in the wages of the capitalist sector), to the terms of trade moving against the capitalist sector. Lewis then made an important observation:

> ...it is not profitable to produce a growing volume of manufactures unless agricultural production is growing simultaneously. This is also why industrial and agrarian revolutions always go together, and why economies in which agriculture is stagnant do not show industrial development.[27]

A rise in food productivity benefits the capitalist sector. Nevertheless, when taking rising demand into account, it is not unlikely that the price of food will not fall as fast as productivity increases. This will force capitalists to pay out a larger part of their profits as wages. Now, if conditions are favourable for the capitalist surplus to grow more rapidly than population, there must come a day when capital accumulation has caught up with labour supply.

For countries confronted with labour scarcity, the question is how the distribution of income would be inside a country and its rate of capital accumulation, when affected by abundant labour at a subsistence wage available elsewhere. Rising wages can be prevented by promoting immigration of unskilled workers (which the labour unions will protest) or by investing in countries with a labour surplus, which is the easiest. What will then happen? It depends on the type of competition between the capital exporting and importing countries. The importation of foreign capital does not raise real wages in countries which have surplus labour, unless the capital results in increased productivity in the commodities which they produce for their own consumption. Obviously, investment in another country will reduce the creation of fixed capital at home and, therefore, reduce the demand for labour, which keeps the wages down. This is offset if the capital export cheapens the things that workers import, or raises wage costs in competing countries. But it is not offset if the capital export raises the costs of imports or reduces costs in competing countries. There are cases where there is surplus labour at home available at subsistence wages, while investment opportunities abroad are more profitable. Lewis observed that many capitalists of these countries rather invest their capital in England or in America.

> Productivity depends also on the human material. Even though the genetic composition of peoples may be much the same, as far as potential productivity may be concerned, their cultural inheritance is very different. Differences in literacy, forms of government, attitudes to work, and social relations generally make a big difference to productivity. Capitalists naturally find it more profitable and safer to invest in countries where the atmosphere is capitalist than they do in different cultures.[28]

Finally, Lewis discusses the case in which country A and B produce competing goods to sell in third markets. Now, if capital is exported in ways which raise subsistence productivity in the capital importing country, the workers in the capital exporting country will benefit, since wages of their rivals will be raised. If, however, it is exported to increase productivity in the exporting sector of the capital importing country, the workers in the capital exporting country will be doubly hit, first by the reduced capital accumulation at home, and then again by the fall in their rivals' prices.

4.4.4 Simon Kuznets

Who hasn't heard of the *Kuznets Curve*; named after Simon Kuznets, the first economist who developed national income accounts at America's National Bureau of Economic Research (NBER)? In 1954, Kuznets was elected President of the American Economic Association. His Presidential address *Economic Growth and Income Inequality*, is summarised below.[29]

Kuznets presented his insights in the relationship between economic growth and income inequality. Its central theme was the character and causes of long-term changes in the personal distribution of income. He analysed income data for the United States, England, and Germany over the period 1875–1950. He concluded that the relative distribution of income, as measured by annual income incidence in rather broad classes, had been moving toward equality. These trends were particularly noticeable since the 1920s, but they likely began before the First World War.

The paper's last part is of special interest to us as it deals with underdeveloped countries, characterised by low average levels of income per capita. Low enough, Kuznets added, to raise the question how the populations in these countries manage to survive. The lower limit of the proportional share in the income structure is higher when the real country-wide per capita income is low than when it is high. This is because the income of the lower brackets could not be much below a fairly sizeable proportion of average income, simply because otherwise the population with the lowest income could not survive.

Kuznets compared the income distribution for the United States and India. The first quintile in India receives 8% of India's total income, which was more than the 6% share of America's first quintile. The second quintile in India received only 9%, the third 11%, and the fourth 16%; whereas in America, the shares of these quintiles were 12%, 16%, and 22% respectively. This is a fairly accurate reflection of income distribution in a rich and in a poor country. There is hardly any middle class in a poor country.

The author is aware of the fact that a mechanistic extrapolation of rich countries' development trajectories is overlooking crucial development preconditions in underdeveloped countries. True, some of these countries used to be economic leaders in the distant past, such as China, India, Mali, Mexico, and Peru. However, during the past two centuries the rate of growth of underdeveloped countries has been a lot lower than the Western World's.

The distribution of income is more unequal in underdeveloped countries. Given their low average incomes, savings can only be done by the ones in the peak of the income pyramid, i.e., by the top 3% or 5%. The combined phenomena of limited investment possibilities for the top-income earners and hardly any welfare policies of the governments, suggest that the distribution of income may even have been widened, further worsened by population increase. The question is whether the political framework, which is controlled by the richest sections of society, can withstand the strain of further widening of income inequality? Kuznets then asks:

> How can either the institutional and political framework of the underdeveloped societies or the process of economic growth and industrialization be modified to favor a sustained rise to higher levels of economic performance and yet avoid the fatally simple remedy of an authoritarian regime that

> would use the population as cannon-fodder in the fight for economic achievement?[30]

Kuznets warns against repeating the process which developed countries went through, in that the preservation of present income inequalities in underdeveloped countries would be necessary to get economic growth going. The answer should not be free markets, foreign investment, and progressive taxation, as they may trigger capital flight and leaving the government with insufficient resources for its capital formation. However, Kuznets does not show the way ahead. Because, as he underscored, we do not know enough about the conditions that characterise present-day underdeveloped countries:

> Without better knowledge of the trends of secular income structure and of the factors that determine them, our understanding of the whole process of economic growth is limited; and any insight we may derive from observing changes in countrywide aggregates over time will be defective if these changes are not translated into movements of shares of the various income groups.[31]

More knowledge of the process of economic growth was required and better insights in demography, technological progress, and social frameworks; all these disciplines impinge upon the operation of economic forces. Effective work in these fields, concluded Kuznets, calls for a shift from market economics to political and social economy.

Quantitative Aspects of Economic Growth of Nations: VIII—Distribution of Income by Size[32]

In 1963, Kuznets revisited the subject of income inequality and economic growth (this time based upon a broader set of data and many more countries) in a series of essays which he published in *Economic Development and Cultural Change*. In particular, *Quantitative Aspects of Economic Growth of Nations: VIII: Distribution of Income by Size* is relevant for developing countries. Kuznets focused on changes in the income distribution that can be attributed to shifts in the production structure which in turn is indispensable for economic growth. This is, in essence, what Kuznets observed:

> Given a greater degree of structural shifts accompanying vigorous economic growth, and hence significantly greater internal mobility, there is likely to be

> more income mobility ... in which some groups, perhaps previously low in the scale, may be rising, and others, perhaps previously high in the scale, may be declining. One would tend to assume that internal income mobility is more limited in stagnant, slowly growing societies than in rapidly growing countries; and there are some implications also for the trends in income mobility over the long time span of growth within a country.[33]

A post-WWII broad-based international comparison of 32 developed and underdeveloped countries revealed that the low-income groups in the underdeveloped countries received shares in total income as high as those in the low-income groups in the developed countries; but the upper-income brackets in the underdeveloped countries received much higher shares in total income than they did in developed countries. Consequently the distribution of incomes below the top brackets must have been less unequal in the underdeveloped than in the developed countries.

What factors contributed to income inequality in less developed countries? Kuznets distinguishes the following: (a) property income received by households; and (b) participation income of entrepreneurs and employees, distinguished further by industry or occupation. Regarding (a) Kuznets argued that since the share of property in total income is no lower in the less developed than in the more developed countries, the contribution of these incomes to inequality in the overall size distribution would seem to be the same in both groups of countries. But it is not the same, since, among others, the equalizing effect of economic mobility as a result of economic growth, is more prominent in developed countries. The persistence in the identity of the upper-income groups, and hence the cumulative effect on wealth concentration, have been greater in the underdeveloped than in the developed countries. As a result, there is a wider inequality in the distribution of income in the underdeveloped countries. Regarding the incomes in modern sectors of the economy, the author makes interesting observations:

> Given the relatively low level of productivity in the A sector [Agriculture; PdH] in the less developed countries and regions—which, combined with the large share of the A sector, is what makes these countries and regions less developed—and given the existence of <u>some</u> modern sectors even in the less developed countries and regions, there is an element of technological necessity in the incomes in these modern sectors being large multiples of incomes in the A sector. Otherwise the people engaged in the modern sectors could not operate efficiently. For example, an adequately qualified engineer, physician, university professor, government or business executive, could not

> function effectively except at a given absolute standard of living and hence income- which may be a high multiple of the countrywide per worker income in an underdeveloped country. In this sense, underdeveloped countries and regions cannot afford income equality, or even as little income inequality as the higher income, more developed areas.[34]

Now, what are the long-term trends? Kuznets analysed trends for developed countries over a period spanning the middle of the nineteenth century to the middle of the twentieth century. The first trend concerns the narrowing of inequality in the size distribution of income, if judged by the decline in the shares of upper income groups. However, the narrowing is less marked if judged by the rise in the shares of the lower income groups. The second trend concerns the influence of taxes. Given the growing impact of progressive taxes in most developed countries, the trend towards equality is the result of a decline in the shares of the upper income groups and a rise in the shares of the lower groups. When did the trend toward narrower inequality start? The answer is that both world wars seem to have had a narrowing effect in all countries.

In the past, income inequality in the developed countries was no narrower than it is in the underdeveloped countries now. True, developed countries had a much higher per capita income in the 1920s and 1930s than do most underdeveloped countries of today. Kuznets then observed that the pattern of distribution of income by size in underdeveloped countries is not unusual, in that—not so long ago- it was found in the developed countries, and that the change in the latter may have begun rapidly and quite recently.

What are the changes in the process of economic growth that reduce the inequality of incomes of developed economies? The industrialisation process triggered a decline in the agricultural labour force; hence the product per worker in that sector increased. Second, the proportion of independent entrepreneurs in the labour force declined and that of salaried employees increased; the former had higher incomes than those of the salaried employees. A third factor is that the share of property income declined. There were also other factors that contributed to the narrowing of inequality. The egalitarian philosophy, concomitant with modern economic growth, exercised pressure that limited income inequality. In addition, there were legislative decisions, such as equal access to education, health, taxation of inheritance, progressive income tax, social security, full employment policy—all of them reflective of a stronger hold of government over economic issues—that had an equalizing effect.

He ended the essay as follows: ‘In particular, we need to be aware of the stresses and strains to which income inequalities give rise so that, in concentrating on the purely economic aspects like generation of savings or effective demand, we do not overlook the effects of the cleavages created in the social and political structures that are indispensable for sustained economic growth.'[35]

4.4.5 *Walt Whitman Rostow*

In the early 1970s, I studied development economics and, surely, Rostow's *The Stages of Economic Growth* formed a central part of the curriculum.[36] Reading Rostow's book was easy and uplifting because of its internal logic, and of the optimistic spirit it radiated.

The book's subtitle: *a non-communist manifesto* is clearly reflective of Truman's *Point Four*—America's fear of the ongoing arms race, and the Soviet Union's expansionist ambitions through introducing developing countries 'a model of an inhumane political organization.'[37] Regarding *Point Four*, Truman had said: 'Communist propaganda holds that the free nations are incapable of providing a decent standard of living for the millions of people in under-developed areas of the earth. The Point Four Program will be one of our principal ways of demonstrating the complete falsity of that charge.'[38] Rostow's book is reflective of the mood during the Cold War. He did not foresee, nor other scholars, the collapse of the Soviet Union. Neither did he consider the possibility that many developing countries would remain stagnant, or whose central government would collapse. But he was spot-on in predicting that developing countries could *take off*:

> ...looking ahead some sixty years it can be said with reasonable confidence that the world will contain many new nations which have achieved maturity. They may not be rich in terms of consumption per head ... but they will have the capacity to apply to their resources the full capabilities of modern science and technology.[39]

He wondered whether economic growth should be analysed in terms of broad aggregates such as Gross Domestic Product, or should these aggregates be linked to movements in the sectors and sub-sectors within which new technologies are absorbed efficiently in an economy? The author chose the second method of analysis, since the successive stages of growth emerged with reasonable clarity in the economic growth history of developed countries.[40] Rostow acknowledged that not all developing countries were ready for the *take-off* stage. Nonetheless, progress made was sufficient in each of them to state that the development job could be done. However, birth rates should be brought down, and adequate support (read: aid) from advanced nations should be sustained.

Rostow distinguishes five stages of economic growth: (a) the traditional society; (b) preconditions for take-off; (c) take-off; (d) maturity; and (e) the age of high mass-consumption.[41] The traditional society is characterised by limited productivity. In these societies there may be periods of relative growth, but there is a limit beyond which growth cannot continue, barred by an economic and technological ceiling. The *preconditions for take-off* become manifest when the insights of modern science translate into new production functions in agriculture and industry. The society fends off diminishing returns in its 'march of compound interest.'

In 1952, well before Rostow published *The Stages of Economic Growth*, Alexander Gerschenkron (1904–1978) published *Economic Backwardness in Historical Perspective*.[42] Economic backwardness was the basis for his model of late-comer economic development. Gerschenkron analysed the economic modernisation processes of European late-comer countries (compared to England) in the nineteenth and early twentieth century, such as Germany, France, Italy, Austria, Bulgaria, and Russia. He argued that their economic backwardness played a positive role in inducing systematic substitution for supposed prerequisites for industrial growth. For example, state intervention did compensate for the inadequate supply of capital, skilled labour, entrepreneurship, or technological capacity, which—in various combinations—were characteristics in follower countries wishing to modernise their economies.

England took off on the basis of Adam Smith's free market ideology. Germany's economic development was made possible by credit provision on a large scale by banks to finance Germany's industrialisation process. Only when industrial development could commence on a large scale did the tension between pre-industrialisation conditions and the benefits expected from industrialisation become sufficiently strong to overcome the existing obstacles to industrial progress. Russia, which started its modernisation process later than Germany, required an even larger and more direct state compensatory role compared to Germany.

Gerschenkron's analysis rejected England's example as *the* standard pattern of industrial development, depriving the accumulation of capital of its crucial role in promoting a country's economic development. Disadvantageous initial conditions of e.g., access to capital could be overcome, argued the author, through new institutional arrangements, such as the establishment of large banks. Success was indicated by more rapid growth in later developers, triggered by a *spurt* in industrial expansion, accompanied by a modernisation spirit. Unlike Rostow's stages of economic growth, Gerschenkron sketched a different picture: each late-comer demonstrated a distinctive process of economic growth. In short, there was no uniform staged process, as Rostow proposed. Gerschenkron argued that the lesson of the nineteenth century was that the policies toward the backward countries were unlikely to be successful if they ignored the basic peculiarities, the native element, of economic backwardness. There is no iron law of historical economic development.

Over time, he further refined his model leading to interesting hypotheses, useful to late-comer developing countries. Here they are: '(1) Relative backwardness creates a tension between the promise of economic development, as achieved elsewhere, and the continuity of stagnation. Such a tension takes political form and motivates institutional innovation, whose product becomes an appropriate substitution for the absent preconditions for growth; (2) the greater the degree of backwardness, the more intervention is required in the market economy, as demonstrated in e.g., Russia's modernisation process, to channel capital and entrepreneurial leadership to nascent industries. Also, the more coercive and comprehensive were the measures required to reduce domestic consumption and allow national saving; (3) the more backward the economy, the more likely were a series of additional characteristics: an emphasis upon domestic production of producers' goods rather than consumers' goods; the use of capital intensive rather than labor intensive methods of production; emergence of larger scale production units at the level

(*continued*)

(continued)

both of the firm as well as the individual plant; and dependence upon borrowed, advanced technology rather than use of indigenous techniques; (4) the more backward the country, the less likely was the agricultural sector to provide a growing market to industry, and the more dependent was industry upon growing productivity and inter-industrial sales for its expansion. Such unbalanced growth was frequently feasible through state participation.'[43]

A mood of ***modernisation*** is ushered in: 'The idea spreads not merely that economic progress is possible, but that economic progress is a necessary condition for some other purpose: be it national dignity, private profit, the general welfare, or a better life for children. Education, for some at least, broadens and changes to suit the needs of modern economic activity.'[44]

The decisive factor in this transition is often political: the building of a centralised national state, or opposition to the colonial power, was in many cases the decisive factor in the creation of the preconditions.[45] In political terms: the take-off is the interval when the old powers and the resistance to growth are defeated. Rising real incomes in agriculture constitute an important stimulus to new industrial sectors that are essential to the take-off. A second precondition for take-off is that the government has to take care of social overhead capital. Government does not need to own the means of production, but it must be capable of organising the nation so that commercial markets develop. It must maintain a tax- and fiscal system that channels resources into modern uses, and it must lead the way through the entire spectrum of national policy ranging from the establishment of tariffs, education, to public health.

A *take-off* requires three conditions: (a) a rise in the rate of productive investment from, say, 5% to over 10%; (b) the development of a manufacturing sector; and (c) the existence or quick emergence of a political, social, and institutional framework which exploits the impulses to expansion, implying a considerable capability to mobilise capital from savings and taxes. The shift of income flowing into more productive hands is also aided by banks and capital markets. The take-off periods have been marked by the extension of banking institutions which expanded the supply of working capital, and entrepreneurs ploughing back their profits into new investments. The proceeds from exports helped to finance the import of capital goods and to serve the foreign debt. Leading sectors in the take-off are: (a) primary growth sectors; (b) supplementary sectors (e.g. coal, iron, and engineering); (c) derived-growth sectors, e.g., housing. New elites emerge building a modern industrial society. In non-economic terms, the take-off usually witnesses a definitive social, political, and cultural victory of those who modernise the economy.

After a long period of sustained progress, the *drive to maturity* ensues. The engine of the transition is a rise in the investment rate to a higher level (i.e., 10–20%). Subsequently, the society enters the international field. Formerly imported goods are now produced at home, while new import requirements develop. New export commodities pay for these imports. Rostow estimates that maturity sets in roughly sixty years after take-off. Modernisation involves a lot of working capital. Now, how is this generated? It is to be done by creating higher productivity in agriculture and in mining. Agriculture is supposed to: (a) supply more food, (b) feed the growing urban population, and (c) meet the foreign exchange bill to pay for capital development. The rate of increase in agriculture's output sets a limit within which the transition to modernisation proceeds.

The *drive to maturity* stage involves a differentiated industrial process, with new leading sectors gathering momentum to supplant the original leading sectors. The process of moving to maturity lays the basis for the kind of political and social pressures that led to that long succession of humane modifications starting with Britain's factory legislation of the 1840s, down through Bismarck's concessions, Lloyd George's reforms and the American progressive era.

During the age of *high mass-consumption*, the balance of attention shifts from supply to demand. Three major objectives emerge: (a) the pursuit of external power and influence, (b) the welfare state, including income redistribution and increased leisure, and (c) the expansion of consumption.

What Next?

Various problems, said Rostow, face us, such as the problem of North-South relations, and the establishment of an arms control system.

Regarding the North-South issue Rostow argued: '...Britain and Western Europe have the resources and the pool of technical assistance to play a major ... role in making sure the underdeveloped areas of the non-Communist world move through the preconditions and through take-off without succumbing to.... Communism.'[46] He proposed that the level of external aid should be increased and sustained for a long period, also given the rapid population growth in the developing world. This is Rostow's final statement:

> For those who would prefer to see the aspiring societies of the world not follow this peculiar road to modernization—in Asia, the Middle East, Africa, and Latin America—the communist technique for mobilizing power and resources poses a formidable problem, almost certainly what historians will judge the central challenge of our time; that is, the challenge of creating, in association with the non-Communist politicians and peoples of the preconditions and early take-off areas, a partnership which will see them through into sustained growth on a political and social basis which keeps open the possibilities of progressive, democratic development.[47]

4.4.6 Hollis Chenery

Hollis Chenery wrote, with the help of Allan Strout, *Foreign Assistance and Economic Development*, in which the two-gap model is elaborated.[48]

Chenery and Strout present the investment-savings gap—and the foreign exchange gap model. In short, the 'two-gap' model, which attempts to assess the potential contribution of foreign aid or capital flows to an economy. Foreign aid, including private investment, is a separate factor of production, whose productivity and allocation provides one of the central problems for a theory of development. Securing sustained development through the effective use of foreign aid has been demonstrated by, e.g., Greece, Israel, Taiwan, and the Philippines. The authors present a theoretical framework designed to analyse the development process with external assistance. Like Rostow, they identify phases of growth, but—unlike Rostow—accompanied by a theoretical model which they apply to actual developments of developing countries.

Without external help, a country must either shoulder the development bill itself or from imports paid by its exports. If one or more of them cannot be achieved, growth will be frustrated. Foreign aid can help to relieve these constraints. The additional resources, produced through more rapid growth, must be used to make good the deficiencies which were temporarily overcome through outside assistance.

There are two questions regarding the sequence: (a) what is the extent to which foreign resources can actually substitute for missing local factors; and (b) what further steps will countries take, needed to reduce their dependence on aid? External resources can contribute to the mobilisation and allocation of productive resources. Aggregate growth models usually focus on the savings limit, which in a closed economy also sets the investment limit. When external financing is available, one needs to examine other limits, ranging from the limited supply of skilled labour, to the ability to increase investment. Developing countries have raised their level of investment much more rapidly than their saving level. Sustained rates of investment of 12–15% per year are common, while typical saving rates are only 6–8%. Another limiting factor is a country's inability to change its productive structure to meet the changing pattern of internal and external demand. The more rapid the growth rate, the larger the reallocation of labour and capital needed to prevent bottlenecks from cropping up. In cases of acute shortages of imported goods, the economy is unable to transform potential saving into investment, precisely because of insufficient supplies of investment goods.

For the short run, the authors apply the Harrod-Domar growth model to determine the growth pattern. For the long run, they use a model based on the neoclassical view that domestic resources can be substituted for imports to the extent required by changing demands with diminishing productivity. This latter model has the effect of reducing the aid requirement. Since most developing countries fall between the two extremes, the use of both models for projections indicates the probable limits to the range of aid requirements.

As mentioned, two resource limits apply: skills and saving, leading to investment-limited growth. The authors consider the possibilities for achieving self-sustaining growth with a balance-of-payments limit: trade-limited growth. The complete model that they propose includes all potential limits. The model is applied to a sample of 31 countries for the period 1957–1962. The median capital-output ratio and saving rate suggest that, without external aid, the growth rate of developing countries would be about 3.4%, or less than 1% per capita.

Regarding investment-limited growth, this is based on the Harrod-Domar assumption that a specified amount of investment is needed to increase output. There is a limit to the absorptive capacity to invest, such as a skills limit. The saving limit is designed to include not only the marginal propensity to save but also the government's ability to increase total saving by changes in the tax structure and by other policies. The saving limit is a function of total GNP rather than of per capita income.

The target growth rate reflects the practice of summing up the principal goal of development in a given rate of increase in GNP. It also reflects the fact that foreign assistance is limited and is unlikely to be available to finance growth rates above 6–7%. Since the average terms of external loans are largely based on the country's future economic prospects, this puts a limit on the total amount which it can borrow. The authors also assume that aid is sufficiently limited (or expensive) to make the recipient unwilling to increase aid merely to increase consumption without also securing some GNP rise. It is also assumed that the country tries to maximise consumption until the target growth rate is attained.

The authors distinguish three phases of the development process. Phase I is characterised by investment-limited growth and by an accelerating growth rate of GNP. The increase in GNP will be limited, first by the ability to invest and, subsequently, by the target growth rate if the investment rate reaches a level required to sustain it. For example, achieving a 10% investment growth rate requires that during Phase I nearly half of the increased investment be financed by external capital. External assistance fills *the finance gap* between investment and saving, permitting the higher growth rate. Phase I ends in the year when investment reaches a level adequate to sustain the target growth rate.

During Phase II the marginal saving rate must exceed the investment rate as required by the growth target. The saving rate will have risen to eliminate the capital inflow. The rate of capital will decline. In Phase III inequalities become equalities and limits are redundant.

As for trade-limited growth, the growth process, with a varying inflow of capital, requires a continual adjustment in imports and exports to make the trade gap equal to the desired gap between investment and saving. Although in Phase I the rising capital inflow as needed reduces the pressure on the balance-of-payments, the tapering off of the capital inflow in Phase II requires exports to rise more rapidly than imports. The authors rightly note that, in practice many countries could not bring this required adjustment about. The resulting trade gap is often structural; it can only be reduced over time, without reducing the rate of growth, by a redirection of investment and the creation of new exports. But a rapid increase in new exports is limited by the productive capacity as well as by organisational and institutional limitations.

When the capital inflow, as determined by the saving-investment gap, is greater than the minimum trade gap, the two gaps can be equated by having imports in excess of the specified minimum, or exports less than the assumed maximum. Once a target growth in GNP is attained, exports must rise more rapidly than imports if aid is to be reduced. As noted, in Phase III the initial inequalities become equalities and the limits become redundant. To complete the transition to self-sustaining growth, total capital required is the sum of the capital requirements for each phase. In the early phases, external capital is determined by the cumulative difference between investment and savings. In subsequent phases it is the cumulative difference between imports and exports.[49]

The productivity of an increment in external resources supplied to a developing country can be measured by the corresponding increase in consumption or total income which it triggered. As the length of time increases, the productivity of assistance in Phase II rises because of the additional saving generated, while the productivity in Phase III falls. However, for long-term development policy it is more useful to consider the total assistance needed to complete the transition to self-sustaining growth. Median performance requires a total capital inflow of more than 2.5 times the initial GNP, and a period of 43 years to complete the transition to self-sustaining growth.

Three central issues for assistance policy are: (a) measurement of the effectiveness of external assistance; (b) policies which recipient countries follow to make best use of these resources; and (c) a basis for allocating assistance among countries. In the short-run, aid effectiveness depends on the use made to relieve shortages of skills, saving, and imported commodities. Aid productivity is measured by the increase in output resulting from the fuller use of domestic resources. In the long-run, the use made of the initial increase in output becomes more important. However, the economy may continue to be dependent on external assistance indefinitely, unless the additional output is allocated to increase saving and reduce the trade gap. Over the entire period of the transition to self-sustaining growth, the use made of successive GNP growth is probably more important than the efficiency with which external assistance is used.

Critical elements in the development sequence are: (a) getting an initial increase in the rate of growth; (b) channeling the increments in income into increased saving; and (c) allocating investment to avoid balance-of-payments bottlenecks. These long-term aspects are more important than the efficiency with which external capital is used in the short run. The long-run effectiveness of assistance is also likely to be increased by supporting as high a growth rate as the economy can achieve, without a substantial deterioration in the efficiency of capital use.

The conclusion is that the achievement of a high growth rate, even if initially supported by large amounts of external capital, is likely to be the most important element in long-term aid effectiveness. The countries with rapidly increasing saving rates (such as Taiwan, the Philippines, Israel, and Greece), demonstrate the speed with which aid-sustained growth can be transformed into self-sustained growth once rapid development has taken hold.

The growth policy for developing countries focus should vary according to the principal limitations to growth. In Phase I the focus should be on increasing output. Phase I can be completed by most countries in a decade, if the increase in investment is accompanied by sufficient improvement in skills to benefit from additional capital. As Phase I is completed, the rate of increase in investment can be allowed to fall toward a feasible target of GNP growth. The focus should then be on changes in the productive structure, and channeling an adequate fraction of increased income into saving. Since substantial import substitution is required to prevent the ratio of imports to GNP from rising, export growth is necessary to reduce external aid. The transition may take more than 20 years, since it is unlikely that developing countries can meet all the requirements of skill formation, institution building, investment allocation, etc., in less than one generation.

Regarding donors, their aid objectives are: (a) economic and social development of the recipient; (b) maintenance of political stability in countries having a special tie with the donor; and (c) export promotion. The most simple form of aid is project aid. This becomes increasingly inappropriate as the development process gets underway. In these circumstances, assistance is more effective if the range of commodities supplied be broadened to permit the recipient's pattern of investment and production is directed to its comparative advantage. A program approach is becoming increasingly feasible in these circumstances. In Phase III, where the balance-of-payments is the limiting factor, priority should be given to import-substitution and to increased exports. In this situation, donor controls should be concerned with the efficient use of foreign exchange resources. Allocation of resources should primarily be done on the basis of expected development performance. True, the varying political objectives of the donors complicate matters. Where reliable statistics are available, an alternative procedure would be to establish minimum overall performance standards for each country and to share the aid burden among interested donors through a consortium.

4.5 Dissenters

Having learned what the first generation proposed, one may conclude that what was proposed made a lot of sense. Their proposals radiated an upbeat spirit: economic growth and development of poor countries could indeed be achieved, provided these countries and their donors would act as prescribed. The first generation economists wielded quite some influence in development policy circles at the time, but there were other economists who begged to differ.

The earliest dissenter was, no doubt, Peter Bauer (1915–2002) whose *Dissent on Development* is a classic.[50] But when the book came out, it was disregarded because Bauer's opinions about what to do and what not, were then politically incorrect. He was a lone voice in criticising first generation's insights.[51] Bauer turned their development theories on their head, so to speak, inspired by what he had learned from studying Malaysian rubber tappers and West African small traders.[52] In both cases he witnessed the power of incentives triggered by trade for economic development, and the important part played by small traders (thereby recognising the role of the informal sector) in a country's commercial life, and the role that international trade played in introducing new ideas.

Bauer underscored the benefits of the market; he rejected development planning. He also recognised the importance of non-economic factors in the development process. He argued that in the explanation of economic growth, cultural and political factors were generally more important than the economic factors proposed by development economists. He refuted the vicious circle of poverty, since all countries had started their development while being poor. He downplayed the negative development effects of rapid population growth.[53] Bauer was not in favour of foreign aid, arguing that it was not given to the people who needed it. Aid was a subsidy given to governments, making them stronger and more dictatorial.

Amartya Sen summarised Bauer's views well. He said that Bauer was convinced that there was: (a) an overemphasis on the limitation of resources in the poorer countries, a limitation he thought could be overcome much more easily than the established views tended to assume; (b) an under-emphasis on the role of exchange, both in general and in domestic trade in particular; and (c) an inadequate recognition of how institutions influenced economic behaviour, with profound effects on the economy and society.[54]

Myint was also not enthusiastic about the first generation's theories: 'Looking at these new theories which became popular during the 1950s, such as the 'vicious circle', the 'take-off' or the 'big push', it does not seem to me that these have stood up any better to the test of realism. The weakness of these new theories is that they try to apply to all the underdeveloped countries a composite model of *the* underdeveloped country incorporating in it certain special features of some one or the other type of underdeveloped country ... the number of the underdeveloped countries to which this model might apply becomes severely limited to one or two countries such as India and possibly Pakistan.'[55]

Paul Krugman was even more unforgiving. He argued that the first generation's theories were:

> ...at first unable, and later unwilling, to codify [their insight; PdH] in clear, internally consistent models. At the same time the expected standard of rigor in economic thinking was steadily rising. The result was that development economics as a distinct field was crowded out of the mainstream economics. Indeed, the ideas of high development theory (of the 1950s) came to seem not so much wrong as incomprehensible.[56]

Easterly observed in *The Elusive Quest for Growth* that most first generation development models were simply wrong. Easterly's panacea is that people only respond to incentives, in line with Steven Landsburg's quip: 'People respond to incentives; all the rest is commentary.'[57] But Easterly admitted that it is devilishly difficult to get the incentives right for creating growth.[58]

4.5.1 *The Dirigiste Dogma*

Deepak Lal characterised the first generation's emphasis on government's principal development role as the *Dirigiste Dogma*, explained in the box below.[59]

Needless to say, Lal is a true zealot of neoclassical economics. *The Poverty of 'Development Economics'* contains an elaborate critique of the

> The essential elements of the *Dirigiste Dogma* ... can be briefly stated. The major one is the belief that the price mechanism, or the working of a market economy, needs to be supplanted (and not merely supplemented) by various forms of direct government control, both national and international, to promote economic development.... The essential task of governments is seen as charting and implementing a 'strategy' for rapid and equitable growth which attaches prime importance to macro-economic accounting aggregates such as savings, the balance of payments, and the relative balance between broadly defined 'sectors' such as 'industry' and 'agriculture'. The third element is the belief that the classical nineteenth century liberal case for free trade is invalid for developing countries, and thus government restriction of international trade and payments is necessary for development. Finally, it is believed that, to alleviate poverty and improve domestic income distribution, massive and continuing government intervention is required to redistribute assets and to manipulate the returns to different types of labour and capital through passive price and (if possible) wage controls—and through controls which influence the composition of commodities produced and imported—so that scarce resources are used to meet the so-called 'basic needs' of the poor rather than the luxurious 'wants' of the rich.[60]

first generation's assumptions and proposed approaches. Dirigisme, argues Lal, hinders rather than promotes economic growth and the fight against poverty. The most serious current distortions in many developing economies, argues Lal, are not those flowing from the inevitable imperfections of a market economy but the policy-induced, and thus far from inevitable, distortions created by irrational dirigisme.[61]

4.5.2 *Failed Industrialisation*

Regarding the professed industrialisation drive, Krugman ironically observes that most developing countries were quite successful at developing industrial bases, but since these industries were highly inefficient, industrialisation turned out not to have much to do with development.[62]

Justin Lin argues in *Demystifying the Chinese Economy* that capital-intensive industries in developing countries typically lack viability, defying the comparative advantages these countries do have. He concludes that most of them are agrarian economies that have little surplus for capital accumulation. So, these countries have high capital costs due to their scarcity, and limited foreign exchange reserves. Now, investing in capital-intensive industries, in which the country does not have a comparative advantage, takes a lot of time and capital. Given the limited foreign exchange reserves, it is difficult to import expensive equipment and machinery. Governments that prioritise capital-intensive industries, and also wish that they be profitable, have to artificially lower the interest rate and undervalue foreign currencies. This is not all. Prices of raw materials and wages will have to be suppressed. And, since wages are low, the government also has to drive down the prices of food, clothes, housing, transport and related services.[63]

For developing countries having an abundance of labor and scarcity of capital, Lin argues that the most dynamic industrial sectors that enjoy a comparative advantage are labour-intensive industries. In addition, enterprises in labor-intensive sectors demand less capital because the capital inputs are smaller. Technology can be imported from advanced countries to avoid technological and marketing risks. After all, there is a glaring technological gap between developing and developed countries. The former can make use of this gap to reduce the cost and accelerate the pace of technological innovation, giving full play to the advantage of late starters.[64]

In sum, the industrialisation process is perceived as inefficient, capital-intensive, creating an inadequate demand for labour, and a cost to government's finances.

4.5.3 The Financing Gap and Aid

Easterly criticised the 'financing gap dogma', i.e., that aid could fill the gap. He investigated whether there was a positive statistical association between aid and investment, and the question whether an additional 1% of GDP in aid would cause an increase of 1% of GDP in investment. Easterly's analysis involved eighty-eight developing countries over the period 1965–1995. It appeared that only seventeen of the eighty-eight countries analysed had a positive statistical association between aid and investment. Easterly argues that aid will not cause its recipients to increase their investment; instead, they will use aid to buy more consumer goods. Having aid increase with country saving is the opposite of the current system, where a country with lower saving has a higher financing gap, and gets more aid.[65]

Howard White argues that several countries in Africa have experienced negative income growth during the 1980s, despite high and rising aid inflows, contrary to what the two-gap model says.[66] Griffin and Enos were critical as well:

> ...given a target rate of growth in the developing country, foreign aid will permit higher consumption, and domestic savings will simply be a residual, that is, the difference between desired investment and the amount of foreign aid available. Thus the foundations of models of the Chenery-Strout type are weak, since one would expect, on theoretical grounds to find an inverse association between foreign aid and domestic saving.[67]

4.6 Conclusion

The first generation of development economists did not sufficiently take into consideration the specific policy context of each developing country, their inadequate government capacity, the importance of the developmental role of the agricultural sector, and they disregarded the role of the market in the efficient allocation of resources. The principal actor on whom the first generation had put their hopes, i.e., government, had failed to deliver the development goods. It had become clear that where government had taken the place of the market, it resulted in distorted prices, wages, interest rates, and exchange rates. A second generation of development economists emerged, in the good-old spirit of neoclassical economics, with the main objective to get the prices right.[68]

4.7 Development Theories in the Marxist Tradition

Neo-Marxist theories identify which factors perpetuate—or even deepen—the divide between rich and poor countries. When I was young, the dependency school of thought was popular among development economics students, including myself. At the time, André Gunder Frank (1929–2005) was the development economics professor at Amsterdam University, my alma mater. We all had read Frank's works, but also the works of Walter Rodney (1942–1980), Paul Baran (1926–2011), Ernest Mandel (1923–1995), and Immanuel Wallerstein.[69]

Now, what hindering factors were at play, according to neo-Marxist thinkers? Thirlwall and Pacheco-López summarise them well:

- The dependence of the periphery on foreign capital and the expropriation of the surplus by the centre;
- the dependence on foreign technology;
- terms of trade deterioration;
- mechanisms that reduce real wages in developing countries to below what they would otherwise be;
- various sociocultural aspects of neocolonialism that thwart the drive for independence and self-reliance.[70]

Terms like centre and periphery, exploitation, terms-of-trade deterioration, neocolonialism, and self-reliance, are indeed typical neo-Marxist terms. Unequal development, they suggest, is characteristic of the global capitalistic system, or modern world-system, as Immanuel Wallerstein would say.[71] Ongoing exploitation explains why the capitalist systems prevail and why, therefore, dependent, peripheral countries are poor, will stay poor, or even become poorer.

Theotônio dos Santos provided a clear description of dependency:

> ...by dependence we mean a situation in which the economy of certain countries is conditioned by the development and expansion of another country to which the former is subjected. The relation is such that some countries (the dominant ones) can expand and can be self-sustaining, while others (the dependent ones) can do this only as a reflection of expansion, which can have either a positive or a negative effect on their intermediate development.[72]

In his description, Dos Santos included the possibility that dependent, peripheral countries may benefit from the expansion of central, dominant countries, be it during their intermediate development process. This is not typical for the neo-Marxist literature, in which the outlook for exploited, peripheral societies is simply grim because the world-capitalist system is divided in winners and losers.

Dependency is not necessarily a direct consequence of the influence of colonial powers, it can also be the result of industrial power, concentrated in rich countries at the centre. Ongoing sophistication of production processes, combined with economies of scale, helped companies to spread their influence on a wider scale. Multinational companies emerged on the world stage, they took control of a large chunk of industrial and technological power, thereby perpetuating dependency. The elites of peripheral countries shared the interests of foreign investors and businesses, which did not particularly help to promote domestic industrialisation and development. Dos Santos and others argue that dependency was not only the result of exploitative foreign influence, dependency was also supported by the powers that be within the peripheral countries.[73]

Raúl Prebisch's centre-periphery model is often associated with neo-Marxist thinking. This is incorrect, as Prebisch applies a Keynesian outlook when analysing regional differences in growth rates as a result of unequal terms of trade, and what could be done to redress the situation. In other words, Prebisch's intention was to shed countries' peripheral status through industrialisation in order to correct the disequilibrium between incomes at the centre and the periphery (see Chap. 7).

There cannot be any doubt, however, about the Marxist inspiration of the works of, e.g., Paul Baran, Samir Amin, and André Gunder Frank: the international capitalist system perpetuates the process of exploitation. Like in Marx's theory, labour is central in neo-Marxist's analyses. Surplus created by labour is successively siphoned off by small middlemen, larger companies and, ultimately, by foreign firms (i.e., multinational corporations) in rich countries that expropriate the surplus value. The toiling masses are left with the crumbs, while they were the ones to have produced this surplus.

This is what Deirdre McCloskey observes about the supposed exploitative effects of imperialism:

> 'Yet imperialism, it can be shown, did not much help the British, or the First World generally, to an industrial revolution and modern economic growth. True, the doctrine that imperialism made the West rich at the expense of the East and South is held passionately by the left in the West and by nearly everyone elsewhere. In short, the average person in Britain got little or nothing out of the British Empire.... What were the vaunted benefits to the British people? Essentially nothing of material worth. They got bananas on their kitchen tables, as I said, that they would have got anyway by free trade—the Swedes did, via London or Amsterdam -or at slightly higher cost if trade had not been entirely free.'[74]

Economic development, analysed from the vantage point of poor, peripheral countries is not going up but going down. It is adding to the peripheral country's underdevelopment. Frank, for example, goes back to the colonial era which, according to him, distorted the economic structure of colonies, through the exploitation of the colonies' valuable materials and domestic labour. Former colonies remained in the firm grip of the former colonisers, in that they were supposed to continue to provide the raw materials for their former masters. Industrial development was effectively blocked, and grossly limited the development of more productive economic investments in these former colonies.

The weakness of neo-Marxist development theories is that they suggest that developing countries face one overriding hindrance to growth: exploitative global capitalism. However, there are other possible limiting factors involved. Moreover, these theories cannot explain how it was possible that, despite supposed exploitative global capitalism, quite a number of former colonies and other poor countries have been able to grow and develop, often in a spectacular fashion.

Notes

1. For example, the World Bank's *World Development Report* 2009 uses terms like balanced growth, unbalanced growth, and cumulative causation, introduced by Ragnar Nurkse, Albert Hirschman, and Gunnar Myrdal respectively.
2. Not everyone agreed. Take Griffin and Enos. They argue: 'To the extent that foreign assistance is biased in favor of capital-intensive technology, it has a tendency to increase the receiving country's subsequent need for capital, prejudice exports, raise the capital-output ratio, and reduce the rate of growth.' Griffin, K. and Enos, J. (1970) Foreign Assistance: Objectives and Consequences. In *Economic Development and Cultural Change*, Vol. 18, No.3, April, 323.
3. UNIDO (2012) *Climbing the Stairways of Development: Structural Change as the Driver of Economic Growth.* Policy Brief, May.
4. Adelman, I. (1984) Beyond Export-led Growth. In *World Development*, 12(9): 937–949. Adelman compared the relative merits of two alternative open development strategies: (a) export-led industrialisation; and (b) agricultural-demand-led industrialisation (ADLI) by means of several simulation experiments. The results supported the ADLI approach on all counts.

5. Deepak Lal observes: 'Keynesian models of thought were seen as relevant to the problems of development. Both the central theoretical concern of Keynesian economics –namely the determinants of the level of economic activity rather than the relative prices of commodities and factors of production- and its distinctive method—namely national income-expenditure analysis—were enthusiastically adopted by development economists.' Source: Lal, D. (2000) *The Poverty of 'Development Economics'*. Cambridge: The MIT Press, 8.
6. Meier, G. (2001) The Old Generation of Development Economists and the New. In *Frontiers of Development Economics*. Ed: Meier, G., Stiglitz, J. New York: Oxford University Press, 15.
7. Little, I. (1982) *Economic Development; Theory, Policy, and International Relations*. New York: Basic Books, 30.
8. Ibid., 127.
9. Suppose the target growth rate is 4% and the required capital-output rate is 3, then the required savings rate should be 12%. If the actual savings rate was lower than that, there obviously was a gap to fill. This could be done by borrowing money or by donor contributions.
10. *Economic Development*, 41.
11. *The Old Generation of Development Economists and the New*, 16.
12. Tinbergen, J. (1967) *Development Planning*. London: Weidenfeld and Nicholson. Tinbergen consistently referred to foreign trade in relevant sections of *Development Planning*.
13. Harberger, A. (1983) The Cost-Benefit Approach to Development Economics. In *World Development*, Vol. 11, No. 10, 866.
14. Hirschman, A. (1958) *The Strategy of Economic Development*. New Haven: Yale University Press.
15. De Haan, P. (2016) *From Keynes to Piketty; The Century that Shook Up Economics*. London: Palgrave Macmillan, 233.
16. Lal, D., Myint, H. (1996) *The Political Economy of Poverty, Equity, and Growth*. Oxford: Oxford University Press, 307.
17. Thirlwall, A., Pacheco-López, P (2017) *Economics of Development*. Tenth Edition. London: Palgrave Macmillan, 104.
18. Ibid., 106–107.
19. This is what William Easterly had to say about Domar's model: 'To sum up, Domar's model was not intended as a growth model, made no sense as a growth model, and was repudiated as a growth model over forty years ago by its creator. So it was ironic that Domar's growth model became, and continues to be today, the most widely applied growth model in economic history.' Easterly adds on the same page: 'Although Domar assumed that production capacity was proportional to the stock of machinery, he admitted the assumption was unrealistic and eleven years later, in 1957, he

disavowed the theory.' Source: Easterly W. (2002) *The Elusive Quest for Growth; Economists' Adventures and Misadventures in the Tropics.* Cambridge: The MIT Press, 28.

Gardner Ackley had a comparable opinion. In his *Macroeconomic Theory* he wrote: '...Domar did not pretend to provide a theory of growth, but only to indicate one significant aspect of the *problem of growth*, and to compute, on simplified assumptions, what the necessary rate of growth would have to be in order to avoid the accumulation of excess capacity which would inhibit growth.' Ackley, G. (1961) *Macroeconomic Theory.* New York: The Macmillan Company, 517.

20. Rosenstein-Rodan, P. (1943) Problems of Industrialisation of Eastern and South-Eastern Europe. In *The Economic Journal*, Vol. 53, No.210/211 (Jun.- Sep.) 202–211.
21. Ibid., 208–209.
22. Nurkse, R. (1953) *Problems of Capital Formation in Underdeveloped Countries.* Oxford: Basil Blackwell.
23. Ibid., 11.
24. In a footnote on page 17, Nurkse quotes Joseph Spengler who made relevant observations about the conditions for industrial progress: 'Industrial progress is markedly dependent upon (a) the relative number of imaginative and energetic innovators and entrepreneurs present in the population, (b) the extent to which these qualified persons are empowered to make and execute relevant decisions, and (c) the degree to which these individuals are free of hampering legal and institutional arrangements. In the past this distribution has been most favourable in countries possessing a comparatively strong 'middle class' that enjoyed sufficient support at the hands of the state; while countries lacking a sufficiently strong middle class have had to depend upon the state to provide entrepreneurial leadership in so far as possible.'
25. This is what Myint argued: 'How far is the Southeast Asian experience applicable to other underdeveloped countries outside the region? I think that it may be of some relevance to the other smaller and less densely populated export economies, notably in West Africa. There, also, expansion in the exports of primary products still offers the most promising engine of economic development both as a source of foreign exchange earnings to finance the new import-substituting industries and, even more important, as the method of drawing the under-utilized natural resources of the subsistence sector into the money economy.' Source Myint. H. Economic Theory and Development Policy. In: *Economica*, Vol. 34, No. 134 (May 1967), 123.
26. Lewis, A. (1954) Economic Development with Unlimited Supplies of Labour. In *The Manchester School of Economics and Social Studies*, 22 (May).

27. Ibid., 173.
28. Ibid.,179.
29. Kuznets, S. (1955) Economic Growth and Income Inequality. In *The American Economic Review*, Vol. XLV, nr. 1, March.
30. Ibid., 25.
31. Ibid., 27.
32. Kuznets, S. Quantitative Aspects of Economic Growth of Nations: VIII: Distribution of Income by Size. In *Economic Development and Cultural Change*, Volume XI, Number 2, Part II. January 1963.
33. Ibid., 9–10.
34. Ibid., 49.
35. Ibid., 69.
36. Rostow, W. (1971) *The Stages of Economic Growth; a Non-Communist Manifesto*. Cambridge: Cambridge University Press, 2nd Edition.
37. Although Alexander Gerschenkron did not agree with Rostow's stages of economic growth, he shared Rostow's anti-Soviet sentiment. Gerschenkron observed that 'There are no four lane highways through the parks of industrial progress. The road may lead from backwardness to dictatorship and from dictatorship to war. In conditions of a 'bipolar world' this sinister sequence is modified and aggrandized by deliberate imitation of Soviet policies by other backward countries and by their voluntary incorporation in the Soviet orbit.' Source: Gerschenkron, A. (1962) *Economic Backwardness in Historical Perspective; a Book of Essays*. Cambridge: The Belknap Press, 29.
38. Wickstead, M. (2015) *Aid and Development; a Brief Introduction*. Oxford: Oxford University Press, 18.
39. *The Stages of Economic Growth*, 127.
40. Rostow jokingly remarked that without appropriate disaggregation, the study of growth is Hamlet without the Prince, or playing piano while wearing mittens.
41. Rostow was not the first economist who proposed various stages of economic growth. For example, well before Rostow, the French economist Anne-Robert Jacques Turgot (1727–1781) identified four stages of growth. Source: Hoyng, A. (2011). *Turgot & Smith; Een Paar Apart*, 14. And Colin Clark distinguished between primary, secondary, and tertiary production in *The Conditions of Economic Progress*. London: Macmillan (1940).
42. Gerschenkron, A. (1952) Economic Backwardness in Historical Perspective. In *The Progress of Underdeveloped Areas*, Ed. B. Hoselitz. Chicago: University of Chicago Press.
43. Fishlow, A. (2001) Review of *Economic Backwardness in Historical Perspective: A book of Essays*.

44. *The Stages of Economic Growth*, 6.
45. The beginning of take-off can be traced to a particular sharp stimulus, such as Germany in 1848, Japan's 1868 Meji Restoration, and India's independence in 1947. It may also come about by technological innovation, or the opening up of markets.
46. Ibid., 137.
47. Ibid., 164.
48. Chenery, H., Strout A. Foreign Assistance and Economic Development. In *The American Economic Review*, Vol. LVI, No. 4, September 1966, 679–733.
49. In section B of their article the authors apply their model to the transition in Pakistan.
50. Bauer, P. (1971) *Dissent on Development.* Cambridge: Harvard University Press.
51. Bauer's favourite toast among friends was: 'Death to our enemies', to which he added: 'which would make the bubonic plague look like a minor media event.'
52. Bauer, P. (1948) *The Rubber Industry.* London: Longmans, Green &co; Bauer, P. (1954) *West African Trade.* Cambridge: Cambridge University Press.
53. He did not foresee that more and more people, who become more prosperous, negatively affect the earth's regeneration capacity.
54. Sen, A. How Does Development Happen?. In *Peter Bauer and the Economics of Prosperity* (2009). New Delhi: Academic Foundation, 52.
55. Myint, H. Economic Theory and Development Policy. In *Economica*, New Series, Vol.34, No. 134 (May 1967), 120.
56. *The Old Generation of Development Economists and the New*, 15–16. Krugman, however, changed his views on the first generation, as described in Chap. 5.
57. *The Elusive Quest for Growth*, xii.
58. Ibid., 288.
59. *The Poverty of 'Development Economics'*, 5.
60. Ibid., 5.
61. Ibid., 103.
62. Krugman, P. (1992) Toward a Counter-Counterrevolution in Development Theory. In *Proceedings of the World Bank Annual Conference on Development Economics.* Washington: World Bank, 28.
63. Lin, J. (2012) *Demystifying the Chinese Economy.* Cambridge: Cambridge University Press, 75–76.
64. Ibid., 135.
65. *The Elusive Quest for Growth*, 39.

66. White, H. The Macroeconomic Impact of Development Aid: A Critical Survey. In *The Journal of Development Studies*, Vol. 28, No.2, Jan. 1992, 175.
67. Griffin, K, Enos, J. (1970) Foreign Assistance: Objectives and Consequences. In *Economic Development and Cultural Change*, Vol. 18, No.3, April, 320. It should be noted that White argued on page 184 of *The Macroeconomic Impact of Development Aid* that in Griffin and Enos's analysis no allowance is made for the possible effect that aid will have on savings by increasing income through a multiplier effect or its impact on other economic variables.
68. Meier quotes a *bon mot* of Peter Timmer who said that getting the prices right would not guarantee economic development, but getting the prices wrong frequently is the end of development. Source: *The Old Generation and the New*, 17.
69. Baran, P. (1957) *The Political Economy of Growth*. New York: Monthly Review Press; Rodney, W. (1972) How Europe Underdeveloped Africa. London: Bogle-L'Ouverture Publications; Frank, A. (1967) *Capitalism and Underdevelopment in Latin America*. New York: Monthly Review Press; Mandel, E. (1963) Marxist Economic Theory. Brussels: New Left Press.
70. *Economics of Development*, 300.
71. Wallerstein, I. (1974) *The Modern World-System, Vol. I: Capitalist Agriculture and the Origins of the European World-Economy in the Sixteenth Century*. New York/London: Academic Press.
72. Dos Santos, T. (1970) The Structure of Dependence. In *American Economic Review, Papers and Proceedings*, 60(2): 234–236.
73. Dos Santos, T. (1973) The Crisis of Development Theory and the Problem of Dependence in Latin America. In Bernstein, H. (ed.) *Underdevelopment and Development*. Harmondsworth: Penguin.
74. McCloskey, D. (2010) *Bourgeois Dignity; Why Economics Can't Explain the Modern World*. Chicago: Chicago University Press, 231–237.

References

Ackley, G. (1961). *Macroeconomic Theory*. New York: The Macmillan Company.

Adelman, I. (1984). Beyond Export-led Growth. *World Development, 12*(9), 937–949.

Baran, P. (1957). *The Political Economy of Growth*. New York: Monthly Review Press.

Bauer, P. (1948). *The Rubber Industry*. London: Longmans, Green & co.

Bauer, P. (1954). *West African Trade*. Cambridge: Cambridge University Press.

Bauer, P. (1971). *Dissent on Development*. Cambridge: Harvard University Press.

Berendsen, B., Dietz, T., Schulte Nordholt, H., & van der Veen, R. (Eds.). (2013). *Asian Tigers, African Lions: Comparing the Development Performance of Southeast Asia and Africa*. Leiden: Koninklijke Brill.

Chenery, H., & Strout, A. (September 1966). Foreign Assistance and Economic Development. *The American Economic Review, LVI*(4), 679–733.

Clark, C. (1940). *The Conditions of Economic Progress*. London: Macmillan.

De Haan, P. (2016). *From Keynes to Piketty: The Century that Shook Up Economics*. London: Palgrave Macmillan.

Dos Santos, T. (1970). The Structure of Dependence. *American Economic Review, Papers and Proceedings, 60*(2), 231–236.

Dos Santos, T. (1973). The Crisis of Development Theory and the Problem of Dependence in Latin America. In H. Bernstein (Ed.), *Underdevelopment and Development*. Harmondsworth: Penguin.

Easterly, W. (2002). *The Elusive Quest for Growth: Economists' Adventures and Misadventures in the Tropics*. Cambridge: The MIT Press.

Fishlow, A. (2001). Review of *Economic Backwardness in Historical Perspective: A Book of Essays*.

Frank, A. (1967). *Capitalism and Underdevelopment in Latin America*. New York: Monthly Review Press.

Gerschenkron, A. (1952). Economic Backwardness in Historical Perspective. In B. Hoselitz (Ed.), *The Progress of Underdeveloped Areas*. Chicago: University of Chicago Press.

Griffin, K., & Enos, J. (1970). Foreign Assistance: Objectives and Consequences. *Economic Development and Cultural Change, 18*(3), 313–327.

Harberger, A. (1983). The Cost-Benefit Approach to Development Economics. *World Development, 11*(10), 864–866.

Hirschman, A. (1958). *The Strategy of Economic Development*. New Haven: Yale University Press.

Hoyng, A. (2011). *Turgot & Smith: Een Paar Apart*. Doctoral thesis.

Krugman, P. (1992). Toward a Counter-Counterrevolution in Development Theory. In *Proceedings of the World Bank Annual Conference on Development Economics*. Washington: World Bank.

Kuznets, S. (1955). Economic Growth and Income Inequality. *The American Economic Review, XLV*(1), 1–28.

Kuznets, S. (1963). Quantitative Aspects of Economic Growth of Nations: VIII: Distribution of Income by Size. *Economic Development and Cultural Change, XI*(2), 1–80.

Lal, D. (2000). *The Poverty of 'Development Economics'*. Cambridge: The MIT Press.

Lal, D., & Myint, H. (1996). *The Political Economy of Poverty, Equity, and Growth*. Oxford: Oxford University Press.

Lewis, A. (1954). Economic Development with Unlimited Supplies of Labour. *The Manchester School of Economics and Social Studies, 22*(2), 139–191.
Lin, J. (2012). *Demystifying the Chinese Economy*. Cambridge: Cambridge University Press.
Little, I. (1982). *Economic Development: Theory, Policy, and International Relations*. New York: Basic Books.
Mandel, E. (1963). *Marxist Economic Theory*. Brussels: New Left Press.
McCloskey, D. (2010). *Bourgeois Dignity: Why Economics Can't Explain the Modern World*. Chicago: Chicago University Press.
Meier, G. (2001). The Old Generation of Development Economists and the New. In G. Meier & J. Stiglitz (Eds.), *Frontiers of Development Economics*. New York: Oxford University Press.
Myint, H. (1967). Economic Theory and Development Policy. *Economica, 34*(13), 117–130.
Nurkse, R. (1953). *Problems of Capital Formation in Underdeveloped Countries*. Oxford: Basil Blackwell.
Rodney, W. (1972). *How Europe Underdeveloped Africa*. London: Bogle-L'Ouverture Publications.
Rosenstein-Rodan, P. (1943). Problems of Industrialisation of Eastern and South-Eastern Europe. *The Economic Journal, 53*(210/211), 202–213.
Rostow, W. (1971). *The Stages of Economic Growth: A Non-Communist Manifesto* (2nd ed.). Cambridge: Cambridge University Press.
Sen, A. (2009). How Does Development Happen? In *Peter Bauer and the Economics of Prosperity*. Academic Foundation: New Delhi.
Thirlwall, A., & Pacheco-López, P. (2017). *Economics of Development* (10th ed.). London: Palgrave Macmillan.
Tinbergen, J. (1967). *Development Planning*. London: Weidenfeld and Nicholson.
UNIDO. (2012). Climbing the Stairways of Development: Structural Change as the Driver of Economic Growth. *Policy Brief*, May.
Wallerstein, I. (1974). *The Modern World-System, Vol. I: Capitalist Agriculture and the Origins of the European World-Economy in the Sixteenth Century*. New York and London: Academic Press.
White, H. (1992). The Macroeconomic Impact of Development Aid: A Critical Survey. *The Journal of Development Studies, 28*(2), 163–240.
Wickstead, M. (2015). *Aid and Development: A Brief Introduction*. Oxford: Oxford University Press.
World Bank. (2009). *World Development Report 2009 Reshaping Economic Geography*. Washington: World Bank.

CHAPTER 5

The Second Generation of Development Economists

5.1 Introduction

Ricardo Hausmann, Lant Pritchett and Dani Rodrik argue that the 1960s were a good time for developing countries, the 1970s to a slightly lesser extent, while the 1980s were pretty disastrous.[1] This catchy statement requires an explanation. On 15 August 1971, America ended the fixed exchange rate between the dollar and gold on which the Bretton Woods international monetary system was based. Two years later, OPEC raised the price of oil dramatically and repeated it in 1979, which earned their members a lot of so-called petro-dollars, but oil-importing countries were on the losing end. In developed countries interest rates went up, and so did inflation. Economic growth slowed down and unemployment soared—*stagflation* was the result. Consequently, international trade plummeted, pushing down prices of developing countries' export commodities. Neoclassical economics emulated Keynesian economics, since Keynesians did not know how to address *stagflation*. Given their renewed prominence, neoclassical economists influenced the way development economists approached the economic challenges of developing countries.

The unfavourable global economic developments contributed to the exposure of the shortcomings of the first generation's proposals. In addition, governments of many developing countries were ineffective—or simply incompetent—in absorbing international shocks, achieving sustained economic growth, and creating sufficient employment opportunities for their rapidly growing population. Moreover, government policies often

P. de Haan, *Whatever Happened to the Third World?*,
https://doi.org/10.1007/978-3-030-39613-8_5

hindered rather than promoted the free functioning of markets, taking away the necessary incentives for entrepreneurs to invest and produce.[2] After all, farmers, investors, and businessmen in developing countries are not different in their behaviour from those in developed countries: they respond to price and market incentives like anybody else.

Economic growth sputtered, poverty increased, state-owned enterprises made losses. In many developing countries import-substitution resulted in adverse economic effects. The development of the agricultural sector was neglected. All told, government of the typical developing country was unable to implement all the development tasks it was supposed to fulfill. The time for visionary comprehensive development models, like the first generation's, was over. The time was ripe for down-to-earth neoclassical economic analysis and policy advice.

The second generation's mantra was: remove price distortions in order to *get the prices right*, since the central challenge for any developing country was to allocate their scarce resources with a view to maximise economic growth while minimising the use of foreign exchange. Second generation economists were convinced that this was necessary to get the economies of developing economies going again. After all, getting the prices wrong frequently meant a nasty spark in the wheel of development and the beginning of crisis.

Getting the prices right was perhaps necessary, but it was not sufficient. As the implementation of the Washington Consensus philosophy (described below) demonstrated, there was too much reliance on the market and too little appreciation for the market-correcting role of government.

5.2 The Philosophy

The second generation was based upon the neoclassical philosophy of economic rationality, self-interest, and small government. The focus was on the micro level rather than on comprehensive macro models. International aid had still a role to play, but it did not any longer occupy the prominent position it had in the first generation's proposals.

The first thing to do was to remove price distortions and trade protection measures. It was also felt that it weren't so much initial conditions but differences in *policies* that explained the poor performance of developing countries. In other words: a country was not poor because of a vicious circle of poverty; no, it was poor because its policies were poor.

Indeed, policy mattered. The consensus was to aim at policy reform.[3] The goal of promoting domestic industrialisation could best be achieved by export expansion. Economists pointed to the success of the Asian Tiger countries applying export-led growth policies, benefitting from external economic opportunities. Their policy was—after a period of protecting the emerging industrial sector from foreign competition—to concentrate on export promotion, privatisation of state-owned enterprises, while responding to market and price incentives. The Asian Tigers demonstrated that they could very well compete with developed countries, offering a broad range of manufactured goods, including quite sophisticated ones. This is what Anne Krueger observes, including the useful role that aid could play in the process:

> The empirical evidence from both the 'success stories' and the failures among the developing countries is that policies that accompany export-oriented activities, including especially their emphasis on incentives rather than direct controls and on the relatively uniform across-the-board treatment of alternative industries, are more conducive to growth than are import-substitution policies accompanied by specific, direct controls and determination of industry-specific incentives and allocations .... A legitimate and desirable function of foreign aid should therefore be to encourage and facilitate the very difficult process of transition from the latter to the former policies.[4]

The second generation moved, as Gerald Meier observes, away from the first generation's 'grand theories' towards a microeconomic approach. Disaggregated micro-studies were undertaken in which the units of analysis were, for example, agricultural production and household units. These studies constituted the basis of specific sectoral or fiscal policies, and the basis of guiding policy in the macroeconomic domain. Studies in the field of agriculture presented evidence that misguided agricultural pricing policies had an adverse effect on the gap between rural and urban incomes, on the incentives to produce food and export crops, and on employment opportunities in farming and rural industries.[5]

Empirical data became widely available, allowing model building around e.g., household behaviour and the impact of human capital investments in education and health. The question of *how* capital was allocated in an efficient manner was more relevant than the *level* of capital accumulation, as the first generation had proposed. Second generation economists argued that the saving rate was less relevant than the question in which productive activities capital was invested. They referred to India—the country registered high saving rates, yet its growth was slow.[6]

The financial sector had also been neglected by the first generation. The typical developing country suffered from financial bottlenecks and financial repression. The second generation studied the possibilities of improving financial systems, so that banks and money—and capital markets could function properly. In other words, a financial environment was to be developed in which there would be efficient financial intermediation between savers and investors, and in which the system would ensure the efficient allocation of investment funds.

Development Economics: A Sub-discipline?

The simplest description of development economics is that what development economists do. This description does not really help to understand what exactly they do. As noted, the neo-classical doctrine says that the postulates of rationality and the principles of maximisation are universally applicable, so there was no need for a sub-discipline of development economics. However, Christopher Bliss presents a different view:

> General economic principles are precisely too general to give us insights into applications for less developed economies. Alone, the parts of economic theory and method they apply more or less universally tell us less than we need in particular applications. To give them life they have to be enlarged and translated. When this is done a specialty is created. Development economics consists in part of the refinement of general economics to deal with questions that arose in the context of development, and partly of certain special ideas that have proved useful in studying developing countries.[7]

This is what Anthony Thirlwall and Penélope Pacheco-López observe:

> While it might be argued that the basic microeconomic assumptions about how people behave are similar for all countries, developing countries still differ structurally from rich ones and therefore require different models. The differences between the two sets of countries are large, particularly in relation to resource allocation and matters relating to long-term growth.[8]

Ian Little had this to say about development economics:

> As the differences mount, perhaps the term [development economics, PdH] will disappear, and we shall speak only of economists specializing in particular groups of countries that do have a lot in common. Development economics will then have ceased to exist. But in the past, there has been a perception of sufficient homogeneity, even if it was sometimes misleading.[9]

Anne Krueger predicts that development economics might evolve into an applied field:

> Once it is recognized that individuals respond to incentives, and that 'market failure' is the result of inappropriate incentives rather than of nonresponsiveness, the separateness of development economics as a field largely disappears. Instead, it becomes an applied field, in which the tools and insights of labor economics, agricultural economics, international economics, public finance and other fields are addressed to the special questions and policy issues that arise in the context of development.[10]

This is what Syed Naqvi succinctly argues:

> Development economics is the only branch of economics that attempts to understand and explain the nature of the development process.[11]

Gerald Meier sums up as follows:

> But as long as the developing countries have characteristics that distinguish them from industrial countries, a subdiscipline of development economics will be relevant. And even though there is a set of basic economic principles, their particular application to any one country will depend on the economic structure, institutions, political regime, administrative capacity, culture, and history of the particular country.[12]

5.3 The Washington Consensus

The 1980s and the 1990s were traumatic decades for many developing countries. Gradually it became clear that getting the prices right had not necessarily brought about economic growth. Let me explain. During the 1970s, most Latin American governments had borrowed heavily—their public sector spending almost doubled (see Chap. 2). In 1982 Mexico defaulted and soon after, other large Latin American countries also had to call in financial help. During the 1980s and 1990s, most African

Given the worrying financial and economic situation to be addressed, most of the Washington Consensus proposals make sense at first sight. The proposals reflect some elements of the reforms that Latin American countries had embarked on during the 1980s.[13] The analysis was that in the development process, the market ought to play a more prominent role, and government a less prominent one. The Table 5.1 below contains ten original and ten augmented elements of the Washington Consensus.

Table 5.1 Rules of good behavior for the promotion of economic growth

Original Washington Consensus	*'Augmented' Washington Consensus (additions to the original 10 items)*
1. Fiscal discipline	11. Corporate governance
2. Reorientation of public expenditures	12. Anticorruption
3. Tax reform	13. Flexible labor markets
4. Interest rate liberalization	14. Adherence to WTO disciplines
5. Unified and competitive exchange rates	15. Adherence to international financial codes and standards
6. Trade liberalization	16. 'Prudent' capital-account opening
7. Openness to direct foreign investment	17. Non-intermediate exchange rate regimes
8. Privatization	18. Independent central banks/inflation targeting
9. Deregulation	19. Social safety nets
10. Secure property rights	20. Targeted poverty reduction

Source: Rodrik, D. (2007) *One Economics, Many Recipes; Globalization, Institutions, and Economic Growth*. Princeton: Princeton University Press, 17

Joseph Stiglitz is critical of the Washington Consensus. He argues that markets are inherently imperfect. The objective of structural reform, he argues, should have been to construct a well-performing economy, given the limitations in information, the costs of setting up markets, and the persistent irrationalities of individuals.

The original Washington Consensus 'dose' had overlooked the harsh effects on the poor population, and, surely, they suffered most. Social safety nets and targeted poverty reduction formed integral parts of the 'augmented' Washington Consensus. The idea behind the augmented version is that promoting market-oriented growth is one thing, but if this is not embedded in the necessary institutional reforms, the poor will remain poor and economic growth will not be sustained.

Dani Rodrik observes that the IMF and WB had difficulties in designing *tailor-made* financial and institutional approaches to overcoming the financial, economic, and institutional challenges of each specific developing country. Instead, the they prescribed a *one-size-fits-all* approach. Yet Rodrik argues: 'No one can seriously oppose the introduction of proper accounting standards or improved prudential supervision of financial intermediaries. The more serious concern with regard to IFI [International Financial Institutions; PdH] conditionality is that such standards will act as the wedge with which a broader set of institutional preferences, friendly to open capital accounts, deregulated labor markets, arm′s-length finance, and American-style corporate governance, and hostile to industrial policies—will be imposed on the recipient countries.'[14]

Rodrik did not suggest that the Washington Consensus was a 'silly' approach; no, '... it is the result of systematic thinking about the multiple, often complementary reforms needed to establish property rights, put market incentives to work, and maintain macroeconomic stability.'[15] However, there might be better ways of achieving the Washington Consensus goals. The Asian Tiger countries developed along the lines of the following principles: (1) fiscal conservatism; (2) investment in human resources; and (3) export orientation. They were embedded in institutional arrangements, in line with the countries' specific institutional environment. The Washington Consensus became a 'damaged brand'. It would have been better, as Rodrik suggests, instead of completing a long laundry list of reforms, to identify the most binding constraints, and once they had been addressed successfully, they would be superseded by others.

economies did not grow at all; their economies shrank. There was an urgent need to restore order in governments' finances, and do away with overvalued national currencies. Fundamental policy reform was required, including trimming down overextended governments.

By necessity, addressing government failure remained the main objective; a good second one was creating conditions for the market to play its allocative role. The way forward, it was thought, was to move from inward-looking strategies towards liberalisation of foreign trade; to introduce stabilisation programs; to privatise state-owned enterprises, and to let prices be set by the market—in short the Washington Consensus philosophy.

The International Monetary Fund (IMF), the World Bank (WB)—and in their slipstream bilateral donor agencies—were prepared to help with stabilisation credits (IMF) and structural adjustment loans (WB), under the strict condition that recipient countries would implement the Washington Consensus 'recipe', elaborated in the box below.

5.4 Growth Theories Revisited

During the second generation's era, scholarly interest in economic growth revived. This was important for developing countries because understanding what the sources of economic growth would be, helps to invest in them. And if successful, it would contribute to economic growth, the creation of jobs and higher per capita incomes. Economic growth also makes it affordable for governments to invest in people's abilities (i.e., education, technical training), and higher incomes help people to invest in themselves. Last but not least, economic growth helps to lift the poor out of poverty.

The most important question in economics is also the most difficult one: why do some countries stay poor while others grow rich? Economists have not yet been able to fully understand growth: where does it come from; what are precisely the sources that trigger growth? What we do know is that sustained economic growth started in the eighteenth century. Before that time, economies were rather stationary; i.e., there were periods during which there was limited growth, but after a while it petered out. The history since the Industrial Revolution also taught us that economic growth had something to do with technological progress; technology greatly helped to boost productivity and to produce new ideas.

5.4.1 From Harrod-Domar to Solow

As mentioned in Chap. 4, development economists initially used the Harrod-Domar growth model. Robert Solow (and Trevor Swan's comparable model) broadened the understanding of growth by introducing three propositions: (1) in the long-run steady state, output growth is determined by the rate of growth of the labour force plus the rate of growth of labour productivity. Ouput growth is independent of the ratio of saving and investment to GDP[16]; (2) the level of per capita income does depend on the saving and investment ratio to GDP (the level of per capita income varies positively with the saving-investment ratio and negatively with the rate of growth of the population); (3) if there is an inverse relation across countries between the capital-labour ratio—and the productivity of capital, tastes (i.e., savings behaviour) and technology are the same across countries—poor countries with a small amount of capital per head should grow faster than rich countries with a lot of capital per head, leading to the *convergence of per capita incomes* and living standards across the world.[17]

The neoclassical assumption of diminishing returns to capital, is a central assumption in Solow's model.

Diminishing returns to capital imply that the more machines you add to each worker, the return to each machine will become lower. But the economic history of developed countries proved that there were no

Gunnar Myrdal (1898–1987) rejected Solow's long-term equilibrium perspective. His *cumulative causation* hypothesis projected that there would be areas that will prosper while others decline.[18] For example, changes in supply may be expected to react on demand in such a way as to counteract the tendency towards equilibrium. For example: migration from one region to another will lower human capital as well as the number of entrepreneurs in the former. Both will depress the demand for products, adding to the downward slope of the demand curve, while development in the latter will stimulate demand for products, adding to the demand for production and labour. In the prospering area, a sort of multiplier-accelerator mechanism will be at play which results in increasing returns. Hence, there is no tendency to arrive at an equilibrium situation.

Where regional imbalances occur, Myrdal observed that developed countries try to redress these imbalances. But in many poor countries regional inequalities have been magnified, as a result of political power in the hands of the rich.

diminishing returns. Developed economies, like the United States (Solow applied his theory to the US, by the way), have grown on average 1.9% over the past two centuries. So the question arose: how come? Solow concluded that it was technological progress that did the trick. In other words: technological progress compensated diminishing returns, resulting in constant economic growth over the long haul. Each worker became more productive thanks to new technological applications.

As mentioned, growth is created by an effective combination of growth of the labour force and the rate of growth of labour productivity as a result of technological progress, which is treated as a residual exogenous factor.[19] Some economists, such as Arnold Harberger, saw the residual technological progress factor as a composite of the effects of different forces: (1) improvement in the quality of labour through education; (2) reallocation of resources from low-productivity uses to higher uses, either through normal market forces, or through the reduction of barriers or distortions; (3) exploitation of economies of scale; and (4) improved ways of combining resources to produce goods and services, not just at the level of new machines or processes, but also by relatively mundane adjustments at the level of the factory or the farm.[20]

We have seen that a key prediction of Solow's model was *converging* of per capita incomes across the world. William Easterly explained: 'Any country that starts out with low capital will offset this unlucky heritage with very high returns to capital. Since international finance capital flows to countries with the highest rate of return, international financial capital will flow to this high-return and low-capital country. The unlucky country will catch up to the more fortunate countries, erasing the memory of its unlucky beginnings.'[21] But in most cases, this did not happen. Poor countries did *not* grow faster than rich countries. After 1981, Latin America and Africa did even worse.[22]

Easterly had already observed that the Harrod-Domar growth model was inadequate to explain growth (see Chap. 4). Solow's model seemed more useful. But were there diminishing returns to capital? New theories (see below) argue that the answer is no. The change in the Solow vision, adds Easterly, was to make technology, and other things that make a given amount of labour go further, *respond to incentives*. Easterly explains that diminishing returns require one ingredient of production to be in fixed supply, like the labour force. But profit-seeking entrepreneurs will find ways to get around the constraint of fixed labour. They have a clear incentive to look for labour-saving new technologies. The effect of incentives on growth was a fundamental change from the Solow framework in which technological progress determined economic growth in the long run.[23]

5.4.2 New Endogenous Growth Theory

Studies appeared that, indeed, could not find convergence of per capita incomes in the world economy, as Solow predicted. New endogenous growth theory attempted to provide a response to this unexplained phenomenon; i.e., why the difference in living standards in the world economy seemed so persistent. Economics Nobel Laureate Paul Romer is a prominent representative of the new endogenous growth theory, along with Robert Lucas, and Sergio Rebelo.[24]

Now, suppose there are no diminishing returns to capital but—instead—constant returns, implying a constancy of the capital-output ratio. This means that the capital-output ratio will not rise when more investment takes place. At the same time this means that the saving and investment to GDP ratio *does* matter for growth. So, it was no longer the growth of the *exogenous factors* (the growth of the labour force and technological progress) that explained growth. Under the new assumption, saving and investment—both *endogenous factors*—explain growth. In addition, the new endogenous growth theory accorded more weight to another endogenous factor—human capital formation: investing in people to create healthy and better educated economic actors becoming more productive. These healthier and better educated people 'embody' technical progress, so to speak. The acquisition of knowledge, triggers constant or even *increasing* returns.

New knowledge is created by new ideas, learning by doing, and by investing in education, research and development. The new endogenous growth theory also focuses on positive spillover effects of a knowledge-based economy, as knowledge may very well trigger an increasing marginal product. This insight meant that the earlier emphasis on physical capital accumulation was giving way to human capital formation, through education, skills training, institutions, and research and development.

In Romer's own words: 'The rate of investment and the rate of return on capital may increase rather than decrease with increases in the capital stock. The level of per capita output in different countries need not converge; growth may be persistently slower in less-developed countries and may even fail to take place at all. These results do not depend on any kind of exogenously specified technical change or differences between countries .... What is crucial for all of the results is a departure from the usual assumption of diminishing returns.'[25] Regarding the role of knowledge, Romer argues: 'The creation of new knowledge by one firm is assumed to have a positive external effect on the production possibilities of other firms because knowledge cannot be perfectly patented or kept secret. Most important, production of consumption goods as a function of the stock of knowledge and other inputs exhibits increasing returns; more precisely, knowledge may have an increasing marginal product.'[26]

In sum, the constant or increasing returns phenomenon is the cornerstone of the new endogenous growth theory. This new, ideas-based, theory says that ideas and investments in human capital and knowledge are both significant contributors to economic growth, preventing the marginal product of capital from falling and the capital-output ratio from rising.

Deepak Lal and Hla Myint did not find endogenous growth theories persuasive enough. The reasons being:

> ... their implausible assumption that there are externalities from physical and human capital, so that there are strictly constant returns to capital, ... and partly because they involve merely mathematical tinkering within the standard Solow-Swan model without any fundamental rethinking of its building blocks.[27]

According to them, it was M.F. Scott who did this rethinking. The Scott model belongs to the so-called generalised capital accumulation approach that considers capital accumulation as broadly defined to include all forms of investment (such as adding to material capital, increasing health, discipline, skill and education, and moving labour into more productive occupations) which lead income over time. This wider notion of investment as the prime mover of growth does make growth endogenous, facilitating 'the discussion on growth policy by emphasizing the relative returns from alternative investments or currently available resources.'[28]

Contrary to the Solow model, Scott maintains that there are no diminishing returns to cumulative gross investment. However, there could indeed be diminishing returns to the *rate* of investment. Scott also argues that there is no need to invoke any exogenous technical progress to explain growth, since growth—due to capital and technical progress—is both the result of investment in the sense of the cost, in terms of consumption foregone, of propelling the economy forward instead of leaving in a stationary state.

Within Scott's proposed model, the rate of increase of income is a function of two variables: total savings and growth of the labour force. He furthermore argues that the economy's technology is best depicted by a set of inexhaustible investment opportunities. Scott recognises that catching up is possible as a result of new inventions. However, the set of investment opportunities may shrink or expand; there is no rule that says that there would be a constant set. Scott provides an empirical analysis of the conformity of the growth experience of developed countries in terms of his model. According to Lal and Myint, all of Scott's statistical tests demonstrate that his model can explain a very large part in growth performance of developed countries.[29]

It is not surprising that the Lal and Myint liked Scott's model since it emphasises that it is differences in the level and returns on investment which are the proximate determinants of differences in growth rates. This is, by and large, what Lal and Myint's 21 country-analysis also brought to light; that it is the efficiency of externally-directed investments (i.e., moving to free trade leads to a higher rate of growth) which plays a prominent part in explaining faster growth. But not the only part. Institutions also matter; in particular the stability of property rights also contribute to sustainable growth. The authors added that the main sources of growth (i.e., entrepreneurship, productivity, and thrift) can best be fostered within an economic framework that maintains stable property rights.

5.4.2.1 Convergence

The new endogenous growth theory attempts to explain growth rate differences between countries. The test for the new endogenous growth theory was to see whether or not poor countries would grow faster than rich ones. In other words, whether there was an inverse relation between the growth of output and the *initial* level of per capita income. If this was *not* the case, then the outcome would confirm the new growth theory's assertion that the marginal product of capital does not decline.

There are many factors that can prevent the marginal product of capital from falling as countries invest more and get richer, such as education, research and development, and trade, so that the endogenous factor investment does matter for long-run growth, and not Solow's exogenous factor of technological progress. As mentioned, Solow predicts that poor countries grow faster than rich countries, leading to a convergence of per capita incomes, while the new endogenous growth theory implies a different outcome.

Now, the literature speaks of unconditional convergence if poor countries grow faster than rich ones; however, without allowing for any other economic, social, or political differences between them. Obviously, this is an unrealistic assumption. Thirlwall and Pacheco-López rightly observe that there can never be the presumption of unconditional convergence; only one of *conditional convergence*, which implies holding constant all other factors that influence the growth of per capita income. For example, a study undertaken in 1992 by Robert Barro and Xavier Sala-i-Martin, introduced the notion of conditional convergence of countries' levels of income, where the institutional policy mix is similar between them.[30] They found convergence of levels of income between US states since 1840. The authors suggest that convergence can happen when the institutional, political, and policy setting of countries is similar.

In 1995, both scholars presented a model that combined elements of endogenous growth with the convergence implications of the Solow model.[31] In the long run, the authors argue, the world growth rate is driven by discoveries in the technologically leading economies. Followers converge toward the leaders because copying is cheaper than innovation. However, as the pool of copiable material decreases, the costs of imitation tend to rise and, consequently, the followers' growth rate tends to fall. Hence a pattern of conditional convergence emerges. In the long run, the

Rodrik (2013) found that if only the manufacturing sector of countries is considered, there is evidence of ***unconditional convergence***, taking a sample of over 100 developed and developing countries since 1990. This is not surprising, observe Thirlwall and Pacheco-López, because manufacturing industries produce tradable goods subject to competitive pressure in a global environment where there is scope for technological transfer and the absorption of new knowledge. Traditional agriculture and non-trade goods do not share these characteristics. This suggests that lack of unconditional convergence across countries has to do with the structural characteristics of countries and particularly the relative shares of traded and non-traded goods.[32]

authors conclude, all economies grow at the rate of discovery in the leading economies. In this model, the rate of discovery plays the role that the exogenous rate of technical change plays in the Solow model. copying inventions.

Angus Maddison (1926–2010) had this to say about the relevance of the distinction between conditional and unconditional convergence:

> The new growth theory has been useful in re-emphasising a number of fundamental issues concerning the interrelation of technical progress, economies of scale and formation of physical and human capital. The distinction between the 'conditional' convergence of countries where the institutional policy mix is similar and repudiation of the idea of 'unconditional' convergence (on a global scale) is useful and is one way of bringing attention to the interaction of 'proximate' and 'ultimate' causal influences. It is a fundamental point ... and it is central to North's (1990) attempt to develop a broader view of growth causality.[33]

As mentioned in Chap. 1, Branko Milanovic concludes that due to the increase of mean incomes in Asian countries, the income gaps between countries have actually been narrowing. If this trend of economic convergence continues, not only will it lead to shrinking global inequality but it will, indirectly, also give relatively greater salience to inequality within nations.[34]

5.5 Empirical Studies

In explaining growth, important variables turned out to be the ones that have traditionally been at the heart of mainstream growth theory: investment and capital accumulation. For example, over the period 1960–1994, Abdelhak Senhadji concludes—on the basis of a study involving 66 countries (including 44 developing countries)—that, indeed, capital accumulation was by far the most important contributing factor to growth in all the countries.[35] In East Asia total factor productivity also contributed to growth, but it in a limited way.

The outcome of similar studies is that the principal source of growth in developing counties consisted of increased factor inputs, helped by a healthier and better educated work force. Total factor productivity did not contribute as much, compared to that in developed countries. Resource transfers from agriculture to industry were also important contributors to growth. These transfers will become more important once the ability of the industrial sector to absorb surplus labour will increase.[36] In sum, more capital and industry's ability to absorb surplus labour triggered growth; capital formation was the most important contributing factor.

However, cross-country analyses reach conflicting conclusions. Intercountry growth differences remain unexplained, caused by, among others, limited availability of data, unequal preconditions for development, and countries' heterogeneity in their structure and institutions.[37]

It is difficult to characterise the growth of many developing countries by a single time trend, simply because growth is a volatile phenomenon. As we saw in Chap. 1, the economies of developing countries do not grow in a steady, linear manner. Given their volatility, it makes sense to find out what the causes would be for growth accelerations and growth slowdowns. Moreover, the experience with the Washington Consensus one-size-fits-all approach learns that a tailor-made approach would be better. Such an approach requires an analysis of the factors that explain a particular country's poor growth performance. In other words, a so-called spray-gun approach may not address the *binding constraints* hard enough to turn the country's economy around. It is much better to undertake 'growth diagnostics', which locates the binding constraints on economic performance, and address them directly. An example: as investment is an important factor in long term growth, it makes sense to ask why is investment low in a particular developing country? Once the diagnosis is done, targeted reform policies can be applied (while others are ruled out) to take away the constraint involved.

5.6 Asia and sub-Saharan Africa Compared

Cross-country comparative studies were undertaken to better understand why certain development policies worked better than others, such as Lal and Myint's 21-countries study, seeking links between economic and political characteristics and economic growth. Another one is entitled *Asian Tigers, African Lions.*[38] Its central question is why, since independence, sub-Saharan African (SSA) countries have not become richer, while countries in Southeast Asia have. The question is the more puzzling when one realises that as late as 1980, average income levels in SSA and Southeast Asia were similar. A sample of four Asian and four African countries was put together in Asian-African pairs, to analyse their respective growth trajectories.[39] The outcome was interesting, in that critical turning points (i.e., the year in which average incomes started to increase in a sustained manner in combination with sustained poverty reduction) were identified in most Southeast Asian countries, while they were absent in all four African countries.

A major area of policy, associated with these turning points, was state-led rural and agricultural development which triggered higher incomes for peasant farmers.[40] This policy was absent in the SSA countries—rural and agricultural development was neglected. Political realities in Southeast Asia forced Asian elites to take the interests of peasant farmers seriously, either in view of potential communist threats, or of concerns on the part of liberalising post-revolutionary states (i.e., Vietnam) to avoid alienating their mass support base. In all of the Southeast Asian cases there has been considerable state involvement in the economy with respect to agriculture: fertiliser and credit subsidies, provision for subsidised purchase of crops when market prices fell below guaranteed minimum levels, and restrictions on the import and export of food.[41]

The spectacular economic growth of Southeast Asian countries went hand in hand with equally spectacular poverty reduction. In 2005, the percentage of Southeast Asia's population living on less than the equivalent of US$ 1.25 per day was 19%, against 39% in 1990. In contrast, the percentages for SSA were 51% in 2005 against 58% in 1990.[42] Sustained economic growth, in combination with poverty reduction, was also associated with sound macroeconomic management and economic freedom for peasant farmers and small entrepreneurs.

The authors of *Asian Tigers, African Lions* conclude that there are three preconditions for a developing economy's take-off: (1) macroeconomic stability; (2) economic freedom for peasants and small entrepreneurs; and (3) massive pro-poor public spending. However, what was not analysed is a sensitive, arguably politically-incorrect, element. In *Economics of Development*, this element is described as follows: 'Other countries may lack the psychological conditions required for modernization, built on individualism and the competitive spirit, coupled with a strong work ethic, rationalism and scientific thought, which characterized the Industrial Revolutions of eighteenth- and nineteenth-century Europe, and which played a large part in the emergence of the newly industrialized Southeast Asian countries in the latter half of the twentieth century.'[43]

The methodological weakness of cross-country studies is that factors that had not been taken into consideration, may also have had an influence on economic growth. Ironically, some scholars argue that empirical studies measure without theory. A growing number of economic development studies take history as the basis for the quest for growth, as elaborated in Chap. 6. This historical vantage point may be the most promising approach to the understanding of economic growth, as economic historians take phenomena like culture and politics on board, which both impinge upon a country's economic growth or stagnation for that matter.

5.7 Dissenters

Is it true that once a developing country got the prices right, as second generation development economists maintained, the country's economic future would be brighter? Markets, under the right assumptions, may indeed function well in directing the efficient allocation of scarce resources. However, during the second generation's era studies appeared in which price distortions in developing countries were criticised: imperfect information, protectionism, and rent-seeking hindered the efficient allocation of investment funds. In short, new market failures were exposed.

Stiglitz, for example, observes that market imperfections exist as a result of imperfect information of buyers and sellers. This imperfect information is particularly notorious in the agriculture and finance sectors.[44] In addition, the question can be raised whether the market can stand the test of societal acceptance; i.e., is the income distribution, as a result of the free functioning of the market, socially acceptable? Correction of these market failures was called for.

Another dissenter is Ha-Joon Chang. Instead of using the term 'neoclassical economics', Chang uses 'neoliberalism'. Chang fires his first salvo by stating that: 'Neoliberalism simply has not been able to generate rapid growth.'[45] He refers to the poor economic record of developing countries caused by neoliberal policies forced upon them. In addition, the more serious issue, according to Chang, is that economic growth that was gained as a result of neoliberal policies was disappointingly low in comparison with the previous, interventionist, period between 1950 and 1970s. He substantiates his argument as follows:

> Per capita income growth in the developed countries slowed from 3.2% to 2.2% between the interventionist period 1960–1980 and the neoliberal period of 1980–99, while that in the developing countries halved from 3% to 1.5%—and without the strong growth performance during the last two decades by China and India, two countries that have definitely not followed the neoliberal recipe, the 1.5% rate would have been close to 1% .... In this period, economic growth basically evaporated in Latin America, with the annual growth rate of per capita income crashing from 3.1% in the period 1960–80 to 0.6% between 1980 and 1999 .... Per capita income has actually been shrinking in the Middle East and North Africa (at the annual rate of −0.2%) and in Sub Saharan Africa (at the annual rate of −0.7%) during the last two decades, whereas they grew at the rates of 2.5% and 2% respectively during 1960–80.[46]

I am afraid that Chang did not consider the question what state-led development of the typical developing country had contributed to economic growth. For example, was it wise to concentrate on capital-intensive industrialisation while neglecting the agricultural sector and the need to create jobs? And why had the public sector of many developing countries expanded beyond financial affordability? Chang also does not take into consideration the positive influence of the *Golden Age* (1950–1973) on economic growth and the trade balance of developing countries, thanks to the high demand of their export commodities.

In line with new endogenous growth theory, William Easterly argues that knowledge—and its spread—is an important growth ingredient. However, poor countries are typically trapped by a vicious circle of having a small knowledge base which does not create the *incentives* to invest more into knowledge, which in turn perpetuates the vicious circle. A pure laissez-faire policy may indeed leave the economy in a vicious circle. Markets will often need an injection through government subsidies to start the knowledge ball rolling.[47]

5.8 The Best of the Two Generations

Had the proposals of the first generation been off the mark? Ironically, some of the second generation's suggestions make the first generations' credible again. Even Krugman who, as we saw in Chap. 4, was critical about the first generation, observes:

> What was ironic was that a competitive neoclassical orthodoxy settled in on the development front just as the orthodoxy was breaking up in other fields .... We can now see that whatever bad policies may have been implemented in the name of high development theory, the theory itself makes quite a lot of sense. Indeed, in some ways it was a remarkable anticipation of ideas that would come to analytical fruition thirty years later in the field, for example, of international trade and economic growth.[48]

Krugman proposes a counter-counter revolution in development theory. The first generation developed the 'high development theory', as Krugman calls it. Its weakness was the failure to translate its proposed approaches into formal models. While the first generation proposed some counterproductive economic policies (described in Chap. 4), nonetheless, a set of core ideas of this generation deserved to be recognised after all. What high development theory did not see (but here and there implied), and what new trade theory and new growth theory *did* see, was the phenomenon of increasing returns.[49] What high development theory also did not see was economies of scale. Yet, what had been overlooked, argues Krugman, was what some first generation economists indeed said—or implied—regarding external economies, strategic complementarity, and economic development at large; these issues remain valid.[50]

During the course of the 1970s, the Third World started to fall apart, in the sense that East Asian countries really took off, while most other developing countries did not. So, the question arose what was it that helped the successful ones to forge ahead? What these countries did was to successfully combine central elements of fist generation *and* second generation development economics, as elaborately described in *The East Asian Miracle*, summarised below.[51]

5.8.1 *The East Asian Miracle*

Peter Berger (1929–2017) wrote a bestseller, entitled *The Capitalist Revolution*.[52] He explained that he did not start writing his book with a pro-capitalist bias. Yet, he added that the sheer pressure of empirical evidence led him to his pro-capitalist position. *The Capitalist Revolution* contains various references to the impressive economic success of the Four Asian Tigers: Hong Kong, South Korea, Singapore, and Taiwan. The turning point in Berger's thinking occurred somewhere during the 1970s when he realised what these four countries had been able to achieve. This experience made it difficult for him to remain even-handed between capitalist and socialist development models.

Berger was only partly right in suggesting that a capitalist approach explains the Four Tigers' rapid economic growth. *The East Asian Miracle* provides a broader analysis of the successful post-WWII economic growth of the Four Tigers, plus Indonesia, Japan, Malaysia, and Thailand. The report refers to these eight countries as High-Performing Asian Economies (HPAEs). The policies applied by them were a mix of state-led and market-led policies. What the first generation of development economists emphasised (i.e., state-led development, in particular investments in industrialisation), and what the second generation had to say (i.e., getting the prices right) was applied by HPAEs. In addition, the institutional context within which these policies were implemented was as important to their success as the policies themselves.[53]

The East Asian Miracle, promoted and funded by the government of Japan, but researched and written by World Bank staff, concludes that most of HPAEs' spectacular growth was due to superior accumulation of physical and human capital.[54] The eight countries did not apply one 'East Asian model'; no, each of them applied a mix of policies suited to their own political, cultural, and historical context—they were thus country-specific.

Common Threads

All HIPAEs combined rapid and sustained economic growth with a reasonable income distribution. They all underwent rapid demographic transitions (i.e., lowering population growth rates), boasted strong and productive agricultural sectors and increased their exports rapidly. The HPAEs also differed from other developing countries, in that they registered high rates of private investment combined with a rising pool of educated people, thanks to public investments in primary and secondary education. Last but not least, their productivity improved dramatically, explained by a combination of success at allocating capital to high-yielding investments, and technologically catching up.

From 1965 to 1990, all twenty-three economies of East Asia grew faster than all other regions in the world.[55] The income distribution of the HPAEs greatly improved compared to other countries. Absolute poverty declined: in Indonesia, for example, from 58% in 1960 to 17% in 1990, and in Malaysia from 37% to less than 5% over the same period.

Human welfare also improved. Primary and secondary education, as well as vocational training were promoted, resulting in an appropriately trained labour force. The emphasis on education, facilitated the supply of qualified personnel and satisfied the wealth-sharing objective, since better educated people typically earn higher incomes.

Getting the Basics Right

The HPAEs did not so much get the prices right; they got the *basics* right. What was involved? Private domestic investment thrived along with rapidly growing human capital. High saving levels sustained high investment levels. The agricultural sector achieved rapid growth and rapid productivity improvement.

Some HPAEs started their economic growth trajectory already equipped with an educated population and a high-quality civil service wielding considerable power. The report's authors observed that there was little that is 'miraculous' about HPAEs' superior record of growth; it was largely due to superior accumulation of physical and human capital.[56] Macroeconomic management was unusually good and its performance was stable, providing a solid base for private investment. Fiscal deficits were limited and inflation was kept in check. The integrity of the banking system was enhanced. All HPAEs kept price distortions in check. All of them welcomed foreign ideas and technology.

The Role of Government

In most HPAEs government played an active developmental role, including the development of specific industries (the descriptions of South Korea's and Singapore's development in Chap. 2 are illustrative). This was done, among others, through subsidised credit to selected industries, and the protection of domestic import substitutes. This was not all; subsidising declining industries, establishing government banks, investing in applied research, establishing export targets, and developing export promotion institutions were also done.

The report's authors wondered whether government interventions were good for growth or not. They concluded that in a few countries, mainly in Northeast Asia (in Southeast Asia governments intervened less), government interventions resulted in higher growth than otherwise would have occurred. But the prerequisites for success were so rigorous that policymakers trying to follow similar paths in other developing countries, often met with failure.[57] The combination of macroeconomic stability, high levels of domestic savings, capital and human resources accumulation, efficient allocation of resources, export promotion, plus rapid technological catch-up, explain HPAEs success.

Institutions

Institutions play a crucial role in HPAEs' development. Unlike protection of property rights, transaction costs, enforcement of contracts (terms frequently used by institutional economists), the authors analysed institutions in the context of wealth-sharing programs designed to include the middle class and the poor in HPAEs' economic growth processes. The important role played by a meritocratic civil service was also highlighted, as well as institutions and mechanisms, such as deliberation councils, that promoted the sharing of information and win the support of the business community. The political leadership promoted mechanisms that increased upward economic and social mobility, rather than the introduction of redistributive policies.

As for a meritocratic civil service, it should enjoy 'technocratic insulation' to ensure formulation of policies in accordance with national goals with a minimum of lobbying from politicians and interest groups. Competency, status, and competitive salaries breed integrity. Most successful were Japan, Hong Kong, Singapore, Taiwan, China, and South Korea. In the other HPAEs the civil service was not capable enough to insulate itself from outside influence. Bluntly stated, the bureaucracies of Indonesia, Malaysia, and Thailand may not have been free from corrupt practices.

Comments

It would have been interesting to have the 1993 *The East Asian Miracle* exercise repeated a decade later. Since 1993, countries like Indonesia, Thailand, Malaysia, and South Korea were hit hard by the 1997 Asian financial crisis. These countries had established high real interest rates to attract capital inflows and foreign direct investment. They also had liberalised their capital account, thus permitting destabilising short-term capital outflows which eventually led to financial contagion. This was not foreseen by the study since the macroeconomic and monetary policies applied by the HPAES were judged as balanced. But they appeared not to be so balanced. It must be admitted that recovery from the financial crisis started in 1999; only two years after the crisis broke out. The authors also failed to pay attention to Japan's ongoing deflation; what exactly caused it, what was done about it, and why did it continue for such a long time? Political unrest broke out in Thailand, Malaysia, and Indonesia. Had economic growth not been shared enough or did graft and corruption play an important explanatory role? All interesting political-economic research questions which would have deserved a renewed analysis.

Alice Amsden is critical about *The East Asian Miracle*. She argues that the report reflects the Bank's development philosophy rather than a truly independent analysis of East Asia's economic success.[58] Amsden observes that the report widened the debate within bank circles on the role of the state in economic development; a debate, she adds, that was overshadowed by the neoliberal Washington Consensus. The report radiated, as Amsden admits, a good understanding of East Asian institutions, and also how deviations from the free market model had promoted development. Nonetheless, the report's overall conclusion was that the HPAEs thanked their spectacular growth above all to a market-friendly approach, including getting the basics right. The Bank's error was that it believed to be possible to disentangle the 'macro' basics (i.e., investment, education, exports) from their 'micro' foundations and supporting institutions. Once macro and micro are integrated, growth becomes complex and the Bank's attempt to attribute most of East Asia's development to market fundamentalism becomes misleading. The author provides various examples of successful state-led investments and interventions in HPAE countries.

How could the Bank transfer the East Asian model to countries that have remained underdeveloped? This is Amsden's answer: 'This cannot be done by force-feeding one East Asian model to all poor countries, as the Bank has tried to do with its 'market-friendly' approach. But a step in the right direction would have been to begin to explore and analyze systematically which of East Asia's supporting institutions has served investment, education, and exports especially well with an eye toward what must be done to modify these institutions to make them work elsewhere.'[59]

Krugman argues that there was no miracle involved in East Asia's growth.[60] He argues that the rapid growth in output in these economies was driven mainly by the rapid growth in inputs. In Krugman's regressions, there was no total factor productivity growth or technical progress, as measured by the residual in Solow's growth model. He concludes that East Asia's growth is not sustainable.

Krugman was proven wrong not only by the economic developments since, but also by Singapore's former Prime Minister Lee Kwan Yew, who observed that Singapore's annual rate of capital accumulation had exceeded 40% for four decades, and yet the return on capital had not declined. This is impossible without technological progress. How come? Justin Lin provides an explanation: '... the reason that we see low or no residual in the growth of developing countries is that their technological progress relies on technology borrowings, mainly through imports of capital goods. In other words the cost of technological progress is counted as a capital input. So, there is no residual in the statistics. But this definitely does not mean that there is no technological progress, because the import of better equipment also suggests improvement in technology.'[61]

5.9 Conclusion

Gradually, the notion dawned that historical, geographical, political, institutional, and cultural factors also play crucial roles in a country's development. These factors became more and more integrated in the work of economic geographers, institutional economists, and economic historians, as elaborated in Chap. 6. Indeed, development economics needed inputs of other disciplines to better understand what it is that makes economies grow and, based on this understanding, provide sensible policy advice to developing countries and donor countries alike. Keith Griffin and John Enos (both economists) rightly observed: 'But because of our ignorance of subjects other than economics, we may say little of consequence about foreign assistance; and because of our skepticism, what we do say may be what Sheridan called a 'string of uncharitable sentiments.''[62] The overall conclusion must be that economists, while explaining a lot about economic growth, should not pretend to have all the answers.

Notes

1. Hausmann, R., Pritchett, L., Rodrik, D. *Growth Accelerations.* Cambridge: NBER Working Paper 10566, June 2004, 14.
2. Justin Lin argues that many state-sponsored enterprises are not viable because they are in the wrong sectors, in which the country has absolutely no comparative advantage. 'But most economists working in the developed countries, with the implicit assumption of enterprise viability, only see the distortions in the market and government's interventions in resource allocation and firm management—and assume these distortions are the main reasons for the poor performance in the socialist and transition economies'. Source: Lin, J. (2012) *Demystifying the Chinese Economy.* Cambridge: Cambridge University Press, 270.
3. Meier, G. (2001) The Old Generation of Development Economists and the New. In *Frontiers of Development Economics.* Ed: Meier, G. and Stiglitz, J. New York: Oxford University Press, 23.
4. Krueger, A. (1981) Loans to Assist the Transition to Outward-Looking Policies. In *World Economy*, vol. 4, no. 3, September, 280.
5. *The Old Generation of Development Economists and the New*, 22.
6. Ibid., 18.
7. Bliss, C. (1989) Trade and Development. In Hollis Chenery and T. Srinivasan, eds. *Handbook of Development Economics*, Vol.2. Amsterdam: North Holland, 1188.
8. Thirlwall, A. and Pacheco-López, P. (2017) *Economics of Development*, Tenth Edition. London: Palgrave Macmillan, 8.
9. Little, I. (1982) *Economic Development; Theory, Policy, and International Relations.* New York: Basic Books, 16.
10. Krueger, A. (1986) Aid in the Development Process. In *World Bank Research Observer* 1 (1), 62.
11. Naqvi, S. (1996) The Significance of Development Economics. In *World Development*, 24 (6), 975–987.
12. *The Old Generation of Development Economists and the New*, 39.
13. Williamson, J. (1990) What Washington Means by Policy Reform. In *Latin American Adjustment: How Much Has Happened?* Ed. J. Williamson. Washington: Institute for International Economics.
14. Ibid., 182–183.
15. Ibid., 22.
16. This is so because a higher savings or investment ratio is offset by a higher capital-output ratio or lower productivity of capital, because of the neoclassical assumption of diminishing returns to capital.
17. *Economics of Development*, 109. On the same page, the authors conclude that the model is designed to show that an economy will tend towards a

long-run equilibrium capital-labour ratio at which output (or income) per head is also in equilibrium, so that output, capital and labour all grow at the same rate. The model therefore predicts long-term equilibrium at the natural rate.

18. Myrdal, G. (1957) *Economic Theory and Underdeveloped Regions.* London: Methuen.
19. *The Economist's* Free Exchange column of 14 April 2018 quoted Moses Abramovitz's quip about this residual factor: it was 'a measure of our ignorance'. Abramovitz (1912–2000) added that that it was also 'some sort of indication where we need to concentrate our attention'. He had discovered that in the first half of the twentieth century between 80% and 90% of the growth of output per head in the American economy could not be accounted for by capital increase. So, something unidentified should explain this growth.
20. Harberger, A. (1983) The Cost-Benefit Approach to Development Economics. In *World Development*, Vol. 11, No. 10, 864.
21. Easterly, W. (2002) *The Elusive Quest for Growth; Economists' Adventures and Misadventures in the Tropics.* Cambridge: The MIT Press, 56.
22. I repeat here Easterly's observation, included in Chap. 1. Easterly provides the following developments: 'For the period 1960–1999, the poorest countries did significantly worse than the rich countries, with the poorest two-fifths barely mastering positive growth. The poorest four-fifth of countries in 1960 ... roughly correspond to what later became known as the Third World. Seventy percent of these Third World countries grew more slowly over the whole period than the median growth of 2.4 percent per capita for the richest countries. They were falling behind, not catching up.' Source: *The Elusive Quest for Growth*, 60.
23. Ibid., 146.
24. Lucas, R. (1988) On the Mechanics of Economic Development. In *Journal of Monetary Economics*, 22(1): 3–42. Romer, P. (1986) Increasing Returns and Long-Run Growth. In *Journal of Political Economy*, 94(5): 1002–1037. Romer, P. (1990) Endogenous Technical Change. In *Journal of Political Economy*, 98(5): 71–102.

    Romer, P. (1994) The Origins of Endogenous Growth. In *Journal of Economic Perspectives*, (Winter), 3–22.

    Rebelo, S. (1991) Long-run Policy Analysis and Long-run Growth. In *Journal of Political Economy*, 99(3): 500–521.
25. Romer, P. Increasing Returns and long-Run Growth. In *Journal of Political Economy*, 1986, Vol. 94, no.5, 1003.
26. Ibid., 1003.
27. Lal, D. and Myint, H. (1996) *The Political Economy of Poverty, Equity, and Growth.* Oxford: Oxford University Press, 76.

28. Ibid., 77.
29. Ibid., 77, 78.
30. Barro, R, Sala-i-Martin, X. (1992) Convergence. *Journal of Political Economy*, 100 (2).
31. Barro, R. and Sala-i-Martin, X. Technological Diffusion, Convergence, and Growth. Cambridge: *NBER Working Paper No. 5151*, June 1995.
32. Ibid., 131. Rodrik, D. (2013) Unconditional Convergence in Manufacturing. In *Journal of Economic Perspectives*, 128(8), 165–204.
33. Maddison, A. (1995) *Monitoring the World Economy 1880–1992*. Paris: OECD, 49.
34. Milanovic, B. (2016) *Global Inequality, a New Approach for the Age of Globalization*. Cambridge: The Belknap Press, 5.
35. Senhadji, A. (2000) Sources of Economic Growth: An Extensive Growth Accounting Exercise. In *IMF Staff Papers*, 47(1), 129–157.
36. *Economics of Development*, 123.
37. Ibid., 131.
38. Berendsen, B., Dietz, T., Schulte Nordholt, H., van der Veen, R., Eds: (2013) *Asian Tigers, African Lions; Comparing the Development Performance of Southeast Asia and Africa*. Leiden: Koninklijke Brill.
39. Cambodia, Indonesia, Malaysia, Vietnam, Kenya, Nigeria, Tanzania, and Uganda.
40. Thirlwall and Pacheco-López observe: 'If there is an overriding factor that explains why some countries developed before others, and why some countries are still backward without a significant industrial sector, it lies in the condition of agriculture, which, in the early stages of development, is the sector that must release factors of production for other activities and provide the purchasing power over industrial goods.' Source: *Economics of Development*, 22.
41. The attention given to the role of the state, in combination with political realities on the ground, is reflective of the approach taken by *new political economy* which attempts to endogenise the decisions of politicians, bureaucrats, and administrators.
42. *Asian Tigers, African Lions*, 30.
43. *Economics of Development*, 22.
44. Stiglitz, J. (1989). Markets, Market Failures, and Development. In *American Economic Review*, 79 (2, May), 197–203.
45. Ha-Joon Chang (Ed.) (2004) *Rethinking Development Economics*. London: Anthem Press, 6.
46. Ibid., 6.
47. *The Elusive Quest for Growth*, 150.

48. Krugman, P. (1992) Toward a Counter-Counterrevolution in Development Theory. In *Proceedings of the World Bank Annual Conference on Development Economics*. Washington: World Bank, 29.
49. Krugman makes interesting observations in comparing the new growth theory with high development theory: 'New growth theory has been preoccupied with a different question than high development theory: how to explain the persistence of growth rather than how to get it started. And it is notable that new growth models tend to assume that the economy has only one sector, or that all sectors are symmetric. By contrast, high development theory had a core preoccupation with the difference between modern sectors that were presumed to be characterized by economies of scale and traditional sectors that were not.' Source: Ibid., 31.
50. Krugman, referring to Rosenstein-Rodan's 1943 paper *Problems of Industrialization of Eastern and South-Eastern Europe*, argues: 'We begin with Rosenstein-Rodan (1943). In his seminal paper he illustrated his argument for coordinated investment by imagining a country in which 20,000 (!) 'unemployed workers ... are taken from the land and put into a large new shoe factory. They receive wages substantially higher than their previous income *in natura*.' Rosenstein-Rodan then goes on to argue that this investment is likely to be unprofitable in isolation but profitable if accompanied by similar investments in many other industries. Both crucial assumptions are clearly present: the assumption of economies of scale, embodied in the assertion that the factory must be established at such a large scale, and the assumption that these workers can be drawn elastically from among the unemployed or poorly paid agricultural workers.' Source: Ibid., 21.
51. *The East Asian Miracle; Economic Growth and Public Policy*. New York: Oxford University Press (1993).
52. Berger, P. (1987) *The Capitalist Revolution: Fifty Propositions about Poverty, Equality and Liberty*. Aldershot: Gower.
53. The role of institutions in the development process is elaborated by the next generation of development economists, presented in Chap. 6.
54. Regarding Japan's funding role, Rodrik observes that Japan felt that World Bank advice given to developing countries relied too much on the American preference for a free market model and under-played the role of the state in promoting industrialization and development. Source: Rodrik, D. (2011) *The Globalization Paradox*. New York: W.W. Norton, 144.
55. Nonetheless, Botswana, Egypt, Gabon, and Lesotho also performed very well. In fact, Botswana's GDP per capita growth was fastest of all, thus outperforming all HPAEs.
56. *The East Asian Miracle*, 5. Alwyn Young confirms that there was not really a 'miracle' involved. He applied the production function model to demon-

strate that no miraculous development had taken place in the Asian countries as studied. His paper shows that, indeed, their economic growth had been spectacular between 1966 and 1990, but most of it can be explained by the rapid growth of factor accumulation. Young adds that there was nothing abnormal about the growth of total factor productivity as they are closely approximated by the historical performance of many OECD and Latin American economies. Source: Young, A. The Tyranny of Numbers: Confronting the Statistical Realities of the East Asian Growth Experience. In *The Quarterly Journal of Economics*, August 1995.

57. Ibid., 6.
58. Amsden, A. Why Isn't the Whole World Experimenting with the East Asian Model to Develop?: Review of The East Asian Miracle. In *World Development*, Vol. 22, No. 4, 627–633, 1994. Amsden argues on p. 630 that the genesis of *The East Asian Miracle* study started with the Japan World Bank Delegation's frustration with what it saw as the Bank's obsessive emphasis on free market policies despite contrary East Asian evidence.
59. Ibid., 628.
60. Krugman, P. The Myth of Asia's Miracle. In *Foreign Affairs*, 73 (6), 62–78; 1994.
61. *Demystifying the Chinese Economy*. Cambridge: Cambridge University Press, 145.
62. Griffin, K. and Enos, J. (1970) Foreign Assistance: Objectives and Consequences. In *Economic Development and Cultural Change*, Vol. 18, No.3, April, 313. By the way, Sheridan was an eighteenth century Irish satirist.

References

Amsden, A. (1994). Why Isn't the Whole World Experimenting with the East Asian Model to Develop? Review of the East Asian Miracle. *World Development, 22*(4), 627–633.

Barro, R., & Sala-i-Martin, X. (1992). Convergence. *Journal of Political Economy, 100*(2), 223–251.

Barro, R., & Sala-i-Martin, X. (1995). *Technological Diffusion, Convergence, and Growth.* NBER Working Paper No. 5151. Cambridge: National Bureau of Economic Research.

Berendsen, B., Dietz, T., Schulte Nordholt, H., & van der Veen, R. (Eds.). (2013). *Asian Tigers, African Lions; Comparing the Development Performance of Southeast Asia and Africa.* Leiden: Koninklijke Brill.

Berger, P. (1987). *The Capitalist Revolution: Fifty Propositions About Poverty, Equality and Liberty.* Aldershot: Gower.

Bliss, C. (1989). Trade and Development. In H. Chenery & T. Srinivasan (Eds.), *Handbook of Development Economics, Vol. 2*. New York: North Holland.

Chang, H.-J. (Ed.). (2004). *Rethinking Development Economics*. London: Anthem Press.

Easterly, W. (2002). *The Elusive Quest for Growth; Economists' Adventures and Misadventures in the Tropics*. Cambridge: The MIT Press.

Free Exchange. (2018, April 14). *The Economist*.

Griffin, K., & Enos, J. (1970). Foreign Assistance: Objectives and Consequences. *Economic Development and Cultural Change, 18*(3), 313–327.

Harberger, A. (1983). The Cost-Benefit Approach to Development Economics. *World Development, 11*(10), 863–873.

Hausmann, R., Pritchett, L., & Rodrik, D. (2004). *Growth Accelerations*. NBER Working Paper 10566. Cambridge: National Bureau of Economic Research.

Krueger, A. (1981). Loans to Assist the Transition to Outward-Looking Policies. *World Economy, 4*(3), 271–282.

Krueger, A. (1986). Aid in the Development Process. *World Bank Research Observer, 1*(1), 57–78.

Krugman, P. (1992). Toward a Counter-Counterrevolution in Development Theory. In *Proceedings of the World Bank Annual Conference on Development Economics*. Washington: World Bank.

Krugman, P. (1994). The Myth of Asia's Miracle. *Foreign Affairs, 73*(6), 62–78.

Lal, D., & Myint, H. (1996). *The Political Economy of Poverty, Equity, and Growth*. Oxford: Oxford University Press.

Lin, J. (2012). *Demystifying the Chinese Economy*. Cambridge: Cambridge University Press.

Little, I. (1982). *Economic Development; Theory, Policy, and International Relations*. New York: Basic Books.

Lucas, R. (1988). On the Mechanics of Economic Development. *Journal of Monetary Economics, 22*(1), 3–42.

Maddison, A. (1995). *Monitoring the World Economy 1880–1992*. Paris: OECD.

Meier, G. (2001). The Old Generation of Development Economists and the New. In G. Meier & J. Stiglitz (Eds.), *Frontiers of Development Economics*. New York: Oxford University Press.

Milanovic, B. (2016). *Global Inequality, a New Approach for the Age of Globalization*. Cambridge: The Belknap Press.

Myrdal, G. (1957). *Economic Theory and Underdeveloped Regions*. London: Methuen.

Naqvi, S. (1996). The Significance of Development Economics. *World Development, 24*(6), 975–987.

Rebelo, S. (1991). Long-run Policy Analysis and Long-run Growth. *Journal of Political Economy, 99*(3), 500–521.

Rodrik, D. (2007). *One Economics, Many Recipes; Globalization, Institutions, and Economic Growth.* Princeton: Princeton University Press.

Rodrik, D. (2011). *The Globalization Paradox.* New York: W.W. Norton.

Rodrik, D. (2013). Unconditional Convergence in Manufacturing. *Journal of Economic Perspectives, 128*(8), 165–204.

Romer, P. (1986). Increasing Returns and Long-Run Growth. *Journal of Political Economy, 94*(5), 1002–1037.

Romer, P. (1990). Endogenous Technical Change. *Journal of Political Economy, 98*(5), 71–102.

Romer, P. (1994). The Origins of Endogenous Growth. *Journal of Economic Perspectives, 8*(1), 3–22.

Senhadji, A. (2000). Sources of Economic Growth: An Extensive Growth Accounting Exercise. *In: IMF Staff Papers, 47*(1), 129–157.

Stiglitz, J. (1989). Markets, Market Failures, and Development. *American Economic Review, 79*(2), 197–203.

The East Asian Miracle; Economic Growth and Public Policy. (1993). New York: Oxford University Press.

Thirlwall, A., & Pacheco-López, P. (2017). *Economics of Development* (10th ed.). London: Palgrave Macmillan.

Williamson, J. (1990). What Washington Means by Policy Reform. In J. Williamson (Ed.), *Latin American Adjustment: How Much Has Happened?* Washington: Institute for International Economics.

Young, A. (1995). The Tyranny of Numbers: Confronting the Statistical Realities of the East Asian Growth Experience. *The Quarterly Journal of Economics, 110*(442), 641–680.(continued)**(continued)**

CHAPTER 6

Main Components of the Third Generation

6.1 Introduction

Contemporary development economics, unlike in the past, cannot be brought under a common denominator. Now there are various influential schools of thought, ranging from new institutional economics, economic geography, new political economics, economic anthropology, to economic history.[1]

In Chap. 5, the evolution of growth theories from Solow's growth model to the ideas-based endogenous growth model is described. Progress has been made in this realm, in that modern growth theory includes more possible sources of growth than older growth models.

Regarding the interplay between macroeconomic and microeconomic dynamics, an integrated framework is proposed by Philippe Aghion and Peter Howitt.[2] Its purpose is to better understand the macroeconomic structure of growth but also the many microeconomic issues regarding incentives, policies, and institutions that interact with economic growth. By focussing on the influences of quality improving innovations[3] in a model where entrepreneurs introduce new technologies that render previous technologies obsolete, it helps to understand why economic actors in some societies gain from growth, while in others they are blocked by those who would lose.

We have seen that the second generation of development economists based their analyses on the neoclassical philosophy of rationality, self-interest, and small government. Their focus was directed at the micro

P. de Haan, *Whatever Happened to the Third World?*,
https://doi.org/10.1007/978-3-030-39613-8_6

level, analysing a wide variety of economic activities in developing country settings, lifting the scientific level of development economics considerably. Disaggregated micro-studies were undertaken in which the units of analysis were, for example, agricultural production and household units, constituting the basis of specific sectoral or fiscal policies and also of more adequately guiding policy in the macroeconomic domain. Just one example of such a study would be De Janvry, Murgai, and Sadoulet's paper: *Rural Development and Rural Poverty*.[4] The 2014 edition of *The Handbook of Economic Growth* contains many more high-quality contributions to development economics focusing on the micro level. For example, the chapters dealing with trust, economic growth and well-being; the one on family ties; and on technology diffusion can be mentioned.[5] This also applies to the chapters about health and economic growth; the growth of cities, and—not to be overlooked—the one on agglomeration and innovation. In short, the new insights in all these subjects contribute to a better understanding of economic growth.

One of the central assumptions in economics is that humans act in an economically rational manner. This assumption is challenged by behavioural economics. Research undertaken by, for example, Economics Nobel Laureate Daniel Kahneman (who is a psychologist, by the way), the late Amos Tversky, and Richard Tahler (2017 Economics Nobel Laureate), explore the systematic ways in which human beings act irrationally.[6] One of their insights is that the economic system shapes individual preferences and behaviour (in contrast to standard theory, which assumes preferences as given), making individuals more selfish or more short-sighted than they might be otherwise.

Not only do new theoretical and empirical analyses and models abound, promising techniques have also been developed and are being applied widely. One technique that catches the eye and that is useful for development practitioners—often acting on the basis of untested fashionable development notions—is Randomised Control Trials (RCTs). Two of the three 2019 Economics Nobel laureates, Abhijit Banerjee and Esther Duflo (both professors at the Massachusetts Institute of Technology), present a host of RCT results in their book *Poor Economics*.[7] The authors cofounded and manage the Abdul Lateef Jameel Poverty Action Lab. This lab is an action network of affiliated professionals across the globe who are united by their use of RCTs to answer questions critical to poverty alleviation. Banerjee and Duflo argue that with the help of RCTs it is possible to make significant progress in alleviating poverty through the accumulation of a set of small steps, each well thought out, carefully tested, and judiciously implemented.[8] Harvard professor, Michael Kremer was the third laureate, having applied RCT's for the first time in a developing country setting. Another promising technique is the instrumental variables technique, which helps to improve the analysis of cause and effect. Instrumental variables help to isolate causal relationships. The purpose of instrumental variables is to ensure that the omission of factors from an analysis does not end up producing inaccurate results.[9]

Angus Maddison (1926–2010) distinguished the following four causal influences which go a long way to explain why large increases in per capita output have been feasible: (i) technological progress; (ii) accumulation of physical capital in which technical progress usually needs to be embodied; (iii) improvement in human skills, education, organising ability; and (iv) closer integration of individual national economies through trade in goods and services. There are more of these causal influences, added Maddison, such as economies of scale, major changes in the structure of employment and output, and the relative scarcity or abundance of natural resources. However, the author realised that one had to dig deeper to better understand development or stagnation, through considering institutional, social, and policy influences.[10] This chapter indeed deals with these influences.

Since it is impossible to pay attention to all contemporary schools of thought, I have chosen to present new institutional economics, economic history, and new economic geography, since each of them play prominent roles in research and debate about the factors explaining economic growth.

6.2 New Institutional Economics

One cannot maintain that the role of institutions in the development process was not recognised by earlier generations of economists. Way back in the eighteenth century, Adam Smith (1723–1790) had something to say about institutions.[11] In *The Wealth of Nations*, he observed: 'The political institutions of the English colonies have been more favourable to the improvement and cultivation of this land than those of any of the other three nations [Spain, Portugal, and France; PdH].'[12]

It was new institutional economist Douglass North (1920–2015) who drew attention to the important role institutions play in economic development. Together with Ronald Coase and Oliver Williamson, he founded the International Society for New Institutional Economics.[13] New institutional economics presents a missing link in economic theory, i.e., the relevance of institutions in explaining economic growth, or stagnation, through time.

6.2.1 The Role of Institutions

North argues that in order to get the prices right, and to get the policies right, it was particularly important to get the institutions right. Now, how did North define institutions? He offered a very broad definition: institutions constitute the constraints that structure human interaction. These constraints can be formal (such as laws, rules, the Constitution) and informal (such as norms, belief systems, and conventions), and their enforcement mechanisms. Together they define the incentive structure embodied in institutions of societies. This incentive structure determines a society's economic growth or stagnation. Institutions define the rules of the game, whereas households, firms, and government organisations are the players of that game.

6.2.2 Path Dependency

Economic change may be of a revolutionary nature. However, as a rule, change is an incremental process. Hence institutions typically evolve gradually, following a certain path—economic development is path dependent. A telling example of path dependency is given in the box below by Melissa Dell's analysis of the 'mita' system applied by Spanish colonisers in Bolivia and Peru.

> Sometimes institutions cast their long shadows across centuries. Development is, as North said, path-dependent. A recent study confirmed this observation once again. In 2010, Melissa Dell published an in-depth analysis of persistent effects of Peru's mining *mita*.[14] Her analysis is the more interesting since its focus is on 'channels of persistence', in Dell's own words. The author studied the long-term impact of the mining mita, which was a forced-labour system that was instituted in 1573 by the Spanish colonisers in Peru and Bolivia. The mita required that over 200 indigenous communities to send one-seventh of their adult male population to work in the Potosí silver

(*continued*)

(continued)

mines in Bolivia, and in the Huancavelica mercury mines in Peru. Some districts fell under this regime, while on the other side of the boundary, other districts were exempt. So, the mita system offered the possibility to establish the long-term effects that the mita system had on the affected districts, and how the unaffected ones fared.

Dell concludes that the long-term mita effects lower household consumption by around 25% and increase childhood stunting by around 6 percentage points.[15] She also analysed how the districts fared that fell outside the mita system. There, haciendas (rural estates with forced-labour force) could develop. The establishment of haciendas was restricted in districts falling under the mita system; there, communal land tenure was promoted. The author concludes that long-term presence of politically influential large landowners (holding secure property rights) in non-mita districts, provided a stable land-tenure system, but it also encouraged market participation and the provision of public goods, such as roads and education. Dell adds that large landowners—while they did not aim to promote economic prosperity for the masses—did shield individuals from exploitation by a highly extractive state and did ensure the provision of public goods. This was not the case in mita districts; to date access to education is lower and the districts are less integrated into Peru's road network.

Dell observes that her analysis also provides microeconomic evidence confirming what other studies also demonstrated: a relationship between historical institutions and contemporary economic outcomes. The outcomes of her analysis confirm what others, such as Acemoglu, Johnson, and Robinson already concluded, i.e., that extractive historical institutions influence long-run economic prosperity.[16]

6.2.3 Transaction Costs

Transaction costs are the costs of enforcing the terms of contracts. When it is costly transact, institutions do matter. North observed that transaction costs do not play a role in neoclassical models. The world portrayed in these models is frictionless, in which institutions do not exist, and all changes occur through perfectly functioning markets. Markets always clear, and since agents do not make systematic errors, full employment equilibrium is the normal state of affairs. In such an ideal situation, the costs of acquiring information and the costs involved in transactions do not exist. In such a world, institutions do not matter. But in the real world transaction costs do exist.[17] These costs are now incorporated in neoclassical models. For example, De Janvry, Murgai and Sadoulet emphasise the absence of roads, markets, and credit, resulting in increasing transactions costs (and hence market failures) for farmers in marketing their produce.[18]

North refuted the neoclassical doctrine, because it cannot explain millennia of inefficient forms of exchange. As described in Chap. 5, neoclassical growth theory focuses on technological change. Instead, North emphasised the prominent explanatory role of institutions in economic growth.

6.2.4 *Property Rights*

Property rights play a vital role in economic markets. Without these rights, and their protection, people will not be prepared to invest, or to apply new technologies; they will not innovate.

Regarding the vital role of property rights, Deirdre McCloskey begs to differ. She argues in *Bourgeois Dignity* that it was something else that triggered spectacular economic growth during the Industrial Revolution.[19] After having demonstrated that secure property rights had been established long before the onset of the Industrial Revolution—and in many other countries besides England—McCloskey concludes that there was little news in British property rights around 1700 that can explain its subsequent economic success. Instead: 'A government of a more popular nature, and political liberty, and above all the energy and vigor that a new deal brought forth from England's bourgeoisie, were what mattered.'[20]

Economic growth did not occur because of a lack of property rights, but because of a lack of massive innovation, and that in turn because of a lack of bourgeois dignity and liberty, and a lack of widespread education. In short, argues McCloskey, what explains the modern world is not investment but innovation, triggered by discovery, invention, and creativity.

Initially, North proposed that institutions determined economic performance, and that relative price changes were the source of institutional change. This was, in essence, an efficient explanation: changes in relative prices create incentives to design more efficient institutions. However, the historical persistence of inefficient institutions could not be explained. How could these inefficient institutions persist? The answer is to be found in the inefficiency of political 'markets', which North elaborated in *Institutions, institutional Change, and Economic Performance.*[21] He argues that high transaction costs and errors in the perception of participants in inefficient political markets can produce property rights that hinder, instead of promote, economic growth. These property rights can result in the creation of new organisations designed to prosper under existing laws, which—consequently—lack incentives to create more efficient economic rules. Private gain is made at the cost of overall economic growth. Organisations that develop in this type of institutional framework will become more effective in making the society even more unproductive, and the basic institutional structure even less conducive to productive activity.

But what about societies that prosper? This is how North answered the question: if economies realise the gains from trade by creating relatively efficient institutions, it is because the private objective of those with the bargaining power to alter institutions, produces institutional solutions that evolve into socially and economically efficient ones. However, the capture by organisations of the gains from trade for all parties to a transaction requires the development of a state as a coercive power, able to monitor property rights and the enforcement of contracts. North concluded that the inability of most societies to develop effective, low-cost enforcement of contracts is the most important source of both historical stagnation and underdevelopment of many developing countries. The other side of the coin is that institutions also constitute the main underlying determinant of sustained economic growth.

6.2.5 *Types of Societies*

North was the lead-author of a World Bank paper entitled: *Limited Access Orders in the Developing World.*[22] The authors of the paper describe three types of societies in historical perspective: (i) the primitive order society (POS); (ii) the limited access order society (LAOS); and (iii) the open access society (OAS). Since the world has left POS behind, the LAOS and

OAS were elaborated. North et al. observe that aid donors' development policies often fail because they try to transplant elements of the OAS, such as competition, markets, and democracy, directly into the LAOS. Needless to say that these policies threaten the privileged position of LAOS elites who are in control, and challenge the very logic on which the LAOS is based. Attempts to, for example, remove corruption or to create the rule of law can destabilise a LAOS and generate resistance from the elites. In other words, a LAOS bars access to valuable political and economic functions to ensure income for the elites. The status-quo is maintained by this privileged group through controlling violence and by maintaining stability. And there is more: the LAOS also frustrates the creation of organisations of potentially competing societal groups. The LAOS deliberately closes off political and economic possibilities for others than the happy few. Developing countries saddled with a natural resource curse, typically qualify as a LAOS. It is the elites who control the proceeds from their country's natural resources, and wield political power to consolidate their position.

The history of development demonstrated that a LAOS can evolve into an OAS. There is a tipping point after which this can take place. Such a tipping point comes when open access in the economic or political domain results in sufficient power of the new entrants to press the elites to accept them. These elites give in when they realise that their interests are better served by allowing the new entrants in. Once this stage is reached, rapid changes will take place, extending to ever-larger segments of society. A mature LAOS state must create new institutions that provide services for newly emerging organisations, including the protection and enforcement of their property rights. Now, the tipping point comes when open access in one dimension (economic or political) commands sufficient power to press successfully for open access to the other dimension.[23]

6.2.6 Why Nations Fail

North was not the only one to underscore the importance of the interplay between economic and political institutions; the latter defined as institutions that include the power and capacity of the state to regulate and govern a society. Daron Acemoglu and James Robinson apply the same interplay in *Why Nations Fail*.[24] In addition, the authors make a distinction between inclusive and extractive institutions. Extractive economic institutions are designed to extract income and wealth from one subset of society to benefit a different subset. Inclusive economic institutions feature secure property rights, an unbiased system of law, and provision of public services that provide a level playing field in which people can exchange and contract; it also must permit the entry of new businesses and allow people to choose their careers.[25] Inclusive political institutions pave the way for inclusive economic institutions. Once this happens, countries will prosper, while extractive political institutions, favouring the happy few only, perpetuate economic stagnation. So, as Acemoglu and Robinson conclude, countries differ in their economic evolution precisely because their institutions differ.

There is also, the authors argue, an exogenous cause of a difference in institutions: the way in which colonisers settled in countries in the past. The potential mortality rate (high in Africa and parts of Latin America, but lower in other colonies) determined the degree of settlement, which in turn determined the characteristics of early institutions in the colonies. These early institutions determined the development of current institutions. In Africa, 'extractive states' were created that produced extractive institutions. Their main function was to take out valuable raw materials and send them to the colonising country to be processed. These extractive states neither had an interest in economic development, nor in the protection of private property rights. Extractive institutions induce leaders to plunder. In such environments, society's produce is captured by parasitical elites which in turn discourage investment and innovation. The elites control politics and the economy. In short: extractive institutions are the norm and failure is the rule.

Acemoglu and Robinson observe that Africa's development has been hampered by two historical factors: (i) slavery, which encouraged the development of extractive political—and economic institutions; and (ii) the use of colonial legislation and institutions to eliminate the development of African commercial agriculture. The history of Sierra Leone provides a good example.

At the time of colonisation, slavery was endemic, with possibly 50% of the population working as slaves. Sierra Leone's cocoa and coffee farmers did not compete with whites during colonial times; yet their incomes were still expropriated via a marketing board, which the British had installed. The British colonisers introduced indirect rule in Sierra Leone: a hereditary aristocracy replaced a situation where chiefs required popular support. What emerged was a rigid system with chiefs holding office for life, beholden to their patrons in Freetown, and thus far less accountable to the people they ruled.[26]

Given adverse climatic conditions in Africa (including high mortality rates), colonists did not stay long, nor did they settle in large numbers. However, where many of them settled permanently, such as in North America, Australia, New Zealand, and even in Hong Kong and Singapore, they established inclusive institutions that protected private property rights and political checks and balances. After independence, these institutions persisted and, as a result, the newly independent countries prospered. After all, without firmly established property rights and the rule of law, who would be interested to take risks and invest?

6.2.7 *Institutions and Geography*

Acemoglu and Robinson refute geography's influence on the development of countries, but not entirely. Historical developments demonstrate that countries that were prosperous in the distant past (such as Mali and Peru) are no longer prosperous; they underwent a so-called institutional reversal. In contrast, erstwhile poor countries prospered; they now belong to the league of rich nations. The reversal of economic fortunes was triggered by the opportunity to industrialise which was taken by countries that had good institutions. The authors argue that it is institutions that matter: Africa is poor, not because of geography, but because of poor institutions. However, the authors admit that geography—and the climate associated with it—did affect the type of colonisation, and thus also the ensuing institutional framework.

Rodrik et al. analysed the influence of geography and institutions on income levels. They found that the direct impact of geographic variables in their analysis on income was either insignificant or non-robust. They conclude that, in the end, it is the quality of institutions which is 'the only positive and significant determinant of income levels.'[27] But they also admit that it is fair to say that scholarly opinion remains divided on the significance of geography as a direct determinant of income levels.

Jeffrey Sachs, for example, argues that the role of geography and resource endowments should not be underestimated. This statement is the sub-heading of a brief article *Institutions Matter but Not for Everything*.[28] A deadly disease, such as malaria, has the ability to cut off economic development. Sachs disagrees with Acemoglu and Robinson who neglected the fact that malaria in sub-Saharan Africa had dramatically lowered the returns on foreign investment and raised the transaction costs of international trade, migration, and tourism in malarial regions. Sachs admits that it is probably true that when human capital is high enough in any location, physical capital will be attracted by it as a complementary production factor. Compare this to the situation of remote countries that also have few skilled workers; these workers will very probably emigrate. True, admits Sachs, 'good institutions certainly matter, and bad institutions can sound the death knell of development even in favorable environments. But poor physical endowments may also hamper development.'[29]

Development thinking should return to the basics of development: *both* institutions and resource endowments are critical. Some geographical areas are simply too unfavourable to attract investors, and thus would be in need of international assistance to get out of the poverty trap. Sachs concludes that by freeing our thinking from one-factor explanations and understanding that poverty may have as much to do with malaria as with a country's exchange rate, we will become much more creative and expansive in our approach to the poorest countries.[30]

6.2.8 *Markets Require Institutions*

As noted, North argued that to get the prices right, one had to get the institutions right. Prices are established at markets. Markets are not something magical; they require institutions to make them function properly. Rodrik and Subramanian identify various types of institutions that are required to create, regulate, and stabilise markets.[31] For example, protection of property rights and binding contracts are indispensable when establishing a market. There should also be regulating institutions to establish and control the market's rules of the game. On a higher plateau, institutions are needed to ensure macroeconomic stability. To legitimise the free functioning of the market, social insurance and conflict management institutions should be in place.

This is quite a list, requiring a solid degree of political and economic maturity to have them put in place. And this is precisely what is lacking in the typical poor developing country: property rights are not well defined, nor protected, regulatory authorities are absent or lack the power to function properly, trust and social cohesion are phenomena in short supply, neither the institutions to manage social conflicts, nor the rule of law and clean government are in place.

The list of things to legitimise the market prompts the question: how on earth can these institutions ever evolve in poor countries? There is no recipe book available, since each country's customs, political organisation, geographic characteristics and historical trajectory, is unique. Hence during the development process, institutions will evolve in a tailor-made fashion. Along the way, political opposition can be expected from those who stand to lose from institutional change. There is also the so-called bargaining problem, which means the difficulty that gainers from institutional change have in compensating the losers. All told, it depends on a country's economic and political dynamics (or the lack thereof) whether, or not, institutional development will take place.

6.2.9 Measurement Challenges

From a methodological point of view, the question arises how does one measure institutions and institutional development? Or, how to prove that one institution is more efficient than another? There are various difficulties, such as the requirement to treat institutional variables as exogenous factors, while institutional development typically is the result of an endogenous process. Another complication is the fact that institutional variables are interconnected, i.e., one variable, such as ideas, influences another. Hence it is difficult to isolate the contribution that one particular variable would have made to development. As Charles Jones and Paul Romer observe: '...we are far from a simple formal model that can describe how institutions evolve. However, a model that allows for ideas suggests that institutions are more complicated and matter more than the neoclassical model once suggested...a key point is that the institutions that underlie the production and distribution of new ideas have evolved over time, dramatically so in the last couple of centuries. Growth driven by the discovery of new ideas...must be understood to occur in the context of institutions such as universities and laws supporting intellectual property rights that have been evolving, that are almost surely not yet optimal, and that will continue to change in the future.'[32]

Different measures have been developed such as an aggregate governance index, a measure of property rights and risk of appropriation, an index of democracy, political rights and civil liberties, measurement of political instability, a perception of corruption index, the extent of economic freedom, and an index of social division. Also, various empirical studies on the role of institutions have been undertaken. One of them is Stephen Knack and Philip Keefer's *Why Don't Poor Countries catch Up?*[33] The authors attempted to measure the impact of the institutional environment on the development of Third World countries. They conclude that deficient institutions underlie the falling back of poor countries compared to the growth of developed countries. While admitting the methodological difficulties in measuring the influence of institutions, the authors conclude that human capital acquisition, machinery, and foreign investment, as well as foreign trade are the main vehicles for international transmission and absorption of technology. They conclude, in a careful fashion, that an explanation for insufficient levels of any of these may be poor institutions. If this is the case, breakdowns in foreign investment or human capital accumulation should be considered as proximate, but not fundamental, to the causes of low growth rates and the failure to catch up.[34]

6.2.10 *Chicken and Egg*

Do institutions promote growth, or does growth promote the evolution of institutions? Edward Glaeser et al. investigate this question and conclude that it is not institutions that promote growth; it is the other way around: economic growth leads to institutional improvement.[35] Their article presents basic econometric regression analyses, and additional evidence which, together, suggest that: (i) human capital is a more basic source of growth than institutions; (ii) poor countries get out of poverty through sound economic policies; and (iii) they subsequently improve their political institutions. Growth may be feasible without immediate institutional improvement, but will ultimately lead to it.

Glaeser et al. provide the example of North Korea's and South Korea's growth trajectories. Prior to the Korean War, both countries were obviously part of one country, so it is difficult to think of them as having different histories. They were both exceptionally poor in 1950 and both were dictatorships. Starting 1980, South Korea transformed itself into a democracy, while North Korea remained a dictatorship. South Korean leaders chose capitalism and secure property rights, and the country grew rapidly, reaching a per capita income of $37,600.- in 2015. The North Korean dictator chose socialism, and the country only reached a level of per capita income of $1700.- in the same year.[36] While on average, looking over the half century between 1950 and 2000, South Korea obviously had better institutions as measured by constraints on the executive. These institutions are the outcome of economic growth after 1950 rather than its cause. So, the authors conclude, it would be wrong to attribute South Korea's growth to these institutions rather than the choice made by its leaders.[37]

Rodrik observes that there is as yet no unique mapping of institutional development. It all depends on the local context: what works well in one, may not work in another country. Regarding the role of aid in poor countries' economic development, Rodrik says that in successful developing countries, the proposed development policy by economists and aid agencies 'has largely failed to live up to its promise.'[38] He goes even further by noting that economists' ability to design growth strategies is extremely limited indeed:

> Basically anything goes, and it is up to imaginative politicians to come up with recipes that will work. We have very limited advice to give them ex ante, even though we are in the possession of many tools to evaluate the consequences of their policy decisions ex post.[39]

6.2.11 Democracy, Autocracy and Institutions

A popular opinion is that autocratic regimes are better at stimulating economic growth than democracies. After all, autocrats endowed with the right development vision, are not hindered by political opponents to push their policies through. This is an opinion vented by pundits who may have had the economic performance of e.g., Singapore, China, and Rwanda in mind.[40] But is this correct; are autocracies more successful economic performers than democratic nation-states? Various studies conclude otherwise. Democracies score better in long-term economic growth than less democratically functioning regimes. Rodrik, for example, argues that democratically governed countries show more resilience in dealing with external shocks than less democratically governed ones.[41] He emphasises the relevance of decentralised political systems in fostering even better institutions: 'But I would argue that the most reliable forms of such mechanisms are participatory political institutions. Indeed, it is helpful to think of participatory political institutions as *metainstitutions* that elicit and aggregate local knowledge and thereby build better institutions.'[42]

Robert Barro is more nuanced in his analysis of the relationship between democracy and economic growth. He argues that this relationship is lightly negative, although not significant in statistical terms. He concludes that: '...democracy is not the key to economic growth...advanced Western countries would contribute more to the welfare of poor nations by exporting their economic systems, notably, property rights and free markets, rather than their political systems, which typically developed after reasonable standards of living have been attained.'[43]

A large study conducted in 2015 by Acemoglu, Naidu, Restrepo, and Robinson concludes that democratisation, i.e., the process of transition to democracy, increases GDP per capacity by about 20% in the long-run.[44] It is in democracies that free media can inform citizens who can hold government to account for its actions. Acemoglu et al. also demonstrate that democracy contributes to future economic development by increasing investment, encouraging economic reforms, improving the provision of public goods, like schooling and health care, and reducing social unrest.

6.2.12 Conclusion

Now, what conclusion can we draw regarding the role of institutions in the development of poor countries? First of all, new institutional economists discovered a crucial missing link in growth theories: institutions do matter when analysing long-term processes of economic growth or stagnation. This discovery is taken on board by development economists who deal with two basic questions: how to get economic growth started in poor countries and, two, how to sustain it.

Research on these two questions has brought to light that, by and large, to get economic growth started, institutions may not yet matter as much. But institutions are important to sustain economic growth. This insight was proposed by Glaeser et al. and by Ricardo Hausmann and colleagues, who—as described in Chap. 1—analysed growth accelerations.[45] They conclude that to get growth started, growth diagnostics will unearth what the binding constraints to growth of a particular poor country would be. Relaxing these specific constraints does not involve wide-ranging institutional reform. This reform will gradually take shape, not in a *one-size-fits-all* manner, but moulded by the country's unique historical, political, and cultural context. A good conclusion, I believe, is the one Jones and Romer offer: 'There is very broad agreement that differences in institutions must be the fundamental source of the wide differences in growth rates observed for countries at low levels of income and for the low income and TFP [total factor productivity; PdH] levels themselves.'[46]

6.3 Economic History

Economists understand even less about economic growth than about business cycles. I took this bold statement from a Free Exchange column in *The Economist*.[47] Apart from economics, there are various other influences that may explain growth, ranging from culture, politics, institutions, geography, to history. Now, regarding history, Jeffrey Williamson argues that economic history is far better equipped to educate contemporary debate in the less developed world than it was in the 1950s and 1960s.[48] The Free Exchange column mentions that the historical approach to the question of growth may be, in some ways, the most promising, as it pays due attention to the role of culture and politics that both may promote or constrain economic growth. However, the same column also argues that economic historians are held back by a paucity of data, nor have they managed to arrive at a shared understanding of the nature of economic growth. Deirdre McCloskey provides an eloquent observation on this lack of a shared understanding in *Bourgeois Dignity*:

> The book tests the traditional stories against the actually-happened, setting aside the stories that in light of the recent findings of scientific history don't seem to work very well. A surprisingly large number of stories don't. Not Marx and his classes. Not Max Weber and his Protestants. Not Fernand Braudel and his mafia-style capitalists. Not Douglass North and his institutions. Not the mathematical theories of endogenous growth and its capital accumulation. Not the left-wing's theory of working-class struggle, or the right-wing's theory of spiritual decline.[49]

This quotation prompts the question: if all these theories don't tell the story, what does? McCloskey's answer is that it is *ideas*: talk and ethics and ideas caused innovation, which in turn triggered hitherto unprecedented economic growth. It was the innovative bourgeoisie that promoted growth.[50] Another quote from *Bourgeois Dignity* provides a clearer picture of what she means:

> In particular, three centuries ago in places like Holland and England the talk and thought about the middle class began to alter. Ordinary conversation about innovation and markets became more approving. The high theorists were emboldened to rethink their prejudice against the bourgeoisie, a prejudice by then millennia old. …The North Sea talk at length radically altered the local economy and politics and rhetoric. In northwestern Europe around 1700 the general opinion shifted in favor of the bourgeoisie, and especially in favour of its marketing and innovating.[51]

Apart from McCloskey's, there are of course other approaches. Besides neo-Marxist interpretations of the history of economic growth (see Chap. 4), evolutionary growth models come to mind, as proposed by, for example, Richard Nelson and Sidney Winter.[52] Evolutionary models have not been able to influence mainstream economics much. The Darwinian approach explains economic growth in a reproductive Darwinian perspective. Oded Galor is a representative of this approach. The basic idea is that the agents who are doing well in the economy, and thus act as the agents of economic growth, will also have differential reproduction rates. Hence their share in the population keeps rising. The cultural traits which these people represent can be characterised as middle class, bourgeois values.[53]

However, other economic historians, such as Joel Mokyr, observe that in Darwinian models culture is assumed to be set for life; there is little room in these models for learning, persuasion, or imitation.[54] Mokyr underscores the important part that culture plays in the history of economic growth as, before him, it was done by David Landes (1924–2013). In 1998, Landes published his monumental *The Wealth and Poverty of Nations.*[55] The question he addressed was how societies deal with adverse conditions. If we learn anything of the history of economic development, Landes argued, it is that culture makes all the difference. He maintained that the driving force has been Western civilisation and its dissemination: the knowledge, the techniques, the political and social ideologies. Landes was not the first historian who emphasised the role played by culture; he got his inspiration from Max Weber (1864–1920). Landes argued that if we learn anything from the history of economic development, it is that culture makes all the difference, adding that Max Weber was right on![56]

In the course of the last century, economists gave up on culture's role in economic growth. In 1970, Robert Solow quipped that attempts to explain growth with variables such as culture ended up 'in a blaze of amateur sociology.' Since then, the mood has changed, in that culture is recognised as, indeed, an important element in the explanation of economic growth through time. After all, many dynamic economic phenomena cannot be explained without the role culture plays in the process. As Mokyr argues, culture is not a static concept; it is evolving and impinges upon nations' growth trajectories. The question remains, however, when and how cultures change.

It is simply impossible to present a comprehensive overview of what economic historians contributed to the understanding of economic growth. I have chosen two works of prominent economic historians who, I believe, provide interesting interpretations of the history of economic growth. The first work is Oded Galor's *From Stagnation to Growth: Unified*

Growth Theory, and the second one is Joel Mokyr's *Long-term Economic Growth and the History of Technology*.[57]

Galor presents a comprehensive historical economic development trajectory in which demographic development, human capital formation, and technological progress promote economic growth. The author also integrates contemporary insights in institutions and geography's role in explaining economic growth. The subtitle of Galor's book *Unified Growth Theory*, is reflective of Galor's theory: revealing the underlying micro foundations that are consistent with the economic growth process over the entire history of the human species. In other words, Galor sets himself the ambitious task of designing a unified theory of growth that intends to explain economic growth in subsequent stages over the entire course of human history.

Joel Mokyr is equally ambitious, in that he attempts to answer ten 'deep' questions regarding the Industrial Revolution. These questions range from what would explain the location of the Industrial Revolution, the timing, the role of technology, demography, human capital, and institutions involved, whether modern economic growth is due to culture, when did the 'Great Divergence' really start, to—finally—the question whether the Industrial Revolution was inevitable. Mokyr provides answers in *Long-term Economic Growth and the History of Technology*.

6.3.1 From Stagnation to Growth: Unified Growth Theory

Galor argues that recent growth theories, such as Solow's exogenous growth theory as well as the endogenous growth theory, fail to include growth processes of less developed countries. The reason is that both theories are inspired by modern economic growth achieved by Western countries and their offshoots: North America, Australia, New Zealand, and Japan. This resulted in growth theories that are only consistent with a small fragment of human history.[58]

Galor presents a more appropriate growth theory. He identifies three stages of growth: the Malthusian Epoch, the Post-Malthusian Regime, and the Sustained Growth Regime, paying special attention to population and human capital issues. In a nutshell, Galor's reasoning is as follows. In the past two centuries, the pace of technological progress increased significantly in association with the process of industrialisation. Various regions in the world departed from the so-called Malthusian trap and initially experienced a steep rise in the growth rates of per capita income *and* population. The increasing rate of technological progress in the second phase of the Industrial Revolution, and its interaction with human capital formation, ultimately led to the demographic transition. This transition liberated the gains in productivity from the counterbalancing effects of population growth. The subsequent decline in population growth, and the associated enhancement in technological progress plus human capital formation, led to the emergence of the modern state of sustained economic growth.

Galor presents four questions: (i) what accounts for the sudden take-off from stagnation to growth in some countries and the persistent stagnation in others; (ii) why has the positive link between income per capita and population growth reversed its course in some economies but not in others; (iii) why have the differences in per capita incomes across countries increased so markedly in the last two centuries; and (iv) has the transition to a state of sustained economic growth in advanced economies adversely affected the process of development in less-developed economies?

Galor referred to the attempts in physics to develop a unified field theory that are based on the conviction that all physical phenomena should ultimately be explained by some underlying unity. The term *unified field theory* was coined by Einstein whose research on relativity had led him to the hypothesis that it should be possible to find a unifying theory for electromagnetic and gravitational forces.

During the Malthusian Epoch technological progress throughout the world was insignificant, and so was population growth. During the first phase of the Industrial Revolution income per capita and population in England increased.[59] The growing number of people could be employed in unskilled jobs. However, during the second phase of the Industrial Revolution, technological progress triggered demand for better educated personnel.[60] This inspired parents to invest more in their offspring's education but also in limiting the number of children. This process resulted in the demographic transition: the rise in aggregate income was not counterbalanced by population growth. This development enabled technological progress to take off from the Malthusian Epoch onto sustained increase in income per capita. In addition, improved medical technologies and health infrastructure promoted higher life expectancy.

The Post-Malthusian Regime started in the beginning of the nineteenth century, while the take-off of less developed regions only started at the beginning of the last century. Towards the end of the nineteenth century, the Post-Malthusian Regime ended with the decline in population in Western countries and its offshoots. In less developed regions (except Africa) population decline only began in the second half of the twentieth century. While technological leader countries experienced a steady increase in per capita income, technological followers experienced a *rapid* increase in their income.

6.3.2 Demographic Transition in Less-Developed Countries

During the nineteenth century, less developed economies had experienced a decline in industrialisation. This was caused by the adverse effect of their increased population, but also triggered by globalisation and colonialism, forcing them to specialise in the production of raw materials, while the colonisers boosted their industrial sector. The take-off of less developed economies was associated with increased industrialisation, like it did in Western economies. Less-developed economies that made the transition to a state of sustained economic growth in recent decades, such as the Asian Tigers, industrialised very rapidly indeed.

Their industrialisation process was characterised by a gradual increase in the relative importance of human capital. In the 1970s, educational attainment increased significantly in Latin America and Asia in tandem with a decline in population growth, ushering in the demographic transition in both continents. Most African countries have not reached that stage yet. The demographic transition enhanced growth through three channels: (i) reduction of the dilution of the stock of capital and land; (ii) enhancement of human capital investment; and (iii) alternation of the age distribution of the population which temporarily increased the size of the labour force relative to the entire population.

As noted, the process of human capital accumulation in developed as well as less developed regions preceded the onset of the demographic transition. This suggests that the rise in the demand for human capital in the process of industrialisation and the subsequent accumulation of human capital played a crucial role in the demographic transition and the movement towards sustained economic growth.

During the nineteenth century, international trade expanded significantly, triggered by industrialisation and a result of the reduction of trade barriers and transportation costs. The gold standard ensured its smooth functioning. By the end of the nineteenth century, Britain and northwest Europe became net importers of primary products and net exporters of manufactured goods.[61] Exports from Asia, Latin America, and Africa were principally primary products.

The difference in timing of the take-off between advanced and less developed countries, and the corresponding variations in the timing of the demographic transition, explain the great divergence in income per capita as well as population growth between them. This generated three 'convergence clubs': (i) poor countries, in the vicinity of the Malthusian equilibrium; (ii) rich countries, in the vicinity of the sustained growth equilibrium; and (iii) others that attempted to graduate from one 'club' to a superior one. The overall growth process is thus characterised by multiple growth regimes. The ratio of GDP per capita in the richest region (Western offshoots) and the poorest region (Africa) has widened considerably from a modest 3:1 ratio in 1820 to a 18:1 ratio in 2001. Regarding the distribution of world population, Western Europe's share declined from 14.8% in 1870 to only 6.6% in 1998, while Asia's share reached 57.4% and that of Africa 12.8%.

6.3.3 *Unified Growth Theory*

A unified theory, according to Galor, unveils the underlying microfoundations that are consistent with the entire process of economic development, enhancing the confidence in the viability of growth theories, its predictions and policy implications, while improving the understanding of the driving forces that led to the recent transition from stagnation to growth and the Great Divergence.[62]

Empirical evidence suggests that the rise in the demand for human capital is the most significant force behind the demographic transition. It is a critical building block in unified theories. Once income rises, the income elasticity with respect to child quality is greater than that with respect to child quantity, which results in a decline in fertility along with a rise in the investment in each child. The decline in fertility during the demographic transition occurred in a period in which increased income per capita was intensified, while declining mortality maintained the trend that already existed in the century that preceded the demographic transition. Historical evidence indicates that the take-off from the Malthusian epoch to a state of sustained growth was a gradual process; i.e., there was no quantum leap in income per capita.

The first unified growth theory was developed by Galor and Weil. The theory was built on the interaction between the Malthusian elements, the engines of technological progress, the origin of human capital formation, and the determinants of parental choice regarding quality and quantity of offspring. Their theory suggests that the transition from stagnation to growth is an inevitable by-product of the Malthusian interaction between population and technology, its impact on the demand for human capital, and the subsequent demographic transition. The timing of the transition differs across countries, due to initial variations in geographical factors and historical accidents and their manifestation in variations in institutional, demographic, and cultural factors, trade patterns, colonial status, as well as in disparity in public policy.[63]

6.3.4 *Unified Evolutionary Growth Theory*

The theory's main hypotheses, which should not surprise the attentive reader, are as follows:

1. during the initial phase of the Malthusian epoch, the growth rate of output per capita is nearly zero and the growth rate of population and literacy rates is miniscule, reflective of the sluggish pace of technological progress, the low number of people with high valuation for child quality, and the slow pace of the evolutionary process;
2. prior to the Industrial Revolution, the process of natural selection increased the number of people with higher valuation for quality, gradually increasing the level of investment in human capital, permitting a slow output growth per capita; and,
3. the acceleration in the rate of technological progress, re-enforced by the investment in human capital of appropriately educated human capital in the Post-Malthusian Regime, which generated a universal investment in human capital, a demographic transition, and a rapid pace of economic growth.

Charles Darwin argued that it is not the strongest of the species that survive, nor the most intelligent, but the one most responsive to change.

Darwin's insight inspired the unified evolutionary growth theory, as it demonstrates that the Malthusian epoch stimulated a process of natural selection that generated an evolutionary advantage to human traits that were complementary to the growth process. This selection process, and its effect on investment in human capital, stimulated technological progress and triggered a reinforcing interaction between investment in human capital and technological progress that brought about the demographic transition and, subsequently, the state of sustained economic growth.

6.3.5 *Differential Takeoffs and the Great Divergence*

Has the transition to a state of sustained economic growth in advanced economies caused the Great Divergence? Institutional and cultural factors have been proposed by, as we saw, North and Landes. There are others who emphasise the relevance of geographical factors, such as location, climate, natural resources, prevalence of diseases. Research by a combination of institution-minded and geography-oriented scholars provided evidence that variations in the contemporary growth process across countries can be attributed to institutional factors, whereas geographical factors are secondary, operating primarily via variations in institutions.

During the second phase of the Industrial Revolution, international trade enhanced the specialisation of industrial economies in the production of industrial-skilled intensive goods. In non-industrial countries international trade resulted in the production of unskilled-intensive, non-industrial goods. Hence the absence of demand for skilled human capital there has not led to the investment in the quality of the population. Instead, the gains from trade resulted in population growth, rather than in an increase in income.

So international trade affected the distribution of population, skills, and technologies in the world economy. Trade has been a significant force behind the Great Divergence in income per capita across countries. For example, Galor and Mountford suggest that the expansion of international trade in the nineteenth century has played a major role in the timing of demographic transitions across countries.[64] While in industrial countries the gains from trade were primarily directed towards investment in education and output growth, a large slice of the trade gains in non-industrialised countries went into population growth. Over the past two centuries, it has been a significant determinant of the distribution of world population and a prime cause of the Great Divergence.

A comparison between the UK and India since the nineteenth century is a case in point. Industrialisation in the UK accelerated, leading to a significant increase in the demand for skilled labour; a demographic transition took place and a transition towards a state of sustained economic growth ensued. However, in India trade played a not so helpful role.

The period 1813–1850 was a period of transition for India: from exporter of manufactured products (textiles) into a supplier of primary products. Trade with the UK was fundamental in the decline in India's industrialisation. This delayed the demographic transition in India and its economic development.

6.3.6 Conclusions

At the beginning of his book Galor presented four questions: (i) what accounts for the sudden take-off from stagnation to growth in some countries and the persistent stagnation in others; (ii) why has the positive link between income per capita and population growth reversed its course in some economies but not in others; (iii) why have the differences in per capita incomes across countries increased so markedly in the last two centuries; and (iv) has the transition to a state of sustained economic growth in advanced economies adversely affected the process of development in less developed economies?

Regarding questions one and two, i.e., the sudden take-off of some countries and the reversal of the positive link between income per capita and population growth, Galor concludes that the transition from stagnation to growth is an inevitable by-product of the inherent Malthusian interaction between population and technology and its ultimate impact on the demand for human capital and, thereby, on the onset of the demographic transition. As for question three and four, i.e., the increasing income gap between rich and poor countries, and whether the economic growth of advanced countries negatively impacted on less developed economies, in general terms Galor concludes: 'Variations in the timing of the transition across countries and regions reflect initial differences in geographical factors and historical accidents and their manifestation in variations in institutional, demographic and cultural factors, trade patterns, colonial status, and public policy.'[65]

6.4 Long-Term Economic Growth and the History of Technology

Oded Galor is a representative of the reproductive Darwinian approach. However, Joel Mokyr, argues that in Darwinian models culture is presented as a *static* phenomenon, to be set for life at conception. In these models there is little room for learning, persuasion, or imitation.[66] The important *dynamic* part played by culture is a leading notion in Mokyr's analysis of the history of economic growth.

Mokyr starts his book with the following questions: what explains the location of the Industrial Revolution, and its timing? If sustained growth is the normal state of the economy, is the experience of the past two centuries revolutionary? What was the role of technology, demography, human capital, and institutions in bringing about modern growth? What about the role of culture? When did the 'Great Divergence' really start; and, finally, was the Industrial Revolution inevitable?

Regarding technology, Solow treats technology as an exogenous factor in his growth model. However, over the last two centuries, technology is central to the dynamic of the economy. Before the Industrial Revolution economies registered economic growth without changes in technology. Growth was promoted by the presence of peace, law and order, improved communications, trust, and enforceable property rights. Before 1750, economic history was about this kind of growth, such as Imperial Rome and medieval Italian and Flemish cities. They were based on commercial progress—so-called Smithian Growth.

The Industrial Revolution is not to be seen as the beginning of growth, but as the time at which technology assumed an ever-increasing weight in the generation of growth. It must not be confused with the demographic transition, which came later and whose relationship with technological progress is complex and poorly understood. A decomposition of growth into a technology component and a trade-and-institutions component must take into account the interaction between them. Mokyr proposes a framework to understand how and why new technology emerges (through a dynamic relationship between prescriptive and propositional knowledge), how it was limited before the eighteenth century, after which it was liberated from its constraints. The author argues that technological modernity means an economy in which sustained technological progress is the principal engine of growth. Mokyr quipped: 'Knowledge opens doors, but it does not force society to walk through them.'[67]

6.4.1 A Historical Theory of Technology

The motivation for technological progress is rarely purely economic. The basic unit of analysis of technology is the technique contained in a sort of cookbook with technical recipes. Society's production possibilities are bound by what society knows. Mokyr distinguishes two types of knowledge: (i) prescriptive knowledge; and (ii) propositional knowledge—together they constitute the set of ***useful knowledge*** (a term coined by Simon Kuznets, by the way). Prescriptive knowledge includes techniques like any recipe: they comprise instructions that allow people to construct and produce. Propositional knowledge, on the other hand, contains a set of propositions about the physical world. The distinction between them can be clarified by patent law, which permits the patenting of inventions (additions to prescriptive knowledge) but not of discoveries (additions to proportional knowledge). Knowledge is mostly cumulative and evolutionary.

Some scholars maintain that the Industrial Revolution was a purely British affair. However, many technological elements of this revolution were the result of a joint international effort in which other innovations collaborated. Yet most successful economic applications of the new technology appeared in Britain. Its technological precociousness was a function of three factors: (i) Britain was at peace in a period when the Continent was in upheaval; (ii) British entrepreneurs adopted new inventions; and, (iii) Britain had developed appropriate institutions. Britain had a healthier public finance system, well-defined property rights on land, and a power structure that favoured the rich and propertied classes. It also had the flexibility to adapt its economic and legal institutions without political violence and disruptions. In short, laissez faire eclipsed mercantilist paternalism.

Joseph Needham (1900–1995) taught biochemistry at Cambridge University. Living in England, that had brought about the Industrial Revolution, Needham thought that all advanced technologies had been developed in England or in other European countries. It so happened that he had a female student, Lu Gwei-djen, in his lab whose father was a professor of history of science at Peking University. Lu had learned a lot from her father. When Needham once told his

(*continued*)

(continued)

students that a certain technology was invented in Europe, she corrected him by telling that the invention had taken place in China; she could even tell Needham in which book he could find it.

This information triggered his curiosity. He started to study the history of Chinese science and technology. During WWII, Needham was posted as British cultural counsellor in Chongqing. During his travels in China, Li Yuese (Needham's Chinese name) collected a lot of historical materials, which now belong to Cambridge University's Needham Library.

Needham studied in which year a certain technology, tool or machine was invented. He discovered that before the fifteenth and sixteenth centuries technology flowed one way: from East to West. After all, China had invented cast iron, the plough, the stirrup, gunpowder, printing, and the magnetic compass, among others. But in the sixteenth and seventeenth centuries, some technologies started to flow from West to East. After the middle of the eighteenth century, the flow was exclusively from West to East. This insight constituted the basis for the *Needham Puzzle*: why had China been so technologically advanced compared to other countries, and why was China not any longer ahead of the rest of the world?

Justin Lin deals with the question in *Demystifying the Chinese Economy*.[68] He proposes a theory to unravel the Needham puzzle. Lin goes back to the Industrial Revolution. The defining phenomenon of it was the *acceleration* of technological innovation. This is why the gap between China and the West became ever wider. On top of it, England developed many more new industries such as the chemical, automobile, aerospace, and information technology industries.

Lin introduces the technology distribution curve (shaped like a Bell curve), divided in low technology at the left half, and high technology at the right half of the curve. Factors like talent, newly developed material (such as steel) and knowledge move the technology distribution curve to the right, meaning that the more a country avails of these three factors, the greater the chance that new technological inventions will ensue. Lin proposes three hypotheses: (i) the

(continued)

(continued)

more trials and errors that are carried out, the greater the probability of inventing a new technology; (ii) the more advanced the current technology, the lower the probability of inventing a new technology; and (iii) after the discovery of one technology (e.g., steel) more tools were invented one after the other. Based on these hypotheses, Lin answers three questions:

1. Why was China advanced in premodern times? At the time, invention was based on experience. China had a large population, and the larger the population the larger the number of craftsmen and peasants, and the greater the chance for inventions. Hence, abundant human resources laid the basis for technological progress in those early days.
2. Why did China lag behind Europe in modern times? In Europe after the eighteenth century, invention was based on *experiment* and no longer on experience. Trials and errors were now mainly based on intentional experiments. A scientist in a lab can do more trials than thousands of craftsmen and peasants. So population was no longer an issue. To counter the diminishing experiment results effect, European countries increased basic research, triggering more technological innovation. The precondition for basic research was the Scientific Revolution that took place in the West, even before the Industrial Revolution. The Scientific Revolution contributed to the Industrial Revolution in two ways: it introduced a revolution in methodology (i.e., controlled experiment replaced experience as the basis for trial and error), and it facilitated the shift to the right of the technology distribution curve.
3. Why did a Scientific Revolution did not also take place in China? Modern science uses mathematical models to formalise its hypotheses, and uses controlled or reproducible experiments to test them. Mathematical language is much better than natural languages in disseminating new knowledge. China had a bureaucratic system whereas Europe had a feudal system, more favourable to mercantilist values. With the collapse of the feudal system,

(*continued*)

(continued)

capitalism and modern science could fully emerge. In China, merchants had a low position in the Confucian system; they were barred from the civil service examination system. China also did not promote the development of good mathematicians nor did it warm to scientific experiments. True, when the civil service examinations were introduced by the Qin Dynasty, mathematics was one of the subjects. However, towards the end of the sixteenth century, Emperor Shenzong decided that mathematics was of little use and scrapped the subject. Without people mastering mathematical tools, the Scientific Revolution could not take place in China.

China's initial prosperity had a lot to do with its civil service system. And when the basis for technological innovation shifted from experience to experiment, like it did in Europe, the system lost its superiority; worse, it even hindered scientific and technological progress. The key issue, concludes Lin, is the absence of the Scientific Revolution in China, without which the Industrial Revolution could not have happened. And without the Industrial Revolution, technology could not accelerate. That is why capitalism, though sprouting in China, failed to develop there fully since the eighteenth century until recently.

After the first wave (1765–1790) of inventions, the persistence of technological change transformed the Industrial Revolution into the Great Divergence. The second wave of inventions was the critical period: after 1830, growth of income per capita accelerated around 1.1 percent per year, while income growth during the Industrial Revolution's beginning period was modest. From 1830 onwards, the modern sector expanded rapidly since the new technology was applied more broadly. Economic growth accelerated, and by the mid-1840s there was clear-cut evidence that the British standard of living was rising, even for the working classes.

6.4.2 *The Intellectual Roots of the Industrial Revolution*

The essence of the Industrial Revolution was technological. Why is it that the inventions did not peter out after a while? The answer is that well before the start of the Industrial Revolution, changes had taken place in the intellectual sphere in Europe. After 1870, the influence of science proper on some branches of production became decisive. The success of the Industrial Revolution must be found in the area of useful knowledge, whose development started in Europe before 1750.

What mattered was the culture of the generation and diffusion of propositional knowledge. This knowledge became more and more tested, either by experiment or through the performance of the techniques based on them. In addition, natural philosophers increasingly understood that the main purpose of knowledge was to improve mankind's material condition.

The Enlightenment was the central intellectual change in Europe before the Industrial Revolution. Mokyr introduces the term *Industrial Enlightenment.* Representatives of the Enlightenment created the attitudes, institutions, and mechanisms through which new useful knowledge was created and put to good use. Francis Bacon (1561–1626) had argued that one could attain material progress through controlling nature, and that one could only harness nature by understanding her. Adam Smith's (1723–1790) division of labour was another Enlightenment notion. Nothing of the sort can be detected in the Ottoman Empire, India, China, and Africa. Mokyr then concludes, in rather exuberant phrasing, that the difference was the ability to break out of the circle of concavity and negative feedback, and slash the upper bound on income that the limitations of knowledge and institutions had set on practically all economies until then.[69]

Another dimension of the Industrial Enlightenment was access to existing knowledge. From the need to rationalise and standardise weights and measures, and the insistence on writing in vernacular language (rather than in Latin), to the launching of academies and to the *Grande Encyclopedie*, the notion of diffusion became the center of attention among intellectuals. Technical and engineering data and books appeared, such as a detailed description of the functioning of windmills. Scientific societies sprung up throughout Europe. In the Netherlands, rich but increasingly technologically backward, heroic efforts were established to infuse the economy with more innovativeness.[70]

6.4.3 The Emergence of Technological Modernity

Since the second half of the nineteenth century, change had become the norm. Now, how do we explain this change in technological dynamics? A phase transition occurs when a model switches from one equilibrium to another. In such models one equilibrium is characterised by rapid investment, which raises the demand for skills. The positive feedback occurs because, as Galor had argued, the increase in the rate of return to human capital induces parents to invest more in their children and have fewer children which in turn raises the rate of return on physical capital that triggers investment.

The question is whether the ideas that count are a monotonic function of population size, or whether they are generated by a negligible fraction of the population? The population growth in Britain was almost zero in the first half of the eighteenth century and, while it took off there during the post-1750 era, the same was true for Ireland, where no Industrial Revolution had taken place. Most endogenous historical growth models depend on the notion that investment in human capital is critical to economic take-off. But in France, fertility was already down when inventions took place there. In Britain, fertility only dropped in the mid-1870s.

The idea that nineteenth century education and literacy emerged as a response to a need for a trained labour force is misleading. It is a fair question to ask how many inventors and technically able people were needed to generate sustained technological progress? Mokyr argues that it were self-made mechanics and technicians that made the Industrial Revolution possible by generating a stream of micro-inventions. They created the opportunities by providing the competence to carry out new instructions. It may well be that the best model to explain technological progress is the level of education and sophistication of a small elite of engineers, mechanics, and chemists.

The dynamics between propositional and prescriptive knowledge is important. As these two co-evolved, they enriched one another, eventually creating the phase transition. When powerful enough, this mechanism can account for the change in stability of the entire system. The positive feedback from prescriptive to propositional knowledge took a variety of forms. The most celebrated example is the connection between steam power and thermodynamics. Rankine's *Manual of the Steam Engine* (1859) made the latter accessible to engineers and led to many improvements in actual machines.[71]

As the total body of useful knowledge is expanding dramatically, it is only with the help of increasingly sophisticated search engines that needles of useful knowledge can be retrieved from a haystack of cosmic magnitude. Kuznets felt that the essence of modern growth was the increasing reliance of technology on modern science. Inside the black box of technology, there is a smaller one called R&D.

6.4.4 *Institutions and Technological Progress*

Why is it that some societies are more inclined to generate new knowledge and others not? Before 1750, there was negative institutional feedback. Opportunists acted as rent seekers. Wealth was redistributed rather than enlarged. Smithian growth was confined to cities were trade took place. The Industrial Enlightenment meant that the old rent-seeking traditions were increasingly viewed as both unfair and inefficient. Mercantilism had been a game of international competition between rival political entities, through subsidising exports and raw materials imports and imposing tariffs on finished goods. The French Revolution did more than anything else to transform Enlightenment ideas into institutional changes, paving the way for economic growth. The institutional changes between 1770 and 1815 saw to it that the revolution was not followed by a surge in rent-seeking and violence that could have reversed the process.

Three kinds of institutions were important in facilitating sustained technological progress: (i) those that provided for connections between people concerned with propositional knowledge and the ones on the production side; (ii) those that set the agenda of research to generate new propositional knowledge that could be transformed into new techniques; and (iii) institutions that created incentives for innovative people to spend resources in order to map this knowledge into new techniques, and specifically weakening social and political resistance against these new techniques.

Regarding connections between those concerned with propositional knowledge and those involved in the production of machines and the like, technical subjects penetrated school curricula; textbooks of applied science and professional journals appeared. Universities increasingly combined teaching *and* research; as a result research and development grew which contributed to the development and application of new techniques. As for institutions offering incentives, property rights were secured and so were patents. For example, the American patent system exhibited many characteristics of a market: inventors responded to demand conditions, they secured the gains from their inventions.[72] There are other institutions that promote new techniques, but there had to be the propositional knowledge on which the inventions rested.[73]

6.4.5 *Technology, Growth, and the Rise of the Occident*

In economic history everything is a matter of degree; there are no absolutes and Mokyr's interpretation is not generally accepted. Many believe that continuity was at play, rather than something radical and deep that changed Western society between 1760 and 1830. The Industrial Revolution itself was not a period of rapid economic growth, but it set into motion an economic process that, by the middle of the nineteenth century, created a material world that demonstrated a dynamic not hitherto experienced. And it proved to be sustainable. The gap between rich and poor countries became bigger than ever; the Great Divergence train stormed on, so to speak.

Referring to the questions at the beginning of the book, Mokyr answered them as follows. How did the West do it, and when? By 1750, the gap between rich and poor was very small indeed. Around 1500, European soil already contained 'seeds' of the future divergence. Something had changed in Europe before the Industrial Revolution that established the economic dynamic in the West, but not elsewhere.[74]

Then, the question *where* did it happen? In 1750, Europe was in many respects already deeply different from other continents. It had Calvin, Newton, Galileo, Spinoza, Descartes, and Bacon. It had commercial capitalism thriving in Atlantic ports, a well-functioning monetary system, and the ability of rulers to tax their subjects. It had universities, parliaments, embryonic financial institutions, microscopes, printing presses, and colonies. Its agriculture was becoming productive thanks to a rotating system of cultivation. It had conquered the plague; it had navigational instruments and maps.

Many of these European features could also be found in other societies, especially in China and Japan. The difference with Europe was not that large. For example, the Ching dynasty had law and order, a meritocratic bureaucracy, peace, and long-distance trade. But what other countries and continents did not have, and Europe did have, was the Industrial Enlightenment. This affected the two central elements of the Industrial Revolution: technology and institutions, and how they influenced one another.

Mokyr's emphasis on the Enlightenment illustrates how economists should also think about culture, since culture mattered a lot to economic development in two ways: (i) the metaphysical beliefs that people held about their environment and nature; and (ii) their attitudes toward the relationship between production and useful knowledge. Mokyr argues that it should also include their beliefs about the possibility of progress and their notions of economic freedom, property, and novelty.

The Enlightenment may have been the *missing link* that economic historians have hitherto overlooked. Many institutional elements were already there in the Middle-Ages, but they did not trigger modern growth, precisely because of technological constraints. Bacon's idea that the understanding of nature leads to its control, was central to the emergence of modern economic growth. The eighteenth century Enlightenment brought many of the institutional elements of an orderly and civil society, together with the growing realisation that economic activity is not a zero-sum game and that redistributions and rent-seeking are costly to society.[75]

Useful knowledge grows because in each society there are people who are creative and original, motivated by some combination of greed, ambition, curiosity, and altruism. All of them can be seen to be operating among the people who helped make the Industrial Revolution. In order to be translated from personal predilections to facts on the ground, and from there to economic growth, Mokyr argues that an environment that produced the correct incentives and the proper access to knowledge had to be there. It was the uniqueness of the European Enlightenment that created that kind of environment.

6.4.6 Conclusion

The Economist's Free Exchange column observed, as noted, that economic historians are held back by a paucity of data, nor have they managed to arrive at a shared understanding of the nature of economic growth. This latter observation would certainly be accepted by Mokyr, who argued that in economic history everything is a matter of degree; there are no absolutes.

The lack of a shared understanding between economic historians is confirmed by Galor's and Mokyr's respective interpretation of the origins of economic growth. In Galor's view it is, in essence, the historical interplay between technological progress, population growth, and human capital development that can be applied to analyse the successive stages of economic growth. By contrast, Mokyr's vantage point is the relationship between culture, technological progress and institutions. Mokyr delved deep into the origins of the Enlightenment and identified the great personalities who brought it about, triggering the Industrial Enlightenment. He, like McCloskey, elaborately underscored that culture and ideas make all the difference. This is not the one and only explanation of what inspired economic growth, but it is an insight not to be overlooked.

Although they do not present a shared understanding of the history of economic growth, Galor and Mokyr agree nonetheless that analysing the onset of the Industrial Revolution is key to understanding what happened since; they both use terms, such as demographic transition and the great divergence. Both of them also integrate political, institutional, and geographical factors into their analyses; factors missing in standard economic growth models to date. These three factors help to better capture—and better explain—the process of economic growth over the past two centuries

Although modern economic growth has begun to reach most of the world, McCloskey once argued that if we had a better understanding of its economic, political, institutional, and geographical causes, we could do a better job of encouraging it to spread to the relatively few remaining holdouts.

6.5 New Economic Geography

Well before the onset of the first generation of development economists, geographers paid attention to the question why some countries were rich and most others were poor. In Chap. 3, a summary of *Civilization and Climate* was presented, written by Ellsworth Huntington, a renowned geographer at the time. However, since then the role played by geography in development was rather neglected. Only much later, another remarkable book drew the attention of scholars and of the general readership. Jared Diamond's *Guns, Germs and Steel* became a bestseller.[76] He argues that Eurasia forms a very large territory, whose axis stretches from West to East, and thus provides similar climatic conditions for promoting the relative rapid spread of agricultural practices and related technological inventions. Comparing this with Africa and the America's, their respective axis runs vertically from North to South, thus encompassing varying climatic conditions (including tropical ones), which limited the spread of crops that thrive in cooler climates. Tropical climates exert a negative influence on agricultural productivity. Moreover, as Diamond adds, the spread of agricultural practices in both continents was greatly hampered by barring deserts and, for the America's, the extreme narrowness of Central America.

It was Paul Krugman who was instrumental in reviving interest in economic geography, underscoring the role of geography in explaining prosperity and poverty. Krugman was awarded the 2008 Economics Nobel Prize for his work on new economic geography.

Before dealing with Krugman's insights, I present some of the findings of a study conducted by Gallup et al.[77] One of the authors' objectives was to present counter-arguments to the popular notion that it were institutions that mattered in explaining economic growth. In their view, difference in economic performance cannot only be explained by the quality of institutions, as discussed in the first section this chapter. They provide evidence that geography plays an important role in shaping the distribution of world income and economic growth. The authors conclude, among others, that: (i) countries located close to the sea had higher per capita incomes than landlocked countries; (ii) tropical countries—with the exception of Hong Kong, part of Taiwan and Singapore—are poorer than non-tropical countries; and (iii) coastal, temperate regions of the Northern hemisphere have the highest income per square kilometer of land. After all, regions near the sea have lower transport costs, hence they can benefit from international trade and specialisation. As discussed in Chap. 2, the fastest growing developing countries based their growth on labour-intensive manufactured exports located in coastal regions. China is the example *par excellence* in this realm. The greater densities of population in countries close to the sea, triggered agglomeration economies and increasing returns.

Gallup et al. also found that per capita income is positively related to the proportion of the population close to the sea, but negatively related to (i) location in the tropics; (ii) the killer disease malaria; (iii) distance; and (iv) export costs. The growth of income is 1.2% less in countries severely affected by malaria than in non-tropical countries.[78] As for export costs, the authors calculated, for example, that shipping a six-meter-long container from Rotterdam, the Netherlands, to Dar-es-Salaam, Tanzania, did cost $1400.- while shipping the same container from Dar-es-Salaam to Kigali, Rwanda, (less than one-third of the distance) would cost $2500.-.[79] The implication of these findings is that policy makers should pay more attention to the developmental barriers associated with geography, poor health, low agricultural productivity, and high transportation costs.

6.5.1 *Increasing Returns and Economic Geography*

In *Increasing Returns and Economic Geography*, Krugman observes that location of production factors occupies a relatively small part of standard economic analysis.[80] When one thinks of it, this is puzzling since most factors involved in manufacturing are often concentrated in only a few clusters of metropolitan areas. Krugman wonders why and when does manufacturing become concentrated in a few regions, with the remaining regions playing a peripheral role of agricultural suppliers to the manufacturing centre.

He designed a model consisting of two countries in which there are two kinds of production: agriculture and manufacturing and their respective wage rates. Transportation costs constitute an integral—but important—part of the model. Agriculture is characterised by constant returns to scale and by intense use of immobile land—its geographical distribution is determined by the availability of suitable land. Manufacturing is characterised, not surprisingly, by increasing returns to scale and modest use of land. Regarding externalities, Krugman assumes that externalities, that sometimes lead to the emergence of a core-periphery pattern, are in fact pecuniary externalities associated with either demand or supply linkages, rather than purely technological spillovers.

> Over the past decade… it has become a familiar point that in the presence of imperfect competition and increasing returns, pecuniary externalities matter; for example, if one firm's actions affect the demand for the product of another firm whose price exceeds marginal cost, this is as much a 'real' externality as if one firm's research and development spills over into the general knowledge pool.[81]

Now, where will manufacturing take place? The preferred locations will be where there is a large nearby demand, as production there obviously minimises transportation costs.[82] Other locations will then be served from these centrally located sites. So manufactures production will concentrate where there is a large market (i.e., agglomeration economies). But equally so, the market will be large where manufactures production is concentrated.[83] This process will be reinforced by a so-called forward linkage, in that it will be more desirable to live and produce near a concentration of manufacturing production because it will be less expensive to buy the goods that this location provides—centripetal forces are then at play. Krugman describes what may happen:

> But now let the society spend a higher fraction of income on nonagricultural goods and services; let the factory system and eventually mass production

> emerge, and with them economies of large-scale production; and let canals, railroads, and finally automobiles lower transportation costs. Then the tie of production to distribution of land will be broken. A region with a relatively large nonrural population will be an attractive place to produce both because of the large local market and because of the availability of the goods and services produced there. This will attract still more population, at the expense of regions with smaller initial production, and the process will feed on itself until the whole of the nonrural population is concentrated in a few regions.[84]

This development suggests that the details of the geography that emerges, i.e., which regions end up with the population, depend on initial conditions. If one region has slightly more population than another, and when transportation costs fall below a certain level, this region ends up gaining population at the other region's expense. However, had the distribution of population been slightly different, the outcome might have been the reverse.

The remainder of Krugman's paper is devoted to the application of the 'two region' model; a variant on the monopolistic competition framework.[85] The empirical value of Krugman's model has been substantial. It is being applied in, among others, town planning and clustering of economic activities.

In 1995, Krugman and Anthony Venables published a paper entitled *Globalization and Inequality of Nations*.[86] Its central argument is that when transport costs fall below a critical value, a core-periphery spontaneously forms, and nations that find themselves in the periphery suffer a decline in real income. But, then, at still lower transport costs, there is a convergence of real incomes, in which peripheral nations gain and core nations may lose. The authors observe that those who remember the debate over the New International Economic Order during the 1970s, their insight sounds surprising. After all, the mainstream view at the time was that integration of world markets would create a rise in living standards of rich nations at the expense of the poor. However, developments since have changed the outlook rather dramatically, as erstwhile peripheral nations have gained at the expense of those belonging to the core.

Krugman and Venables present a world in which each region can produce two kinds of goods: agricultural goods that are produced with constant returns to scale and manufactured goods that are subject to increasing returns. The manufacturing sector produces both final goods for consumers and intermediate goods as inputs in the production of other manufactures. They assume that all countries are equally proficient in both sectors. They also assume that, initially, transportation costs between the two are very high. Then they introduce gradually reducing transportation costs. This opens up the possibility of trade between the two countries. A circular process ensues, leading to regional differentiation. The country with the larger manufacturing sector offers an attractive place for the production of intermediate goods. And when the country produces a greater variety of intermediate goods than the other, better access to these goods will mean lower costs of production of final goods, leading to a further shift of manufacturing to that region—agglomeration of manufacturing will take place there. Hence when transportation costs fall below a certain critical point, the world economy will spontaneously organise itself into an industrial core and a deindustrialised periphery. But if transportation costs continue to fall, the importance of being close to markets and suppliers will also decline. Peripheral countries offer potential producers the advantage of lower wages.[87] Again, at some point the decline in transportation costs will be sufficient that the lower wage rate in the periphery more than offsets the disadvantage of being remote from markets and supplies. At this point manufacturing will have an incentive to move out from the core to the periphery again, resulting in the convergence of wage rates.[88]

6.5.2 *Reshaping Economic Geography*

It is perhaps no surprise that one year after Krugman was awarded the Economics Noble Prize, the World Bank devoted its 2009 World Development Report to economic geography. The report's title is *Reshaping Economic Geography*.[89] Its principal message is that although worldwide economic development is quite unbalanced, development can still be more inclusive and sustainable. The report's purpose was to re-energise geography's place in understanding economic and human development.

The message of *Reshaping Economic Geography* is that economic growth will be unbalanced: do not try to spread out economic activities, because that will not work, but do not forget to invest in human welfare. An example: the European Union (EU) tried to stimulate economically lagging areas through its so-called cohesion policy. However, the results showed little effectiveness of interventions in improving economic performance of these areas. Ireland followed a different policy; the Irish government promoted *national* economic growth. From being one of Europe's poorest countries, it became one of the richest. The report underscored that between 1985 and 1995, in the EU the rising inequality of before-tax market incomes was partially offset by progressive tax and transfer policies.

Development can still be inclusive, in that even people who start their lives far away from economic opportunities, can benefit from the growing concentration of wealth in agglomerations. The key policy challenge is to speed up economic divergence while reducing the time for welfare convergence.

Part I of the report describes its conceptual framework in three dimensions (i) density; (ii) distance; and (iii) division—the 3-D's: higher densities due to urbanisation, shorter distances as people and businesses move to cities, and fewer divisions as economic borders are thinned and world markets are entered. The 3-D's constitute the required changes that will help developing countries to prosper.

What happened in the developed world is now being repeated in the most dynamic economies of the developing world. After all, the report argues (in an evolutionary fashion), that in the past America and Japan reshaped their economic geography along these lines and that China is reshaping its economic geography now.

Regarding the question what works, the report provides proposals, along the lines of the 3-D's from the local level upwards. For example, density works most powerfully at the local level, while distance is the most critical element at the national level. Division, the third D, is the most important dimension at the international level. Governments can step in to reduce spatial disparities through (again) three instruments: institutions (which should be spatially blind and universal in coverage),[90] infrastructure (to promote spatial connections), and incentives (spatially targeted interventions). In various instances more than one instrument has to be applied. For example, when dealing with sizeable concentrations of the poor in lagging areas, spatially blind institutions, that promote the mobility of labour and capital and ensure the provision of basic services, must be supported by policies to improve the access of entrepreneurs in lagging areas to markets.

The report cites an example from Bangladesh. The bridge over the Jamuna River opened market access for producers in the Northwest around the Rajshahi division. Built at a cost of $1 billion, this bridge provides the first road and rail link between the Northwest, an intermediate area, with the more developed East which includes the national capital region. Better market access and reduced input prices encouraged farmers to diversify into high-yielding crops, such as modern varieties of rice and vegetables. The government has complemented connective infrastructure policies with spatially blind institutions to improve coverage of social services such as immunisation.

Incentives to promote economic investments in lagging areas have been widely used by countries to accelerate national economic growth. They seem to work better when they reinforce market signals and address coordination failures. They are less successful when governments pick the places to support growth. More often than not, geographically targeted incentives would not even be necessary if the policy objective was to integrate leading and lagging areas, rather than promote industry in economically unfavourable places.

The report examines the most important policy issues of economic geography, from the local, via the national, on to the international level. A common element in policy debates on urbanisation, area development, and globalisation is over-emphasising geographic targeting; i.e., what to do in rural areas or in slums; what to do in lagging states or remote areas; and what to do in landlocked countries. The report calls for rebalancing these policy discussions to include all the instruments of integration, such as institutions that unify, infrastructure that connects, and interventions that target.

6.5.3 Does the Report Reshape Economic Geography?

Did *Reshaping Economic Geography* re-energise geography's place in the understanding of economic development? An international group of geographers dealt with this question.[91] Their short answer is that the report appears academically narrow and historically shallow. They admit that it is to some extent 'sour grapes' when they conclude that the report claims to be reshaping economic geography while ignoring the work of geographers. The report mainly refers to recent economic geography literature—in particular Krugman's—while scarcely citing any contemporary geographers, neither early analysts of the relationships between space, economy and society, nor subsequent critics and innovators.

The report presents singular models, as if any situation would fit into them. The many examples fit into these models; but what about exceptions to the rule? They are not explored; positivism trumps realism, in the words of the geographers. Qualitative analyses are also rare in the report; embeddedness and differences between geographical areas is lost, including relationships between local, regional, and national levels.[92] Regarding these relationships, the geographers observe that the transference of poverty from rural to urban areas is hidden in the report; nor were social and environmental effects taken on board.

There are also inconsistencies. Human capital is treated as an endogenous factor. However, if human capital must be considered as endogenous to growth, how can it be consistent to state that natural and social capital should be treated as exogenous, as the report does? The geographers also wonder how inclusion (a principal objective of the report) can be examined without spending too much time considering the social and environmental aspects of this inclusion?

The report quotes Deng Xiaoping's statement: 'If all of China is to become prosperous, some areas must get rich before others', underscoring the report's proposed spatially unbalanced growth. Although policymakers in developing countries have been aware of the impossibility of spatially balanced growth, they nevertheless weighed this against the dangers of social and political instability, as elaborated in a report of the Asian Development Bank.[93] Understanding regional inequalities as an effect of social and power relations would make it clear that it is also no accident that certain regions become poor and stay poor; in fact, there are political interests that benefit from regional inequalities. These interests are over-represented in the institutions that reproduce these inequalities. This observation is frequently lost out of sight in the report. The geographers observe that the socio-political causes of regional inequality are invisible in the report.

In sum, the geographers conclude:

> …*Reshaping Economic Geography* is a disappointment. It does a disservice to economic geography (at least as done by many geographers) and it eludes many or most of the interesting debates in development geography. …In the Report… the appropriate management of the economy precedes all else and issues of power, politics and embeddedness, so creatively worked by development *and* economic geographers, have little purchase. Certainly they seem not to have complicated the arrow that… seems to run straight from economic first principles to development outcomes.[94]

6.5.4 Conclusion

Geography again forms an integral part of the research and debate about economic growth; this renewed attention for the 'Geographical Divide' has been squarely taken on board. Location, climate, tropical diseases, population densities, geological endowments, transportation and communication costs, all impinge upon economic growth. However, not exclusively; other factors also play their part, such as institutions, history, and the quality of economic policies. Nonetheless, Krugman's models are, in his own words, remarkably powerful in their ability to yield simple intuition-building treatments of seemingly intractable issues. The model he and Venables developed shows how the core-periphery paradigm could be turned upside down once transportation costs drop; indeed, a contemporary development, as demonstrated by e.g., China's economic development.

There is no shared understanding to date about the decisive force of institutions or geography in explaining economic growth, or stagnation for that matter. At any event, development economists now pay more attention to what economic geographers have to say about geography's role in the development process. *Reshaping Economic Geography* was a firm step into the right direction, although a somewhat biased step, in that it was more the result of what economists contributed than what economic geographers could have contributed to the report.

6.6 Overall Conclusion

Development economics in its widest sense has developed a few firm insights. One of them is that institutions matter in the development of an economy, and certainly in sustaining it. Institutional reform is a not a question of one-size-fits all; it is moulded by each country's specific historical, political, and cultural context. One dilemma concerning institutions is that institutional development is a messy term; it involves a lot and it is difficult to measure. North—aware of the challenges involved—said that the promise of a unified growth model is there, but we may never have definite answers to all our questions.

Economic historians integrate political, institutional, and geographical factors into their analyses. These factors certainly help in better capturing and explaining the history of economic growth. Although economic historians have not reached a shared understanding of the nature of economic growth, on one aspect they agree: the Industrial Revolution dramatically changed the interplay between culture, technological innovation, population growth, human capital formation, and institutions.

As mentioned, location, climate, tropical diseases, population densities, geological endowments, transportation costs, what have you, impinge upon economic growth. True, but the other factors presented in this chapter also play their respective parts.

If there is one thing that this chapter confirms, it is McCloskey's observation that economics can't explain the modern world. I would like to slightly rephrase her observation: economics alone cannot explain the modern world. Economic growth is about economic yard sticks and phenomena such as GDP, income per capita, income and wealth distribution, investment and saving rates, taxes, and market prices. All of them explain a lot about the dynamics of economic growth, but not everything.

The challenge is to capture economic growth in its widest sense. Indeed, Maddison observed that if we are to explain why the economic growth experience of nations has been so diverse, and why income spreads are now so wide, it is necessary to go beyond proximate and measurable elements of causality and consider institutional, social or policy influences which may retard or encourage economic development.[95] I believe that John Hicks formulated economists' predicament best:

> The more characteristic economic problems are problems of change, or growth and retrogression, and of fluctuation. The extent to which these can

be reduced into scientific terms is rather limited; for at every stage in an economic process new things are happening, things which have not happened before—at the most they are rather like what has happened before. We need a theory that will help us with these problems; but it is impossible to believe that it can ever be a complete theory. It is bound, by its very nature, to be fragmentary. It is commonly called 'dynamic' in contrast to 'static'; but that is a name which now seems to me to be better avoided. For 'dynamics', in its original sense, is a branch of mechanics; and the problem to which the economic counterpart (if it is a counterpart) refers, is not mechanical. As economics pushes on beyond 'static' it becomes less like science, and more like history.[96]

Perhaps Hicks was right after all, when he argued that given the fact that economies are prone to change, retrogression, or fluctuation, and the extent to which these can be reduced into scientific terms is rather limited. One way or the other, insights of other sciences need to be incorporated to eventually arrive at a growth model that not only better explains what factors cause growth, but also accurately predicts its future trajectory.

Appendix: Population Issues

Since the end of WWII, the world's population increased spectacularly to around 7.6 billion. Two-thirds live in developing countries. Demographic experts at the UN estimated that by the end of this century the world's population might reach between 9.6 billion and 13.2 billion. Somewhere in between, the UN projects that by 2100, the world's population would be around 11.2 billion.

Contrary to the UN projections, Darrell Bricker and John Ibbitson conclude in *Empty Planet* that the world population may reach around 8 billion, after which it will reverse.[97] They argue that the UN's projection is far too high, as it underestimates how fast fertility will decline. It is, however, fair to note that the United Nations Population Division did not only present the 10 to 13 billion projection; it also presented other, in their view less likely, scenario's. In the so-called low variant scenario, women produce half a baby less than initially predicted. In this scenario, the planet's population would peak at 8.5 billion around 2050, and would then start to decline rapidly. Indeed, so rapidly that by the end of this century the world's entire population would be down to around 7 billion.

In June 2019, the UN revised its above-mentioned 10 to 13 billion projection downwards. The UN now estimates that the world will contain a little over 9.7 billion people in 2050, and just under 10.9 billion at the turn of the century.

Fertility's replacement rate is 2.1, at which the population remains stable. Nearly all high-income countries have sub-replacement fertility rates—the average is 1.7. Only in poor countries fertility is still high enough to fuel rapid population growth. In sub-Saharan Africa it is 4.8; in heavily-indebted poor countries it is even 4.9. Hence pre-industrial fertility rates persist only in the poorest parts of the poorest countries.[98]

Conventional wisdom has it that birth rates in developed economies started to decline after the postwar *baby boom*. However, Bricker and Ibbitson argue that in some countries these rates had already been declining for more than a century. In around 20 countries, such as Japan, South Korea, Spain, Italy, and some Eastern European countries, population is declining. By 2050, the number of countries with declining populations will have doubled to around forty.

The rate of increase in the world population is slowing down. In the coming decades it will slow down even more; it will stop and then reverse as a result of a declining mortality rate combined with a declining birth rate.[99]

The Vienna-based Wittgenstein Centre presents a range, taking into consideration the influence of education and other social indicators. In this realm, Rosling et al. report that the number of people living in extreme poverty has almost halved, that 60% of girls in all low-income countries finish primary school, and that, worldwide, 30-year old women have, on average, spent 9 years in school.[100] If progress in them would stall, says the Wittgenstein Centre, the global population would indeed reach 12 billion by 2100. However, if current progress in these indicators continues, it will peak at 9.4 billion in 2075, after which it will drop to 8.9 billion by 2100. And if progress is even bigger, the world's population will peak around 9 billion and decline back to 7 billion.[101]

Worldwide, the number of children has already stopped increasing. Rosling concluded that 2000 was the year of 'peak child'. Since then, the worldwide fertility rate is going down.[102] To date, half of married women in developing countries use any form of birth control. Some commentators quipped, paraphrasing Francis Fukuyama's bestseller *The End of History and the Last Man*, that the world could be heading for the end of demography and the last man.

Falling Fertility Rates

Reduction in fertility happens when incomes and living conditions improve, when people move from rural areas to cities, and—above all—when women are literate and have access to education and contraceptives. More years in school means fewer babies—learning reduces fertility, not the other way around. In Ethiopia, for example, a household survey in 2005 found that the fertility rate for women with no formal schooling was 6.1. But for women with secondary education or more, it was only 2.0.[103]

The reasons for falling fertility rates of women who received education:

- Education improves work opportunities for women which makes having children more costly in terms of income forgone;
- educated women want their own children to be educated, which raises the cost of having children;
- education and literacy make women more receptive to information about contraception;
- education and employment delay marriage and the time available to rear children;
- education improves the status, bargaining power and independence of women, encouraging and enabling them to make their own choices.[104]

The million dollar question is: when will the birth rate drop? Even if fertility rates decline, birth rates may not decline in the same proportion. This is because of the simple fact that the young age structure of the population of most developing countries was triggered by high fertility rates in the past. So, there are now many young couples creating families of their own. Another question is when the so-called *demographic transition* will take place. This transition happens when death rates and birth rates fall together. This took place in Western Europe during the Industrial Revolution. In the typical developing country, the death rate fell rather dramatically thanks to improvements in public health, while the birth rates did not follow suit. In various cultures having many children is highly valued.

Demographic Dividend

A possible positive effect of population growth is the demographic dividend, consisting of a large group of young people and a much smaller group of old people depending on the young.[105] This may also speed up technological progress as young people are more conducive to new ideas. Another possible advantage may be that the pressure resulting from rapid population growth triggers incentives to increase the economy's productivity. What remains is the challenge whether the young will be able to earn a decent income when entering the labour market. *The Growth Report* observes:

> In a significant number of countries, the demographics run directly counter to the global trend: high fertility; reduced longevity in some cases, due to diseases like HIV/AIDS; and an increasingly youthful population. This raises the danger of widespread youth unemployment. To avert this danger, countries need to grow faster. Migration, while not alone sufficient to solve the problem of youth unemployment, would also benefit those host countries with an aging population. Well-managed long-term migration and well-supervised programs of temporary migration for work should be part of twenty-first century globalization.[106]

Notes

1. In *From Keynes to Piketty* (2016), I included a summary of Karl Polanyi's classic *The Great Transformation* (1944). Polanyi (1886–1964) was an anthropological economist. He developed the Substantivist school of thought. Source: De Haan, P. (2016) *From Keynes to Piketty; The Century that Shook up Economics*. London: Palgrave Macmillan, 164–172.
2. Aghion, P., Hewitt, P. (2005) Growth with Quality-Improving Innovations: An integrated Framework. In Aghion, P., Durlauf, S. (Eds) *The Handbook of Economic Growth*. Amsterdam: Elsevier, Vol. I, Part A, 67–110.

3. Also referred to as the 'Schumpeterian' growth paradigm. The incorporation of this paradigm into the model is helpful in understanding: '(i) why liberalization policies (in particular an increase in product market competition) should affect productivity growth differently in sectors or countries at different stages of technological development.... and (ii) why the organizations or institutions that maximize growth, or that are actually chosen by societies, also vary with the distance to the frontier.', Ibid., 84. This frontier term means that the extent of productivity growth would depend on a country's distance to the world technology frontier: the closer a country is to this frontier, the higher is the effect on its rate of productivity growth.
4. De Janvry A., Murgai, R., Sadoulet, E. *Rural Development and Rural Poverty.* Paper prepared for Handbook of Agricultural Economics, June 1999.
5. Aghion, P., Durlauf, S. Eds. (2014) *The Handbook of Economic Growth*; Vols. 2A and 2B. Amsterdam: Elsevier.
6. In 2011, Kahneman wrote a bestseller entitled *Thinking, Fast and Slow.* New York: Farrar, Straus and Giroux. On page 269 Kahneman explains how he got involved in behavioural economics: 'One day in the early 1970s, Amos handed me a mimeographed essay by a Swiss economist named Bruno Frey, which discussed the psychological assumptions of economic theory...Bruno Frey barely recalls writing the piece, but I can still recite its first sentence: 'The agent of economic theory is rational, selfish, and his tastes do not change.' I was astonished. My economist colleagues worked in the building next door, but I had not appreciated the profound difference between our intellectual worlds. To a psychologist, it is self-evident that people are neither fully rational nor completely selfish, and that their tastes are anything but stable.... Here was an opportunity for an interesting conversation across the boundaries of the disciplines. I did not anticipate that my career would be defined by that conversation.' On page 374, Kahneman observes about the rational agent model: 'Theories can survive for a long time after conclusive evidence falsifies them, and the rational agent model certainly survived the evidence we have seen, and much other evidence as well.'

   In 1992, Richard Tahler published *The Winner's Curse: Paradoxes and Anomalies of Economic Life.* Princeton: Princeton University Press.
7. Banerjee, A., Duflo, E. (2011) *Poor Economics; a Radical Rethinking of the Way to Fight Global Poverty.* New York: Public Affairs. William Easterly is less enthusiastic about RCTs. He observes that: 'RCTs are infeasible for many of the big questions in development, like the economy-wide effects of good institutions or good macroeconomic policies.' He concludes that 'embracing RCTs has led development researchers to lower their ambi-

tions.' Source: *Poor Economics*, 236. By 1979, trials to find out what type of approach or assistance works for the poor were already undertaken by the Bangladesh Rehabilitation Committee (BRAC). I became involved in supporting BRAC way back in 1979, when I started to work for NOVIB, a Dutch funding organisation. I was amazed to discover that at the time BRAC already had a research and evaluation department to, indeed, find out which approach worked and which one not. In sum, BRAC was way ahead in designing, testing, and delivering development assistance programmes aimed at improving the livelihood of Bangladesh's poor.

8. Ibid., 15. Originally developed in the medical sciences, RCT attempts to clarify whether (development) interventions work and how they can be made more effective. To explain why interventions work, one needs theory.
9. Critics of this technique argue that the causal effects that instrumental strategies identify, are uninteresting because they often give answers to narrow questions. But enthusiasts of this technique argue that accurate answers to narrower questions are more useful than unreliable answers to wider questions. This reminds me of Keynes's quip about rigorous statistics. He observed that that it was better to be roughly right than precisely wrong.
10. Maddison, A. (1995) *Monitoring the World Economy 1880–1992.* Paris: OECD, 33, 50.
11. Smith's contemporary, Irish philosopher and politician Edmund Burke (1729–1797) saw institutions as the embodiment of collective wisdom and the bulwark of civilisation, standing between decency and anarchy.
12. Smith, A. (1937) *The Wealth of Nations.* New York: Modern Library, 538–539.
13. Before the onset of new institutional economics, there was the old institutional economics school. The eccentric institutionalist Thorstein Veblen (1857–1929) was a representative of old institutional economics. This school of thought maintained that economic systems evolved as a result of adjustments to existing institutions, provoked by technological change.
14. Dell, M. The Persistent Effects of Peru's Mining Mita. *Econometrics*, Vol. 78, No. 6 (November, 2010), 1863–1903.
15. Ibid., 1899.
16. Acemoglu, D., Johnson, S., Robinson, J. (2001) The Colonial Origins of Comparative Development: An Empirical Investigation. In *American Economic Review*, 91, 1369–1401.
17. In 1970, around 45% of America's national income was devoted to transaction costs, such as banking, insurance, finance, and costs of lawyers, accountants. Source: Wallis, J., North, D. (1986) Measuring the Transaction Sector in the American Economy 1870–1970. In Engerman, S., Gallman R. (eds) *Long-Term Factors in American Economic Growth.*

Chicago: University of Chicago Press. As noted, multi-sectoral neoclassical models include sectors for transport, banking, insurance, mediation, and the like.
18. *Rural Development and Rural Poverty*, 16.
19. McCloskey, D. (2010) *Bourgeois Dignity; Why Economics Can't Explain the Modern World*. Chicago: Chicago University Press.
20. Ibid., 315.
21. North, D. (1990) *Institutions, Institutional Change and Economic Performance*. Cambridge: Cambridge University Press.
22. North, D. et al. (2007) Limited Access Orders in the Developing World. A New Approach to the Problems of Development. *World Bank Working Paper 4359*. Washington: World Bank.
23. The repeal of the Corn Laws in England is a telling example in this realm. David Ricardo campaigned for the repeal of the Corn Laws, in which he, and others with him, was successful in 1846 when these laws were indeed repealed. Industrialists benefitted from them to the detriment of the landed gentry.
24. Acemoglu, D., Robinson, J. (2012) *Why Nations Fail: The Origins of Power, Prosperity and Poverty*. New York: Crown Publishers.
25. Ibid., 74–75.
26. Ibid., 341.
27. Rodrik, D., Subramanian, A., Trebbi, E. (2004) Institutions Rule: The Primacy of Institutions over Geography and Integration in Economic Development. In *Journal of Economic Growth*, 9(2): 131–165.
28. Sachs, J. Institutions Matter but Not for Everything; The Role of geography and resource endowments in development shouldn't be underestimated. In *Finance & Development*, June 2003.
29. Ibid., 39.
30. Ibid., 41.
31. Rodrik, D., Subramanian, A. (2008) The Primacy of Institutions and what This Does and Does Not Mean. In Secondi, G. (ed) *The Development Economics Reader*. London: Routledge.
32. Jones, C., Romer, P. The New Kaldor Facts: Ideas, Institutions, Population, and Human Capital. In *American Economic Journal: Macroeconomics* 2010, 2:1, 228. The authors argue on page 242: 'Institutions are themselves ideas—inventions that shape the allocation of resources, and the search for better institutions is unending.'
33. Keefer, P., Knack, S. Why Don't Poor Countries Catch Up? A Cross-National Test of an Institutional Explanation. In *Economic Enquiry*, Vol. XXXXV, July 1997, 590–602.
34. In their 1995 article Institutions and Economic Development which was published in *Economic and Politics*, 7(3), Keefer and Knack analysed the

impact of property rights on economic growth across counties over the period 1974–1989. They apply composite indices of contract enforceability and expropriation risk. They find that there was a strong positive effect of property rights on economic growth.

35. Glaeser, E., La Porta, R., Lopez-de-Salinas, F., Shleifer, A. (2004) Do Institutions Cause Growth? In *Journal of Economic Growth*, 271–303.
36. Source: CIA Factbook.
37. Ibid., 3–4.
38. Rodrik, D. (2007) *One Economics, Many Recipes; Globalization, Institutions and economic Growth*. Princeton: Princeton University Press, 85.
39. Ibid., 88.
40. *New York Times* columnist Thomas Friedman, for example, noted the following in one of his columns: 'One-party non-democracy certainly has its drawbacks. But when it is led by a reasonably enlightened group of people, as China is today, it can also have great advantages. That one party can just impose the politically difficult but critically important policies needed to move a society forward in the twenty-first century.'
41. In addition, Rodrik observes: 'Longstanding democracies such as India, Costa Rica, Malta, and Mauritius have experienced significantly less volatility than countries like Syria, Chile, or Iran.' Source: *One Economics, Many Recipes*, 172–173.
42. Ibid., 166.
43. Barro, R. (2008) Democracy and Growth. In Secondi, G. (Ed.) *The Development Economics Reader*. London: Routledge.
44. Acemoglu, D., Naidu, S., Restrepo, P., Robinson, J. (1 May 2015) *Democracy Does Cause Growth*. Can be downloaded via www.economist.com/democracy15.
45. Hausmann, R., Pritchett, L., Rodrik, D. Growth Accelerations. Cambridge: *NBER Working Paper Series 10566*, June 2004.
46. *The New Kaldor Facts: Ideas, Institutions, Population, and Human Capital*, 238.
47. Free Exchange, *The Economist*, 14 April 2018, 66.
48. Williamson, J. (1991) *Inequality, Poverty and History*. Cambridge: Basil Blackwell, 2–3.
49. McCloskey, D. (2010) *Bourgeois Dignity; Why Economics Can't Explain the Modern World*. Chicago: Chicago University Press, xii.
50. McCloskey defined bourgeoisie in a wide sense: 'as the hiring or owning of professional or educated class', 3. Ideas take up a prominent position in contemporary growth theories. Jones and Romer observe that, apart from institutions, population and human capital, ideas are now at the centre of growth theory. The authors continue by explaining that: 'Ideas

introduce scale effects. They also change the feasible and optimal economic institutions. The institutional implications have attracted more attention, but the scale effects are more important for understanding the big sweep of human history.' Source: *The New Kaldor Facts: Ideas, Institutions, Population, and Human Capital*, 226–227.

51. *Bourgeois Dignity*, 7.
52. Nelson, R., Winter, S. (1982) *An Evolutionary Theory of Economic Change*. Cambridge: The Belknap Press.
53. One also finds an emphasis on successful economic agents in Allen, R. (2009) *The British Industrial Revolution in Global Perspective*. Cambridge: Cambridge University Press. Allen writes on page 14: 'Culture possibly became more secular and more concerned with economic success. People could read and calculate. They chased after new products and worked to get the money to buy them. …While the eighteenth century was not the same as the twenty-first, modern attitudes and attributes were ascendant. Many had economic roots, and they furthered the growth of the economy.' And on page 261 Allen observes: 'The expansion of literacy occurred in the middle ranks of society—shopkeepers, tradesmen, artisans and proto-industrial workers—and many inventors came from this group.'
54. Mokyr, J. (2017) *A Culture of Growth; the Origins of the Modern Economy*. Princeton: Princeton University Press, 23.
55. Landes, D. (1998) *The Wealth and Poverty of Nations: Why Some are so Rich and Others are so Poor*. New York: W. W. Norton.
56. Ibid., 516. On page 178 Landes observed: 'Weber's argument, as I see it, is that in that place and time (northern Europe, sixteenth to eighteenth centuries), religion encouraged the appearance in numbers of a personality type that had been exceptional and adventitious before; and that this type created a new economy (a new mode of production) that we know as (industrial) capitalism.'
57. Galor, O. (2005) From Stagnation to Growth: Unified Growth Theory. In Aghion, P., Durlauf, S. (Eds.) *The Handbook of Economic Growth*. Vol. 1, Part A. Amsterdam: Elsevier, 172–293.

    Mokyr, J. (2005) Long-term Economic Growth and the History of Technology. In Aghion, P., Durlauf, S. (Eds) *The Handbook of Economic Growth*. Vol. 1, Part B. Amsterdam: Elsevier, 1113–1180.
58. The author argues that unless the factors that promoted the transition of the currently developed economies into a state of sustained economic growth could be identified, and their implications would be modified to account for the differences in the growth structure of less developed economies, any attempt to explain the obstacles faced by less developed countries to reach a stage of sustained economic growth would be futile.

59. Britain's early industrialisation occurred without direct state intervention and developed successfully within a *laissez-faire* framework.
60. Education may initially have been inspired by non-industrial reasons. England initiated a sequence of reforms in its education system since the 1830s and literacy rates gradually increased. Later on, in light of the industrial competition from other countries, such as France and Germany, British capitalists started to recognise the importance of technical education for the provision of skilled workers. However, the pure laissez-faire policy failed in developing a proper educational system, and capitalists demanded government intervention in the provision of education. Source: *From Stagnation to Growth*, 207.
61. UK's proportion of foreign trade to national income had swollen to 51.5% in the period 1909–1913.
62. *From Stagnation to Growth*, 219.
63. The theory is translated into a mathematical model presented in pp. 239–252.
64. Galor, O., Mountford, A. (2003) *Trading Population for Productivity*. Providence: Brown University.
65. *From Stagnation to Growth*, 284.
66. Mokyr, J. (2017) *A Culture of Growth*. Princeton: Princeton University Press, 23.
67. *Long-term Economic Growth and the History of Technology*, 1126.
68. Lin, J. (2012) *Demystifying the Chinese Economy*. Cambridge: Cambridge University Press, 30–53.
69. Ibid., 1135.
70. *Long-term Economic Growth and the History of Technology*, 1142–1143. For example, *Felix Meritis* in Amsterdam, and *Athenea* high schools throughout Holland taught mathematics, astronomy, and physics.
71. Another example is food canning and the evolution of bacteriology. The canning of food led to a prolonged scientific debate about what caused food to spoil. Pasteur ended the debate in the early 1860s.
72. Abraham Lincoln (1809–1865) once said that what the patent system did was to add the fuel of interest to the fire of genius.
73. Surely, there was opposition to new techniques, like the Luddites and protests against steam engines and mechanical sawmills. And there were riots such as the Captain Swing riots of 1830–1832. They slowed down the adoption of technology altogether. Riots were just one of the manifestations against technological progress. Mass labour protests constituted others.
74. Mokyr's *A Culture of Growth*, which covers the period 1500–1700, is about the 'seeds' that were planted during these two centuries. The author concludes: 'To see the true importance of the European

Enlightenment in the economic development that followed it, recall that it involved two highly innovative and complementary ideas: the concept that knowledge and the understanding of nature can and should be used to advance the material conditions of humanity, and the belief that power and government are there not to serve the rich and powerful but society at large. The combination of these two and the triumph in the market for ideas created a massive synergy that led to the economic sea changes we observe, from industrialization and the growth of physical and human capital to the discovery and mastery of natural forces and resources that were still beyond imagining in 1750.' Source: *A Culture of Growth*, 341.
75. *Long-term Economic Growth and the History of Technology*, 1173.
76. Diamond, J. (1998) *Guns, Germs and Steel; A short History of Everybody for the last 13,000 Years*. London: Vintage.
77. Gallup, J., Sachs, J., Mellinger, A. (1998) Geography and Economic Development. In Pleskovic, B., Stiglitz, J. (Eds) *Annual World Bank Conference on Development Economics 1998*. Washington: World Bank.
78. Thirlwall, A., Pacheco-López, P. (2017) *Economics of Development*. Tenth Edition. London: Palgrave Macmillan, 300.
79. 'Given these findings, it is hardly surprising that Africa has some of the poorest and most stagnant economies in the world. Geography is stacked against it.' Source: *Economics of Development*, 300.
80. Krugman, P. (1991) Increasing Returns and Economic Geography. In *The Journal of Political Economy*, Volume 99, Issue 3.
81. Ibid., 485.
82. Johann Heinrich von Thünen (1783–1850) developed his agricultural location theory, based upon an analysis of his own agricultural estates in Mecklenburg, Germany. Von Thünen concluded that the intensity of production of a particular crop declines with the distance to the market. Every farmer wants to be as close as possible to the market. The location of crops or live stock is determined by: (i) the market price; (ii) transport costs; and (iii) its yield per hectare. A concentric circles production pattern ensues around the market centre. Spectacular developments in transportation, allowing perishable products to be transported at long distances in a short period of time, meant that von Thünen's theory is no longer applicable as originally conceived.
83. This is a nice example of circular causation; a term coined by Gunnar Myrdal.
84. Krugman, P. (1991) Increasing Returns and Economic Geography. In *The Journal of Political Economy*, Volume 99, Issue 3, 487.
85. Perhaps to Krugman's own surprise, the framework as applied proved to be, in his own words: 'remarkably powerful in its ability to yield simple intuition-building treatments of seemingly intractable issues.', Ibid., 487.

Krugman concluded: 'The model does illustrate… how tools drawn from industrial organization theory can help to formalize and sharpen the insights of a much neglected field. Thus I hope that this paper will be a stimulus to a revival of research into regional economics and economic geography.' Ibid., 498.

86. Krugman, P., Venables, A. Globalization and the Inequality of Nations. In *The Quarterly Journal of Economics*, Vol. CX, Issue 4, November 1995, 857–880.
87. Wages in the core country will have risen as a result of increasing demand for labour in the manufacturing sector and a smaller proportion of manufactures have to be imported, reducing the consumer price index.
88. The analysis could be extended, according to the authors, through getting more geography in it; i.e., the integration of a multi-region setting. Secondly, the model now excludes capital mobility; in fact, it includes no capital. So it would make sense to add capital movements. And, finally, the model should be tested with the help of real numbers.
89. World Development Report 2009 *Reshaping Economic Geography*. Washington: World Bank.
90. The report explains in great detail what institutions encompass. The term is used to categorise policies that are not explicitly designed with spatial considerations, but that have effects and outcomes that may vary across locations. These include national policies such as the income tax system, intergovernmental fiscal relations, and governance of land and housing markets, as well as education, health care, basic water and sanitation.
91. *The World Development Report 2009 'reshapes economic geography': geographical reflections*. Journal compilation ©Royal Geographical Society (with the Institute of British Geographers), 2009. The group consisted of Jonathan Rigg, Anthony Bebbington, Katherine Gough, Deborah Bryceson, Jytte Agergaard, Niels Fold and Cecilia Tacoli.
92. Regarding embeddedness, while some institutions may be spatially blind (as proposed by the report), all are culturally embedded and culturally consequential.
93. ADB (2007) *Key Indicators 2007: Inequality in Asia*. Manila: Asian Development Bank.
94. *The World Development Report 2009 'reshapes economic geography': geographical reflections*, 134.
95. Maddison, A. (1995) *Monitoring the World Economy 1820–1992*. Paris: OECD, 50.
96. Hicks, J. (1979) *Causality in Economics*. Oxford: Blackwell, xi.
97. Bricker, D., Ibbitson, J. (2019) *Empty Planet; The Shock of Global Population Decline*. London: Robinson.

98. *The Economist*, 2 February, 2019, 50.
99. The authors argue that the drop in birth rates is also caused by the increasing rate of urbanisation: 'It removes the need for young brawn to work the farm and makes children, instead, an economic liability, and it empowers women, who invariably choose to have fewer children once they have control over their own bodies. Those two factors became entrenched in the developed world in the nineteenth and twentieth centuries. But now these forces are at work in developing societies as well.' Source: *Empty Planet*, 29.
100. Rosling, H., Rosling, O. and Rosling Rönnlund, A. (2018) *Factfulness; Ten Reasons We're Wrong About the World-and Why Things are Better Than You think*. London, Sceptre 3–5.
101. *The Economist*, 50.
102. *Factfulness*, 84–85.
103. *The Economist*, 52.
104. *Economics of Development*, 310.
105. South Korea's economy was boosted by the doubling of its population from 20 million in 1950 to 40 million in 1985. However, this did not happen in the Philippines, and most Latin American countries that also registered rapid population growth but sluggish economic growth at the time.
106. *The Growth Report; Strategies for Sustained Growth and Development*. Washington: World Bank (2008), 11.

References

Acemoglu, D., & Robinson, J. (2012). *Why Nations Fail: The Origins of Power, Prosperity and Poverty*. New York: Crown Publishers.

Acemoglu, D., Johnson, S., & Robinson, J. (2001). The Colonial Origins of Comparative Development: An Empirical Investigation. *American Economic Review*, 91.

Acemoglu, D., Naidu, S., Restrepo, P., & Robinson, J. (2015, May 1). *Democracy Does Cause Growth*. http://www.economist.com/democracy

ADB. (2007). *Key Indicators 2007: Inequality in Asia*. Manila: Asian Development Bank.

Aghion, P., & Durlauf, S. (Eds.). (2014). *The Handbook of Economic Growth*. Vols. 2A and 2B. Amsterdam: Elsevier.

Aghion, P., & Hewitt, P. (2005). Growth with Quality-Improving Innovations: An Integrated Framework. In P. Aghion & S. Durlauf (Eds.), *The Handbook of Economic Growth*. Vol. I, Part A. Amsterdam: Elsevier.

Allen, R. (2009). *The British Industrial Revolution in Global Perspective.* Cambridge: Cambridge University Press.

Banerjee, A., & Duflo, E. (2011). *Poor Economics; A Radical Rethinking of the Way to Fight Global Poverty.* New York: Public Affairs.

Barro, R. (2008). Democracy and Growth. In G. Secondi (Ed.), *The Development Economics Reader.* London: Routledge.

Bricker, D., & Ibbitson, J. (2019). *Empty Planet; The Shock of Global Population Decline.* London: Robinson.

De Haan, P. (2016). *From Keynes to Piketty; The Century that Shook up Economics.* London: Palgrave Macmillan.

De Janvry, A., Murgai, R., & Sadoulet, E. (1999, June). *Rural Development and Rural Poverty.* Paper prepared for Handbook of Agricultural Economics.

Dell, M. (2010, November). The Persistent Effects of Peru's Mining Mita. *Econometrics, 78*(6).

Diamond, J. (1998). *Guns, Germs and Steel; A short History of Everybody for the Last 13,000 Years.* London: Vintage.

Gallup, J., Sachs, J., & Mellinger, A. (1998). Geography and Economic Development. In B. Pleskovic & J. Stiglitz (Eds.), *Annual World Bank Conference on Development Economics 1998.* Washington: World Bank.

Galor, O. (2005). From Stagnation to Growth: Unified Growth Theory. In P. Aghion & S. Durlauf (Eds.), *The Handbook of Economic Growth.* Vol. 1, Part A. Amsterdam: Elsevier.

Galor, O., & Mountford, A. (2003). *Trading Population for Productivity.* Providence: Brown University.

Glaeser, E., La Porta, R., Lopez-de-Salinas, F., & Shleifer, A. (2004). Do Institutions Cause Growth? *Journal of Economic Growth.*

Hausmann, R., Pritchett, L., & Rodrik, D. (2004, June). *Growth Accelerations.* Cambridge: NBER Working Paper Series 10566.

Hicks, J. (1979). *Causality in Economics.* Oxford: Basil Blackwell.

Jones, C., & Romer, P. (2010). The New Kaldor Facts: Ideas, Institutions, Population, and Human Capital. *American Economic Journal: Macroeconomics, 2*, 1.

Kahneman, D. (2012). *Thinking, Fast and Slow.* New York: Farrar, Straus and Giroux.

Keefer, P., & Knack, S. (1997, July). Why Don't Poor Countries Catch Up? A Cross-National Test of an Institutional Explanation. *Economic Enquiry, XXXXV.*

Krugman, P. (1991). Increasing Returns and Economic Geography. *The Journal of Political Economy, 99*(3).

Krugman, P., & Venables, A. (1995, November). Globalization and the Inequality of Nations. *The Quarterly Journal of Economics, CX*(4).

Landes, D. (1998). *The Wealth and Poverty of Nations: Why Some Are so Rich and Others Are so Poor.* New York: W. W. Norton.
Lin, J. (2012). *Demystifying the Chinese Economy.* Cambridge: Cambridge University Press.
Maddison, A. (1995). *Monitoring the World Economy 1820–1992.* Paris: OECD.
McCloskey, D. (2010). *Bourgeois Dignity; Why Economics Can't Explain the Modern World.* Chicago: Chicago University Press.
Mokyr, J. (2005). Long-Term Economic Growth and the History of Technology. In P. Aghion & S. Durlauf (Eds.), *The Handbook of Economic Growth.* Vol. 1, Part B. Amsterdam: Elsevier.
Mokyr, J. (2017). *A Culture of Growth; the Origins of the Modern Economy.* Princeton: Princeton University Press.
Nelson, R., & Winter, S. (1982). *An Evolutionary Theory of Economic Change.* Cambridge: The Belknap Press.
North, D. (1990). *Institutions, Institutional Change and Economic Performance.* Cambridge: Cambridge University Press.
North, D., Wallis, J., Webb, S., & Weingast, B. (2007). *Limited Access Orders in the Developing World. A New Approach to the Problems of Development.* World Bank Working Paper 4359. Washington: World Bank.
Rodrik, D. (2007). *One Economics, Many Recipes; Globalization, Institutions and Economic Growth.* Princeton: Princeton University Press.
Rodrik, D., & Subramanian, A. (2008). The Primacy of Institutions and What This Does and Does Not Mean. In G. Secondi (Ed.), *The Development Economics Reader.* London: Routledge.
Rodrik, D., Subramanian, A., & Trebbi, E. (2004). Institutions Rule: The Primacy of Institutions over Geography and Integration in Economic Development. *Journal of Economic Growth, 9*(2).
Rosling, H., Rosling, O., & Rosling Rönnlund, A. (2018). *Factfulness; Ten Reasons We're Wrong About the World—And Why Things Are Better Than You Think.* London: Spectre.
Sachs, J. (2003, June). Institutions Matter but Not for Everything; The Role of Geography and Resource Endowments in Development Shouldn't Be Underestimated. *Finance & Development.*
Smith, A. (1937). *The Wealth of Nations.* New York: Modern Library.
Thaler, R. (1992). *The Winner's Curse: Paradoxes and Anomalies of Economic Life.* Princeton: Princeton University Press.
The Growth Report; Strategies for Sustained Growth and Development. (2008). Washington: World Bank.
The World Development Report 2009 'Reshapes Economic Geography': Geographical Reflections. (2009). Journal Compilation ©Royal Geographical Society (with the Institute of British Geographers).

Thirlwall, A., & Pacheco-López, P. (2017). *Economics of Development* (10th ed.). London: Palgrave Macmillan.
Wallis, J., & North, D. (1986). Measuring the Transaction Sector in the American Economy 1870–1970. In S. Engerman & R. Gallman (Eds.), *Long-Term Factors in American Economic Growth.* Chicago: University of Chicago Press.
Williamson, J. (1991). *Inequality, Poverty and History.* Cambridge: Basil Blackwell.
World Bank. (2009). *World Development Report 2009 Reshaping Economic Geography.* Washington: World Bank.

CHAPTER 7

Trade, Globalisation and Development

7.1 Introduction

International trade and globalisation constitute solid subjects of analysis in economics. In fact, Adam Smith (1723–1790) was the first economist to write about the benefits of free trade. Since Smith's views on the subject, international trade theory evolved. Globalisation is a more recent phenomenon, as Maddison's quotation below underlines:

> The degree of integration of different parts of the world has grown dramatically since 1820 and the increased openness has had an important impact on growth potential. In 1820 exports were only 1 per cent of world product. By 1913, the ratio had risen to 8.7 per cent. By then it was meaningful to speak of an interactive 'world' economy, rather than an aggregate of countries, any of which had little knowledge or contact with foreign technology. There was a very bad patch from 1913 to 1950, a period of neomercantilism, when the trade ratio declined, but after 1950, it moved sharply upward. By 1992, it had risen to 13.5 per cent.[1]

Maddison mentioned 'a very bad patch from 1913 to 1950'. Indeed, before World War II (WWII), not just rich countries but also many colonies suffered from the negative effects of the Great Depression and protectionist measures taken by the former. Prices of colonies' export products dropped dramatically. When many former colonies gained independence, the mood was, therefore, one of export pessimism. To achieve sustainable increases in income and output it was thought that

P. de Haan, *Whatever Happened to the Third World?*,
https://doi.org/10.1007/978-3-030-39613-8_7

industrialisation, through capital accumulation, was a better bet than to rely on the continued export of raw materials and minerals, the demand for which was inelastic anyway. And domestic industrialisation would substitute expensive imports.

However, the irony was that the 1950s and the 1960s were decades during which the prices of raw materials and mineral exports soared, triggered by spectacular economic growth in America, Europe, and Japan. The import-substitution drive turned out to be less successful. Meanwhile, developing countries, especially in East Asia, which had adopted an export-orientation, registered high economic growth figures benefitting from international trade. This wetted the appetite of other developing countries to follow their example.

Globalisation encompasses more than international trade. It includes the international flow of ideas and knowledge, sharing of cultures, and the global environmental movement. Globalisation contributed to international economic growth and cheaper consumer goods. Globalisation also contributed to the reduction of poverty. Many people benefitted, but not everybody. However, there are downsides to globalisation, initially neglected by free trade-minded policymakers and economists. But not by politicians who gained popular support from globalisation-skeptics and from people who lost their jobs as a result of international competition.

Since the establishment in 1947 of the General Agreement on Tariffs and Trade (GATT), measures were taken to gradually break down tariff walls so as to promote international trade. In addition, technological progress, the lowering of transportation and communication costs, and the spread of private capital flows, broadened the horizon of trade and investment. In short, national markets became more and more integrated into the globalised world market, through trade in goods and services, international capital flows, and labour migration. The question is whether developing countries benefitted. The answers are to be found at the end of this chapter.

7.2 International Trade Theories

International trade is not, as mercantilists would have it, a *zero-sum game*. It can function as an engine of growth, as already underscored by classical economists. The most prominent one, David Ricardo (1772–1823), developed *the law of comparative advantage*. He presented his famous example of trade between England and Portugal, in which England exports cloth to Portugal in exchange for Portugal's wine. Although both countries were able to produce cloth and wine, England had a comparative advantage in producing cloth and Portugal in making wine. So, if England were to specialise in the production of cloth and Portugal in producing wine, both countries would be better off, as England can exchange cloth for more wine, and Portugal can exchange its wine for more cloth than in a situation where there was no international trade. In sum, specialisation acted as a source of economic progress. An additional bonus was that thanks to trade between the two countries, the people in both can stop producing things they are not good at, sparing them frustration.

Ricardo's law of comparative advantage had a great influence. However, Ricardo's law is a *static* one, i.e., once the decision to specialise in cloth and wine will have been made, no further gains are foreseen. Ricardo assumed continuous full employment. But if in a particular situation this is not the case, the gains from international trade may be offset by losses from unemployment. In a situation in which there is no balanced trade, one trade partner ends up in payment deficits. In order to restore the balance, imports will then have to be restricted and foreign exchange saved, resulting in a contraction of the economy.

A more recent contribution to international trade economics came from two Swedish economists: Eli Heckscher (1879–1952) and his pupil Bertil Ohlin (1899–1979). The *Hekscher-Ohlin Theorem* says that poor countries, with a combination of an abundant labour force and scarce capital, will find it cheaper to produce and export labour-intensive goods, whereas rich countries, endowed with more capital goods but with a limited labour supply, would produce and export capital-intensive goods. One of the advantages for poor countries would be that demand for unskilled labour compared to skilled labour will increase, which will limit the wage gap between rich and poor countries. At first sight a compelling theorem. But is it? The mistake is often made that abundant labour is cheap labour. This is not necessarily the case. All depends on labour's productivity. Capital-abundant economies may still export relatively labour-intensive goods. For example, the Netherlands, a capital-abundant country, is a formidable exporter of labour-intensive agricultural products, such as vegetables and flowers. Poor countries may also feel the pain of competition from other poor countries' exports: Mexico benefits from exporting labour-intensive goods to America, but at the same time suffers from labour-intensive imports from China, which has a dampening effect on the wages of Mexico's labour-intensive industries. Capital inflows, in the form of foreign direct investment, may trigger the demand for skilled workers in poor countries and so contributes to a widening of the wage gap in these countries, rather than narrowing the gap as predicted by Hekscher-Ohlin's Theorem.

Then, there is the Stolper-Samuelson Theorem, developed by Wolgang Stolper (1912–2002) and Paul Samuelson (1915–2009).[2] Its central theme is that international trade necessarily lowers the real wage of the scarce factor expressed in terms of any good. The authors use a simple framework of two homogeneous factors which are freely mobile between two domestic industries. While elimination of tariffs might cause the money wage to fall, the resulting reduction in the prices of the goods workers buy with their wages was presumed larger. The real wage was thus to rise, at least in terms of imported goods and most likely overall, although the effect would depend on the relative importance of imported and exported goods in workers' total expenditure. This theorem also demonstrates that a productive factor's ability to relocate from an import-competing to an export industry does not prevent a loss in real income due to expanded trade. The basic message of the theorem is that even when free trade raises national income, some factors may lose in the absence of compensation by the government. Given contemporary international trade developments, the Stolper-Samuelson Theorem may well enjoy renewed interest.

Raúl Prebisch's (1901–1986) point of departure was peripheral Latin America, where the benefits from increased productivity had not reached. Industrialisation is the answer to obtain the benefits of technical progress, said Prebisch. Productivity increases imply lowering prices. If prices had been reduced in proportion to increased productivity, the reduction should have been less in the case of primary products than in those of manufactures, so that—as the disparity between productivities increased—the price relationship between the two should have shown a steady improvement in favour of the countries of the periphery. However, the price relationship became more and more unfavourable for primary products.[3] The increase of incomes in countries of the industrialised centre was larger than the increase in their productivity. More precisely: the average income *per capita* had risen more in industrial centres than in primary product producer countries of the periphery.

Prices of primary products rise more rapidly than industrial products in the upswing, but they fall more in the downswing, so that in the course of the business cycle the gap between prices of the two is progressively widened.[4] Since prices do not keep pace with productivity, industrialisation is the only means by which Latin–American countries may obtain the advantages of technical progress. If productivity in agriculture can be increased by technical progress and if real wages can be raised by industrialisation and by social legislation, the disequilibrium between incomes at the centre and the periphery can be corrected. If imports need to be restricted to the export earnings, this can be done by sacrificing part of the exports in order to increase industrial production as a substitute for imports. The substitution of internal production for imports requires the raising of tariffs caused by the higher costs of internal production. This increase also requires capital imports which could be financed through international financial institutions, especially during a downswing period when gold reserves and saving levels are low.

Apart from Ricardo's *static* comparative advantage theorem, international trade can also trigger *dynamic* effects. It depends on what a country specialises in: natural resources or manufacturing. Manufacturing triggers technological progress which in turn promotes faster growth.

As we saw in Chap. 6, Paul Krugman and Anthony Venables argue in *Globalization and Inequality of Nations*[5] that a core-periphery spontaneously forms when transport costs fall below a critical value. Nations that find themselves in the periphery suffer a decline in real income. But at still lower transport costs there is a convergence of real incomes, in which peripheral nations gain and core nations may lose. This is contrary to what Prebisch argued at the time. Since then, developments have changed the outlook rather dramatically, as erstwhile peripheral nations have gained at the expense of those belonging to the core.

7.3 Globalisation

Globalisation is, as noted, not exclusively an economic phenomenon; it encompasses more things, such as the international flow of ideas and knowledge, sharing of cultures, global civil society, and the global environmental movement. As regards the economic dimension, the first globalisation wave started around 1870 and ended abruptly in 1914, when the First World War broke out. The second globalisation wave started after the end of WWII, from which developing countries also benefitted.

It seemed as if the supporters of globalisation would have the upper hand—globalisation was here to stay. In 2004, Jagdish Bhagwati published *In Defense of Globalisation*, and in that same year, the influential *Financial Times* columnist Martin Wolf followed suit with *Why Globalization Works*.[6] Indeed, the world economy had grown at an unprecedented pace. Nothing in history came closer to this achievement. The lowering of trade barriers, transportation and communication costs definitely helped to boost the international flow of traded goods and services.

Between 1950 and the early 1970s—the Golden Age—the world economy (developed *and* developing countries together) grew at approx. 3% per year on a per capita basis boosted by a large expansion of international trade, monetary stability, and acceleration of technical progress. True, during the second half of the 1970s and early 1980s the world economy's growth underwent a dip, caused by the sharp increase in the price of oil, the Latin American debt crisis, and the end of the Bretton Woods system. However, around the middle of the 1980s growth resumed its upward swing, with international trade exceeding 50% of global GDP, up from around 20% in the mid-1960s. Globalisation was humming along, not in the least spurred by the fall of the Berlin Wall in 1989 and, in 2001, by China's membership of the World Trade Organisation. For example, China's exports grew on average 6.4% per year. By 2009 the volume of its foreign trade exceeded $2.2 trillion, a 107-fold jump in thirty years.[7]

How did these developments influence the developing world? Since the early 1950s, the export of developing countries trailed behind the export of industrialised countries. However, in recent years emerging economies, in particular China and India, are doing much better, benefitting from the lowering of trade barriers and from the change in the composition of their exports from primary products to (semi)-manufactured goods.[8] In 2008, the weight of developing and emerging economies in the global economy tipped over the 50% mark for the first time. In 2013, the Asian and Pacific region's world market share of (semi)-manufactures was 24.5%, while their share of high-tech exports was 30.6%. In short, large emerging economies, like Brazil, China, and India, play an ever more important role in international trade, to the detriment of traditional industrial economies.[9] The story of sub-Saharan Africa (SSA) is quite different: in 2018, its market share of world manufactured exports was only 1.1%.[10]

In addition, instead of integrating the entire supply chain as was done in the past, developing countries now join international production arrangements to become competitive and subsequently industrialise by getting more jobs inside international value chains.[11] As Richard Baldwin argues: 'Twenty-first century globalization, by contrast, is not just happening at the sector level; it is also happening at the level of production stages and occupations.'[12]

> 'Korea switched from the twentieth-century import substitution strategy to the twenty-first-century global value chain strategy. The 1997 financial crisis was the catalyst, but the realities of global competition were the basis. The world auto sector had become so scale-intensive, and the costs of R&D had mounted so high, that no company could survive by relying on a fully national supply chain. By the 2000s, Korea's car sector was a full-on member of the global value chain club. Yet because it built a supply chain *before* the second unbundling, Korea is now a headquarters economy rather than a factory economy.'[13]

Consumers worldwide benefitted from globalisation. And so did transnational corporations (TNCs). By 2009, it was estimated that there were 82,000 TNCs in operation, controlling more than 810,000 subsidiaries worldwide. A few examples: American TNCs control more than 50% of the international banana trade. Five European TNCs control around 90% of tea sold in industrialised countries, and the two largest coffee brewers control 20% of the international market.[14]

7.3.1 The Downside of Globalisation

Surely, globalisation contributed to international economic growth, lowering of prices of consumer goods and, not in the least, to poverty reduction. But globalisation was not beneficial to all; not everybody enjoyed an improvement of their income.[15] As an ILO report sourly observes: 'There is no point to a globalization that reduces the price of a child's shoes, but costs the father his job.'[16]

In particular, manufacturing jobs in industrialised countries were lost; be it that not all job losses can be blamed on globalisation; technological progress played a more important part.[17] Job losses did not only occur in industrialised countries. Thirlwall and Pacheco-López cite examples of job losses in developing countries. For instance, in Kenya cotton farming and textile production have both been hard hit by trade liberalisation. Cotton production fell by 70% between mid-1980s and mid-1990s and textile employment fell from 120,000 to 85,000 during the same period. Since the first North American Free Trade Area (NAFTA) was signed in 1994, two million Mexican maize farmers lost their jobs because they could not compete against subsidised maize from the USA.[18]

In sum, workers lost their employment, and income and wealth inequality increased, as predicted by the Stolper-Samuelson Theorem. In addition, in industrialised countries labour markets changed: job security is no longer a given, and more and more work is done by short-term contract workers. Middle-management jobs are being slashed; automation and robotics take their toll as well. As *The Growth Report* concluded way back in 2008: 'The Commission thinks governments should try harder to spread the benefits of globalization more equitably and to protect people from economic dislocation, whatever the cause. Support for an open global economy depends upon it.'[19]

> '...globalization is a force both for good and bad. Ideally, he or she, even when reading about some aspects that seem 'good', should be on alert for thinking about some aspects what the drawbacks or 'bad' effects may lurk behind them ... Our ability to comprehend and include the 'goods' and all the 'bads' and to give them a subjective weighting will, in the last analysis, determine how we feel about globalization.'[20]

Fundamental questions will have to be answered: will the ones who lost their job find another one; will they then earn the same income, and what about the distribution of income and wealth? Ethical questions can also be asked about jobs triggered by globalisation: what about child labour, draconian and hazardous work conditions, poor wages, what have you.

The destabilising consequences of *financial* globalisation, which took flight after the Bretton Woods system collapsed in August 1971, must also be taken into consideration. Many developing countries did not benefit as much from financial globalisation as expected. In fact, it backfired because not all the necessary safeguards were in place. Dani Rodrik argues that a long list of requirements needs to be satisfied before one can conclude that free trade would indeed improve a society's well-being.[21] He observes that: '...this broader perspective [on the implications of free trade; PdH] also helps to distinguish pure protectionism from legitimate and well-grounded opposition to free trade. A deserving argument against free trade must overcome at least one of the two hurdles mentioned above: the economic gains from freer trade must remain small compared to the distributional costs; and trade must entail practices that violate prevailing norms and social contracts at home.'[22]

Apart from economic considerations there is also an important political-psychological aspect at play. Some people in industrialised countries fear that the cultural and social environment they used to live in is being affected by globalising forces beyond their control. New political parties, often of a populist variety, have emerged and eat away the support that established political parties used to enjoy. Populism represents a retreat both from multilateralism and democracy, and a fresh call for protectionism. But, let us take a step back and present when and why the freeing up of international trade started.

7.4 The Institutions of Multilateralism

Towards the end of WWII, sensible political leaders were determined to prevent the catastrophic pollical decisions made during the first half of the twentieth century, which put an end to the first wave of globalisation and led to destructive protectionism,[23] the Great Depression, and two World Wars. Sound decisions were taken that, indeed, greatly helped to prevent a repetition of these devastating events.

In July 1944, US President Roosevelt invited 44 countries to Bretton Woods, New Hampshire, to agree on the establishment of the International Monetary Fund (IMF) and the World Bank (WB). These two institutions formed a solid basis for the postwar international economic system inspired by multilateralism, i.e., rule-setting through international organisations, based upon the principle of non-discrimination. The General Agreement on Tariffs and Trade (GATT) was to promote free trade.

7.4.1 GATT

In 1946 the US and other industrialised countries bordering the Atlantic Ocean, took the initiative to establish GATT. Their intention was to cut tariffs between them. In 1947 this initiative led to the establishment of GATT in Geneva, Switzerland, supported by twenty-three industrialised countries. Most of the twenty-three member countries were heavily involved in the reconstruction of their infrastructure and their economies.

They very much welcomed GATT which was to promote trade and settle disputes among the members.

Under the GATT, domestic policy considerations always had the upper hand. GATT signatories adhered to the most-favoured nation (MFN) principle, which ensured that tariff and trade favours to one country applied to all member countries. GATT did not include services, nor agriculture. This limitation did not prevent world trade to grow annually with an average of 7% between 1948 and 1990. Indeed, GATT paved the way for the creation of the modern trade regime.

Initially, GATT was not (yet) concerned with the needs of developing countries. Moreover, at the time most of the GATT members still controlled parts of Asia, Africa, and Latin America. As Edgar Dosman observes: '…the GATT addressed the interests of the advanced powers: lowering trade barriers in industrial goods and services where they had a comparative advantage, while ignoring agriculture and textiles where developing countries had an advantage.'[24] Rodrik argues in this realm: 'Agriculture was kept out of GATT negotiations and remained riddled with tariff and non-tariff barriers—most infamously in the form of variable import quotas aimed at stabilizing domestic prices at levels much higher than in exporting countries.'[25]

By 1965, West Germany and Japan had joined GATT. Meanwhile, tensions between industrialised country GATT members and developing countries rose. The latter argued that GATT lacked a broader framework combining trade and development. In particular, GATT did not have a facility for stable and acceptable prices for agricultural exports. In 1964, GATT adopted a specific legal framework within which the concerns of developing countries could be addressed. However, on the question of improved access to industrialised country markets and commodity price stabilisation, no action was taken or legally binding commitments made.[26] In short, GATT increasingly became a target of criticism from developing countries, as their concerns were not properly addressed by GATT. It was felt, not unjustified, that the post-WWII international institutional structure functioned primarily to defend the interests of industrialised countries to maintain the *status quo*.

The typical developing country was more and more plagued by declining exports, a lack of investment funds, declining aid, more debt, and trade barriers. In addition, it had no control over shipping and insurance services. But GATT denied the skewed power relations. Some GATT members argued that the chief obstacles to Third World development were internal rather than external. Developing countries started to lobby for the establishment of a separate organisation to deal explicitly with their problems around trade, commodity price stabilisation, finance, and development.

7.4.2 UNCTAD

In the early 1960s the UN convened the Cairo Conference between developed and developing countries to discuss trade, investment, and economic development. The conference resulted in a declaration that spelled out a common program dealing with internal and external obstacles to development. In addition, the meeting endorsed a special UN conference to discuss these issues.

The fact that this to-be-held conference was agreed upon was a reflection of the changing power relations. Thirty-six developing countries had sent delegates to Cairo. In 1961, the Non-Aligned Movement (NAM) had been established in former Yugoslavia. The NAM agreed that trade and development needed international action and that a united stance during the Cairo Conference would be a step in the right direction. During the 1963 preparatory meeting for the special UN conference, the group of 77 NAM nations (G-77) emerged as a solid, united group.

In 1964, UNCTAD I was held in Geneva, which resulted in the birth of the United Nations Conference on Trade and Development (UNCTAD). This new UN institution provided a forum for industrialised and developing countries to participate in, and benefit from, the international economy. UNCTAD's objectives were to: (i) create better access to the markets of industrialised countries through the reduction of trade barriers; (ii) establish a system which would help stabilise commodity prices; and (iii) to compensate developing countries for fluctuations in their export earnings and the deterioration of their terms of trade.

UNCTAD gave developing countries the platform and institution to pursue their trade priorities. However, they did not necessarily share the same priorities, which obviously limited their bargaining power. Given the fact that Raúl Prebisch was instrumental in UNCTAD's establishment, his prominent role—and that of the G-77—in the difficult birth and early years of UNCTAD is described below in some detail to give UNCTAD's story an additional flavour.[27]

Prebisch and UNCTAD

There were economists who were digging a bit deeper in analysing the development challenges obtaining. One of them was former Argentinean central banker Raúl Prebisch. He argued, as explained above, that industrialised and developing countries were unequal trading partners. Developing countries were at the losing end of trade deals while industrialised countries were gaining—developing countries were suffering from declining terms of trade.

Prebisch was appointed by UN Secretary General U Thant to lead UNCTAD. Initially, there was opposition to his nomination, given his alleged leftist image, but in the end he got the position.[28]

For UNCTAD I, five themes were agreed upon: (i) trade in commodities; (ii) trade in manufactures; (iii) financing and invisibles (shipping and insurance) related to trade; (iv) new institutions; and (v) regional problems. Prebisch drafted the preparatory UNCTAD I report.

After Kennedy's assassination on 22 November 1963, America's initial positive mood towards developing countries changed for a more reserved position. Dosman describes Prebisch's curious meeting with Walt Rostow, the author of *The Stages of Economic Growth*, who at the time was chair of President Johnson's Policy Planning Council and advisor on North-South relations:

> The interview was an important opportunity for Raúl to introduce his UNCTAD I report and to listen and respond to US concerns. Instead, Rostow declared that UNCTAD was on the wrong track altogether—that Latin American countries, for example, should rely more on import-substitution industrialization than trying to export manufactured goods to foreign markets. Prebisch thought he was joking—import substitution within the closed markets after the Great Depression had produced Latin America's current dilemma of protected and inefficient industries for local markets—and asked whether this was US trade strategy in the current Kennedy Round of the GATT. Challenged and unable to respond, Rostow transformed into Mr. Hyde, and his earlier professional tone turned to threats. The best advice for developing countries was 'remedying their own internal deficiencies' and helping the United States develop new technologies with faster growth. In this way 'old industries like textiles will gradually wither away on their own' and transfer production to the Third World. In any case the US administration was unable to do much for UNCTAD since 'protectionist lobbies are protected by Congress and fiats established by the State Department can do little about it.'[29]

Prebisch's objective with UNCTAD was to close the projected $20 billion trade gap between poor and rich countries, which hindered the economic prospects of the former. He argued that all countries, rich and poor, shared a long-term self-interest in overcoming poverty.

GATT's position was that it acknowledged a difference of mandate between them and UNCTAD: GATT had a narrower focus, i.e., to lower tariffs. It would not negotiate commodity agreements; this was for the UN and its agencies to tackle. The World Bank and a handful of industrialised countries were in support of UNCTAD's objectives. However, other industrialised countries, led by America, felt that UNCTAD's proposed policies were simply too radical. They pointed to the shortcomings of developing countries themselves in doing something about the trade gap. Yet, the overall position of industrialised countries was not outright negative.

During the conference it appeared that the G-77 group was not as united as intended. After all, the 77 countries were very different in size, level of development, and culture. In addition, some African countries already had trade deals with the European Economic Community through the 1963 Yaoundé Convention. Still others, such as former French African colonies, had special trade and monetary relationships with their former coloniser. However, in the end unity was forged as the G-77 member states understood that only a united position would give them the necessary clout during negotiations. But this triggered a strong opposition of developed countries. A deadlock loomed. Some sourly observed that UNCTAD actually meant Under No Circumstances Take Any Decision.

Prebisch saw this deadlock coming and organised private meetings with representatives of all relevant groups. After some arms twisting and concessions, a workable compromise was arrived at the end of UNCTAD I: (i) every three or four years a conference would be held where the entire global trading community would meet; (ii) a new international trade entity could be established under UN auspices, including a Trade and Development Board acting as a standing committee; and (iii) day-to-day affairs would be handled by a permanent secretariat to be based in Geneva, reporting directly to the UN Secretary General. Even skeptical British weekly *The Economist* wrote on 6 June 1964:

> Prebisch and the countries he represents are no longer outsiders. A new force is the emerging leadership of the poor. Some delegates from the developing countries and Dr Prebisch himself, are a match for the best the

> industrial world can put up…As the likely head of the new UN trade secretariat, Dr Prebisch will have his foot in the door and he is not one to take it out again.

Dosman captured the sentiment about UNCTAD well: 'UNCTAD was set up to rethink and recast the rules-of-the-game in international trade, leading the campaign for a world economic order with less unequal power relationships. Prebisch was not neutral, just as the IMF, World Bank, and the GATT were not neutral. If these established bodies defended the interests of developed countries, UNCTAD would be unapologetic in promoting new rules to benefit the Third World.'[30]

Only concrete results would underpin UNCTAD's *raison d'être*. For example, cocoa seemed an appropriate commodity for the establishment of an international commodity agreement to stabilise cocoa export prices. But international cocoa dealers lobbied their governments to block it.

UNCTAD II

On 1 February 1968, UNCTAD II was opened by Prime Minister Indira Gandhi in New Delhi, India. Since UNCTAD I, very few concrete results had been achieved. UNCTAD was losing political goodwill. The original spirit of multilateralism had made way for bilateralism. In short, the political and economic environment was now less conducive than during UNCTAD I, as America was drawn more and more into the Vietnam War, France was struggling with student uprisings, the UK was heading towards a recession, and the Soviet Union crushed the 1968 'Prague Spring'.

UNCTAD II was to launch a global strategy of development. During the conference, Presbisch launched his idea of a New International Economic Order (NIEO).[31] This 'global compact' was to consist of a durable ethic of cooperation that would safeguard the international community in the long run. It was hoped that after the oil producing countries dramatically increased the price of oil, that this would also imply a boost for developing countries, in that OPEC members would side with them in international negotiations. It was not to be. Oil-importing developing countries in particular had to pay a heavy price, in that their international debts soared. In sum, NIEO went nowhere.

During UNCTAD II the Generalised System of Preferences (GSP) was tabled to promote developing countries' exports of manufactured and semi-manufactured products through non-reciprocal treatment. GSP was accepted in principle. Nonetheless, industrialised—and G-77 countries pronounced the UNCTAD II conference as a failure. The political and economic interests of the 131 participating countries were simply too different to expect substantial agreements between them. *The Washington Post* captured the attitude of developed countries during the conference: 'We don't need them-they need us.'[32] Prebisch was disillusioned and resigned from UNCTAD in March 1969. In hindsight, the verdict on UNCTAD II was too harsh, as it led the way to the 1968 International Sugar Agreement. In addition, by 1990 $70 billion worth of G-77 trade was GSP-related.

What is the verdict on Prebisch? 'All great statesmen end in failure'; this is what one Dutch Prime Minister (PM) replied to a journalist's question when it would be time for the PM to resign. Prebisch was by any standard an international statesman. His biographer Edgar Dosman concluded that, despite all his talents and gifts, Prebisch had seen most of his great projects, such as UNCTAD, fail or not meet his own expectations.[33] Nonetheless, Dosman's final verdict is not as harsh:

> Prebisch was never neutral; he was a driving force in development thought and diplomacy who changed the vocabulary of international politics and cast a long shadow over the twentieth century.... Prebisch's idealism carried him into the top international group of people who make history rather than endure it and continues to animate his followers in the struggle for global equity and justice.[34]

Beyond UNCTAD II

Since UNCTAD II, every four years conferences were held; in 2016, the most recent one was held in Nairobi, Kenya. The question is: what has UNCTAD been able to achieve? Some analysts maintain that GSP is arguably UNCTAD's principal achievement.[35] Another one is the higher proportion (than originally envisaged) of IMF's Special Drawing Rights reserved for developing countries.[36] There was also the adoption of the Integrated Programme for Commodities, which was to cover principal commodity exports, including arrangements for the stabilisation of commodity prices. In 1980 the Common Fund for Commodities (CFC) was established (it went into effect in 1989) with the intention to finance international buffer stocks and internationally coordinated national stocks. CFC would also finance measures for commodity development and promote coordination and consultation on commodity issues.[37] However, CFC functions primarily in providing technical assistance to developing country commodity producers. Its website mentions that: '...direct interventions to dampen fluctuations in commodity prices are no longer considered a viable option. Alternatives are not to mitigate the fluctuations but to reduce the impact they have on the lives of poor producers and consumers.'[38]

Perhaps the fact that UNCTAD is a UN institution, in which ministries of foreign affairs of member-countries participate, explains why UNCTAD has not been able to achieve more since its inception. Issues such as international trade and international finance are the domain of ministers of trade resp. finance, who typically stay away from UN fora.

To date, UNCTAD has 194 member states, proportionally represented in the Trade and Development Board, which manages UNCTAD's work between two conferences. Its secretariat is still based in Geneva. UNCTAD joins the WTO in the International Trade Centre; a technical cooperation centre dealing with operational aspects of trade development.

All told, UNCTAD plays a smaller role as a political forum than in the 1960s and 1970s. UNCTAD is focusing more on analyses of developing country trade and foreign investment issues and perspectives. Thirlwall and Pacheco-López conclude about UNCTAD that: 'It had some limited success in persuading developed countries to grant preferential access to the exports of developing countries, but mainly in the field of manufactured goods, benefitting the larger and more advanced developing countries.'[39]

7.4.3 GATT, UNCTAD, and the WTO

After UNCTAD was established, there were two international institutions dealing with trade and development—GATT and UNCTAD. How did they fare before the establishment in 1995 of the World Trade Organisation (WTO)? GATT broadened its focus by including more and more developing countries and making headlines through its various 'Rounds' of negotiations of which, arguably, the Kennedy Round and Uruguay Round are the best-known. Both Rounds had direct relevance for developing countries, since they were not required to offer tariff concessions during the negotiations under GATT's MFA rule.

The Kennedy Round

A prominent inspiration for the Kennedy Round was the adoption of the US Expansion Act in 1962 which allowed the White House to directly enter into mutual tariff negotiations. The Kennedy Round (1964–1967)—during which $40 billion on tariffs were scrapped or reduced—included attention for trade interests of developing countries, triggered by UNCTAD I.

GATT attempted to hijack UNCTAD's role. On 4 May 1964, in the midst of UNCTAD I, GATT started the Kennedy Round with an impressive ceremony in which G-77 countries formed the majority. It was agreed to discuss measures regarding the expansion of trade of developing countries to promote their economic development. Also measures were to be taken regarding access to markets for agricultural and other primary export products, which so far had been excluded from GATT. However, the results on agriculture were poor.[40] Despite all pronounced intentions, developing countries played a minor role during the negotiations. Nevertheless, they benefitted from substantial tariff cuts, particularly in non-agricultural products. As mentioned, they were absolved from GATT's reciprocity principle. So they could benefit from tariff cuts from industrialised countries without granting the same tariff cuts to them. This was, arguably, the result of UNCTAD's call for a better trade deal for developing countries.

The Uruguay Round

The Uruguay Round (1986–1994) was the last one under GATT auspices. This Round took much more time than the Kennedy Round. It started in September 1986 in Punta del Este, Uruguay, and ended in 1994. Its scope was much wider than previous Rounds, as it included non-tariff barriers, trade in services, intellectual property rights, and trade in agricultural products and textiles.

No less than 123 countries participated. Fourteen countries, among them Australia, Indonesia, Brazil, and Canada (the Cairns Group) were not prepared to sign any agreement unless something was done about agricultural products. The result was The Agreement on Agriculture, which continues to be the most substantial trade liberalisation agreement in these products. The agreement was to: (i) improve market access for agricultural products through phasing out import quotas and converting them into tariffs and subsidies; (ii) reduce domestic support of agriculture by way of price-distorting subsidies and quotas; (iii) eliminate over time export subsidies; and (iv) harmonise sanitary and phytosanitary measures between member countries. The Multi-Fiber Arrangement, which governed trade in textiles and clothing, would be phased out within a decade.[41]

This is what Stiglitz observes about the so-called 'Grand Bargain', which constituted the basis of the Uruguay Round negotiations:

> The Uruguay Round had been based on what became known as the 'Grand Bargain', in which the developed countries promised to liberalize trade in agriculture and textiles (that is labor-intensive goods of interest to exporters in developing countries) and, in turn, developing countries agreed to reduce tariffs and accept a range of new rules and obligations on intellectual property rights, investments, and services. Afterward, many developing countries felt that they had been misled into agreeing to the Grand Bargain: the developed countries did not keep their side of the deal. Textile quotas would remain in place for a decade, and no end to agricultural subsidies was in sight.[42]

In April 1994, the Round concluded with the Marrakesh Agreement, paving the way for the creation of the WTO.[43] In addition, it included commitments to reopen negotiations on agriculture and services around the turn of the century. These negotiations started in early 2000, and they were incorporated in the Doha Development Agenda in 2001.

This is what Constantine Michalopoulos concludes on the Rounds: 'However, the average reduction in tariffs following each Round was less favorable to developing countries than to developed ones: 26% compared with an average of 36% on goods of export interest to developed countries after the Kennedy Round...and 26% compared to 33% after the Tokyo Round. This was because many such goods were either exempt from formula cuts or subject to lower than formula cuts.'[44] Despite commitments to reduce export subsidies on the part of developed countries, they have been maintained at high levels. For example, subsidies on dairy products have hurt the production in countries such as Brazil, Jamaica, and Tanzania. And support for EUs beef production resulted in European beef dominating the markets of Benin and Ivory Coast for which Burkina Faso and Mali were once important supplies.[45]

Stiglitz, not surprisingly, is unforgiving about the consequences of the Uruguay Round for developing countries. He argues that the Round made an unlevel playing field even less level. Rich countries had cost poor countries three times more in trade restrictions than they gave in total development aid. In addition, he observes that liberalisation of unskilled labour services would have led to a far greater increase in global efficiency than liberalisation of skilled labour services, the comparative advantage of industrialised countries. Yet, negotiations focused on liberalisation of skill-intensive services.

7.4.4 WTO

In 1995, Jeffrey Sachs and Andrew Warner published an elaborate study entitled *Economic Reform and the Process of Global Integration*.[46] Its principal message was that countries, developed or developing, open to international trade grew 2.45% faster over the longer term than countries that closed themselves from international trade. Their findings were confirmed by scores of other studies heralding the benefits of openness. Rodrik observes that the pursuit of promoting international trade and globalisation became 'a substitute for development strategy.'[47] In short, an ideal environment for the WTO to start working.

At the end of the Uruguay Round, GATT was immersed into the World Trade Organisation, which began its operations on 1 January 1995. The GATT basically consisted of a set of rules concluded by nations, whereas the WTO is an institution whose arrangements are a multilateral agreement settlement mechanism. For example, one such agreement is WTO's Agreement on Sanitary and Phytosanitary Measures. Another one is the Agreement on Safeguards. This allows members to increase import tariffs when a sudden surge in imports puts domestic firms in trouble. The WTO itself does not punish violators, but it allows countries that suffer injury as a result of a violation, to retaliate by imposing trade restrictions on the offending country.

Myles Wickstead summarises WTO's mandate succinctly: 'WTO sets out the principal contractual obligations determining how governments frame and implement domestic trade legislation and regulations, and is also the platform on which trade relations among countries evolve through collective debate and negotiation.'[48]

The WTO is an institutional response to a practical question: how to sustain a mutually beneficial liberal economy in a world of many sovereign states of different economic strength and sophistication, all suffering from protectionist pressures. This time, domestic economic concerns were subservient to international trade and finance rather than during GATT, where it was the other way around: under the GATT, domestic policy considerations always had the upper hand.

WTO introduced a new procedure for dispute settlement, implying that evading its appellate body's decision was impossible, unless it was reversed collectively by every single WTO member. Given WTO's large membership, different trade interests, different safety and other standards, and the fact that decisions had to be made by consensus, it is clear that the WTO had a very difficult task ahead.

The WTO does not do away with the inequality in the power of nations. It is not a system of global government (there is none, by the way), but rather a way of organising and disciplining the unequal capacity for self-help of the member-states. Nonetheless, the WTO offers poor countries a forum of forcing powerful countries to adhere to internationally agreed rules, and also the possibility of greater integration in the international trade system.

This was welcomed by poor countries since they had the ambition to promote their exports. As Baldwin observes: 'When the global value chain revolution started picking up steam, many developing nations realized that trade barriers were harming their chances of getting their share of the offshored jobs.'[49] In addition, exceptions to WTO rules would apply to developing countries and extra exceptions would apply to low-income countries.[50] Consequently, these countries became more willing than in the past to adhere to internationally agreed trading rules to also attract foreign investment. Since the early 1990s, many developing countries made great progress in liberalising their trade regimes. Out of 50 countries analysed, Michalopoulos concludes that 45 of them showed a decline in their average applied rates, frequently more than half.[51]

On the other hand, developing countries face WTO restrictions regarding their own industrial policies. It is now harder for Latin American and African countries to copy the development policies so successfully applied by East Asian countries in the past. This is what Pau Collier observes:

> Without effective temporary protection against the Asian giants, the countries of the bottom billion will not break into new global markets. Their governments will not even try because they lack belief in themselves and expect to fail. I once suggested to a senior civil servant in the trade ministry of one of the countries of the bottom billion that they focus on new global markets. His response was: It's like looking at the sun.[52]

Collier adds that protection against Asia is not about justice, fairness, or resisting globalisation, rather, it is about pulling the marginalised countries aboard.[53] Their history tells us that imports should not be liberalised before the export sector has had the time to boost its productivity and successfully compete in the international market so as to generate sufficient foreign exchange to foot the higher import bill. After all, if imports were to rise faster than exports, balance-of-payments problems would ensue, putting a brake on growth. Under WTO rules export subsidies are not allowed, nor sequencing of appropriate measures on the way to full trade liberalisation. Only the poorest nations are exempt from it. Industrial imitation, successfully done by the same East Asian countries in the past, is also not any longer allowed. But countries that broke these rules in the past such as China and Vietnam, registered spectacular growth figures by promoting foreign direct investment and the export sector, while protecting their domestic markets.

Take China: the country joined the WTO during the first Doha meeting in 2001. China was to be considered a 'non-market economy' for 15 years, which permitted WTO members, such as the EU and America, to use somewhat arbitrary measures in determining whether China was 'dumping' products in their markets.[54] What policies did China apply before joining? The government created high tariff walls. It actively promoted the training of workers and managers, and it promoted the creation of successful demonstration projects. Foreign investors were welcomed. However, the government forced foreign companies into mergers and joint ventures with local companies, although a 25% investment share was enough for foreign investors to gain a joint venture status, subsequently qualifying them for tax incentives. Export subsidies were given to Chinese exporters and China maintained a competitive exchange rate. Rodrik observes:

> Many of these early policies would have run afoul of WTO rules that ban export subsidies and prohibit discrimination in favor of domestic firms, if China had been a member of the organization. Chinese policy makers were not constrained by any external rules in their conducted industrial policies and could act freely to promote industrialization. By the time China did join the WTO in 2001, it had created a strong industrial base, much of which did not need protection or nurturing. China substantially reduced its tariffs in preparation for WTO membership, bringing them down from the high levels of the early 1990s (an average of around 40 percent) to single digits in 2001. Many other industrial policies were also phased out.[55]

WTO's Agreement on Trade Related Intellectual Property Rights (TRIPS) impairs the possibility for developing countries to copy protected advanced technologies used by industrialised countries. Very large countries such as China and India stand to benefit from these rights. But this does not apply to smaller developing countries that may see their ability to educate restricted (because of copy rights) as well as to provide public health to their citizens. As Stiglitz notes: 'No one denies the importance of intellectual property rights. But these rights need to balance the rights and interests of producers against those of users, not only users in developing countries but also researchers in developed countries.'[56]

Tilman Altenburg and Wilfried Lűtkenhorst (A&L) express a more nuanced opinion on the position of developing countries within WTO. They say that, to a considerable degree, these countries are allowed to protect their industries. For example, a good number of their tariffs can still be retained. They can also impose import surcharges when these imports threaten to destabilise the balance-of-payments or when sudden import surges would emerge that may jeopardise local industries. Protective measures are also allowed when their food security is in danger. Regarding foreign investments, governments are allowed to carry out Economic Needs Tests and deny investment licenses when they expect, for example, negative employment effects. The authors' conclusion is that their remaining policy space is still considerable. Especially for modern industrial policy, the field is wide open. However, A&L observe that given the fact that only few poor countries have been able to take advantage of preferential trade agreements, these poor countries' binding constraints are not so much international trade but supply-side constraints and structural problems, such as the increasing economies of scale required for exports.[57]

It was in 1999 in Seattle, Washington, where developing countries voiced their great displeasure about industrialised countries, since they had not done enough in reducing protection of their agricultural products. Their so-called dirty tariffication and continued export subsidies had inflicted a considerable burden on developing countries. The Singapore Round had run into major difficulties over agricultural subsidies, which eventually led to the Doha Round. This 'Development Round', with a special view to address the agricultural demands of developing countries, should have ended in 2005. The Doha Development Agenda had several important implications for TRIPS. The most important one was the declaration on health, in which it was agreed that each WTO member had the right to determine what constitutes a national emergency, and that public health crises relating to HIV/AIDS, TB, or malaria can represent a national emergency. Another point on the agenda was that low-income countries would not be asked to liberalise any of their trade restrictions in either manufactures or agriculture. But it was not to be: the Doha Round was formally abandoned in 2015. Industrialised countries were only prepared to cut agricultural subsidies and trade barriers in exchange for access of their manufactured goods and financial services to the markets of developing countries, to which the latter objected.

Meanwhile, tariff escalation, which leads to higher protection for finished products, is an issue among developing countries, in that, as Michalopoulos observes, low-income countries, including SSA countries, tend to have the highest degree of escalation and hence the highest protection for their final goods producers.[58] However, industralised countries apply them as well, by making exports of the developing countries' processed products more difficult, such as wheat flour, orange juice, vegetable oils and dairy products, clothing, leather and wood products.

The WTO has at least achieved one major victory: the Trade Facilitation Agreement of 2014. This agreement involves a $1 trillion package of reforms of global customs rules and the ease of transporting goods across national borders.

Rodrik wonders whether any model of deep international integration would be sustainable when democratic politics remained organised along national lines. He concludes that it is not.[59]
How do we manage the tension between national democracy and global markets? Rodrik presents the following 'trilemma': 'We cannot have hyperglobalization, democracy and national self-determination. We can have at most two out of three. If we want hyperglobalization and democracy, we need to give up on the nation state. If we must keep the nation state and want hyperglobalization too, then we must forget about democracy. And if we want to combine democracy with the nation state, then it is bye-bye deep globalization.'[60]
The Bretton Woods regime sacrificed hyperglobalization. It allowed countries to dance to their own tune as long as they removed a number of border restrictions on trade and generally treated all their trade partners equally. The Bretton Woods compromise was largely abandoned in the 1980s as the liberalization of capital flows gathered speed and trade agreements began to reach behind national borders.[61]

7.4.5 Regional Trade Agreements

There are many more regional trade agreements than the global ones described above. The WTO listed over 100 regional agreements, whether they are customs unions, free trade agreement; whether they are between developing countries, or between developing and industrialised countries.[62] A customs union applies free trade between the members while applying a common external tariff. A free trade area slashes tariffs between the members but it does not apply a common external tariff. So, the member countries are free to apply their own tariffs for imported goods from without the free trade zone, thus allowing each individual member to benefit from the cheapest imports.

The best-known and most spectacular regional agreement is the European Union (EU). By all standards, the EU is a remarkable success, taking into consideration Europe's dismal political and economic beggar-thy-neighbour history before WWII. The North American Free Trade Area (NAFTA) between the US, Canada, and Mexico was another well-known free trade agreement. Its successor, the United States-Mexico-Canada Agreement (USMCA), may be undermined by the Trump Administration's hostile attitude towards Mexico, and to free trade at large. Although developing countries are involved in quite a few regional trade agreements, the total trade involved is relatively small: almost 50% of all trade among regional trade partners involves the EU; another 13% involved NAFTA.[63]

The developing world is home to dozens of regional trade agreements. MERCOSUR comes to mind, in which Argentina, Bolivia, Brazil, Paraguay, Uruguay, and Venezuela participate. The Association of Southeast Asian Nations (ASEAN) consisting of Brunei, Cambodia, Indonesia, Laos, Malaysia, Myanmar, Philippines, Singapore, Thailand, and Vietnam, is another one. The Southern African Customs Union (SACU) between Botswana, Lesotho, Namibia, South Africa, and Swaziland, also belongs to the better-known regional trade agreements.[64] In early 2018, 44 African nations signed an agreement to establish a free-trade zone between them, entitled the African Free Trade Area. Should the respective parliaments approve, this new free-trade zone will be the largest since WTO's establishment. It is estimated that around 1 billion Africans will be able to trade with each other free of tariffs. However, the two largest African economies, Nigeria and South Africa, did not sign the agreement. Nigeria needed more time to consider, and South Africa's president Ramaphosa said that he would sign the agreement once the South African Parliament would have approved it. Currently, African countries only trade 16% of their total exports with each other.

As regards the Lomé Convention, in 1975, the European Economic Community (now European Union) signed an agreement with initially 46, and now 77, African, Caribbean, and Pacific (ACP) countries. It provided free access to the EU market for all ACP's manufactured goods and 90% of their agricultural exports. This was not all. A Stabex Scheme was also concluded to stabilise the foreign exchange earnings of 12 important commodities. In 2000, Stabex was abolished and replaced by financial support from the European Development Fund (EDF). EU's assistance to ACP countries is now channeled through EDF.

In 2001, the EU launched its *Everything but Arms* (EBA) initiative. 49 Least-developed countries (LDCs) were to benefit from EBA, in that these countries can export all their exportable products (except arms and armaments) to the EU free of any tariff or other trade barrier. Entry into EBA is automatic and EBA has no time limit. In 2013, Euros 4.1 billion were exported from LDCs to the EU.

Negotiations are ongoing between the EU and ACP countries about Economic Partnership Agreements to replace the trade preferences the ACP countries enjoyed since Lomé. The EU wants ACP countries to reduce restrictions on the importation of EU-manufactured goods and services in return for continued access to the EU market for ACP's agricultural exports.

In July 2019, after 20 years of negotiations, the EU and MERCOSUR reached a principle trade agreement, from which some 770 million people could benefit, provided protests from European farmers and environmentalists will be satisfactorily dealt with, and EU's national parliaments as well as the European Parliament will have approved the agreement. The main components of the deal are the slashing of import duties, liberalisation of services across borders, and cross-border investments. Finally, tenders will be open to all participating countries.

7.5 How Developing Countries Fared

Globalisation accelerated from 1980 onwards. It was promoted by tariff reductions, technological advances made in transport and communication, and by decisions taken by large emerging economies, such as China and India, to open their markets to foreign trade and investment.

Poor countries were able to benefit from the potential of their abundant labour to enter into global markets for manufactured goods and services. Manufactures, for example, rose from around 25% of developing country exports in 1980 to more than 80% in 1998. Some 24 developing countries—home to 3 billion people—had doubled their ratio of trade to income over the period 1980–2000.[65] Their average annual growth rate rose from 3% in the 1970s to 5% during the 1990s. This was the good news.

The not so good news was that other developing countries traded less than what they traded towards the end of the 1970s. In other words, they were falling behind. It would be incorrect to blame globalisation alone for disappointing growth. Developing countries themselves also needed to seize the opportunities which globalisation provided, which in various instances they did not. Mancur Olson argued:

> Sometimes the shortcomings of the economic policies and institutions of poor countries make foreign investors and foreign firms unwelcome, or provoke the flight of locally owned capital, or make lending to these countries exceedingly risky. Whether the institutional and policy shortcomings of a country keep capital from having the productivity appropriate to its scarcity or discourage the investments and lending that would equalize the marginal product of capital across countries, they keep it from achieving its potential.[66]

In 2002, the World Bank published a report entitled *Global Economic Prospects and the Developing Countries*.[67] Its message was that if global trade liberalisation would continue, it would offer enormous opportunities for developing countries to expand their trade and increase their welfare. The Bank even calculated how much these countries could possibly benefit. By 2015, world income would be $355 billion higher with merchandise trade liberalisation, of which developing countries would gain $184 billion annually. Nearly 80% of these gains would come from liberalisation of agriculture. The report added that with dynamic benefits included, developing countries' incomes would rise by more than

$500 billion a year, with $390 billion coming from agriculture and $120 billion from textiles and clothing.

Not all analysts agreed to the World Bank's enthusiasm about the benefits of globalisation. Take Dani Rodrik. In 1998, he published *The New Global Economy: Making Openness Work.*[68] He argues that the benefits of trade liberalisation have been greatly exaggerated. What Rodrik proposes is that policymakers should focus on the fundamentals of economic growth, i.e., investment, macroeconomic stability, human resources development and good governance, and not let international economic integration dominate their thinking. Yet, he agrees that successful economies become more open by lowering tariff barriers, but that this does not guarantee success. Rodrik refers to import substitution strategies which had been successfully applied before the early 1970s. They failed since then because they could not sustain macroeconomic stability.

One would indeed expect that there is a positive relationship between trade liberalisation and economic growth. However, this is not necessarily the case. This is what Stiglitz observes:

> Advocates of liberalization cite statistical studies claiming that liberalization enhances growth. But a careful look at the evidence shows something quite different...It is exports—not the removal of trade barriers—that is the driving force of growth. Studies that focus directly on the removal of trade barriers show little relationship between liberalization and growth. The advocates of quick liberalization tried an intellectual sleight of hand, hoping that the broad-brush discussion of the benefits of globalization would suffice to make their case.[69]

This observation confirms why the export-led growth strategies of the Asian Tigers—and more recently China's—were so successful. Nonetheless, the *Globalization, Growth and Poverty* report observes that more globalised developing countries had a better growth performance than less globalized ones. Thirlwall and Pacheco-López present the results of various studies on the relationship between trade liberalisation and growth. The majority of these studies conclude that there is no significant effect of openness on economic growth, although the authors also refer to studies by Greenaway et al. that demonstrate a lagged positive relationship.[70] Regarding the question whether this lagged positive relationship would last, there is no indication that it does. The authors round up as follows:

> In conclusion, there is some evidence that trade liberalization promotes growth and a higher growth of living standards; on the other hand, the results are not always robust, and depend on the measure of liberalization used, the time period taken and the estimation method… In other words, trade liberalization cannot be regarded as a substitute for a comprehensive trade and development strategy. To quote Rodrik (2001): 'deep trade liberalization cannot be relied upon to deliver rates of economic growth and therefore does not deserve the high priority it typically receives in the development strategies pushed by leading organizations.'[71]

Let us now take a look at economic growth and trade over the first two decades of this century. The economies of many SSA countries have been doing well. In Chap. 2, it is mentioned that over the period 2000–2007, two-thirds of SSA's economies grew at more than 5.5% per year. One-third of them even managed to achieve 7% per year, benefitting from China's continued importation of SSA's commodity export products. Indeed, impressive growth figures, implicitly refuting what Rodrik and Stiglitz said about openness and growth. Moreover, these growth percentages did not include the contribution of Africa's informal economies. During the first half of the second decade of this century, economic growth in most SSA countries slowed down; mainly caused by the lowering of commodity prices, and less demand from China. Yet, the IMF is fairly optimistic: it reports that one-third of SSA countries can expect a GDP growth of more than 5% in 2019. Unfortunately, SSA's scores on productivity and income distribution are still very poor indeed, compared to other developing regions.

Now, what are the prospects for the developing world at large? As noted, since 2008 the weight of developing and emerging economies in the global economy tipped over the 50% mark (expressed in PPP terms) for the first time.[72] By 2010, developing countries accounted for around 42% of global merchandise trade; South-South flows made up about half of the total.[73] During a good part of the second decade of this century, world economic growth and trade slowed down, caused by the negative effects of the Great Recession and China's gradual transformation from a manufacturing and export-led economy to one based on services and domestic consumption, resulting in China's economy growing more slowly. Yet, China and, to an increasing extent, India remain attractive export markets for developing countries. However, international trade and world economic growth may be affected by various ongoing trade disputes and by Brexit.

7.5.1 *Trade Liberalisation and Poverty Reduction*

Until recently, it was thought that economic growth, triggered by openness to trade, would improve everybody's living standard. Even the poorest sections of society would benefit, depending on the elasticity of the poverty rate to growth. In short, economic growth was good for the poor. This was the title of a celebrated article published in 2002 by David Dollar and Aart Kraay.[74] They conclude that openness to trade increases income of the poor to the same extent that it increases income of the other households in society.

The World Bank does not any longer agree with this insight. On 1 October 2015, former World Bank President Jim Yong Kim spoke at the United States Institute of Peace and assured his audience that he took issue with those who believe that economic growth alone is 'the rising tide that will lift all boats'. This rather obsolete metaphor suggests that all income earners would benefit from growth, including the poorest. Kim explained that a focus on GDP growth is simplistic. He went on by saying that the Bank rejects 'trickle down' approaches. Kim called on governments to look into growing inequality and to boost 'shared prosperity'. He reminded his audience that the World Bank had two objectives: (i) ending extreme poverty; and (ii) boost shared prosperity. This double objective was to be achieved through economic growth, investing in people, and insuring them so that they do not risk falling back.[75]

What does the literature tell us? In 2005, Branko Milanovic took a large sample of 321 household income surveys from 95 countries in 1993 and 1998, covering 90% of the entire world's population. He concludes that: (i) increased openness reduces the income share of the bottom six deciles; and (ii) the adverse effect of openness on inequality is greater the lower a country's per capita income.[76] But, Milanovic added that at an income per capita of about $7500.- the poor start to benefit relative to the rich. The author concludes: 'openness would therefore seem to have a particularly negative impact on poor and middle-income groups in poor countries—directly opposite to what would be expected from the standard

Hekscher-Ohlin framework.'[77] Another authority on poverty is Martin Ravallion. In a 2006 study he observes: 'It remains clear that there is considerable variation in the rates of poverty reduction at a given rate of expansion of trade volume'. He concludes rather categorically: '...based on the data available from cross-country comparison, it is hard to maintain the view that expanding trade, in general, is a powerful force for poverty reduction in developing countries.'[78]

7.5.2 *Income Distribution*

Opening an economy to international competition will impinge upon the distribution of assets, its rate of return, incomes, and wealth. But what happens to changes in the distribution of income triggered by trade liberalisation? Contrary to what the Hekscher-Ohlin Theorem suggests, it appears that there is a trend of increasing inequality in wages between skilled and unskilled workers in developing countries. How come? If imported products can be sold cheaper in the importing country, the unskilled worker of that country will suffer at best a drop in wages, or at worst lose his or her job. Should imports eclipse exports, balance-of-payments problems will arise, resulting in a contraction of the economy from which the unskilled workers will suffer more since the demand for their services drops. Then, there is the influence of foreign direct investment. And there is a shift in production of relatively sophisticated production processes from industrial to developing countries. These two developments, put together, result in an increase in the demand for skilled workers. Again, the gap between the wages of skilled and unskilled workers will widen. Technological progress taking place in developing countries will trigger demand for skilled workers there—the gap will widen.

Now, what do studies on globalisation and income distribution tell us? In *The Great Convergence*, Richard Baldwin concludes that over the period 1980–2010 globalisation has had a positive effect on poverty, improving the lot of hundreds of millions of people, primarily in lower middle-income and upper middle-income countries. However, during the same period the number of people below the World Bank poverty line increased mainly in low-income African countries: 'These are not nations where the global value chain revolution's magic is working.'[79]

An often quoted study on income and wealth distribution is Branko Milanovic's *Global Inequality*, which I mentioned in Chap. 1. Milanovic adjusted his 2005 insights, summarised above. This is what Milanovic now concludes about income distribution, including to what extent globalisation contributed to improving the incomes of the poor. In his famous elephant-shaped figure, Milanovic shows who gained and who lost out, by plotting percentage gain in income against the original income covering the period 1988–2008—the period of 'high globalisation'.[80] Indeed, the years just before the financial crisis of 2008, were the most globalised years in human history. The emerging global middle class, predominantly from Asian countries, between the 40th and 60th global percentile, benefited a lot.[81] Nonetheless, people belonging to this class are still relatively poor compared to e.g., Western middle class income earners. There is also a group of income earners that has not witnessed any growth in their income. Now, who are these people? They are almost all from rich OECD economies—the lower middle class of the rich world. 'In short, the world's great winners have been the Asian poor and middle classes; the great losers, the lower middle classes of the rich world.'[82]

Regarding the world's very richest 1% (the global plutocrats, as Milanovic calls them), their real income has risen substantially between 1988 and 2008. They clearly belong to the winners. Half of them are Americans; the remainder are almost all from Western Europe, Japan, and Oceania. But we find them also in Brazil, China, South Africa, and Russia. These billionaires combined, own twice as much wealth as exists in all of Africa. The conclusion is that the income gaps between the top and bottom have widened in the rich world, and that globalisation has favoured those in rich countries who were already better-off.[83]

Within nations, inequalities in the rich world have widened during the last three decades. But this also applies to the world as a whole. The percentage gains are always the strongest among the middle classes in emerging economies and the global 1%. And they are always the least among people situated around the 75–90th percentile of the global income distribution—the middle- and lower middle classes in OECD countries.

Between the world's nations, inequality has fallen dramatically, since middle class incomes in China and India have drawn closer to the stagnating incomes of the middle classes in the industrial world.

Now, what about the impact on the poor? Milanovic concludes that, by and large, the great winners have been the Asian poor and middle classes; the great losers, the lower middle classes of the rich world.[84] There is simply no way, Milanovic explains, in which an answer can be given in differentiated terms, since both the actual situation and developments in each country are different, and other factors weigh in as well, such as the quality of a country's institutions, the appropriateness of its economic policies, and development in consumer goods prices.

In March 2018, Valentin Lang and Marina Mendes Tavares published an IMF Working Paper entitled *The Distribution of Gains from Globalization*.[85] They took a panel of 147 developed and developing countries over the period 1970–2014. The authors wanted to find out how important economic globalisation was for explaining changes in income levels and income inequality.

They conclude that in countries where globalisation is low or medium, increasing globalisation leads to higher growth. After all, standard models of endogenous growth (see Chap. 5) suggest that economic integration improves the flow of knowledge and technological diffusion across countries and thus broadens the potential market for innovators. These processes promote incentives for inventing new products and improving productivity, triggering even more growth.

Large gains from globalisation have been reaped in the early stages. However, the marginal returns to globalisation diminished as globalisation increased and, eventually, the gains petered out. As a result, in the globalising world a converging process *between* countries is ongoing, confirming Milanovic's findings. This process is mainly due to China's and India's rapid economic growth over the past four decades.

But what about the results *within* countries? Lang and Mendes Tavares observe that the gains from globalisation were concentrated at the top of income earners without significantly affecting the incomes of the poor in many countries. This meant rising inequality. All told, economic globalisation is positively correlated with income level and negatively correlated with income inequality. In other words: global inequality of incomes between individuals is increasingly driven by within-country inequality and decreasingly by between-country inequality.

Regarding income inequality, a subsample of developing countries indicated that the gains from globalisation also reached the bottom of the income distribution and, thus, reduced poverty there. The authors conclude, after having analysed the effects on the various income deciles: 'There is evidence for a poverty-reducing effect in developing countries and no evidence for income losses in absolute terms for any decile.'[86] This supports the view that globalisation helps reduce poverty in developing countries. Their findings also suggest that there was an important role played by domestic policies aimed at realising more inclusive gains from globalisation.[87]

In the instances where globalisation would lead to greater inequality in poor countries, what can be done about it? The authors argue that since the gains from globalisation for a poor country that starts to globalise are relatively large, the resulting increase in financial resources can be used to finance measures to redress inequality. The government may, for example, decide to apply an income redistribution policy or it can invest in accessible and better education for the poor. After all, higher levels, and a more equal distribution of human capital helps a society to reap the gains from economic openness and distribute these gains more evenly. The authors find some evidence that developing countries that invest more than 3% of their GDP on education, and/or apply redistributive income policies, did indeed help to reduce poverty.

7.5.3 *No Level Playing Field*

This chapter has made it clear, I trust, that opening up a developing country's borders up-front for international trade is not necessarily contributing to its economic growth. Remember that almost all industrial countries developed their economies behind protective walls. This also goes for successful former developing countries such as South Korea, Taiwan, Singapore, and China. These countries all applied an infant industry policy allowing their manufacturing firms to mature before entering the international market. Without this type of protection, a country whose comparative advantage is in agriculture (as in many low-income countries), is destined to have limited growth perspectives.

All was not well regarding fairness in international trade. Industrial countries, the IMF, World Bank, and the WTO presented trade liberalisation to developing countries suggesting that this would be the way forward in their development process. However, they did not always give developing countries a fair deal, which is not surprising given the composition of their respective Boards in which developing countries are underrepresented and in which industrial nations, in particular the US, are overrepresented. Stiglitz observes that the IMF is distorted: it has traditionally been an institution in which creditor interests and views are disproportionally represented. IMF's perspectives are inevitably strongly influenced by the United Sates, given the fact that in IMF's Board, America is the only country with veto power.[88]

America, Canada, the European Union, and Japan charged far higher tariffs (some exceeding 15%) than their average tariff of 3%, for labour-intensive manufactured imports and processed foodstuff.[89] Then, there is the phenomenon of *tariff-escalation*, meaning that processed raw materials, such as cocoa, tea, and coffee, were charged far higher tariffs than those for unprocessed raw materials. This explains why countries like the UK, Switzerland, and the Netherlands still control to a large extent the markets for cocoa, tea, and coffee.

Safeguards are temporary tariffs to allow an industry time to make adjustments to better withstand competition from importers. Dumping duties are supposed to be applied to stop unfair trade practices or selling goods below their cost price. These duties can be used to ban imports and, at the same time, protect local manufacturers. Dumping duties are not only applied by industrial countries, they are also used by developing countries against each other. Technical barriers are also being applied to limit competitive imports. The application of the rules of origin is yet another possibility. Stiglitz cites the example of the US using rules of origin to promote its own exports: '…countries that make shirts using American cotton are given preferences which those who use the least expensive cotton are not.'[90]

Particularly notorious are agricultural subsidies policies of the European Union, Japan, and America. In 2000, for example, the EU provided $913 per cow raised in EU countries and only $8 to each SSA country. Japan did do a lot better; that is from the point of view of the cows: it provided $2700.- for each cow raised in Japan, and just $1.47 to each African person. In addition, subsidised agricultural surpluses were dumped on the international markets with negative effects for agricultural exports of developing countries. US rice farmers receive 72% subsidy. America spends $3.3 billion annually to subsidise American cotton production from which some 25,000 American cotton farmers benefit, to the detriment of 10 million cotton farmers in Burkina Faso, Mali, Chad, and Benin. The protection given to agriculture is also given to many low-value manufactured goods in which developing countries have a comparative advantage—particularly in a wide range of textile goods.[91] One cannot but conclude that the whole world trade system works against the majority of poor developing countries.

7.5.4 *Renewed Protectionism*

Until recently, protectionism was a dirty word. But it no longer seems to be. Way back in 2006, I wrote the following in an essay about globalisation, growth, and poverty:

> Yet the opponents [of globalization, PdH] who form a minority, represent a rather formidable counterforce. This will gain more ground if a world-wide recession would occur.... Labour unions in countries that stand to lose employment opportunities could exert irresistible pressure; protectionism and nationalism could reappear if inequality as well as poverty worldwide will not diminish further. In other words, the process of globalization is not necessarily here to stay, it may very well be interrupted by the counter forces I just mentioned.[92]

A 2007 *PEW Survey of Global Attitudes* observes that enthusiasm for further opening of the global economy was flagging in many advanced economies and in some developing countries. The 2018 IMF Working Paper, summarised above, observes that high-income countries reached the highest level of globalisation towards the end of the first decade of this century and that they are currently experiencing stagnation or even decline in this respect.[93] Meanwhile, two huge regional trade deals in the making: the Transatlantic Trade and Investment Partnership (TTIP) and the Transpacific Partnership (TPP), have been shelved.[94]

Some speak of a process of *deglobalization*, given the fact that in the period 2000–2010 growth in trade has been less than growth in GDP. Moreover, relatively easy industrialisation that promoted China's economic miracle is drying up, and terms like labour migration, free trade, and the free flow of capital trigger political resistance.

In 2011, Rodrik warned that if China's trade surplus would not shrink, the United States would likely resort to trade barriers directed at Chinese exports.[95] Rodrik's warning was spot on: as I was writing this chapter, President Trump announced that the US would increase the import tariffs on steel and aluminum. He added that this could apply to more goods. Retaliation by China, the European Union, Canada, Mexico, Japan and other countries followed suit. Stiglitz argues that the threats to continued globalisation and to the liberal philosophy on which it is based, derive from the shortcomings in addressing the needs of those left behind, and from the failure to have multinational corporations pay their fair share of taxes.[96]

7.5.5 How to Ward Off Protectionism

Until 2008, the world economy continued to grow in a robust manner. In September 2008, the Great Recession broke out. Some commentators argue that the recession was not as 'great' as the term suggests. As mentioned in Chap. 1, Edward Luce observes: 'Although the short-term market turmoil was worldwide, the so-called global recession was primarily an Atlantic one. Most of the rest of the world continued to expand. Indeed, growth in China, the world's largest autocracy, picked up for several years after 2008.'[97]

Now, to ward off a wave of protectionism, China—and India for that matter—could both act as *the* engines of growth for developing countries exporting to them. But more can be done to improve economic growth of poor developing countries. For example, WTO rules that prevent these countries from protecting their infant industries could be scrapped. The same applies to: (i) tariff escalation; (ii) industrialised countries' agricultural subsidies; (iii) technical barriers and rules of origin; and (iv) the application of safeguard and anti-dumping measures that block developing countries' access to the markets of developed countries.

There is more. Take the freeing up of labour markets. Rodrik estimates that the gains to be made would outstrip any other proposal, including the entire package of trade measures under the Doha Round negotiations. Perhaps Rodrik's estimate was on the conservative side. Michael Clemens of the Centre for Global Development, argues that if everyone who wanted to migrate were able to do so, global GDP would double.[98]

Rodrik proposes a temporary work visa scheme of rich countries that would expand their labour force by less than 3%. Skilled and unskilled workers from developing countries would be allowed to work in rich countries for a limited period, say, five years. This would produce an estimated gain of $360 billion annually for the world economy.[99] Lastly, the negative effects of globalisation should be better addressed by governments of affected countries, through financial support to those who lost their jobs, retraining programs, promotion of labour mobility, and employment creating businesses.

7.6 Conclusions

Trade liberalisation, a prominent phenomenon of globalisation, took flight after WWII, and gathered more and more pace ever since, thereby contributing to economic growth of many countries. Industrailised countries and emerging economies benefitted most, poor African countries least. Trade liberalisation contributed to the reduction of poverty in developing countries, but not in all. Trade liberalisation and globalisation are both manifestations of the spirit of multilateralism, which is under threat from political leaders promoting protectionism.

A converging process between countries is ongoing; be it that this is to a large extent due to China's phenomenal economic growth over the past four decades. This converging process may well have geopolitical and economic ramifications in the medium to long term, in that the Western liberalism-inspired Washington Consensus, may be overtaken by the Beijing Consensus.

Global inequality of incomes between individuals is increasingly driven by within-country inequality and decreasingly by between-country inequality.

International trade helped to lower the price of consumer and investment goods. But international trade also cost workers in uncompetitive industries their job. A combination of loss of international competitiveness and technological advances limit job opportunities in industrialised countries, especially hurting middle-income and lower middle-income groups in these countries. Once the downsides of globalisation and international trade became more visible, it resulted in a renewed call for protectionism but also for the need to address growing inequality within countries.

The composition of export products of emerging economies, in particular those of Southeast Asia and the Pacific region, changed rapidly from primary products, via labour-intensive manufactures, to high-tech exports, in tandem with gaining a niche in global value chains.

During the early 1960s, more favourable trade relations with developing countries were considered. UNCTAD offered the most appropriate forum for developing countries' trade and development interests. However, UNCTAD's achievements have been limited.

The history of international trade negotiations since WWII, demonstrates that industrialised countries have not been generous to developing countries. Trade relations are principally dictated by financial interests of the idustrialised world. It proved particularly difficult to create an international level playing field in agriculture and textiles, from which developing countries could have benefitted. Tariff escalation, the application of technical barriers, safeguards and anti-dumping measures further block developing countries' access to the markets of developed countries. In short, the world trade system still works against poor developing countries. It did not help that developing countries themselves applied protectionist policies against products from other developing countries.

Even when markets of industrialised countries were opened for exports from of developing countries, in various instances this did not result in their transformation from raw materials to manufactured goods exporting countries. Trade liberalisation alone may be a necessary condition for economic development of poor countries. However, opening a country to international trade should go together with the implementation of other fundamentals of economic growth, i.e., investment, macroeconomic stability, human resources development, and good governance.

East Asian countries that applied a combination of import-substitution and export promotion policies in a balanced and properly timed manner, achieved economic successes. For an aspiring poor developing country, the East Asian experience suggests that it would be wise to first invest in boosting the productivity of its agricultural sector and its manufacturing sector behind protective walls, before opening the country to the international market.

Freeing up labour migration from poor countries to industrialised countries would not only help improve migrants' incomes, but also their home countries' economic growth through remittances. However, contemporary political sentiments in industrialised countries suggest that promoting labour migration is not realistic.

Notes

1. Maddison, A. (1995) *Monitoring the World Economy 1820–1992*. Paris: OECD, 37.
2. The text on the Stolper-Samuelson Theorem is largely based upon *Protection and Real Wages: the Stolper-Samuelson Theorem*, by Rachel McCulloch. In Szenberg, M. (2005) *Samuelsonian Economics in the 21st Century*.
3. Frederic Benham (1900–1962) sketched a different picture. In 1961 he wrote in *Economic Aid to Underdeveloped Countries* (London: Oxford University Press): 'The belief that international trade consists mainly of the

exchange of manufactured goods from industrial countries against primary products from the underdeveloped countries is quite wrong. If we exclude the trade of the Communist countries (just over 10 percent of the total), more than half the remainder is trade among industrial countries themselves. Some 10 percent is trade among the underdeveloped countries themselves, and less than one-third is trade between them and industrial countries.' 43. On page 46 of the same publication Benham argued: 'All this suggests that the reasons for changes in the export proceeds of any particular commodity can be found only by studying the conditions affecting that particular commodity, and should not be attributed to general fluctuations in the economic activity of the industrial countries.'

4. This observation is confirmed by Paul Cashin and John McDermott: 'Although there is a downward trend in real commodity prices, this is of little policy relevance, because it is small compared with the variability of prices. In contrast, rapid, unexpected and often large movements in commodity prices are an important feature of their behavior. Such movements can have serious consequences for the terms of trade, real incomes, and fiscal positions of commodity-dependent countries, and have profound implications for the achievement of macroeconomic stabilization.' Source: Cashin, P., McDermott, J. The Long-run Behavior of Commodity Prices: Small Trends and Big Volatility. In *IMF Working Paper, Nr. 01/68* (2001).
5. Krugman, P., Venables, A. Globalization and the Inequality of Nations. In *The Quarterly Journal of Economics*, Vol. CX, Issue 4, November 1995, 857–880.
6. Bhagwati, J. (2004) *In Defense of Globalization*. Oxford: Oxford University Press.

   Wolf, M. (2004) *Why Globalization Works*. New Haven: Yale University Press.
7. Lin, J. (2012) *Demystifying the Chinese Economy*. Cambridge: Cambridge University Press, 4.
8. China is exporting products with a higher productivity than what would be expected of its level of per capita income, meaning that it produces and exports sophisticated goods which are typically associated with high-income countries.
9. In 1980, the US represented 22% of the world economy. To date this percentage is down to 15%. In 1980, all traditional industrial economies contributed 60% of the world's GDP. To date they contribute some 30%.
10. UNIDO's *Industrial Development Report 2018*.
11. Baldwin, R. (2016) *The Great Convergence; Information Technology and the New Globalization*. Cambridge: The Belknap Press, 14.
12. Ibid., 11.
13. Ibid., 249.

14. Thirlwall, A., Pacheco-López, P. (2017) *Economics of Development*. Tenth Edition. London: Palgrave Macmillan, 154.
15. '...for nearly a third of a century incomes of most Americans have been essentially stagnant.' Source: Stiglitz, J. (2017) *Globalization and its Discontents, Revisited*. London: Penguin Books, xiii.
16. *A Fair Globalization: Creating Opportunities for All*. Geneva: ILO 2004, 13.
17. *The Economist's* Survey on Globalisation (1 October 2016) noted that the US lost 6 million manufacturing jobs between 1999 and 2006. One-fifth of this drop was due to China's competition. However, the loss in manufacturing jobs in the US, due to technological advances, predates the rise of China as an exporter. Stiglitz, for example, mentions in *Globalization and its Discontents, Revisited*: 'The [American; PdH] steel mills today produce the same amount of steel that they ever have, but with one-sixth the labor force', xix.
18. *Economics of Development*, 499.
19. *The Growth Report*, 7.
20. Milanovic, B. (2016) *Global Inequality, a New Approach for the Age of Globalization*. Cambridge: The Belknap Press, 30.
21. Rodrik, D. (2011) *The Globalization Paradox*. New York: W.W. Norton, 52. On page 53, Rodrik adds that the resources used in international exchanges must be valued at their social opportunity costs rather than at their market price only. If economics were only about profit maximization, it would be just another name for business administration. However, economics is a social science, and society has other means of cost accounting besides market prices.
22. Ibid., 60.
23. Between 1929 and 1934, the volume of world trade declined by two-thirds between. By the way, contrary to conventional wisdom, tariffs constituted a significant barrier to international trade during the first wave of globalisation (1870–1914).
24. Dosman, E. (2008) *The Life and Times of Raúl Prebisch*, 1901–1986. Montreal: McGill-Queen's University Press, 380.
25. *The Globalization Paradox*, 72.
26. Michalopoulos, C. (2017) *Aid, Trade and Development; 50 Years of Globalization*. London: Palgrave Macmillan, 36.
27. I benefitted in describing Prebisch's role from Dosman's biography *The Life and Times of Raúl Prebisch*, 1901–1986.
28. The February 1962 issue of *Fortune* magazine described Prebisch as follows: '...doctrinaire...perhaps the most influential—but not necessarily the soundest—political economist in the hemisphere, with an engaging, vola-

tile personality and a mind as agile as it is capricious…one of those politically minded economists who tailor their economics to fit their objectives.'
29. *The Life and Times of Raúl Prebisch*, 396–397.
30. Ibid., 417.
31. Dosman noted that Prebisch had used the term NIEO for the first time in October 1963, so even before UNCTAD. It gained clarity and precision as he spread his gospel in every possible forum he was invited to; a gospel few wanted to hear, by the way.
32. *The Life and Times of Raúl Prebisch*, 434.
33. Ibid., 501.
34. Ibid., 501–502.
35. Michalopoulos presents a different picture: 'The GSP turned out to be less than it had been touted to be at its inception. It was important for some products, for some countries and for some of the time. …Because it was a voluntary scheme, it meant that developing country suppliers were less certain about market conditions than under contractual arrangements involving bound tariffs in GATT.' And on page 184 he adds: 'They [GSP preferences; PdH] typically exclude 'sensitive' products, which are often the very products of export interest to developing countries.' Source: *Aid, Trade and Development*, 39.
36. Perhaps this is giving UNCTAD too much credit. After all, IMF decisions are only made by the IMF Board. SDR is an international reserve asset created by the IMF in 1969 to supplement its member countries' official reserves. In practice, particularly developing counties make use of SDRs. They see them as a cheap line of credit.
37. Ibid., 47.
38. 'The collapse of the International Tin Agreement and the International Coffee Agreement in 1989 were due in large part to the setting of too high intervention prices and free riding. By 1996, the economic provisions in all major commodity agreements had either lapsed or failed and new market-based approaches to guard against price fluctuations started to be explored and used.' Source: *Aid, Trade and Development*, 48.
39. *Economics of Development*, 519.
40. With the exception of an agreement on higher minimum trading prices for agricultural grains and an international wheat agreement providing for 4.5 million tons of wheat available to the most deserving nations.
41. In the past there were five international commodity agreements for sugar, tin, rubber, cocoa, and coffee. All broke down in the course of time. Ironically, the only agreement that survived is the EU's Common Agricultural Policy, which is not particularly helpful to developing countries.
42. *Making Globalization Work*, 77.

43. 'I heard many stories from delegates [of developing countries at the WTO; PdH] to the effect that they had been pressured to sign the Marrakesh Agreements by the EU and the US or else—meaning lower bilateral aid levels; and that some had not even understood what they were signing.' Source: *Aid, Trade and Development*, 158.
44. Ibid., 38.
45. Ibid., 153.
46. Sachs, J., Warner, A. Economic Reform and the Process of Global Integration. *Brookings Papers on Economic Activity, 1* (1995). According to the authors, a country is closed if at least one of the following criteria applies: (i) an average tariff higher than 40%; (ii) non-tariff barriers covering more than 40% of imports; (iii) a socialist economic system; (iv) a state monopoly; or (v) a black market exchange rate premium in excess of 20%.
47. *The Globalization Paradox*, 167.
48. Wickstead, M. (2015) *Aid and Development*. Oxford: Oxford University Press, 168.
49. *The Great Convergence*, 99.
50. For example, they enjoy the freedom to undertake policies that limit access to their markets or provide support to domestic producers or exporters in ways which are not allowed to other members and they are provided with more time to meet their obligations or commitments under the WTO agreements. Michalopoulos rightly wonders why countries like Singapore and China, registered as developing countries by the WTO, would really need preferential treatment for their exports to penetrate developed country markets. Source: *Aid, Trade and Development*, 135.
51. Ibid., 137.
52. Collier, P. (2007) *The Bottom Billion*. Oxford: Oxford University Press, 183.
53. Ibid., 187.
54. *Aid, Trade and Development*, 227. On page 321 it is mentioned that trade powerhouses like Brazil, China, South Korea or Singapore are all considered 'developing countries' based on WTO's self-selection principle.
55. *The Globalization Paradox*, 154–155.
56. Stiglitz, J. (2002) *Globalization and its Discontent*. New York: W.W. Norton, 245.
57. Altenburg, T., Lütkenhorst, W. (2015) *Industrial Policy in Developing Countries, Failing Markets, Weak States*. Cheltenham: Edward Elgar, 102–103.
58. *Aid, Trade and Development*, 140.
59. Rodrik, D. (2011) *The Globalization Paradox; Democracy and the Future of the World Economy*. New York: W.W. Norton, 83.
60. Ibid., 200.
61. Ibid., 204–205.

62. 'The unfettered proliferation of regional and other PTAs [preferential trade agreements; PdH]—'termites' in the language of Bhagwati...ostensibly consistent with WTO provisions—is undermining the edifice of WTO rules based on the MFN principle, and thus weakening the second leg on which the WTO stands.' Source: *Aid, Trade and Development*, 297–298.
63. *Aid, Trade and Development*, 147. The recently re-negotiated NAFTA deal would increase American GDP by 0.35% and employment by 0.12%, according to the United States International Trade Commission.
64. I worked six years each in Bolivia and Zambia. Bolivia is a member of MERCOSUR, and of Comunidad Andina de Naciones (CAN), of which Colombia, Ecuador, Peru, and Venezuela also form part. Bolivia benefitted from CAN, in that it became a prominent soy bean exporter to other member countries, in particular to Colombia. Then, there was ATPDEA, the so-called war-against-drugs trade agreement between the US and Bolivia, in which, in exchange for the eradication of coca plants, Bolivia gained preferential access to the American market for textiles, leather, and timber. It should be noted that, in the past, Bolivia made much more money from the illegal coca production. Despite all these trade agreements, Bolivia is still a raw materials exporter: in 2017, fuels, ores, and gems together accounted for 71.3% of Bolivia's total export.

    Zambia is a member of COMESA, together with 18 other African countries. Zambia also belongs to the 14-member Southern African Development Community (SADC) which established a free-trade agreement in 2008. The establishment of a single market through the merged COMESA, the East African Community (EAC) and SADC was launched in 2015. Zambia has also duty-free and quota-free access to the EU market under the Everything but Arms (EBA) scheme. It is also eligible for American trade benefits under the Africa Growth and Opportunity Act (AGOA) which provides duty-free and quota-free access to the US market for most goods, including textile and apparel. Like Bolivia, Zambia has not been able to move its exports from raw materials to manufactured goods: in 2017, copper still accounted for 75.7% of Zambia's total export. This is what Thirlwall and Pacheco-López observe: 'The general experience of regional trade agreements in developing countries has been disappointing because they have been inward-looking and protectionist, with trade diversion exceeding trade creation.' Source: *Economics of Development*, 485.
65. Globalization, Growth and Poverty; Building an Inclusive World Economy. Washington: *World Bank Policy Research Report*, January 2002, 5.
66. Olson, M. Big Bills left on the Sidewalk: Why Some Nations are Rich, and Others Poor. In *The Journal of Economic Perspectives*, Vol. 10, No. 2 (Spring, 1996), 15.

67. *Global Economic Prospects and the Developing Countries.* Washington: The World Bank; 2002.
68. Rodrik, D. (1998) *The New Global Economy: Making Openness Work.* Policy Essay No. 24. Baltimore: Johns Hopkins University Press.
69. Stiglitz, J. (2006) *Making Globalization Work.* New York: W.W. Norton.
70. Greenaway, D., Morgan, W., Wright, P. (1998) Trade Reform, Adjustment and Growth: What Does the Evidence Tell Us? In *Economic Journal*, 108 (450): 1547–1561.

    Greenaway, D., Morgan, W., Wright, P. (2002) Trade Liberalisation and Growth in Developing Countries. In *Journal of Development Economics*, 67(1): 229–244.
71. *Economics of Development*, 498.
72. *Perspective on Global Development; Rethinking Development Strategies.* Paris: OECD, (2018), 1.
73. Ibid., 5–6.
74. Dollar, D., Kraay, A. (2002) Growth is Good for the Poor. In *Journal of Economic Growth*, 7 (3), 195–225.
75. The World Bank's *World Development Report 2000/2001* already reflected the Bank's stance of putting the reduction of poverty at the centre of its activities.
76. Milanovic, B. (2005) Can We Discern the effects of Globalization on Income Distribution? In *World Bank Economic Review*, 19(1): 21–44.
77. *Economics of Development*, 503.
78. Ravallion, M. (2006) Looking Beyond Averages in the Trade and Poverty Debate. In *World Development*, 34 (8): 1374–1392.
79. *The Great Convergence*, 105–108.
80. Milanovic, B. (2016) *Global Inequality; a New Approach for the Age of Globalization.* Cambridge: The Belknap Press, 11.
81. It is projected that the global middle class will grow in numbers from 1.8 billion in 2009 to around 3.2 billion in 2020.
82. *Global Inequality*, 20.
83. Ibid., 22.
84. *Global Inequality*, 20.
85. Lang, V.F., Mendes Tavares, M. (2018) The Distribution of Gains from Globalization. *IMF Working Paper*, WP/18/54.
86. Ibid., 27.
87. Ibid., 38. However, Lang and Mendes Tavares warn that the results of the regressions undertaken should be interpreted with caution; among others, because they are based on a dataset that had not been subjected to scholarly scrutiny.
88. *Globalization and its Discontents, Revisited*, 363.

89. It should be mentioned that the export interests of developing countries were also damaged by protectionism of other developing countries.
90. *Making Globalization Work*, 96.
91. *Economics of Development*, 518.
92. De Haan, P. (2006) *Development in Hindsight; The Economics of Common Sense*. Amsterdam: KIT Publishers, 51–52.
93. *The Distribution of Gains from Globalization.*
94. As for TPP, China is pushing the Regional Comprehensive Economic Partnership as an alternative to TPP.
95. *The Globalization Paradox*, 275.
96. 'Apple became emblematic, paying a tax in the United States that was far, far below the 35 percent of its income that is the official tax rate by taking advantage of loopholes in the United Sates tax code and routing of its profits through Irish subsidiaries.' Source: *Globalization and its Discontents, Revisited*, 362.
97. Luce, E. (2017) *The Retreat of Western Liberalism*. London: Little Brown, 83.
98. Special Report on Migration, *The Economist*, 16 November 2019, 3.
99. *The Globalization Paradox*, 268.

References

Altenburg, T., & Lütkenhorst, W. (2015). *Industrial Policy in Developing Countries, Failing Markets, Weak States*. Cheltenham: Edward Elgar.

Baldwin, R. (2016). *The Great Convergence; Information Technology and the New Globalization*. Cambridge: The Belknap Press.

Benham, F. (1961). *Economic Aid to Underdeveloped Countries*. London: Oxford University Press.

Bhagwati, J. (2004). *In Defense of Globalization*. Oxford: Oxford University Press.

Cashin, P., & McDermott, J. (2001). *The Long-Run Behavior of Commodity Prices: Small Trends and Big Volatility*. IMF Working Paper, Nr. 01/68.

Collier, P. (2007). *The Bottom Billion*. Oxford: Oxford University Press.

De Haan, P. (2006). *Development in Hindsight; The Economics of Common Sense*. Amsterdam: KIT Publishers.

Dollar, D., & Kraay, A. (2002). Growth Is Good for the Poor. *Journal of Economic Growth, 7*(3).

Dosman, E. (2008). *The Life and Times of Raúl Prebisch, 1901–1986*. Montreal: McGill-Queen's University Press.

Greenaway, D., Morgan, W., & Wright, P. (2002). Trade, Liberalisation and Growth in Developing Countries. *Journal of Development Economics, 67*(1).

ILO. (2004). *A Fair Globalization: Creating Opportunities for All*. Geneva: ILO.

Krugman, P., & Venables, A. (1995, November). Globalization and the Inequality of Nations. *The Quarterly Journal of Economics, CX*(4).
Lang, V., & Mendes Tavares, M. (2018). *The Distribution of Gains from Globalization.* IMF Working Paper 18/54.
Lin, J. (2012). *Demystifying the Chinese Economy.* Cambridge: Cambridge University Press.
Luce, E. (2017). *The Retreat of Western Liberalism.* London: Little Brown.
Maddison, A. (1995). *Monitoring the World Economy 1820–1992.* Paris: OECD.
McCulloch, R. (2005). Protection and Real Wages: The Stolper-Samuelson Theorem. In M. Szenberg (Ed.), *Samuelsonian Economics in the 21st Century.*
Michalopoulos, C. (2017). *Aid, Trade and Development; 50 Years of Globalization.* London: Palgrave Macmillan.
Milanovic, B. (2005). Can We Discern the Effects of Globalization on Income Distribution? *World Bank Economic Review, 19*(1).
Milanovic, B. (2016). *Global Inequality; A New Approach for the Age of Globalization.* Cambridge: The Belknap Press.
Olson, M. (1996, Spring). Big Bills Left on the Sidewalk: Why Some Nations Are Rich, and Others Poor. *The Journal of Economic Perspectives, 10*(2).
Ravallion, M. (2006). Looking Beyond Averages in the Trade and Poverty Debate. *World Development, 34*(8).
Rodrik, D. (1998). *The New Global Economy: Making Openness Work.* Policy Essay No. 24. Baltimore: Johns Hopkins University Press.
Rodrik, D. (2011). *The Globalization Paradox; Democracy and the Future of the World Economy.* New York: W.W. Norton.
Sachs, J., & Warner, A. (1995). Economic Reform and the Process of Global Integration. *Brookings Papers on Economic Activity, 1.*
Special Report on Migration. (2019). *The Economist*, November 16.
Stiglitz, J. (2002). *Globalization and Its Discontent.* New York: W.W. Norton.
Stiglitz, J. (2006). *Making Globalization Work.* New York: W.W. Norton.
Stiglitz, J. (2017). *Globalization and Its Discontents, Revisited.* London: Penguin Books.
Survey on Globalisation. (2016). *The Economist*, October 1.
The Growth Report; Strategies for Sustained Growth and Development. (2008). Washington: World Bank.
Thirlwall, A., & Pacheco-López, P. (2017). *Economics of Development* (10th ed.). London: Palgrave Macmillan.
UNIDO. (2018). *Industrial Development Report 2018.* Vienna: UNIDO.
Wickstead, M. (2015). *Aid and Development.* Oxford: Oxford University Press.
Wolf, M. (2004). *Why Globalization Works.* New Haven: Yale University Press.
World Bank. (2001). *World Development Report 2000/2001.* Washington: World Bank.
World Bank. (2002). *Globalization, Growth and Poverty; Building an Inclusive World Economy.* World Bank Policy Research Report. Washington: World Bank.

Epilogue

In 2011, Branko Milanovic argued: 'The key challenges of the twenty-first century may be summarized as follows: how to bring Africa up, how to peacefully bring China in, and how to wean Latin America off of its self-obsession and bring it into the real world. And doing all of this while maintaining peace and avoiding ideological crusades.'[1] Milanovic summarised very well how Third World countries had fared and what they should do to continue their upward development, uninterrupted by war and ideological clashes.

Yet, I believe more can be said about the dramatic changes since the term Third World was invented. Hans Rosling demonstrated—without many of us realising it—that the world is now a much better place than 70 years ago. There are now more high-income countries and fewer low-income countries. More people earn a higher income and enjoy a better life than ever before. The number of extremely poor people has fallen from 1.9 billion in 1990 to 836 million in 2015. More babies are vaccinated, more children—including girls—finish school. World fertility is falling, triggering a downward projection of the word population.

Emerging economies such as Brazil, Russia, India, China, and South Africa—the BRICS—are now influential economic and political actors on the world stage. Since 2008, the weight of developing and emerging economies in the global economy tipped over the 50% mark (expressed in PPP terms) for the first time. By 2010, developing countries accounted for around 42% of global merchandise trade. The projection is that around

P. de Haan, *Whatever Happened to the Third World?*,
https://doi.org/10.1007/978-3-030-39613-8

2050, three of the world's five largest economies will be in Asia: China, India, and Japan. America will obviously belong to the top five. But who will be number five—will it be Germany, Indonesia, Russia, or Brazil?

What will this development imply for the international geopolitical order? Due to the spectacular rise of Asia, global economic and political power is shifting from the West to the East; a development not without tensions and risks. The trade dispute between the US and China not just affected their economies, it also impinged upon international trade at large.

Globalisation, a long-time heralded phenomenon, no longer is. Globalisation's downsides, for example visible in industrialised countries' rust belts, are being exploited by politicians of the populist variety, whose political agenda includes anti-immigration and withdrawal from international free trade. In short, the spirit of multilateralism, established after the end of WWII, is making way for one of protectionism. Whether a new wave of protectionism will indeed ensue, we do not know, but it cannot be excluded.

Milanovic suggested that Latin America countries ought to get their act together and join the 'real world'. He clearly implied that the continent was stuck in the middle, as Latin American countries are typically associated with the middle-income trap. Surely, not all middle-income countries are trapped. Some are on the way to becoming high-income countries. But a large number of middle-income countries find it difficult to achieve a high-income status. These countries need to confront the challenges themselves as the bottlenecks to tackle are mainly—to put it in technical terms—endogenous.

Although the number of low-income countries is falling, they need help to overcome the traps as identified by Paul Collier. He also explained why they need help: it is not about justice, fairness, or resisting globalisation; no, it is about pulling the marginalised countries aboard, and to give the 'bottom billion' the opportunity to shed their poverty.

In a growing number of fragile states, the authority of the state is being eroded or, worse, has disappeared into thin air. Benefitting from the void, extremist groups or drug cartels establish strongholds in them. Citizens having lost their job as a result of the chaos, are looking for work elsewhere, joining the swelling numbers of economic migrants. Needless to say that it is in the international community's interest to help restore order in fragile and failed states.

Regarding the contributions of development economics, the first generation of development economists designed appealing 'grand theories' at first sight. However, they were naïve in assuming that fledgling Third World governments could lead the development process. Industrialisation—as strongly recommended by the first generation—was undertaken, but often in the wrong type of industries. Agricultural development was typically neglected, while this sector was to generate the funds to pay for a country's development. The first generation also felt that the market system in newly independent countries did not yet function properly; instead, development planning was to be applied to direct growth and development. With little success, as it turned out.

The second generation found its intellectual inspiration in the efficient allocative function of the market, small government, and other central notions of neoclassical economics. In this spirit, early Washington Consensus assistance programs were designed to help Latin American and African countries that had encountered serious financial problems. However, in the course of their implementation, the programs had to be adjusted to, at least, shield the poor from their negative effects. By and large, the assistance rendered helped debt-ridden developing countries to get back on their feet. However, the ensuing growth was rather modest. By contrast, an increasing number of rapidly growing Asian countries successfully applied useful elements of the first generation (industrialisation) and the second generation (benefiting from market forces).

It had dawned that purely economic analyses could not capture all the sources of economic growth. Other academic disciplines proposed that culture and institutions also played important parts, as well as political development and the historical trajectory of each individual country. If one can speak of a third generation, it is that scholars of different disciplines contributed to a broader understanding of economic growth and development.

Empirical cross-country studies appeared in large numbers, attempting to find out which factors would have contributed to economic growth in the countries concerned. However, these studies met with the ironical observation that empirical studies measure without theory.

Since Harrod-Domar, economic growth theories evolved, via Solow to new endogenous growth theories. Solow's growth model projected a converging process of incomes between poor and rich countries, while endogenous growth theories suggested that the gap could possibly widen between the two. It was Milanovic, who—on empirical grounds—tentatively concluded that, indeed a converging process is ongoing.

As mentioned, economics cannot fully explain growth. Economists apply economic phenomena, such as GDP, income per capita, income and wealth distribution, investment and saving rates, diminishing or increasing returns, taxes, market prices, what have you. All of them explain a lot about the dynamics of economic growth, but not everything. Is the time over for economists constructing grand designs? Was it therefore that the 2019 Economics Nobel Prize was awarded to three economists for their ground-breaking work on randomised control trials? Perhaps the 2019 Nobel laureates were awarded the prize because, as *The Economist* suggested, economists—despite their efforts—do not know how to transform poor countries into rich ones.[2]

Way back in 1979, John Hicks argued: 'The more characteristic economic problems are problems of change, or growth and retrogression, and of fluctuation. The extent to which these can be reduced into scientific terms is rather limited; for at every stage in an economic process new things are happening, things which have not happened before—at the most they are rather like what has happened before. We need a theory that will help us with these problems; but it is impossible to believe that it can ever be a complete theory.'[3]

One way or the other, insights of other sciences need to be incorporated into economics, to eventually arrive at growth models that more comprehensively explain what factors cause growth, and better predict its future trajectory. Whether this will be achieved, I do not know. In this realm, let me quote Douglass North. He once said—aware of the challenges involved—that the promise of a unified growth model is there, but we may never have definite answers to all our questions.

In conclusion, the past 70 years have demonstrated that a lot of good things have happened to the Third World. Word has it that historians are not good at predicting the future. Therefore, they do not like to make predictions; only the brave ones do. One of them is Deirdre McCloskey. She predicts that in 50 years—if things go as they have since 1800—the terribly poor will have become adequately nourished. Slaves and women will be largely free. The environment will be improving. And the ordinary person worldwide will have become bourgeois. Nowadays, although an age of widely circulating tales of impending catastrophe, there are many more reasons to be optimistic about our future. I agree.

Notes

1. Milanovic, B. (2011) *The Haves and Have-Nots; A Brief and Idiosyncratic History of Global Inequalit.* New York: Basic Books, 215.
2. Free Exchange. In: *The Economist*, 23 November 2019, 70.
3. Hick, J. *Causality in Economics.* Oxford: Blackwell, xii.

Index[1]

A
Abdul Lateef Jameel Poverty Action Lab, 194
Abramovitz, M., 187n19
Acemoglu, D., 197, 200–202, 207
Ackley, G., 154n19
Adelman, I., 115, 152n4
Afghanistan, 49, 74
Africa Growth and Opportunity Act (AGOA), 295n64
African, Caribbean, and Pacific (ACP) countries, 25, 26, 277
African Continental Free Trade Area agreement, 58
African Free Trade Area, 276
Africa's development, 201
  manufacturing in, 90n46
Aghion, P., 193, 240n2
Agreement on Agriculture, 269
Agreement on Safeguards, 271
Agricultural development, 15, 177
Agricultural exports, 12, 15, 25, 68, 262, 277, 286
Agricultural pricing policies, 163
Agricultural productivity, 3, 227, 228
Agricultural subsidies, 24, 29, 270, 274, 275, 286, 288
Albania, 43
Algeria, 60, 62, 91n51, 91n52
Allen, R., 245n53
Alliance for Progress, 4, 51, 117
Altenberg, T., 70
America, 9, 39, 102, 106, 130, 170, 202, 210, 264, 287, 297n96
  gap between Africa and, 9
  income distribution, 131, 283
  OPEC's price hike and economy of, 5
  rate of progress, 32n9
Amin, S., 151
Amsden, A., 184, 190n58
Angola, 54, 58

[1] Note: Page numbers followed by 'n' refer to notes.

P. de Haan, *Whatever Happened to the Third World?*,
https://doi.org/10.1007/978-3-030-39613-8

Antigua, 43
Apple, 297n96
Arab Human Development Report (AHDR), 61, 62, 91n53, 91n56
Arab League member-countries, 60
Arab population growth rates, 61
Arab Spring, 2011, 62
Argentina, 51–53, 276
Asia
 per-capita incomes, 10
 political and economic developments in, 45
Asian financial crisis, 1997, 184
Asian Infrastructure Investment Bank (AIIB), 47
Asian middle-income countries, 85, 86
Asian Tiger countries, 16, 163, 167
Assistance policy, 143
Association of Southeast Asian Nations (ASEAN), 276
Augmented Washington Consensus, 167
Australia, 74, 81, 100, 103, 202, 210, 269
Austria, 136

B

Bacon, F., 222, 225, 226
Balanced growth, 113, 118, 119, 123, 124, 152n1
 of underdeveloped countries, 113
Balance of payments, 5, 141, 142, 144, 147, 273, 282
Baldwin, R., 258, 272, 282
Banerjee, A., 194, 241n7
Bangladesh
 economy, 45, 48, 74
Bangladesh Rehabilitation Committee (BRAC), 242n7
Bank of Latin America (CAF), 53
Baran, P., 149, 151
Barbados, 43
Barbuda, 43
Bargaining problem, 204
Barro, R., 174, 206
Batista, F., 51
Bauer, P., 145, 156n51
Beef production, 270
Behavioural economics, 194, 241n6
Beijing Consensus, 46, 47, 289
Benedict, R., 103
Benham, F., 290n3, 291n3
Berendsen, B., 188n38
Berger, P., 181
Berlin Wall, fall of, 6, 258
Bernstein, H., 157n73
Bhagwati, J., 257, 291n6, 295n62
Bilateral and multilateral debt relief, 6
Biogeography, 107
Birth rate and birth control, 239
Bliss, C., 164
Bloomberg, 33n28
Boas, F., 103
Boeke, J. H., 101, 104, 105, 107, 108
 colonial economics, 101, 104
 economic and social needs, 104
Bolivia, 27, 50, 53, 88n19, 196, 197, 276, 295n64
Botswana, 189n55, 276
Bourgeoisie, 198, 208, 244n50
Braudel, F., 208
Brazil, 2–4, 11, 21, 39, 40, 45, 47, 50–54, 57, 258, 269, 270, 276, 283, 294n54
Brazilian Development Bank, 53
Bretton Woods system, 258, 260
Brexit, 7, 21, 27, 281
Bricker, D., 237, 238
BRICS countries, 11, 40
Bulgaria, 136
Burke, E., 242n11
Burkina Faso, 29, 72, 270, 286

C
California, 103
Canada, 5, 25, 74, 81, 269, 276, 285, 287
Capital-abundant economies, 241
Capital accumulation, 113, 115, 116, 121, 128–130, 148, 163, 171, 172, 176, 185, 205, 208, 212, 254
Capital export, 129
Capital growth, 69
Capital intensity, 109, 124
Capital-intensive goods, 255
Capital-intensive industries, 55, 68, 148
Capital investment, 114, 122–125, 163, 212
Capitalism, 21, 48, 99, 105, 106, 108, 109, 152, 205, 221, 225, 245n56
  role in economic growth, 99
Capitalist sector, 107, 128, 129
Capitalist surplus, 128, 129
Capital-surplus oil exporters, 87n3
Captain Swing riots of 1830–1832, 246n73
Cashin, P., 291n4
Castro, F., 51, 52
Catch-up growth, 9
Central African Republic, 72, 74, 93n89
Centrally planned economies, 42, 87n3, 117
Central Provident Fund (CPF), 83
Centre-periphery model, 151
Chad, 29, 74, 286
Chang, H-J., 64–67, 72, 92n64, 179
Chenery, H., 114, 140–145, 149
  assistance policy, 143
  development process, 140, 142, 144
  investment-limited growth, 141, 142
  investment-savings gap and foreign exchange gap models, 140
  trade-limited growth, 141, 142
Cherry production, 88n26
Chile, 51, 53, 71, 86, 88n26, 244n41
Chilean vineyards, 89n28
China
  agricultural growth, 49
  Beijing, 46, 90n40
  Belt and Road Initiative, 46–48, 87n11
  Deng Xiaoping reforms, 11, 40
  economy and economic growth, 7, 9, 11, 12, 21, 27, 29, 30, 40, 46–48, 115, 206, 235, 258, 273, 281, 284, 287–289
  foreign direct investment, 53, 273
  labour-intensive industries, 148
  Scientific Revolution in, 220, 221
Ching dynasty, 225
CIA Factbook, 244n36
Civil wars and its consequences, 13, 62, 73, 75
Clark, C., 155n41
Clemens, M., 36n60, 288
Climate Agreement, 104
Climate change
  impact on societies, 97
  influence on people's productivity, 98
  role in rise and fall of civilisation, 96
Climatic determinism, 103
Closed economy, 127, 141
Coase, Ronald, 195
Cohesion policy, 232
Collier, Sir P., 13, 72–75, 93n89, 93n90, 94n92, 94n94, 272
Colombia, 53, 295n64
Colonial economics, 101, 104

Colonies, 3, 14, 54, 100, 101, 113, 116, 152, 195, 201, 225, 253, 265
COMESA, 295n64
Commodity prices, 4, 7, 22, 32n15, 58, 115, 262, 263, 267, 268, 280, 291n4
Common Fund for Commodities (CFC), 23, 267
Comparative advantage, 20, 29, 55, 144, 148, 186n2, 254, 255, 257, 262, 270, 285, 286
Comunidad Andina de Naciones (CAN), 295n64
Conditional convergence, 174, 175
Confucius, 33n28
Constant or increasing returns phenomenon, 172
Contemporary development economics, 193
Corn Laws, in England, 34n39, 35n40, 243n23
Corporate governance, 167
Corruption, 1, 3, 11, 13, 41, 45, 59, 62, 71, 74, 78, 82, 88n27, 89n36, 90n40, 90n49, 184, 200, 204
Côte-d'Ivoire, 58
Countries classification, 1978–2018
  in percentages, 42
  thresholds and average GNI per capita, 43
  trends, 44–45
Country Policy and Institutional Assessment Index, 93n92
Creative entrepreneurs, 124
Cree communities, 110n14
Cross-country comparative studies, 177
Cuba, 51, 89n32
Cumulative causation hypothesis, 169
Cyclical instability, 32n12

D
Darwin, C., 214, 215
De Haan, P., 153n15, 240n1, 297n92
De Janvry, A., 194, 198
Death rate, 2, 240
Debt repayments, 6
Deglobalization, 287
Deindustrialisation, 32n7
Dell, M., 196, 197
Democratic politics, 12, 69, 275
Democratisation, 47, 207
Demographic dividend, 240
Demographic transition, 18, 181, 211–217, 227, 239
Deng Xiaoping, 11, 40, 234
Dependency, 51, 73, 115, 149, 150, 196
Developed countries
  income inequality, 133, 134, 284
  per capita income growth, 179
  tax regime in, 34n28
Developing countries
  development plan of, 116–118
  economic growth of, 4, 15, 27, 30, 31, 133, 135, 179, 288
  economic shock impact on, 6
  export-led growth, 115
  foreign aid, role in development, 67
  foreign direct investment, 56
  global economic prospects of, 27, 278
  globalisation, impact of, 20, 21, 26, 28, 30, 260, 284
  global merchandise trade, 7
  growth patterns of, 8
  growth policy for, 144
  IMF's Special Drawing Rights for, 23, 267
  impact of agricultural subsidies policies, 286
  lost decades of growth, 5
  marketing transactions, 70

oil imports, 55, 266
real per capita income, 4, 41
redistribution of income and wealth, 10
tax system, 34n28
WTO restrictions, 272
Development
heterogeneous stages of, 104
planning, 116–119, 145
sequence, elements of, 143
Development Decade, 4
Development economics
first generation view, 14–15
second generation view, 15–16
third generation view, 16–17
tropical-colonial conditions, 104
Development Round, 24, 274
Development, scholarly insights
Boeke, 101, 104, 105, 107, 108
Diamond, Jared, 107
Huntington, 84, 103
Krugman, Paul, 106, 108, 147, 180, 185, 189n49
Lal, Deepak, 109, 119, 146, 153n5, 173, 177
Lewis, Arthur, 108, 118, 127–130
Little, Ian, 117, 164
Myint, Hla, 108, 109, 119, 173, 177
Rodrik, Dani, 107, 161, 167, 189n54, 206
Sachs, Jeffrey, 107, 202, 203, 271
Subramaniam, Arvind, 107
Trebbi, Francesco, 107
Developmental state, 116
Developmentalist policies, 3
Diamond, Jared, 107, 227
Dietz, T., 188n38
Diminishing returns to capital, 169–171, 186n16
Dirigiste Dogma, 146–147
Disguised unemployment, 124, 127
Dissenters, 69–70, 145–149, 178–180
Djibouti, 87n11, 88n11, 91n51
Doha Development Agenda, 24, 270, 274
Doha Round, 24, 29, 274, 275, 288
Dollar, D., 10, 281
Domar, E., 120, 121
Domestic industrialisation, 151, 163, 254
Donor countries, 1, 5, 46, 56, 185
Dornbusch, R., 41
Dos Santos, T., 150, 151
Doshi, Rush, 88n13
Dosman, E., 262, 264, 266, 267, 292n27, 293n31
Dowden, R., 59
Drive to maturity, 139
Drug- and human trafficking, 76
Dualism, 101, 104–109
Dualistic economies, 105, 108, 109
Duflo, E., 194
Dumping duties, 29, 286
Durlauf, P., 240n2, 241n5, 245n57

E

East Asian countries, 2, 24, 180, 272, 273, 290
East Asian Miracle, 180–185
East Asian model, 181, 184
East Timor, 49
Easterly, W., 9, 56, 146, 148, 153n19, 170, 179, 187n22, 241n7
Eastern economy, 105
Economic backwardness, 136, 137
Economic convergence, 20, 175
Economic geography
increasing returns and, 19, 228–231
Krugman's insights, 106, 228
per capita income and, 218
policy issues, 233
reshaping, 231–235
3-D's, 232
World Bank report, 231

Economic growth
contribution of globalisation, 21, 254, 259
culture, role in, 18, 208
Darwinian perspective, 18, 209
decisive force of geography in, 19
endogenous and exogenous factors, 210
Harrod-Domar model, 117, 120–121, 141, 168, 170
historical approach to understanding, 18, 208
history of, 18, 208, 209, 217, 227, 236
measurement of inequality, 10
migration of labour and, 127
political, institutional, and geographical factors, 236
relationship between democracy and, 206
relationship between income distribution and, 10
relationship between income inequality and, 130
Rostow's stages of, 137, 155n37
rules of good behavior for promotion of, 166
Solow's model, 169, 170
successive stages of, 135, 226
unlimited supplies of labour, role of, 127
Economic history
demographic transitions, 212–213
endogenous growth theory, 171–175, 179, 210
stages of growth, 135
unified growth theory, 213–214
Economic modernisation processes, 136
Economic policy approaches, Asian developmental model, 49
Economic shocks, 6
Ecuador, 53, 295n64
Education, 10, 15, 34n28, 45, 49, 50, 58, 60, 67, 68, 72, 75, 78, 80–81, 83, 86, 100, 134, 138, 163, 168, 170–172, 174, 182, 184, 195, 197, 198, 211, 215, 223, 238, 239, 246n60, 248n90, 285
Egypt, 11, 40, 91n51, 91n55, 189n55
Eichengreen, B., 93n74
Emerging economies, 7, 9, 21, 26, 27, 30, 40, 49, 258, 278, 280, 283, 289
Endogenous growth theory, 78, 171–175, 179, 210
Endogenous shocks, 6
Engerman, S., 242n17
England, 34n39, 130, 136, 137, 198, 208, 211, 218, 219, 243n23, 246n60, 254, 255
Enos, J., 149, 152n2, 157n67, 185
Equatorial Guinea, 44
Ethical policy, 100
Ethiopia, 58, 59, 239
Urban Productive Safety Net Project, 59
Eurasia, 107, 227
Europe
industrialisation, impact of, 3
OPEC's price hike and economy of, 5
European Development Fund (EDF), 26, 277
European Enlightenment, 226, 246–247n74
European Union (EU), 25–27, 29, 35n40, 62, 232, 270, 273, 276, 277, 285–287, 293n41, 294n43, 295n64
agricultural subsidies policies of, 286
Everything but Arms (EBA) initiative, 277, 295n64

Exploitative global capitalism, 152
Export-led economy, 7, 280
Export-led growth countries, 115
Export-led growth policies, 163
Export subsidies, 269, 270, 273, 274
Extractive economic institutions, 200

F

Failed Sates Index, 91n62
Failed states, 2, 11, 13, 40, 41, 59, 63, 72–77, 85
Failing states, 53, 73, 74, 91n62, 94n92
Fanton, N., 87n4
Fertility rate, 238–240
Fiji, 43
Financial globalisation, 22, 260
Financing gap dogma, 148
First generation development models
  aggregate savings, 118
  balanced and unbalanced growth, 14, 113, 118, 119, 123, 124, 138, 152n1
  Chenery, Hollis, 114, 140–145
  development planning, 116–119, 145
  dissenters, 145–149
  effective use of foreign aid, 140
  foreign aid, 113, 114, 119, 123, 125, 140, 145, 149
  Harrod-Domar model, 117, 120–121, 141
  industrial development, 122, 124, 125, 129, 136, 137, 152
  Kuznets, Simon, 114, 130–132
  Lal, Deepak, 119, 146, 147, 153n5
  Lewis, William Arthur, 108, 113, 117, 118, 127–130
  Ragnar Nurkse, 113, 118, 123–127, 152n1, 154n24
  Rodan, Paul Rosenstein, 113, 119, 121–124
  Rostow, Walt Whitman, 113, 119, 135–140, 155n37, 155n40, 155n41
  role of government, 116
Fiscal expansion, 6
Fishlow, A., 155n43
Food productivity, 129
Forced labour, 128, 196, 197
Foreign aid
  aid objectives, 138
  bilateral aid, 5, 75, 76, 280n43
Foreign capital, 6, 49, 126, 129, 150
Foreign direct investment, in developing countries, 6, 53, 56, 125
Fragile States Index, 34n34, 74, 75
Fragile state, 12–13, 60, 74–76
France, 57, 81, 89n36, 100, 136, 195, 223, 246n60, 266
Frank, A. G., 149, 151, 152
Free trade agreements, 25, 88n26, 276, 295n64
Free-trade zones, 25, 276
Frey, B., 241n6
Friedman, T., 244n40
Fukuyama, F., 239
Fund for Peace, 74

G

G-77 countries, 266, 269
G-77 nonalignment movement, 4
Gabon, 189n55
Gabriel, F., 69
Gallman, R., 242n17
Gallup, J., 228
Galor, O., 18, 209–211, 213–217, 223, 226, 227
Gandhi, I., 266

Garrett, G., 12, 68, 86
General Agreement on Tariffs and Trade (GATT), 22–24, 254, 261–266, 268–271, 293n35
Generalised System of Preferences (GSP), 23, 266, 267, 293n35
George, L., 139
Germany, 4, 68, 81, 130, 136, 156n45, 246n60, 247n82
Gerschenkron, A., 136, 137, 155n37
Ghana, 3, 43, 54, 58, 92n65
Ghani, A., 13, 76
Gini ratio, 10
Glaeser, E., 205, 207
Global compact, 266
Global economic development, 4–30
Global economy, 7, 27, 40, 258, 260, 280, 287
Global income inequality, 9
Globalisation
  benefits, 20, 260, 279
  destabilising consequences of financial, 260
  financial, 22, 260
  first wave (1870–1914), 3, 292n23
  flow of ideas and knowledge, 21, 254, 257
  international trade and, 19, 20, 253, 254, 271, 289, 292n23
  negative aspects of, 284, 288
Global manufacturing value added (MVA), 40
Global production networks and value chains, 71
Global recession, 7, 288
Goh Chok Tong, 84
Gold, D., 89n37
Government, role in development, 116, 119, 146, 182
Grand Bargain, 270
Great Britain, 103
Great Divergence, 18, 210, 213, 215–217, 221, 225, 227
Great Moderation, The, 5
Great Moderation, The, 7
Great Recession, 2008, 7, 27, 56, 288
Greece, 140, 144
Greenaway, D., 280
Green Revolution, 49, 55
Griffin, K., 149, 152n2, 157n67, 185
Gross National Income (GNI) per capita, 41, 43, 44, 87n3, 87n4
Growth Report, 67, 72, 86, 240, 260
Growth slowdown episode, 93n74

H
Hamilton, A., 64
Harberger, A., 117, 170
Harrod, R., 120
Harrod-Domar economic growth model
  in context of developing country, 121
  growth rate of income, 120
  performance of poor countries, 121
Hausmann, R., 8, 161, 207
Hayek, F., 119
Heavily Indebted Poor Country (HIPC) Initiative, 6, 7
Hekscher, E., 255
Hekscher-Ohlin Theorem, 20, 26, 255, 256, 282
Hewitt, P., 240n2
Hicks, J., 236, 237
High alert states, 74
High development theory, 108, 146, 180, 189n49
High-income countries (HIC), 9, 11, 12, 41, 42, 44, 53, 57, 63, 68, 69, 85, 86, 87n3, 238, 287

High-income status, 43, 44, 51, 63, 67, 69, 71
High mass-consumption, 136, 139
High-Performing Asian Economies (HPAEs)
institutions, role of, 183
macroeconomic management, 182
role of government, 182
savings levels and investment levels, 182
Hirschman, A., 118, 152n1
HIV/AIDS epidemic, 8
Hofman, A., 88n25
Hong Kong, 3, 40, 50, 88n18, 181, 183, 202, 228
Howitt, P., 193
Hoyng, A., 155n41
Human capital
accumulation, 205, 212
investments, 163, 212
Human Development Index (HDI), 60, 91n52
Humphrey, William Jackson, 103
Hungary, 43
Huntington, E., 101–103, 110n10, 227
role of climate in civilization development, 102–104
Huntington, S., 84
Hussain, A., 90n47
Hyde, Mr., 264

I

Ibbitson, J., 237, 238
Imperialism, 151
Import substitution, 3, 12, 20, 51, 60, 68, 116, 144, 162, 163, 254, 259, 264, 279, 290
Import-substituting industrialisation (ISI), 51
Incentives, 15–17, 19, 73, 80, 106, 107, 118, 125, 145, 146, 162, 163, 165, 167, 170, 171, 179, 193, 196, 199, 224, 226, 231–233, 240, 273, 284
Inclusive economic institutions, 200, 201
Income distribution, 10, 28, 61, 131, 132, 147, 178, 181, 182, 280, 282–285
Income inequality
capitalist sector and, 128
global, 9
within countries, 10, 30, 284, 289
India
economic growth, 9, 11, 30, 40, 48, 284, 288
income distribution, 131
panchayat legislation, 105
principal export, 48
social policies, 48
Indonesia, 4, 11, 40, 48, 57, 78, 81, 100, 105, 181–184, 269, 276
agricultural life in, 105
Industrial Enlightenment, 222, 224–226
Industrialisation
based on international investment, 122
correlation with agriculture sector, 125, 179
failed, 147–148
models, 122
planned large-scale, 123
Industrialised countries, 22, 25, 28, 30, 31, 87n3, 116, 215, 258–265, 269, 270, 274–276, 288–290
Industrial progress, conditions for, 154n24

Industrial Revolution, 3, 18, 65, 99, 100, 103, 125, 128, 151, 168, 178, 198, 210, 211, 214, 215, 217–223, 225–227, 236, 240
Infant industry policy, 65, 285
Inflation, 5, 6, 44, 52, 53, 58, 60, 86, 87n4, 119, 125, 126, 161, 182
Innovation, 70, 72, 103, 137, 148, 156n45, 174, 193, 194, 198, 201, 208, 218–221, 236
Integrated Programme for Commodities, 267
Interbellum (1918–1939), 115
Interest rates, 5, 6, 32n15, 55, 86, 148, 149, 161, 184
Intermediate inputs, 71
International Coffee Agreement, 293n38
International Development Policy Establishment (IDPE), 64, 92n64
International Monetary Fund (IMF), 5, 6, 16, 32n14, 46, 48, 52, 53, 57, 58, 65, 86, 93n74, 167, 168, 261, 266, 280, 285, 293n36
International Society for New Institutional Economics, 195
International Tin Agreement, 293n38
International trade
  emerging economies, role in, 26
  Hekscher-Ohlin theorem, 255, 256
  of industrialised and developing countries, 26
  institutions, 22–25
  law of comparative advantage, 255
  regional and international factor mobility, 106
  Ricardo's static comparative advantage theorem, 21, 257
  rounds, 24
  Stolper-Samuelson Theorem, 20, 22, 256
  as a zero-sum game, 20, 254
Investment capital, 17
Investment-limited growth, 141, 142
Iran, 11, 40, 62, 244n41
Israel, 60, 140, 144
Israel-Palestine conflict, 62
Italy, 81, 89n36, 136, 238
Ivory Coast, 270

J

Japan
  economy, 4, 45
  funding role, 189n54
  industrialisation in, 3, 262
  post-Meji Restoration, 45
  total factor productivity performance, 45
Johnson, S., 197
Jones, C., 204, 207, 244n50
Jubilee 2000, 6

K

Kahneman, D., 194, 241n6
Kaldor, Sir N., 114, 115
  growth laws, 114, 115
Keefer, P., 204, 243n33, 243n34
Kennedy, J. F., 4, 51, 117, 264
Kennedy Round (1964–1967), 4, 24, 264, 268–270
Kenya, 54, 89n30, 90n40, 267
Kenya cotton farming and textile production, 259
Kenyatta, U., 90n40
Keynes, J. M., 120, 242n9
Kim, J. Y., 281
Knack, S., 204, 243n34
Knowledge-based economy, 70, 171
Kraay, A., 10, 281
Kremer, M., 195
Krueger, A., 163, 165

Krugman, P., 19, 21, 106, 108, 146, 147, 156n56, 180, 185, 189n49, 189n50, 227–231, 234, 235, 247n85, 248n86, 248n85, 257
high development theory, 108, 146, 180, 189n49
Kuznets, Simon, 114, 130–132, 218, 223
comparison of developed and underdeveloped countries, 131–134
income inequalities in underdeveloped countries, 132, 134
relationship between income inequality and economic growth, 130, 132
study of income distribution, 131, 132
trends for developed countries, 134

L

Labour force, 2, 20, 36n60, 59, 61, 115, 120–122, 124, 134, 169–171, 173, 182, 212, 223, 255, 288
skilled and unskilled, 36n60, 282, 288
Labour-intensive export industries, 119
Labour-intensive goods, 20, 255
Labour-intensive manufacturing, 3, 30, 74, 228, 286, 289
Labour migration, 31, 254, 287, 290
Labour productivity, 57, 60, 121, 169, 170
Lal, D., 32n12, 109, 119, 146, 147, 153n5, 172, 173, 177
Landes, D., 209, 215, 245n55, 245n56
Landlocked countries, 73, 228, 233
Lang, V. F., 28, 284, 296n85, 296n87
La Porta, R., 244n35
Latin America
expansionary policies, 52
IMF's 2019 growth projections, 53
middle-income trap, 12, 53, 69, 84
per capita income, 1950, 86
peripheral, 20, 256
political and economic developments in, 45
ports of, 89n27
problem of dualism in, 109
secondary import substitution strategy, 12, 68
Latin American middle-income trap, 12, 69, 85
Latvia, 43
Law of comparative advantage, 20, 254, 255
Lee Kuan Yew, 77–84, 94n104
Less developed countries, 133, 172, 210, 212–213, 245n58
demographic transition in, 212–213
Lewis, W. A., 107, 108, 113, 117, 118, 127–130, 154n26
Libya, 60, 91n51, 91n52
Limited access order societies (LAOS), 17, 109, 199, 200
Lin, J., 12, 68, 87n7, 148, 156n63, 185, 186n2, 219–221, 246n68, 291n7
Lincoln, A., 246n72
Literacy rates, 1, 214, 246n60
adults, 60
Little, I., 9, 33n21, 108, 117, 153n7, 164, 186n9
Livingstone, 102, 110n5
Lockhart, C., 13, 76, 94n103
Lomé Convention, 1975, 277
Lopez-de-Salinas, F., 244n35
Lower middle-income countries, 13, 35n40, 40, 41, 44, 48, 75, 94n98

Low-income countries (LIC), 5, 11–13, 24, 39–41, 44, 45, 49, 59, 63, 72–77, 87n3, 91n62, 94n98, 238, 272, 275, 285
trade restrictions and, 275
Lucas, R., 171, 187n24
Luce, E., 7, 9, 33n16, 288, 297n97
Lütkenhorst, W., 70, 90n45, 93n83, 274, 294n57

M

Maçães, B., 4, 32n8, 87n9
Maddison, A, 8, 32n5, 49, 84, 86, 88n17, 89n32, 92n69, 100, 175, 195, 236, 242n10, 253
Malawi, 2, 89n30
Malaysia, 45, 46, 48, 50, 78, 81, 94n105, 181–184, 188n39, 276
Malaysian investment fund, 45
Mali, 29, 131, 202, 270, 286
Malta, 43, 244n41
Malthus, T., 99, 105
Malthusian Epoch technological progress, 211
Malthusian trap, 210
Mandel, E., 149, 157n69
Manufacturing sector, 19, 32n7, 138, 175, 231, 248n87, 290
Manufacturing value added (MVA), 40
Market-based price mechanism, 119
Marrakesh Agreement, 270, 294n43
Marshall Plan, 4, 116, 117
Martin, Geoffrey, 103, 110n7
Marx, Karl, 99, 208
Massachusetts Institute of Technology (MIT), 41, 194
Mauretania, 43, 91n51
McCloskey, D., 39, 151, 198, 208, 226, 227, 244n49, 244n50
McDermott, J., 291n4
Mead, M., 103
Meier, G., 153n6, 157n68, 163, 186n3
Mellinger, A., 247n77
Mendes Tavares, M., 28, 284, 296n87
Mercantilism, 224
MERCOSUR, 276, 277, 295n64
Meredith, M., 89n36
Metainstitutions, 206
Mexico, 11, 16, 25, 40, 50–52, 54, 68, 86, 131, 165, 255, 256, 276, 287
labour-intensive industries, 256
Michalopoulos, C., 24, 35n42, 270, 272, 275, 293n35, 294n50
Middle East and North Africa (MENA), 9, 45, 60–63, 179
adult literacy, 60
armed conflicts and violence crisis, 60, 62
economic trends, 1975–1998, 60
education and health, 60
employment rate, 61, 62
female labour force participation, 61
general characteristics of, 60
HDI scores, 60
inequality in, 61
labour productivity, 60
manufacturing exports, 61
oil export, 61
population growth, 61
poverty level, 61
status of women, 61–62
Middle-income countries (MIC), 11–13, 39, 40, 42–44, 46, 51, 53, 68–71, 73, 85, 86, 87n3, 282
Middle-income trap
dissenters, 69–70
slowdowns, 70, 92n74
Migration, 10, 59, 61, 127, 169, 202, 240, 254, 290
Milanovic, B., 2, 9, 10, 27–29, 31n3, 39, 88n20, 175, 281–283

Military expenditures, 6, 62
Millennium Development Goals (MDGs), 1, 7
Mineral exports, 115, 254
Mission civilisatric, 100
Mita system, 196, 197
Mobutu, 56, 89n36
Modernisation, 45, 50, 52, 58, 60, 136–139
Mokyr, J., 18, 209, 210, 217, 218, 222, 223, 225–227
Morales, E., 50
Morgan, W., 296n70
Most-favoured nation (MFN) principles, 262, 295n62
Most Seriously Affected (MSA) Countries, 2
Mozambique, 54
Multi-Fiber Arrangement, 269
Multilateral Debt Relief Initiative (MDRI) programs, 6, 7
Multilateralism, 20, 22, 261–277, 289
Multinational corporations, 95n111, 151, 287
Murgai, R., 194, 198, 241n4
Myint, H., 32n12, 108, 109, 111n21, 119, 146, 154n25, 172, 173
Myrdal, G., 152n1, 169, 247n83

N

Naidu, S., 207, 244n44
Naqvi, Syed, 165, 186n11
Nationalism, 120, 287
Needham, Joseph, 218, 219
Needham Puzzle, 219
Nelson, R., 209, 245n52
Neoclassical economics, 46, 146, 149, 161, 162, 179
Neoliberalism, 179
Neo-Marxist development theories, 4, 152
Nepal, 46, 49
Netherlands, 5, 13, 17, 27, 47, 50, 100, 101, 104, 109n3, 222, 228, 255, 286
New Deal America, 116
New Development Bank, 47
New endogenous growth theory, 78, 171–175, 179
New growth theory, 15, 174, 175, 180, 189n49
New institutional economics
  functioning of market, 193–194
  geography's influence, 192–193
  mapping of institutional development, 192–193
  measuring of institutions, 186
  path dependency, 196–197
  property rights, 17
  relationship between democracy and economic growth, 206
  relevance of institutions, 196
  transaction costs, 183
  types of societies, 189–190
New International Economic Order (NIEO), 230, 266, 293n31
New Kaldor Facts, 243n32
Newly independent countries, 14, 15, 39, 55, 81, 113, 114, 202
New world order, 4, 47
New Zealand, 81, 100, 103, 202, 210
Next-11 countries, 11, 40
Nicaragua, 53
Niche markets, 71
Nigeria, 11, 40, 54, 58, 90n39, 90n46, 188n39, 276
Non-Aligned Movement (NAM), 22, 263
North America, *see* America
North American Free Trade Area (NAFTA), 25, 260, 276, 295n63
North Korea, 49, 92n65, 205

North, Douglass, 16, 17, 109, 175, 195–200, 203, 208
North-East coast of the United States, 102
North-South issues, 140
Norway, 74, 94n94
NOVIB, 242n7
Now Developed Countries (NDC), 65
Nurkse, R., 108, 113, 118, 123–127, 152n1, 154n24

O

Official Development Assistance (ODA), 6, 56
Ohlin, B., 255
Oil price changes, 2, 5, 62, 63
Oil shocks of 1970s, 55
Olson, M., 26, 278
OPEC, 4, 5, 161, 266
Open access societies (OAS), 17, 109, 199, 200
Optimistic growth theory, 99
Organisation for Economic Cooperation and Development (OECD), 49, 190n56, 283

P

Pacheco-López, P., 2, 10, 75, 109, 121, 150, 164, 174, 175, 188n40, 259, 268, 279, 295n64
Pakistan, 11, 40, 146, 156n49
Panama, 51, 53
Paris Club, 52
Park, D., 93n74
Peace Corps, 5
Peripheral countries, role in economic development, 152
Peron, J., 52, 53
Peru, 54, 109, 131, 196, 197, 202, 295n64
  mita effects, 196, 197
Petro-dollars, 5, 52, 161
Philippines, the, 11, 40, 48, 140, 144, 249n105, 276
Pleskovic, B., 247n77
Point Four Program, 135
Polanyi, K., 240n1
Poor countries, 3, 8, 15, 20, 24, 26, 31n3, 36–37, 45, 56, 63, 65, 70, 72, 73, 93n89, 99, 101, 113, 116, 120, 121, 123, 131, 145, 149, 152, 169, 170, 174, 179, 184, 202, 203, 205–207, 213, 216, 225, 238, 255, 256, 270, 272, 274, 278, 281, 285, 290
Population growth
  baby boom, 238
  birth rate and birth control, 135, 238–240, 249n99
  demographic dividend, 240
  demographic transition, 181, 211–214, 216, 239
  falling fertility rate, 239–240
  fertility's replacement rate, 238
  rate of increase, 238
  UN estimate, 237
Portugal, 51, 89n36, 195, 254, 255
Post-Malthusian Regime, 210, 212, 214
Poverty, 1, 6–8, 11, 13, 14, 16, 21, 27, 28, 30, 40, 44, 49, 50, 55, 58, 61–63, 67, 70, 73, 75, 77, 87n6, 93n90, 101, 114, 115, 118, 145, 147, 162, 166, 168, 177, 182, 194, 203, 205, 228, 234, 238, 254, 265, 281, 282, 284, 285, 287, 289
Poverty Reduction and Growth Facility (PRGF), 32n14
Poverty Reduction Strategy Paper (PRSP), 6
Prague Spring, 266
Prebisch, R., 20, 21, 51, 151, 256, 257, 263–267, 292n28, 293n31

Preferential trade agreements (PTA), 274, 295n62
Premature deindustrialisation, 32n7
Prescriptive knowledge, 218, 223
Primitive order society (POS), 199
Pritchett, L., 8, 161
Private entrepreneurship, 14
Production (or output)
growth, 32n5
Productivity, 2, 3, 9, 14, 15, 20, 49, 52, 55, 57, 59–61, 64, 67, 70–72, 103, 104, 114, 118, 120, 124–130, 133, 136, 138–141, 143, 168–170, 173, 182, 186n16, 211, 240, 241n3, 256, 257, 272, 278, 280, 284, 290, 291n8
Programme for International Student Assessment (PISA), 49
Property rights, 3, 17, 59, 68, 71, 86, 167, 173, 183, 197–206, 217, 218, 224, 244n34, 269, 270, 274
Propositional knowledge, 217, 218, 222–224
Protectionism, 20, 28–30, 178, 260, 261, 287–289, 297n89
Puerto Rico, 51
Putin, Vladimir, 57

Q

Qatar, 60, 91n51, 91n52

R

Randomised Control Trials (RCTs), 194, 195, 241n7, 242n8
Ravallion, M., 28, 282
Raworth, K., 110n14
Razak, N., 45
Rebelo, S., 171
Refugees, 11, 13, 41, 74, 76
Regional Comprehensive Economic Partnership, 36n56, 297n94
Regional trade agreements, 25–27, 276–277, 295n64
Restrepo, P., 207
Ricardo, D., 20, 21, 34n39, 93, 233n23, 240, 243
Rich and poor countries, gap between
income inequality, 9
supply of goods, 20, 255
Robinson, J., 197, 200–202, 207
Rodan, P. R., 113, 119, 121–124, 189n50
Rodney, W., 149
Rodrik, D., 8, 27, 29, 31n3, 32n7, 36n60, 51, 57, 107, 161, 167, 175, 189n54, 202, 203, 206, 244n41, 260, 262, 271, 273, 275, 279, 280, 287, 288, 292n21
Romer, P., 171, 172, 204, 207, 244n50
Rosenblatt, D., 69
Rosenstein-Rodan, P., 113, 119, 121–124, 189n50
Rosling, H., 1, 238
Rosling-Rönnlund, A., 31n1
Rostow, W. W., 113, 119, 135–140, 155n37, 155n40, 155n41, 264
Rousseff, D., 45
Russia, 4, 11, 40, 47, 57, 62, 136, 137, 283
Russian model of industrialisation, 122
Rwanda, 76, 90n48, 206, 228

S

Sachs, J., 107, 202, 203, 271
Sadoulet, E., 194, 198
Sala-i-Martin, X., 174
Santos, T. dos, 150, 151
Saudi Arabia, 60, 62, 91n51, 91n52
Sauvy, A., 2

Saving rates, 114, 117, 118, 121, 141, 142, 144, 164, 236
Say's law, 124
Schleifer, A., 244n35
Schumpeterian growth paradigm, 241n3
Scientific Revolution, 220, 221
Scott, M. F., 172, 173
Second generation development models
  convergence of per capita incomes, 169, 171, 174
  dissenters, 178–180
  Gerald Meier, 163, 165
  microeconomic assumptions, 164
  new endogenous growth theory, 171–175, 179
  philosophy, 16, 162–165
  Robert Solow model, 168
  saving and investment to GDP ratio, 171
  Scott model, 172
  Washington Consensus, 16, 162, 165–167, 176
Secondary import substitution strategy, 68
Secondi, G., 243n31, 244n43
Sen, A., 8, 145
Senegal, 58
Senhadji, A., 176
Serajuddin, U., 87n4
Sheridan, 185
Shin, K., 93n74
Singapore
  annual per capita income, 78
  annual rate of capital accumulation, 185
  anticorruption law, 82
  democracy and development, 83, 84
  economic development of, 67, 78
  employment and education, 81
  factories, 80
  health insurance schemes, 78
  home-ownership scheme, 83
  industrialisation in, 79
  Lee Administration, 84
  liberty of individuals, 84
  Medisave and Medishield, 83
  National University campus, 81
  service industries, 80
  success factors of, 78
  voting in, 82
  welfare system, 82
Singapore Action Party (PAP), 83, 84
Singapore Bus Service, 83
Singapore Telecom, 80, 83
Singer, H., 126
Slavery, 201
Slums, 12, 68, 88n15, 233
Smith, A., 19, 20, 64, 92n67, 99, 136, 195, 222, 242n12, 253
Social mobility, 105, 119, 183
Solomon Islands, 43
Somalia, 74, 91n58
South Korea
  growth rate, 67
  land reform process, 67
  per capita income, 64, 92n65
Southeast Asian countries, economic growth of, 177
Southern African Customs Union (SACU), 276
Southern African Development Community (SADC), 295n64
South Sudan, 43, 74
Sovereignty gap, 13, 76
Sovereign-wealth funds, 90n48
Soviet Union, collapse of, 135
Spain, 51, 89n36, 195, 238
Spatial imbalances, 118
Specialisation, 215, 228, 255
Spengler, J., 154n24
Sri Lanka, 13, 48

Stagflation, 5, 161
Stagnation/slowdowns, 8, 13, 17–19, 68–70, 93n74, 137, 176, 178, 195, 196, 199, 201, 207, 210–214, 216, 235
State-led development, 3, 60, 179, 181
State-led industrialisation, 71, 92n66
Static comparative advantage theorem, 21, 257
Stehr, Nico, 103
Steinberg, D., 67, 92n72
Stiglitz, J., 29, 166, 178, 270, 274, 279, 280, 285–287, 292n17
Stolper-Samuelson Theorem, 20, 22, 256, 260, 290n2
Storch, H. von, 103
Strout, A., 140
Structural Adjustment Programmes (SAPs), 55, 66
Subramaniam, A., 107, 203
Sub-Saharan Africa (SSA)
  biggest trade partners of, 57
  ease of doing business in, 59
  economic growth and development, 54
  export trade, 258
  food production, 58
  impact of colonisation, 54
  manufacturing sector, 57
  overall economic performance, 58
  poverty rate, 40, 55, 167
  total factor productivity, 59
  trade with Turkey and Indonesia, 57
Subsistence economy, 108, 128
Sudan, 44, 60, 62, 74, 91n51, 91n52, 91n58
Sufficiency principle, 104n14
Sustainable Development Goals (SDGs), 8, 63, 104
Sustained economic growth per capita, 100
Sustained Growth Regime, 210
Sustained productivity growth, 9
Sustained world economic growth, 44
Sweden, 5
Switzerland, 33n28, 74, 89n36, 261, 286
Syria, 40, 62, 74, 91n51, 91n55, 91n58, 244n41
Szenberg, M., 290n2

T
Tahler, Richard, 194, 241n6
Taiwan, 3, 40, 50, 84, 140, 144, 181, 183, 228, 285
Tajikistan, 49
Take-off periods, 139
Tamil Tigers' armed struggle, 13
Tanzania, 3, 48, 54, 58, 74, 188n39, 228, 270
Tariff-escalation phenomenon, 29, 31, 286
Tariff protection, 126
Tavares, Marina Mendes, 28, 284
Technology
  distribution curve, 219, 220
  historical theory of, 218–221
  institutions and, 225
  intellectual roots and Industrial Revolution, 221–222
  Mokyr's insights, 226
  role in economic growth, 21, 48, 67, 97, 130, 159–164, 175, 183–185, 200, 201, 204, 205, 207–216, 226, 270
  Solow's insights, 170, 217
  technological modernity, 217, 222–224
Thailand, 48, 181, 183, 184, 276
Thant, U., 264

Theory of neocolonialist exploitation, 95n111
Third World countries
  agricultural productivity, 55–56
  cancellation of debt, 6
  developmentalist policies, 3
  productivity level, 52, 57, 59, 60
  similarities and obstacles of, 2
Thirlwall, A., 2, 10, 31n2, 75, 109, 121, 150, 164, 174, 175, 188n40, 259, 268, 279, 295n64
Tinbergen, J., 117
Tokyo Round, 270
Topping up scheme, 32n15
Toshimichi, O., 92n66
Total Factor Productivity (TFP), 3, 4, 18, 30, 32n5, 32n9, 45, 51, 52, 59, 60, 69, 90n47, 176, 185, 190n56, 207
Trade liberalisation, 25, 27, 30, 53, 259, 269, 273, 278–282, 285, 289, 290
Trade-limited growth, 141, 142
Trade Related Intellectual Property Rights (TRIPS), 24, 25, 274
Transatlantic Trade and Investment Partnership (TTIP), 28, 287
Transnational corporations (TNCs), 259
Transpacific Partnership (TPP), 28, 36n56, 287, 297n94
Transparency International's Corruption Perception Index, 45
Trebbi, E., 243n27
Trebbi, F., 107
Trebbi, R., 110n18
Truman, H. S., 135
Trump, D., 21, 276
Turgot, Anne-Robert J., 155n41
Turkey, 3, 11, 40, 43, 57, 62
Tversky, A., 194

U
Uganda, 89n39, 188n39
Unbalanced growth, 118, 138, 152n1, 234
Unconditional convergence, 174, 175
Underdeveloped countries
  financing of, 125
  importance of exports, 118
  labour supply in, 121
  role of government in development, 182–183
Unemployment, 5, 7, 10, 12, 62, 63, 68, 80, 105, 109, 121, 124, 127, 161, 240, 255
UNIDO Policy Brief, 115
Unified evolutionary growth theory, 214–215
Unified field theory, 211
Unified growth theory, 210–214
United Arab Emirates (UAE), 60, 91n51
United Nations Conference on Trade and Development (UNCTAD), 4, 15–16, 22, 31, 263–270, 289, 293n31, 293n36
  agreements, 266
  launch of UNCTAD II, 266
  Prebisch's objectives, 265
  role as political forum, 23, 268
United Nations Development Programme (UNDP), 79
United Nations General Assembly, 5, 104
United Nations Population Division, 237
United States Agency for International Development (USAID), 4–5
United States of America. See America, 131
United States-Mexico-Canada Agreement (USMCA), 25, 276

Upper middle-income countries, 13, 40, 42, 43, 87n3, 282
Uruguay, 50, 51, 53, 89n28, 269
Uruguay Round (1986–1994), 24, 268–271
US Expansion Act in 1962, 268

V

Van der Veen, R., 188n38
Van Marle, A., 110n11, 110n13
Veblen, T., 242n13
Venables, A., 230, 231, 235, 257
Venezuela, 40, 53, 74, 85, 276, 295n64
Very sustainable states, 74
Vietnam, 11, 40, 48, 49, 177, 273, 276
Von Thünen, J. H., 247n82

W

Wage gap, 20, 255, 256
Wallerstein, I., 149, 150
Wallis, J., 242n17
War-against-drugs trade agreement, 295n64
Warner, A., 271, 294n46
Washington Consensus, 16, 21, 46, 52, 55, 66, 162, 165–167, 176, 184, 289
Wealth distribution, 7, 33n28, 56, 236, 282
Wealth of poorest, 33n28
Wealth tax, 33n28
Weber, M., 208, 209, 245n56
Western capitalism, 105
Western Europe, 55, 103, 140, 213, 240, 283
Western middle classes, 9, 10, 283
White, H., 149, 157n67
Wickstead, M., 75, 76, 271
Williamson, J., 208
Williamson, O., 195
Winsemius, A., 79
Winter, S., 209
Wolf, M., 258
World Bank (WB)
  on benefits of globalisation, 279
  classification of countries, 41
  ease of doing business ranking, 50
  Global Economic Prospects, 2017, 57, 63
  Structural Adjustment Programmes, 55, 59
World Bank Flagship Report, 90n43
World Development Indicators, 87n6
World Development Report (WDR), 42, 43, 85, 231
World Economic Forum report, 63
World inequality, 9
World population, 213, 215, 237, 238
World's extreme poor, percentage, 40
World Trade Organisation (WTO)
  Agreement on Sanitary and Phytosanitary Measures, 271
  Agreement on Trade Related Intellectual Property Rights (TRIPS), 274
  export subsidies, stand on, 273
  as an institutional response, 271
  national emergency, 275
  position of developing countries within, 274
  procedure for dispute settlement, 24, 271
  restrictions, 23–25, 271, 272

World Trade Organisation (WTO) (*cont.*)
as a system of global government, 272
Trade Facilitation Agreement of 2014, 275
World War II (WWII), 12, 14, 39, 68, 92n73, 101, 113, 253
Wright, P., 296n70

X
Xi Jinping, 47, 88n13

Y
Yaoundé Convention, 1963, 265
Yemen, 40, 62, 74, 91n51, 91n58
Young, A., 189n56, 190n56

Z
Zaïre, 54, 56
Zambia, 6, 27, 57, 110n5, 295n64
Zero-sum game, 20, 254

The manufacturer's authorised representative in the EU is Springer Nature Customer Service Centre GmbH, Europaplatz 3, 69115 Heidelberg, Germany. If you have any concerns regarding our products, please contact ProductSafety@springernature.com

Printed and bound by CPI Group (UK) Ltd, Croydon, CR0 4YY

30/09/2026

02225645-0010